Table of Contents

DATE DUE FOR RETURN

The loan period may be shortened if the item is requested.

Literature and Religion in
Late Medieval and Early Modern Scotland

Essays in Honour of Alasdair A. MacDonald

EDITED BY

Luuk Houwen

PEETERS
LEUVEN – PARIS – WALPOLE, MA
2012

The cover illustration shows the Flight into Egypt from a Book of Hours written and illuminated in French Flanders, c. 1460 (University of Glasgow Library, MS Euing 4, fol. 55)

A catalogue record for this book is available from the Library of Congress.

© 2012 – Peeters – Bondgenotenlaan 153 – B-3000 Leuven – Belgium.
ISBN 978-90-429-2582-3
D/2012/0602/21

i006879945

List of Abbreviations

Adv. Lib.	Advocates' Library
APS	*The Acts of the Parliament of Scotland.* Eds. Cosmo Nelson Innes and Thomas Thomson. 12 vols. Edinburgh: s.n., 1814-75
AV	Authorised Version
BD	*The Book of the Duchess*
BL	British Library
BUK	*Booke of the Universall Kirk of Scotland: Acts and Proceedings of the General Assemblies of the Kirk of Scotland.* Ed. Thomas Thomson. 3 vols. Edinburgh: Bannatyne and Maitland Clubs, 1839-45
2 Chr.	2 Chronicles
CCSL	Corpus Christianorum, Series Latina
CSPS	*Calendar of the State Papers Relating to Scotland.* Eds. William Kenneth Boyd and Henry W. Meikle. Edinburgh: H.M. General Register House, 1936
CSPF Eliz	*Calendar of State Papers, Foreign Series, of the Reign of Elizabeth.* Eds. Joseph Stevenson, et al. 23 vols. London: Longman & Co., 1863
CSP Scot	*Calendar of the State Papers Relating to Scotland, 1509-1603.* Ed. M. J. Thorpe. 2 vols. London: Longman, Brown, Green, Longmans, 1858
DOST	*Dictionary of the Older Scottish Tongue*
DSL	*Dictionary of the Scots Language*
EETS	Early English Text Society
ES	Extra Series
H.M.S.O.	Her Majesty's Stationery Office
LGW	*The Legend of Good Women*
Matt.	Matthew
MED	*Middle English Dictionary*
NHC	Northern Homily Cycle
NIMEV	*A New Index of Middle English Verse.* Eds. Julia Boffey and A. S. G. Edwards. London: British Library, 2005
NLS	National Library of Scotland
NRS	National Records of Scotland, Edinburgh

N&Q	*Notes and Queries*
OS	Ordinary Series
PL	Patrologia Latina
PMLA	*Publications of the Modern Language Association*
OE	*Old English*
OED	*Oxford English Dictionary*
Rev.	Revelations
RSCHS	*Records of the Scottish Church History Society*
RMS	*Registrum Magni Sigilli regum Scotorum,* Eds. John Maitland Thomson, et al. 11 vols. Edinburgh: H.M. General Register House, 1882.
RPC	*The Register of the Privy Council of Scotland.* Eds. Peter Hume Brown and David Masson. Second series. 8 vols. Edinburgh: H.M. General Register House, 1900
RPS	*Records of the Parliaments of Scotland to 1707.* Eds. K. M. Brown and Scottish Parliament Project Team. St Andrews: University of St Andrews, 2007-10
ScL	*Scottish Legends of the Saints*
SEL	*South English Legendary*
SHR	*Scottish Historical Review*
STC	Short Title Catalogue
STS	Scottish Text Society
Tim.	Timothy

List of Contributors

Priscilla Bawcutt is Honorary Professor in the School of English, University of Liverpool.

Jamie Reid Baxter is Honorary Research Fellow in Scottish History, University of Glasgow.

Alexander Broadie is Honorary Professorial Research Fellow, Glasgow University.

Kenneth Dunn is Senior Curator, Manuscripts and Map Collections, National Library of Scotland.

Janet Hadley Williams is Visiting Fellow, School of Cultural Inquiry, Research School of the Humanities and the Arts, CASS, The Australian National University.

Douglas Gray is emeritus Professor of English, Oxford University.

Luuk Houwen is Professor of Medieval English Language and Literature at the Ruhr-Universität Bochum, Germany.

Michael Lynch, formerly Sir William Fraser Professor of Scottish History and Palaeography at the University of Edinburgh, is currently a Professor Emeritus of the same institution.

J. Derek McClure, formerly Senior Lecturer, Department of English, University of Aberdeen.

Nicole Meier is Academic Coordinator and Senior Lecturer, Department of English, American and Celtic Studies, University of Bonn.

Regina Scheibe teaches Medieval English Literatures at the Free University, Berlin.

Michael Twomey is Charles A. Dana Professor of Humanities and Arts, Department of English, Ithaca College, New York, USA.

Introduction

It is a common-place that religious and devotional literature makes up the bulk of medieval vernacular literature. This is true for Middle English and even though the body of extant vernacular literature of medieval Scotland is less extensive in quantity and scope and thus may give one a somewhat distorted view of the historical reality,[1] it is nevertheless substantial enough to warrant special study and it is not for nothing that some scholars feel it deserves 'more critical recognition'.[2] The present volume represents a modest attempt to do just that.

Medieval Scottish religious literature starts with a hagiographical work of the *légendes abrégées* type, the *Scottish Legendary*.[3] It survives only in Cambridge, University Library Gg.II.6 and dates from the end of the fourteenth century. That makes it together with Barbour's *Bruce* one of the earliest extant examples of Middle Scots literature. Although Jacobus de Varagine's *Legenda aurea* is only referred to once,[4] this thirteenth-century legendary is one of its more important sources; others are Vincent of Beauvais's *Speculum historiale* and the *Vitae patrum*. The compiler alleges he assembled the work in an attempt to shun idleness which 'giffis novrysingis to vices' (Prologue, 2-3), at a time when he was too old to exercise the ministry of the Church (Prol. 33-35). About a century later William Caxton justifies his *Golden Legend* using the same argument when he quotes St Jerome as having said that one should always do 'some good work, to the end that the devil find thee not idle'.[5] Unfortunately, not much else is known about the author, except that he must have been a man of the cloth with a possible link with Aberdeenshire. The *Legendary* may not have received much critical attention in the past, but in the present volume Regina Scheibe examines its fascinating Prologue with its somewhat puzzling secular references to the *Disticha Catonis* and *Roman de la*

---

[1]   As noted with respect to late-medieval devotional literature in Scotland by A. A. MacDonald, 'Passion Devotion in Late-Medieval Scotland,' *The Broken Body. Passion Devotion in Late-Medieval Culture*, eds. A. A. MacDonald, H. N. B. Ridderbos and R. M. Schlusemann (Groningen: Forsten, 1998) 109.

[2]   Priscilla Bawcutt, 'Religious Verse in Medieval Scotland,' *A Companion to Medieval Scottish Poetry*, eds. Priscilla J. Bawcutt and Janet Hadley Williams (Cambridge: D.S. Brewer, 2006) 131.

[3]   *Legends of the Saints in the Scottish Dialect of the Fourteenth Century*, ed. W. M. Metcalfe, STS 1st ser. 13/18; 23/25; 35/37, 3 vols. (Edinburgh: Blackwood and Sons, 1888-96).

[4]   The reference occurs in the life of Blasius, XX.17.

[5]   Jacobus de Voragine, *The Golden Legend or Lives of the Saints as Englished by William Caxton*, ed. F. S. Ellis, 7 vols. (New York: AMS Press, 1973) 1.

Rose. She shows that the reference to Cato is not that unusual in hagiographical texts with which the *Distichs* are also occasionally found bound together. An explanation for the reference to the *Roman de la Rose* is less straightforward, but it is argued that by this reference 'the Scottish poet is making the listener/reader not just realize that idleness is affecting man's all important operative forces of will and reason, resulting in a rejection of divine love, and that idleness can be overcome by *fortitude*, a common property of saints, but he is also suggesting that idleness is particularly a sin of the affluent'. Thus the Prologue to *Legend of the Saints* is turned into a means to critique Scottish secular and religious leaders for their idleness, a purpose that is entirely appropriate for hagiographic collections which in the later Middle Ages were sometimes seen as guidebooks on religious behaviour. Moreover, by combining the courtly tradition of idleness with penitential teachings on sloth the compiler manages to broaden the impact of his collection by appealing to both a secular and a religious audience.

Much of the Middle Scots religious and devotional literature is to be found in literary miscellanies. Among them three stand out because of their size and range: the Asloan manuscript (Edinburgh, NLS 16500), London, BL MS Arundel 285 and the Bannatyne manuscript (Edinburgh, NLS Adv. 1.1.6). The compilation of the earliest of these was started by the notary public John Asloan around 1515. It does not only contain numerous religious lyrics but also one of the four extant manuscript copies of William of Touris's *Contemplacioun of Synnaris*.[6] Although the early sixteenth-century date of the manuscript may suggest it belongs to the Renaissance van Buuren observes that its predominantly devotional and moralising contents place it firmly in the Catholic Middle Ages.[7]

Religious verse is also found scattered throughout other manuscripts such as books of hours (EUL, MS Laing III. 17) and protocol books, and even makes an appearance in a manuscript of lecture notes in Latin (Makculloch Manuscript; EUL, MS Laing III.

---

[6]   The others are MS Arundel 285, London, BL Harley MS 6919 and the Bannatyne manuscript. The last is an extract disguised as a Protestant lyric which shows 'how Catholic material could be so processed as to become suitable for Protestant consumption' (A. A. MacDonald, 'Catholic Devotion into Protestant Lyric: The Case of the *Contemplacioun of Synnaris*,' *Innes Review* 35 (1984): 58). The earliest surviving copy is actually a Westminster print by Wynkyn de Worde that dates from 10 July 1499; for a further discussion of this print and its use of Latin quotations between the stanzas in the vernacular, see A. A. MacDonald, 'Political and Religious Instruction in an Eschatological Perspective: The *Contemplacioun of Synnaris* of William of Touris,' *Calliope's Classroom. Studies in Didactic Poetry from Antiquity to the Renaissance*, eds. Annette Harder, A. A. MacDonald and Gerrit J. Reinink (Leuven: Peeters, 2007).

[7]   Catherine C. van Buuren, 'John Asloan and his Manuscript: An Edinburgh Notary and Scribe in the Days of James III, IV and V (c. 1470-c. 1530),' *Stewart Style 1513-1542. Essays on the Court of James V*, ed. Janet Hadley Williams (East Linton: Tuckwell Press, 1996) 50.

149), not to mention many other Latin manuscripts.[8] Less remarkable is the fact that some Middle Scots religious poems are heavily indebted to Latin sources.[9] This is also true for many of the poems in MS Arundel 285, especially those in the second half of the manuscript which, as Bennett noted, 'are versions of Latin prayers that occur regularly in Books of Hours of the period 1450-1550'.[10] Yet, as MacDonald argues, this manuscript was certainly not intended as a Book of Hours, if only because it does not contain a Psalter, Office of Our Lady, or Office of the Dead.[11] Its emphasis on the Passion and its liturgical flavour, on the other hand, are unmistakable. One example of this is Walter Kennedy's *Þe Passioun of Crist*. This is a rather free rendering of Ludolph of Saxony's *Vita Christi* and, as the latter's title reveals, encompasses more than just the Passion, even if the Passion is the central event towards which the rest is but an introduction. Kennedy's *Passioun* may well have been intended for James IV[12] just like other examples of devotional literature like the *Contemplacioun of Synnaris* and John Ireland's *Meroure of Wyssdome,* which Ireland himself calls the 'ABC of Christianity'.[13] Indeed, it has been suggested that the same may also apply to William Dunbar's 'Tabill of Confessioun', the poem with which MS Arundel 285 opens.[14] Another poem that appears to have a liturgical background is Kennedy's 'Ane Ballat of Our Lady' (Asloan MS, ff. 303-304b). It has its source in hymns, sequences and antiphons, largely 'culled from the Office of the Blessed Virgin Mary'.[15] The rhetorical aspects of devotion and more specifically the role the Blessed Virgin plays in these two poems by Kennedy is the subject of an article by Nicole Meier. Meier investigates how 'devotees turn their eyes towards the Blessed Virgin in prayer and ask for intercession' and examines Mary's

---

[8]   Bawcutt, 'Religious Verse,' 121-22.

[9]   For an example see A. A. MacDonald, 'The Latin Original of Robert Henryson's Annunciation Lyric,' *The Renaissance in Scotland. Studies in Literature, Religion, History and Culture*, eds. A. A. MacDonald, Michael Lynch and I. B. Cowan (Leiden: Brill, 1994).

[10]   *Devotional Pieces in Verse and Prose from MS. Arundel 285 and MS. Harleian 6919*, ed. J. A. W. Bennett, STS 3rd ser. 23 (Edinburgh: Scottish Text Society, 1955) xxiv; cf. also Bawcutt, 'Religious Verse,' 122.

[11]   MacDonald, 'Passion Devotion in Scotland,' 115.

[12]   *Ibid.*, 95, 120.

[13]   John Ireland, *The Meroure of Wyssdome Composed for the Use of James IV., King of Scots Books I & II*, ed. Charles MacPherson, STS 2nd ser. 19, vol. 1 (Edinburgh: Blackwood, 1926) 14/13. For the other volumes see John Ireland, *The Meroure of Wyssdome Composed for the Use of James IV., King of Scots, A.D. 1490*, ed. F. Quinn, STS 4th ser. 2, vol. 2 (s.n.: Scottish Text Society, 1965) and John Ireland, *The Meroure of Wyssdome Composed for the Use of James IV., King of Scots Vol.III, Books VI & VII*, ed. Craig McDonald, STS 4th ser. 19, vol. 3 (Aberdeen: Aberdeen University Press, 1990).

[14]   A. A. MacDonald, 'Religious Poetry in Middle Scots,' *The History of Scottish Literature Volume 1: Origins to 1660*, ed. R. D. S. Jack (Aberdeen: Aberdeen University Press, 1988) 95.

[15]   Walter Kennedy, *The Poems of Walter Kennedy*, ed. Nicole Meier, STS 5th ser. 6 (Woodbridge: Scottish Text Society, 2008) 188.

own role as a witness to Christ's death on the Cross. Unlike Mary in Dunbar's 'Hale, sterne superne', however, Kennedy's Mary is approachable; her primary role is that of an intercessor, a *mediatrix* who allows the devotee to petition Christ to forgive him his 'gret trespaß and wyce' (III.67), and this, Meier argues, is in keeping with the other religious lyrics that precede in the Asloan manuscript.

Among the post-Reformation manuscripts containing religious and devotional poetry, the Bannatyne manuscript, the Maitland Folio and the Maitland Quarto stand out. The Bannatyne manuscript was compiled by George Bannatyne between 1565 and 1568. It clearly started its life as a collection of lyrics in four parts, but later a fifth part on fables was added, and much other material was also inserted into the third section of humorous lyrics.[16] Religious lyrics make up the first part, and here are preserved lyrics by Robert Henryson, William Dunbar and Gavin Douglas. The manuscript's post-reformation date also means that this section suffered most censorship: Bannatyne clearly attempted to avoid too hostile a reaction to his collection and altered many a doctrinally sensitive line.[17]

It is to these 'ballatis of theologie' that we have to turn for the Prologue to book ten of Douglas's *Eneados*.[18] To find the Prologue in this section is perhaps a little unexpected, but since its subject matter is the nature of God and the Trinity, the allocation is entirely appropriate. As Douglas Gray observes in 'The Religious Elements in the Poetry of Gavin Douglas', it is the most clearly religious of all the prologues and impresses because of its poetic power and its precision of expression (especially when expounding the nature of the Trinity). In fact, it deserves to be ranked with the prose of John Ireland's *Meroure of Wyssdome* as an example of vernacular theology. The Provost of St Giles and later Bishop of Dunkeld may not generally be regarded as a religious poet but as Douglas Gray demonstrates he should be taken seriously as a religious writer and might even be regarded as a 'kind of early sixteenth-century Christian humanist'.

---

[16] A. A. MacDonald, 'Lyrics in Middle Scots,' *A Companion to the Middle English Lyric*, ed. T. G. Duncan (Woodbridge: D.S. Brewer, 2005) 243, n. 6.

[17] For a discussion of Bannatyne's self-censorship and his possible reasons see A. A. MacDonald, 'Poetry, Politics, and Reformation Censorship in Sixteenth-Century Scotland,' *English Studies* 64 (1983); MacDonald, 'Catholic Devotion & Protestant Lyric'; A. A. MacDonald, 'The Bannatyne Manuscript-A Marian Anthology,' *Innes Review* 37 (1986); and A. A. MacDonald, 'The Printed Book that Never Was: George Bannatyne's Poetic Anthology,' *Boeken in de Late Middeleeuwen: Verslag van de Groningse Codicologendagen 1992*, eds. Jos M. M. Hermans and Klaas van der Hoek (Groningen: Forsten, 1994).

[18] Gavin Douglas, *Virgil's Aeneid Translated into Scottish Verse by Gavin Douglas, Bishop of Dunkeld*, ed. D. F. C. Coldwell, STS 3rd series 25, 27-28, 30, 4 vols. (Edinburgh: William Blackwood & Sons, 1957-64) III, 223-28.

The first few stanzas of Douglas's Prologue to book ten in which he introduces God as Creator are reminiscent of the opening stanzas of Henryson's 'Preaching of the Swallow'[19] and this fable Bannatyne places at the head of the fifth section which encompass 'the fabillis of Esop with diuerß vþir fabillis and poeticall workis maid & Compyld be diuers lernit men'.[20] In 'The Sedentary Swallow in Henryson's The Preaching of the Swallow' an attempt is made to explain why Henryson's swallow does not migrate. When no convincing natural historical arguments present themselves that would explain this extraordinary event other reasons are adduced for the swallow's sedentary inclinations and it is argued that this fable with its cosmological introduction and its emphasis on the debate between the body and the soul is more akin to an exemplum than a fable. It also demonstrates a much tighter unity between the introductory stanzas, the tale and the moralisation than has sometimes been acknowledged and moves easily from the macrocosmic dimension of God and his creation to the microcosmic one of the exemplum proper, thereby making it an equally good candidate for Bannatyne's 'ballatis of theologie' section.

That it pays to look outside both the temporal and the generic boundaries traditionally associated with Medieval and Renaissance literature is demonstrated by Priscilla Bawcutt who looks at some Scottish charms and their ancient religious roots and notes the close correspondence between charms and prayers. She also presents freshly edited texts of two charms that have been preserved in the sixteenth- and seventeenth-century Books of Adjournal which record trials and court decisions. The charms were said to have been used by Agnes Sampson to heal sick people and animals. Agnes Sampson was one of the North Berwick witches burned at the stake for attempting to plot against King James VI on his return from Denmark in 1590. The shorter one of the two also survives in English and is thought to date back to the fifteenth century. Unlike the Scottish version the latter is untouched by the Reformation and in its emphasis on the Passion it resembles the tracts in MS Arundel 285. The second reads a little like a 'doggerel version of the Apostles' Creed'. Another charm appears as two lines in the pastoral section of the *Complaynt of Scotland* where it is barely recognisable as such. It is only when these lines are compared to two charms recorded in the Shetlands in the nineteenth century that its true nature becomes apparent and a further connection can be established between these charms and a medieval English one associated with the healing of horses.

---

[19] Cf. *ibid.*, I, 234 and Robert Henryson, *The Poems of Robert Henryson*, ed. Denton Fox (Oxford: Clarendon Press, 1981) VII.1622-712.

[20] *The Bannatyne Manuscript Writtin in Tyme of Pest 1568*, ed. W. Tod Ritchie, STS 2nd ser. 22, 23, 26; 3rd ser. 5, 4 vols. (Edinburgh: Scottish Text Society, 1928-34) IV, 116.

It is not always easy or indeed sensible to distinguish too rigidly between religious and moral material. This certainly applies to the so-called 'Monologue Recreative' which forms a part of the pastoral middle section of the *Complaynt of Scotland*. This 'prolix orison'[21] partakes in some important ways of the moral-didactic genre of the shepherd's calendar in that, as Michael Twomey notes in his contribution, 'Shepherds' calendars are, like Wedderburn's *Complaynt*, moral treatises touching on an encyclopedic variety of topics surrounding a cosmographical centre. They are presented in the voice of a 'master shepherd' like the one who delivers Wedderburn's 'Monologue'; they refer to the author as *Auctor*, as does Wedderburn; and like Wedderburn their cosmography covers the stars, planets, heavenly manifestations, and weather'. In what follows Twomey investigates the cosmological sources of the 'Monologue Recreative' which, he argues, serve as 'a reminder to Wedderburn's readers of the pastoral ontology of Scottish civilization in cosmography' and in which the shepherd acts 'as a teacher, a repository of Scottish culture, a shepherd of souls'.

The confluence of secular and religious material is also very evident in the *Roit* or *Quheill of Tyme*, a universal history produced by the Observant Franciscan Adam Abell. As Janet Hadley Williams and Kenneth Dunn observe elsewhere in this volume it is only one of a few early-sixteenth century prose works in Scots. According to Alasdair Stewart Abell wrote this work at the Franciscan Friary at Jedburgh, sometime after 1513 and this is broadly confirmed by Hadley Williams and Dunn. It is an abridged translation of Abell's Latin version and has been undertaken 'to *the* hono'r of god *the* wirgin mary and o'r halie fad*ir* sanct francis my merit and alswa plesour to my lord setone.'[22] Like other such works what is important for Abell is 'the interpretation, the providential pattern revealed by historiography, the implicit moral guidance of the "exempla" and the explicit moral guidance which Abell includes for lay readers.'[23] In the Prologue Abell gives his own reasons for the translation: that secular men and women 'may haif plesant and prophetable commonyng'; and religious men 'may fynd mair of prechin and be mair reddy to gife of diuers thingis inquirit solutioune'. Abell's history is preserved in Edinburgh, NLS, MS 1746 and it is the bibliography and provenance of this manuscript that Hadley Williams and Dunn examine in their joint paper. The history of the manuscript starts with the copying of the manuscript at the

---

[21] *The Complaynt of Scotland, c. 1550*, ed. A. M. Stewart, STS 4th ser. 11 (Edinburgh: Scottish Text Society, 1979) 49 (Ch. 6, *actor*).

[22] Alasdair M. Stewart, 'The Final Folios of Adam Abell's *Roit or Quheill of Tyme*: An Observantine Friar's Reflections on the 1520s and 30s,' *Stewart Style 1513-1542. Essays on the Court of James V*, ed. Janet Hadley Williams (East Linton: Tuckwell Press, 1996) 228-29.

[23] *Ibid.*, 230.

friary before the second half of 1537, continues with the possible ownership of the manuscript by the Seton family, and ends in 1935 when Lt. Colonel W. W. Cuninghame of Caprington deposited it at the National Library of Scotland.

If Robert Wedderburn is credited with being the author of the *Complaynt of Scotland* it is his brother John who may have had a hand in the composition of the *Gude and Godlie Ballatis* (1565).[24] Although this work is often referred to as a collection of Psalms in Middle Scots verse — it is sometimes referred to as 'Wedderburn's Psalms' or the 'Psalms of Dundee' — its twenty-two psalms only constitute part of the work which also includes a catechism in prose. Some of its poems have a decidedly Lutheran feel to them; in fact, it has been said the *Gude and Godlie Ballatis* exudes the same spirit as found in Alexander Alesius's *De autore et utilitate psalmorum Oratio* (1541).[25] The earliest known edition dates from 1565 but it has been suggested the material, partly because of its Lutheran flavour, must have circulated several decades earlier.[26] There were several reprints.

The same climate of Reform that was responsible for the publication and the continued popularity of the *Gude and Godlie Ballatis* — by 1621 it had been reprinted four, possibly even five times[27] — also produced a spate of new translations of the Psalms. They were inspired by humanist studies of the Hebrew Bible which coincided with a desire on the part of the Reformers to create what Barbara Lewalski called a Protestant poetics.[28] At the time such Biblical lyrics were considered 'the most elaborate form of

---

[24] MacDonald rules out the other two brothers: James because it is not known for certain that he was a Protestant, moreover, he fled to France after having satirised the times in comedies and tragedies, where he resumed his career as a merchant never to return to Scotland; Robert, on the other hand, is known to have remained a Catholic all his life. See A. A. MacDonald, 'On First Looking into the *Gude and Godlie Ballatis* (1565),' *Older Scots Literature*, ed. Sally Mapstone (Edinburgh: John Donald Publishers, 2005) 232.

[25] R. J. Lyall, 'Alexander Allan (Alesius) and the Development of a Protestant Aesthetics,' *The European Sun: Proceedings of the Seventh International Conference on Medieval and Renaissance Scottish Language and Literature*, eds. Graham D. Caie, Roderick J. Lyall, Sally Mapstone and Kenneth Simpson (East Linton: Tuckwell Press, 2001) 376-77.

[26] A. A. MacDonald, '*Gude and Godlie Ballatis*,' *Dictionary of Scottish Church History and Theology*, eds. Nigel M. de S. Cameron, David F. Wright, David C. Lachman and Donald E. Meek (Edinburgh: Inter-Varsity Press, 1993) 379, and MacDonald, 'On First Looking into the *Gude and Godlie Ballatis*,' 231.

[27] The possible fifth reprint alludes to a fragment which may have been part of a 1597 print; see A. A. MacDonald, 'The *Gude and Godlie Ballatis* (1597): A Ghost no More?,' *Edinburgh Bibliographical Society Transactions* 6.4 (1998).

[28] Cf. Rivkah Zim, *English Metrical Psalms: Poetry as Praise and Prayer, 1535-1601* (Cambridge: Cambridge University Press, 1987) 1, and Barbara Kiefer Lewalski, *Protestant Poetics and the Seventeenth-Century Religious Lyric* (Princeton, NJ: Princeton University Press, 1979).

poetry'.[29] In England Thomas Wyatt and Henry Howard, Earl of Surrey, were among the first Renaissance poets to try their hands at them; in Scotland it was Alexander Scott and Alexander Montgomerie. However, it is the translation of thirty of the Psalms by King James VI that Derrick McClure analyses. James's translations are preserved in London, BL MS Royal 18B xvi, where five psalms are signed 'I[acobus] D[ominus] R[ex] S[cotorum]'.[30] Craigie notes that they are directly based on the Latin versions by the sixteenth-century Biblical scholar Tremellius.[31] Using Psalm 1 as a basis for comparison McClure is able to demonstrate that James's rendering compares favourably with those by Scott and Montgomerie. His other Psalm translations likewise stand out for their metrical range and inventiveness, but McClure cannot find any evidence for any relationship between the suitability of various metres to particular themes or topics, despite James's own careful categorisation in his *Reulis and Cautelis*.

At the very end of the period under consideration we have a poem which in the only printed edition with a title page (1713) is entitled 'Ane godly treatis, callit the first and second cumming of Christ, to the toone of the Winter Night, showing plainly the blindness wherein were [sic] misled of in Popery, and the clear light of the Gospel now manifested in our days to the glory of God, and the comfort of all them that hope for Salvation'. *The Winter Night*, as Jamie Reid-Baxter prefers to call this poem in his paper, is the work of the former Cistercian monk James Anderson who became a presbyterian minister and ended up as commissioner for Dunblane. It consists of 85 stanzas of *rime couée*, and although it is 'almost entirely devoid of literary merit', its historical interest is considerable. The first known printing dates from 1595 but here it is argued the poem was written as early as 1581-82; an incomplete print is extant from 1614. This 'little poem' is dedicated to one of the 'fathers' of the Scottish reformation, John Erskine, Laird of Dune. Like many of the *Gude and Godlie Ballatis* it is a *contrafactum* of a popular song *Winter Night*,[32] and can be shown to have been inspired by

[29] Gijsbert J. Siertsema, 'Translation and Genre in the European Renaissance: Psalms,' *Übersetzung/ Translation / Traduction: ein internationales Handbuch zur Übersetzungsforschung / An International Encyclopedia of Translation Studies / Encyclopédie internationale de la recherche sur la traduction*, eds. Harald Kittel, Juliane House and Brigitte Schultze, vol. 2 (Berlin: W. de Gruyter, 2004) 1455.

[30] *The Poems of James VI of Scotland*, ed. James Craigie, STS, 3rd ser. 22, 26, 2 vols. (Edinburgh: Blackwood, 1955) II, xv.

[31] *Ibid.*, xvi.

[32] Cf. A. A. MacDonald, 'Contrafacta and the *Gude and Godlie Ballatis*,' *Sacred and Profane: Secular and Devotional Interplay in Early Modern British Literature*, eds. Helen Wilcox, Richard Todd and Alasdair A. MacDonald, Annual Bibliography of English Language and Literature (Amsterdam: VU University Press, 1996).

the 'militantly protestant lyrics' of the *Ballatis*. The bulk of the poem is devoted to the signs and tokens of the day of doom in which the Pope embodies the Antichrist. The ten stanzas that make up the concluding prayer hammer home the presbyterian message, with the tulchan bishops of the 1570s and 1580s coming in for severe criticism. The terminology used to attack them — 'dumbe dogs that cannot barke … wastefull Bees that make no warke' — is similar to that used by the *Gude and Godlie Ballatis* for the clergy of the Church of Rome. Reprinted and read for some 130 years *The Winter Night* contributed to the propaganda battle between presbyterianism and episcopacy, and the fact that this battle lasted all the way up to the Presbyterian settlement of 1688 helps to explain the poem's long shelf-life.

Religious and devotional literature is watered by a fount fed by many other disciplines. Two of those are touched upon in this volume. As we have seen, in both Henryson's introductory stanzas to 'The Preaching of the Swallow' and in the opening to Douglas's Prologue to book ten of the *Eneados* God is celebrated as the *Creator Mundi*. Alexander Broadie looks at this act of creation in greater detail. The question that occupied the minds of many a medieval and early modern philosopher and theologian was that of the relation between God's creation of the world and his conservation of it. The Scottish philosopher John Mair (1467–1550) was one of those who tried to answer this vexed question and Broadie argues that for Mair the act of creation is tantamount to that of its preservation and therefore God need not do anything further after the creation in order to preserve the world.

Grand events such as coronations are inevitably invested with meaning and this was certainly the case for Scotland's first Protestant coronation on 29 July 1567 when the infant Prince James, son and heir of Mary, Queen of Scots, was crowned in the parish church of Stirling. The coronation ceremony itself and the ramifications of this revolutionary act, which was accompanied by 'a full-blooded sermon by John Knox based on the second Book of Kings', are discussed by Michael Lynch in the last paper in this volume. Despite some interesting modifications made to the coronation ceremony, what is perhaps most striking is the extent to which it preserves most of the standard ingredients of the medieval one. This served, Lynch argues, to paper over the cracks that arose as a result of internal disagreements among the revolutionaries themselves, yet it also sheds interesting light on the hybrid nature of Scottish Protestantism in its early years. After a detailed analysis of three of the main disagreements among the Reformers Lynch concludes, first, that 'sovereignty counted for more than religion, whether Protestant or Catholic', and second, that 'most convinced Protestants, even if they were intent on purging the 'dregs of papistry', were anxious to preserve the cultural treasury of the past, if sometimes in a new or disguised form — as in the recast version of the Bannatyne Manuscript or as a new-style imperial monarchy'.

This book is dedicated to Professor Alasdair A. MacDonald on the occasion of his retirement from the English Department of the Rijksuniversiteit, Groningen, The Netherlands, where he contributed much to putting medieval studies on the national and international map. In his long and distinguished career he has managed to leave an indelible mark on Scottish studies. He has also been a much valued teacher, colleague and friend. This volume commemorates Alasdair's contribution to Scottish religious and devotional literature, a contribution which, as this Introduction suggests but cannot do full justice to, was considerable. It is hoped the List of Publications that follows will remedy that. Alasdair's publishing career started with an article on 'The Poetry of Sir Richard Maitland of Letinghton' published in the *Transactions of the East Lothian Antiquarian and Field Naturalists' Society* in 1972 and is still going strong to this day. His most recent publication in the Scottish field is an article on the Renaissance monk and composer Robert Carver and his motet 'O bone Jesu'. In this article Alasdair manages to touch upon two of his great interests: religious poetry and music. Since 1972 some hundred and fifty publications saw the light of day, ranging from reviews and brief notes in encyclopaedias to longer learned articles in a wide range of journals, not to mention numerous editions of essay collections and Festschriften. One series of publications in which many of these appeared is *Mediaevalia Groningana* with its subseries *Germania Latina*. It is entirely apposite that this volume should be published in this series of which Alasdair was the editor-in-chief for many years.

Luuk Houwen
Dalheim (Germany), April 2011

1972

'The Poetry of Sir Richard Maitland of Lethington.' *Transactions of the East Lothian Antiquarian and Field Naturalists' Society* 13 (1972): 7-19.

1973

Rev. of *Ballatis of Luve*, ed. John MacQueen (Edinburgh, 1970). *Neophilologus* 57 (1973): 427-28.

Rev. of *The Middle Scots Poets*, ed. A. M. Kinghorn (London, 1970). *Neophilologus* 57 (1973): 107.

1974

Rev. of R. D. S. Jack, *The Italian Influence on Scottish Literature* (Edinburgh, 1972), and *A Choice of Scottish Verse: 1470-1570*, eds. John and Winifred MacQueen (London, 1972). *Neophilologus* 58 (1974): 146-47.

1978

'Recent Editions of the *Kingis Quair*.' *Neophilologus* 62.1 (1978): 145-50.

'The Middle Scots Religious Lyrics.' Ph.D. thesis. University of Edinburgh, 1978.

1980-81

'Illusions Perdues: *The New Ancestors* revisited.' *Dalhousie Review* 60 (1980-81): 703-11.

1981

Rev. of *Medieval English Songs*, eds. E. J. Dobson and F. L. Harrison (London and Boston, 1979). *English Studies* 62 (1981): 479-81.

1982

Rev. of Robert G. Benson, *Medieval Body Language: A Study of the Use of Gesture in Chaucer's Poetry* (Copenhagen, 1980). *English Studies* 63 (1982): 474-75.

1983

'A Meeting of East and West: *The Buke of the Sevyne Sagis*.' *Dutch Quarterly Review* 13 (1983): 232-36.

'Poetry, Politics, and Reformation Censorship in Sixteenth-Century Scotland.' *English Studies* 64 (1983): 410-21.

Rev. of *A Manual of the Writings in Middle English 1050-1500*, eds. J. B. Severs and A. E. Hartung (Connecticut, 1980). *English Studies* 64 (1983): 192.

Rev. of *Scots Saws: From the Folk-Wisdom of Scotland*, ed. David Murison (Edinburgh, 1981). *English Studies* 64 (1983): 94-95.

Rev. of *The Buke of the Sevyne Sagis*, ed. C.C. van Buuren-Veenenbos (Leiden, 1982). *English Studies* 64 (1983): 176-78.

Rev. of Ian S. Ross, *William Dunbar* (Leiden, 1981). *English Studies* 64 (1983): 179-80.

Rev. of Lucy de Bruyn, *Woman and the Devil in Sixteenth-Century Literature* (Tisbury, 1979). *English Studies* 64 (1983): 93-94.

1984

'Approaching Middle English Lyrics.' *Studies in Early Middle English Literature*. Eds. Johan Kerling and Judith C. Perryman. Leiden: Department of English, Leiden University, 1984. 115-28.

'Editing the *Gude and Godlie Ballatis*.' *Papers from the Fifth and Third Philological Symposium*. Ed. Erik Kooper. Utrecht: Department of English, 1984. 107-22.

'Catholic Devotion into Protestant Lyric: The Case of the *Contemplacioun of Synnaris*.' *Innes Review* 35 (1984): 58-87.

'Some Recent Work on George Buchanan.' *English Studies* 65 (1984): 312-15.

'William Dunbar, Andro and Walter Kennedy, and Hary's *Wallace*.' *Neophilologus* 3 (1984): 471-77.

Rev. of Ian Bishop, *Chaucer's 'Troilus and Criseyde': A Critical Study* (Bristol, 1981). *English Studies* 65 (1984): 279-81.

Rev. of *Selections from Hoccleve*, ed. M. C. Seymour (Oxford, 1981) and *Thomas Hoccleve: Selected Poems*, ed. Bernard O'Donoghue (Manchester, 1982). *English Studies* 65 (1984): 277-79.

Rev. of Henrik Specht, *Chaucer's Franklin in the Canterbury Tales: Social and Literary Background of a Chaucerian Character* (Copenhagen, 1981). *English Studies* 65 (1984): 110.

1985

'Some Recent Work on the Early English Drama.' *English Studies* 66 (1985): 162-66.

Rev. of *Assays: Critical Approaches to Medieval and Renaissance Texts, Vols. I and II*, eds. Peggy A. Knapp and Michael A. Stugrin (Pittsburgh, 1981-82). *English Studies* 66 (1985): 363-65.

Rev. of Marianne Powell, *Fabula Docet: Studies in the Background and Interpretation of Henryson's 'Moral Fabillis'* (Odense, 1983). *English Studies* 66 (1985): 461-62.

Rev. of *Poetry of the Stewart Court*, ed. Joan Hughes and W. S. Ramson (Canberra, 1982). *English Studies* 66 (1985): 462-65.

Rev. of A. C. Cawley, Marion Jones, Peter F. MacDonald and David Mills, *The Revels History of Drama in English. Vol. I* (London, 1983). *English Studies* 66 (1985): 365-66.

Rev. of *The Index of Middle English Prose. Handlist I: Henry E. Huntingdon Library,* ed. Ralph Hanna III (Cambridge, 1984). *English Studies* 66 (1985): 380.

Rev. of Barbara Howard Traister, *Heavenly Necromancers: The Magician in English Renaissance Drama* (Columbia, Miss., 1984). *Vivarium* 23 (1985): 157-58.

1986

'Fervent Weather: A Difficulty in Robert Henryson's *Testament of Cresseid*.' *Scottish Language and Literature, Medieval and Renaissance*. Eds. Dietrich Strauss and Horst W. Drescher. Frankfurt am Main: Peter Lang, 1986. 271-80.

'The Bannatyne Manuscript – A Marian Anthology.' *Innes Review* 37 (1986): 36-47.

'The Middle Scots Expansion of *Iesu, Nostra Redemptio*, and a Ghost in the Bannatyne Manuscript.' *Neophilologus* 70 (1986): 472-74.

Rev. of *Thomas of Erceldoune*, ed. Ingeborg Nixon (Copenhagen, 1980-83). *English Studies* 67 (1986): 184-86.

Rev. of *Minor Prose Works of King James VI and I.* Ed. James Craigie. STS, 4th Ser. 14. (Edinburgh: Blackwood, 1982). *The Scottish Historical Review* 65.179 (1986): 85-86.

1987

'William Dunbar, Mediaeval Cosmography, and the Alleged First Reference to the New World in English Literature.' *English Studies* 68 (1987): 377-91.

Rev. of *Middle Scots Poets: a Reference Guide to James I of Scotland, Robert Henryson, William Dunbar, and Gavin Douglas*, eds. Walter Scheps and J. Anna Looney (Boston, Mass., 1986). *English Studies* 68 (1987): 283-85.

1988

'The Middle English Lyrics: An Introduction.' *Companion to Early Middle English Literature*. Eds. N. H. G. E. Veldhoen and H. Aertsen. Amsterdam: Free University Press, 1988. 7-19.

'Religious Poetry in Middle Scots.' *The History of Scottish Literature Volume 1: Origins to 1660*. Ed. R. D. S. Jack. Aberdeen: Aberdeen University Press, 1988. 91-104.

'Chaucer's *Man of Law's Tale* 847: A Reconsideration.' *Chaucer Review* 22 (1988): 246-49.

Rev. of *Robert Henryson, The Poems*, ed. Denton Fox (Oxford, 1987). *English Studies* 69 (1988): 359-60.

1989

'England: Literaturgeschichte: Vorreformatorische Zeit.' *Marienlexikon II: Chaldäer – Greban*. Eds. Remigius Bäumer and L. Scheffczyk. St. Ottilien: EOS-Verlag, 1989. 355-56.

'Geoffrey Chaucer.' *Marienlexikon II: Chaldäer – Greban*. Eds. Remigius Bäumer and L. Scheffczyk. St. Ottilien: EOS-Verlag, 1989. 36.

'Robert Henryson, Orpheus and the *puer senex* Topos.' *In Other Words: Transcultural Studies in Philology, Translation, and Lexicology Presented to Hans Heinrich Meier on the Occasion of his Sixty-Fifth Birthday*. Eds. J. Lachlan MacKenzie and Richard Todd. Dordrecht: Foris, 1989. 117-20.

'William Dunbar.' *Marienlexikon II: Chaldäer – Greban*. Eds. Remigius Bäumer and L. Scheffczyk. St. Ottilien: EOS-Verlag, 1989. 260-61.

Rev. of *Longer Scottish Poems. Vol. I: 1375-1650*, eds. Priscilla Bawcutt and Felicity Riddy, *Vol. II: 1650-1830*, ed. Thomas Crawford, David Hewitt and Alexander Law (Edinburgh, 1987). *English Studies* 70 (1989): 175-77.

Rev. of Daniel Donoghue, *Style in Old English Poetry: the Test of the Auxiliary* (New Haven and London, 1987). *Studies in Language* 13.2 (1989): 525-27.

1990

De literaire cultuur van het laat-middeleeuwse Schotland. Nijmegen: Cicero Press, 1990 [inaugural lecture].

'Dunbar in Paraphrase.' *A Day Estivall: Essays on the Music, Poetry and History of Scotland and England and Poems previously unpublished.* Eds. Alisoun Gardner-Medwin and Janet Hadley Williams. Aberdeen: Aberdeen University Press, 1990. 112-23.

'Vergilius in de Engelse literatuur van de Middeleeuwen.' *Dwergen op de schouders van Reuzen: Studies over de receptie van de Oudheid in de Middeleeuwen.* Eds. Hans van Dijk and E. R. Smits. Groningen: Forsten, 1990. 117-26.

Aertsen, Henk, and A. A. MacDonald, eds. *Companion to Middle English Romance.* Amsterdam: Free University Press, 1990.

'Bede de eerbiedwaardige, en de *uera lex historiae*.' *Madoc* 4 (1990): 149-53.

'The *Court of Sapience* and the *Gude and Godlie Ballatis*.' *Neophilologus* 74 (1990): 608-11.

1991

'Thomas Hoccleve.' *Marienlexikon III: Greco – Laib.* Eds. Remigius Bäumer and L. Scheffczyk. St. Ottilien: EOS-Verlag, 1991. 216.

'Anglo-Scottish Literary Relations: Problems and Possibilities.' *Studies in Scottish Literature* 26 (1991): 172-84.

'Censorship and the Reformation.' *File* 3 (1991): 9-16.

MacDonald, A. A., and A. M. Jansen. 'Dating *The Remedy of Love*: The Limitations of Lexicography.' *Neophilologus* 75 (1991): 619-25.

'John Gower and Seventeenth-Century Wit.' *John Gower Newsletter* 10 (1991): 6-9.

'Mary Stewart's Entry to Edinburgh: an Ambiguous Triumph.' *Innes Review* 42 (1991): 101-10.

'The Sense of Place in Early Scottish Verse: Rhetoric and Reality.' *English Studies* 72 (1991): 12-27.

Rev. of *The Index of Middle English Prose. Handlist III: Manuscripts in the Digby Collection, Bodleian Library, Oxford,* ed. Patrick J. Horner (Cambridge, 1986) and *Handlist V: Manuscripts in the Additional Collection (10001-14000), British Library, London,* eds. Peter Brown and Elton D. Higgs (Cambridge, 1988). *English Studies* 72 (1991): 183-84.

Rev. of Malcolm Godden, *The Making of Piers Plowman* (London and New York, 1991). *English Studies* 72 (1991): 562-63.

Rev. of *The 'Passion Play' from the N-Town Manuscript,* ed. Peter Meredith (London and New York, 1990). *English Studies* 72 (1991): 563.

Rev. of *Mary of Nemmegen,* ed. Margaret M. Raftery (Leiden, 1991). *Millennium* 5 (1991): 173-74.

1992

'John Lydgate.' *Marienlexikon IV: Lajtha – Orangenbaum*. Eds. Remigius Bäumer and L. Scheffczyk. St. Ottilien: EOS-Verlag, 1992. 195-96.

Rev. of Elizabeth Salter, *English and International: Studies in the Literature, Art and Patronage of Medieval England*, eds. Derek Pearsall and Nicolette Zeeman (Cambridge, 1988). *English Studies* 73 (1992): 548-49.

Rev. of Piero Boitani, *The Tragic and the Sublime in Medieval Literature* (Cambridge, 1989). *English Studies* 73 (1992): 568-69.

Rev. of Christine Richardson and Jackie Johnston, *Medieval Drama* (London, 1991). *English Studies* 73 (1992): 569-70.

Rev. of *Der Rheinische Merlin*, ed. Hartmut Beckers et al. (Paderborn, 1991). *Tijdschrift voor Geschiedenis* 105 (1992): 638-39.

Rev. of *This Noble Craft. Proceedings of the Xth Research Symposium of the Dutch and Belgian University Teachers of Old and Middle English and Historical Linguistics, Utrecht 19-20 January, 1989*, ed. Erik Kooper (Amsterdam, 1991). *Millennium* 6 (1992): 69-70.

Rev. of Jean-Jacques Blanchot, William Dunbar (1460?-1520?): Rhétoriqueur Ecossais, 2 vols. (Diss. Paris-Sorbonne, 1987). *Studies in Scottish Literature* 27 (1992): 256-60.

1993

'Douglas, Gavin.' *Dictionary of Scottish Church History and Theology*. Eds. Nigel M. de S. Cameron, et al. Edinburgh: InterVarsity Press, 1993. 253.

'Dunbar, Gavin.' *Dictionary of Scottish Church History and Theology*. Eds. Nigel M. de S. Cameron, et al. Edinburgh: InterVarsity Press, 1993. 260-61.

'Dunbar, William.' *Dictionary of Scottish Church History and Theology*. Eds. Nigel M. de S. Cameron, et al. Edinburgh: InterVarsity Press, 1993. 261.

'*Gude and Godlie Ballatis*.' *Dictionary of Scottish Church History and Theology*. Eds. Nigel M. de S. Cameron, et al. Edinburgh: InterVarsity Press, 1993. 379-80.

'Wedderburn, James.' *Dictionary of Scottish Church History and Theology*. Eds. Nigel M. de S. Cameron, et al. Edinburgh: InterVarsity Press, 1993. 858-59.

'Wedderburn, John.' *Dictionary of Scottish Church History and Theology*. Eds. Nigel M. de S. Cameron, et al. Edinburgh: InterVarsity Press, 1993. 859.

'Lindsay, (Sir) David.' *Dictionary of Scottish Church History and Theology*. Eds. Nigel M. de S. Cameron, et al. Edinburgh: InterVarsity Press, 1993. 485-86.

Rev. of *James Watson's Choice Collection of Comic and Serious Scots Poems*, ed. Harriet Harvey Wood, Vol. I (Edinburgh, 1977), Vol. II (Aberdeen, 1991). *English Studies* 74 (1993): 391-92.

1994

'Alliterative Poetry and Its Context: The Case of William Dunbar.' *Loyal Letters. Studies on Mediaeval Alliterative Poetry and Prose*. Eds. L. A. J. R. Houwen and A. A. MacDonald. Groningen: Forsten, 1994. 261-79.

'The Latin Original of Robert Henryson's Annunciation Lyric.' *The Renaissance in Scotland. Studies in Literature, Religion, History and Culture*. Eds. A. A. MacDonald, Michael Lynch and I. B. Cowan. Leiden: Brill, 1994. 45-65.

'The Printed Book that Never Was: George Bannatyne's Poetic Anthology.' *Boeken in de Late Middeleeuwen: Verslag van de Groningse Codicologendagen 1992*. Eds. Jos M. M. Hermans and Klaas van der Hoek. Groningen: Forsten, 1994. 101-10.

MacDonald, A. A., and J. M. Blom. 'Schottland: Frömmigkeitsgeschichte und Literaturwissenschaft.' *Marienlexikon VI: Scherer – Zypresse; Nachträge*. Eds. Remigius Bäumer and L. Scheffczyk. St. Ottilien: EOS-Verlag, 1994. 63-65.

Houwen, L. A. J. R., and A. A. MacDonald, eds. *Loyal Letters. Studies on Mediaeval Alliterative Poetry and Prose*. Mediaevalia Groningana 15. Groningen: Forsten, 1994.

MacDonald, A. A., Michael Lynch, and Ian B. Cowan, eds. *The Renaissance in Scotland. Studies in Literature, Religion, History and Culture offered to J. Durkan*. Leiden: Brill, 1994.

Rev. of J. A. Burrow, *Langland's Fictions* (Oxford, 1993). *English Studies* 75 (1994): 387-88.

Rev. of *A Wyf Ther Was: Essays in Honour of Paule Mertens-Fonck,* ed. Juliette Dor (Liège, 1992). *Revue belge de philologie et d'histoire* 72.3 (1994): 741-43.

1995

'The Middle English Lyrics: An Introduction.' *Companion to Early Middle English Literature*. Eds. N. H. G. E. Veldhoen and H. Aertsen. Amsterdam: Free University Press, 1995. 7-18.

'The Renaissance Household as Centre of Learning.' *Centres of Learning. Learning and Location in Pre-Modern Europe and the Near East*. Eds. J. W. Drijvers and A. A. MacDonald. Leiden: Brill, 1995. 289-98.

Drijvers, J. W., and A. A. MacDonald, eds. *Centres of Learning. Learning and Location in Pre-Modern Europe and the Near East*. Leiden: Brill, 1995.

Hofstra, Tette, L. A. J. R. Houwen, and A. A. MacDonald, eds. *Pagans and Christians. The Interplay between Christian Latin and Traditional Germanic Cultures in Early Medieval Europe*. Mediaevalia Groningana. Groningen: Forsten, 1995.

Rev. of McClure, J. Derrick, *Scots and its Literature* (Amsterdam and Philadelphia, 1997). *Studies in Language* 21 (1995): 702-03.

1996

'Contrafacta and the *Gude and Godlie Ballatis*.' *Sacred and Profane: Secular and Devotional Interplay in Early Modern British Literature*. Eds. Helen Wilcox, Richard Todd and Alasdair A. MacDonald. Annual Bibliography of English Language and Literature. Amsterdam: VU University Press, 1996. 33-44.

'*Dixit insipiens*: Sir David Lindsay and Renaissance Folly.' *Media Latinitas. A Collection of Essays to Mark the Occasion of the Retirement of L.J. Engels*. Eds. R. I. A. Nip, et al. Steenbrugge, Turnhout: Brepols, 1996. 263-68.

'William Stewart and the Court Poetry of the Reign of James V.' *Stewart Style 1513-1542. Essays on the Court of James V*. Ed. Janet Hadley Williams. East Linton: Tuckwell Press, 1996. 179-200.

Houwen, L. A. J. R., and A. A. MacDonald, eds. *Beda Venerabilis Historian, Monk & Northumbrian*. Mediaevalia Groningana 19. Groningen: Forsten, 1996.

Wilcox, Helen, Richard Todd, and A. A. MacDonald, eds. *Sacred and Profane: Secular and Devotional Interplay in Early Modern British Literature*. Amsterdam: VU University Press, 1996.

1997

Rev. of *Scotland and the Low Countries 1124-1994*, ed. Grant G. Simpson (East Linton, 1996). *Millennium* 11 (1997): 76-77.

Rev. of *The Ellesmere Chaucer: Essays in Interpretation*, ed. Martin M. Stevens and Daniel Woodward (San Marino and Tokyo, 1995). *English Studies* 78 (1997): 573-75.

Rev. of David Stevenson, *Scotland's Last Royal Wedding: The Marriage of James VI and Anne of Denmark*, (Edinburgh, 1997). *Tijdschrift voor Skandinavistiek* 18 (1997): 110-14.

1998

'Early Modern Scottish Literature and the Parameters of Culture.' *The Rose and the Thistle. Essays on the Culture of Late Medieval and Renaissance Scotland*. Ed. S. Mapstone. East Linton: Tuckwell Press, 1998. 77-100.

'Passion Devotion in Late-Medieval Scotland.' *The Broken Body. Passion Devotion in Late-Medieval Culture*. Ed. A. A. MacDonald. Groningen: Forsten, 1998. 109-31.

Houwen, L. A. J. R., and A. A. Macdonald, eds. *Alcuin of York: Scholar at the Carolingian Court. Proceedings of the Third Germania Latina Conference held at the University of Groningen, May 1995*. Mediaevalia Groningana. Groningen: Forsten, 1998.

MacDonald, A. A., H. N. B. Ridderbos, and R. M. Schlusemann, eds. *The Broken Body. Passion Devotion in Late-Medieval Culture*. Mediaevalia Groningana. Groningen: Forsten, 1998.

'The *Gude and Godlie Ballatis* (1597): A Ghost no more?' *Edinburgh Bibliographical Society Transactions* 6.4 (1998): 115-31.

Rev. of Thorlac Turville-Petre, *England the Nation: Language, Literature, and National Identity 1290-1340* (Oxford, 1996). *English Studies* 79 (1998): 470-71.

1999

Rev. of Ronald K.S. Macaulay, *Standards and Variation in Urban Speech: Examples from Lowland Scots* (Amsterdam and Philadelphia, 1997). *Studies in Language* 23 (1999): 466-67.

2000

'The Chapel of Restalrig: Royal Folly or Venerable Shrine?' *The Palace in the Wild: Essays on Vernacular Culture and Humanism in Late-Medieval and Renaissance Scotland*.

Eds. L. A. J. R. Houwen, A. A. MacDonald and S. L. Mapstone. Leuven: Peeters, 2000. 27-59.

Houwen, L. A. J. R., A. A. MacDonald, and S. Mapstone, eds. *The Palace in the Wild: Essays on Vernacular Culture and Humanism in Late-Medieval and Renaissance Scotland*. Mediaevalia Groningana n.s. Leuven: Peeters, 2000.

Rev. of D.D.R. Owen, *William the Lion, 1143-1214: Kingship and Culture* (East Linton, 1997). *Mediaevistik* 13 (2000): 307-09.

2001

'Chivalry as a Catalyst of Cultural Change in Late-Medieval Scotland.' *Tradition and Innovation in an Era of Change / Tradition und Innovation im Übergang zur Frühen Neuzeit*. Eds. Rudolf Suntrup and Jan Veenstra. Frankfurt: Peter Lang, 2001. 151-74.

'The Low Countries.' *The Oxford Companion to Scottish History*. Ed. Michael Lynch. Oxford: OUP, 2001. 398-401.

'Scottish Poetry of the Reign of Mary Stewart.' *The European Sun: Proceedings of the Seventh International Conference on Medieval and Renaissance Scottish Language and Literature*. Eds. Graham Caie, et al. East Linton: Tuckwell Press, 2001. 44-61.

'Sir Richard Maitland and William Dunbar: Textual Symbiosis and Poetic Individuality.' *William Dunbar, 'The Nobill Poyet': Essays in Honour of Priscilla Bawcutt*. Ed. Sally Mapstone. East Linton: Tuckwell Press, 2001. 134-49.

Rev. of *Englishes around the World: Studies in Honour of Manfred Görlach. Vol. I: General Studies, British Isles, North America; Vol.II: Caribbean, Africa, Asia, Australasia*, ed. E.W. Schneider (Amsterdam and Philadelphia, 1997). *Studies in Language* 24 (2001): 750-51.

2002

'The Legend of St Triduana: Piety at the Interface of Pictish and Early Germanic Cultures.' *Current Research in Dutch Universities and Polytechnics on Old English, Middle English and Historical Linguistics. Papers read at the Twenty-Third Research Symposium* Ed. Henk Lemmen. Utrecht, 2002. 24-31.

Rev. of Gordon Kipling, *Enter the King* (Oxford, 1998). *Journal of English and Germanic Philology* 101 (2002): 573-75.

Rev. of *Lyrische Lente: Liederen en gedichten uit het middeleeuwse Europa*, ed. W.P. Gerritsen, trans. W. Wilmink (Amsterdam, 2000). *Millennium* 16 (2002): 171-73.

2003

'The Cultural Repertory of Middle Scots Lyric Verse.' *Cultural Repertoires: Structure, Functions and Dynamics*. Eds. G. J. Dorleijn and H. L. J. Vanstiphout. Leuven: Peeters, 2003. 59-86.

'The Early Reception of German Literature in Scotland.' *Literatur – Geschichte – Literaturgeschichte*. Eds. Nine Miedema and Rudolf Suntrup. Frankfurt am Main: Peter Lang, 2003. 263-76.

'Scottish Culture under James III and James IV.' *Princes and Princely Culture: 1450-1650*. Eds. Martin Gosman, A. A. MacDonald and Arie Johan Vanderjagt. Leiden: Brill, 2003. 147-72.

MacDonald, A. A., Michael W. Twomey, and G. J. Reinink, eds. *Learned Antiquity: Scholarship and Society in the Near East, the Greco-Roman World, and the Early Medieval West*. Groningen Studies in Cultural Change 5. Leuven: Peeters, 2003.

Gosman, Martin, A. A. MacDonald, and Arie Johan Vanderjagt, eds. *Princes and Princely Culture: 1450-1650, Vol. I*. Brill's Studies in Intellectual History. Leiden: Brill, 2003.

Rev. of *The Long Fifteenth Century: Essays for Douglas Gray*, eds. Helen Cooper and Sally Mapstone (Oxford, 1997). *English Studies* 84 (2003): 288-90.

2004

'*The Wyf of Auchtermuchty* and her Dutch Cousin.' *Living in Posterity: Essays in Honour of Bart Westerweel*. Eds. J.F. van Dijkhuizen, et al. Hilversum: Verloren, 2004. 177-83.

MacDonald, A. A., and A. H. Huussen, eds. *Scholarly Environments: Centres of Learning and Institutional Contexts, 1560-1960*. Groningen Studies in Cultural Change 7. Leuven: Peeters, 2004.

MacDonald, A. A., and Michael W. Twomey, eds. *Schooling and Society: The Ordering and Reordering of Knowledge in the Western Middle Ages*. Groningen Studies in Cultural change 6. Leuven: Peeters, 2004.

2005

'Introduction.' *Perspectives on the Older Scottish Tongue*. Eds. C. J. Kay and M. A. Mackay. Edinburgh, 2005. 1-4.

'Lyrics in Middle Scots.' *A Companion to the Middle English Lyric*. Ed. T. G. Duncan. Cambridge: D. S. Brewer, 2005. 242-61.

'A Note on Robert Carver's Motet *O bone Iesu*.' *Notis Musycall: Essays on Music and Scottish Culture in Honour of Kenneth Elliott*. Eds. Gordon Munro, et al. Glasgow: Musica Scotica Trust, 2005. 115-24.

'On First Looking into the *Gude and Godlie Ballatis* (1565).' *Older Scots Literature*. Ed. Sally Mapstone. Edinburgh: John Donald Publishers, 2005. 230-42.

'Scottish Poetry of the Reign of Mary Stewart.' *Een Tuil Orchideeën: Anthologie uit de Tuin der Geesteswetenschappen te Groningen*. Ed. H. T. Bakker. Groningen, 2005. 163-81.

Gosman, Martin, A. A. MacDonald, and Arie Johan Vanderjagt, eds. *Princes and Princely Culture: 1450-1650, Vol. II*. Brill's Studies in Intellectual History. Leiden: Brill, 2005.

MacDonald, A. A., and Kees Dekker, eds. *Rhetoric, Royalty, and Reality: Essays on the Literary Culture of Medieval and Early Modern Scotland*. Mediaevalia Groningana New ser.7. Leuven: Peeters, 2005.

'The *Gude and Godlie Ballatis* Once More.' *Edinburgh Bibliographical Society Transactions* 6.7 (2005): 317-20.

2006

'The Nature and Function of Rhyming Pair-Formations in the English Lexis.' *Current Research in Dutch Universities and Polytechnics on Old English, Middle English and Historical Linguistics. Papers Read at the Twenty-Seventh Research Symposium Held in Utrecht on 16 December 2005.* Ed. Erik Kooper. Utrecht: s.n., 2006. 27-36.

2007

'Political and Religious Instruction in an Eschatological Perspective: The *Contemplacioun of Synnaris* of William of Touris.' *Calliope's Classroom: Studies in Didactic Poetry from Antiquity to the Renaissance.* Eds. Annette Harder, Alasdair A. MacDonald and Gerrit J. Reinink. Leuven: Peeters, 2007. 269-92.

Harder, Annette, Alasdair A. MacDonald, and Gerrit J. Reinink, eds. *Calliope's Classroom: Studies in Didactic Poetry from Antiquity to the Renaissance.* Leuven: Peeters, 2007.

2008

Goodare, Julian, and A. A. MacDonald. 'Michael Lynch and Sixteenth-Century Scotland.' *Sixteenth-Century Scotland: Essays in Honour of Michael Lynch.* Eds. Julian Goodare and A. A. MacDonald. Leiden: Brill 2008. 1-13.

Dekker, Kees, A. A. MacDonald, and Hermann Niebaum, eds. *Northern Voices: Essays on Old Germanic and Related Topics, Offered to Professor Tette Hofstra. Germania Latina VI.* Mediaevalia Groningana New Series, 11. Leuven: Peeters, 2008.

Goodare, Julian, and A. A. MacDonald, eds. *Sixteenth-Century Scotland: Essays in Honour of Michael Lynch.* Brill's Studies in Intellectual History. Leiden: Brill, 2008.

Rev. of Roderick J. Lyall, *Alexander Montgomerie: Poetry, Politics, and Cultural Change in Jacobean Scotland* (Tempe, 2005). *English Studies* 89 (2008): 737-38.

2009

'Allegorical (Dream-) Vision Poetry in Medieval and Early Modern Scotland.' *Himmel auf Erden / Heaven on Earth.* Eds. Rudolf Suntrup and Jan Veenstra. Frankfurt am Main: Peter Lang, 2009. 167-76.

'Florentius Volusenus and Tranquillity of Mind: Some Applications of an Ancient Ideal.' *Christian Humanism. Essays in Honour of Arjo Vanderjagt.* Eds. A. A. MacDonald, Z. R. W. M. von Martels and Jan R. Veenstra. Studies in Medieval and Reformation Traditions. Leiden: Brill, 2009. 119-38.

'The Middle English Lyrics: An Introduction.' *Companion to Early Middle English Literature.* Eds. Bart Veldhoen and Henk Aertsen. 3rd ed. Amsterdam: VU University Press, 2009. 7-19.

MacDonald, A. A., Z. R. W. M. von Martels, and Jan R. Veenstra, eds. *Christian Humanism: Essays in Honour of Arjo Vanderjagt.* Studies in Medieval and Reformation Traditions. Leiden: Brill 2009.

'Johannes Soter and the Vita Caroli Magni (Cologne 1521). Ethiopia comes to Scotland.' *Journal of the Edinburgh Bibliographical Society* 4 (2009): 60-68.

'William Dunbar and Andro Kennedy: A Dental Challenge.' *Medium Ævum* 78 (2009): 118-23.

2010

'A Note on Robert Carver's Motet 'O bone Jesu'.' *Onder Orchideeën. Nieuwe Oogst uit de Tuin der Geesteswetenschappen te Groningen.* Ed. Jacobus van Dijk. Groningen: Barkhuis Publishing, 2010. 113-22.

'The Orchids: A Brief History.' *Onder Orchideeën. Nieuwe Oogst uit de Tuin der Geesteswetenschappen te Groningen.* Ed. Jacobus van Dijk. Groningen: Barkhuis Publishing, 2010. 1-5.

'Idilnes giffis novrysingis to vicis':
The Prologue of the *Scottish Legends of the Saints*

Regina Scheibe

Despite the remarkable popularity of hagiography in the Middle Ages,[1] the *Scottish Legends of the Saints*, compiled in *c.* 1400 and preserved in the early fifteenth-century manuscript Cambridge, University Library, Gg. II. 6, has largely been neglected by modern researchers of medieval English hagiographic writings.[2] John Scahill's and Margaret Rogerson's bibliography *Middle English Saints' Legends*, published in 2005, has just thirteen entries for the Older Scots saints' lives in contrast to the one hundred and twenty-five entries for the *South English Legendary* and the fifty-three entries for the *Northern Homily Cycle*.[3] Seven studies on the Scottish legendary were published *prior* 1900, three between 1903 to 1921, and three between 1985 to 1994.[4] On the contents of these publications, Scahill remarks:

> Despite praise of its literary quality (e.g. in the discussions by Horstmann, **9**, and Wolpers, **35**), little has been published on the *ScL* beyond debate about the now discarded proposal of John Barbour as author; McDiarmid and Stevenson, **268**, have an alternative candidate.[5]

---

[1] See, for instance, Sarah Salih, 'Introduction', in Sarah Salih, ed., *A Companion to Middle English Hagiography* (Woodbridge: D.S. Brewer, 2006) 10-11.

[2] See also Priscilla Bawcutt, 'Religious Verse in Medieval Scotland,' *A Companion to Medieval Scottish Poetry*, eds. Priscilla J. Bawcutt and Janet Hadley Williams (Cambridge: D.S. Brewer, 2006) 120.

[3] John Scahill and Margaret Rogerson, *Middle English Saints' Legends*, Annotated Bibliographies of Old and Middle English Literature 8 (Woodbridge: D.S. Brewer, 2005) 90-94 (*ScL*, entries 258-70), 38-75 (*SEL*, entries 77-202) and 77-89 (*NHC*, entries 204-57).

[4] It should be noted that Scahill's and Rogerson's list is not exhaustive. The following reference is, for instance, not included: M. M. Maxwell Scott, 'Barbour's Legends of the Saints,' *Dublin Review* 3rd ser. 34 (1887), in which Scott comments on the sequence of the legends and discusses the legend of St Machar, to mention just two of his concerns.

[5] Scahill and Rogerson, *Saints' Legends* 90. The references are to *Altenglische Legenden, Neue Folge*, ed. Carl Horstmann (Heilbronn: Henninger, 1881); Theodor Wolpers, *Die englische Heiligenlegende des Mittelalters: Eine Formgeschichte des Legendenerzählens von der spätantiken lateinischen Tradition bis zur Mitte des 16. Jahrhunderts* (Tübingen: Niemeyer, 1964); John Barbour, *Barbour's Bruce*, eds. M. P. McDiarmid and J. A. C. Stevenson, STS, 4th series, 15, 12, 13, 3 vols. (Edinburgh: Blackwood, Pillans & Wilson, 1980, 1981, 1985). On extremely feeble grounds, McDiarmid (I, 4) suggests that the poet 'may well be

So far no one has provided a detailed analysis of the prologue to the fifty legends, of the concept of sin which permeates the *vitae*, and of the collection's sources, narratological qualities, or has studied the work from the modern perspectives of gender-related, post-colonial or psychoanalytical literary theories, to mention just a few of the possible approaches to the collection. To shed some light on the function of the prologue, its contents and structure will be related to the narrator's main concern and concept of idleness, which, according to the author's claim, provide the justification for his compilation of fifty legends.

With his reference to the popular *Disticha Catonis* and *Roman de la Rose*, the anonymous poet begins his work in a strikingly secular tone:

> CATONE sais, þat suthfaste thing is,
> þat Idilnes giffis novrysingis
> to vicis. þare-for, quha-sa wil be
> vertuise suld Idilnes fle,
> as sais 'the romance of þe rose,'
> but settyng to of ony glose,
> þat, thru þe vicis of ydilnes,
> gret foly, quhile, & vantones
> syndry hartis enteris withine,
> & gerris men ofte sic thing begyne,
> þat þai ma nocht fra thyne be brocht,
> fra þai þare-in beset þare thocht. [Prologue, 1-12[6]]

The author's reference to Cato is in line with the medieval hagiographers's common practice of citing from classical sources.[7] The Early Scots paraphrase of one of Cato's maxims seems to be a free rendering of the second distich of Book I of the *Disticha Catonis*, possibly composed in the third century:

> Plus vigila semper neu somno deditus esto;
> nam diuturna quies vitiis alimenta ministrat.[8]

---

the Heriot, almost certainly of Midlothian, whom Dunbar interposes between Eglinton and Wyntoun', for which see the review by Klaus Bitterling, *Anglia* 107 (1989): 204-05.

[6] All references are to *Legends of the Saints in the Scottish Dialect of the Fourteenth Century*, ed. W. M. Metcalfe, STS 1st ser. 13/18; 23/25; 35/37, 3 vols. (Edinburgh: Blackwood and Sons, 1888-96).

[7] Michael Goodich, 'A Note on Sainthood in the Hagiographical Prologue,' *History and Theory* 20.2 (1981): 174, repr. in Michael Goodich, *Lives and Miracles of the Saints: Studies in Medieval Latin Hagiography*, Variorum Collected Studies Series (Aldershot: Ashgate/Variorum, 2004).

[8] *Disticha catonis*, ed. Marcus Boas (Amsterdam: North-Holland Publishing, 1952) 35 (i.2); or '*Dicta Catonis*', in *Minor Latin Poets*, eds. & trans. J. Wight Duff and A. M. Duff, Loeb Classical Library, rev. ed. (Cambridge, MA: Harvard University Press, 1982) 596 (I.2).

Michael E. Goodich suggests that such citations from classical sources 'were perhaps based upon *florilegia*'.[9] However, the *Disticha Catonis* was standard reading in medieval grammar schools and, as has been indicated elsewhere, the Scottish author was obviously well versed in Latin.[10] The Latin work was also translated into various vernacular languages, among them Middle English, and would hence have been accessible to a wider audience or readership.[11] Occasionally, the *Disticha Catonis* is preserved alongside hagiographic collections. In the well-known, late fourteenth-century, Vernon MS (Oxford, Bodleian Library, MS Eng. poet. a.1.), copies of saints' legends from the *Northern Homily Cycle*, the *South English Legendary*, the first English translations of nine lives from the *Legenda aurea* and several Miracles of Our Lady[12] as well as other devotional texts are found alongside *Cato Minor* and *Cato Major*; and among the texts of the mid-fifteenth-century London, BL MS Arundel 168 are William Paris's verse life of Christine, a verse life of Dorothy, John Capgrave's life of Katherine of Alexandria, and Benedict Burgh's translation of Cato's *Morals*.[13] The Scottish poet restricts himself to a

---

9   Goodich, 'Note on Sainthood,' 174.

10   Regina Scheibe, 'Aspects of the Snake in the *Legends of the Saints*,' *Bryght Lanternis: Essays on the Language and Literature of Medieval and Renaissance Scotland*, eds. J. Derrick McClure and Michael R.G. Spiller (Aberdeen: Aberdeen UP, 1989): *passim*.

11   M. Curry Woods and Rita Copeland, 'Classroom and Confession,' *The Cambridge History of Medieval English Literature*, ed. David Wallace (Cambridge: Cambridge University Press, 1999) 380-81. Note that lines one to two of the Scottish prologue are also proverbial; see B. J. Whiting, *Proverbs, Sentences, and Proverbial Phrases from English Writings Mainly Before 1500* (Cambridge: Harvard University Press, 1968) I6. Wenzel refers to the Latin proverb 'Otiositas est mater vitiorum et noverca virtutum' and notes that it is usually ascribed to Bernard of Clairvaux 'and found as "otiositas mater nugarum, noverca virtutem" in [Bernard's] *De consideratione*, II, 13 (PL 182: 756)': Siegfried Wenzel, *The Sin of Sloth: Acedia in Medieval Thought and Literature* (Chapel Hill: University of North Carolina Press, 1967) 102, 229, n. 72, and 235, n. 21.

12   Mary Beth Long, 'Corpora and Manuscripts, Authors and Audiences,' *A Companion to Middle English Hagiography*, ed. Sarah Salih (Woodbridge: D.S. Brewer, 2006) 53.

13   Note here, for instance, the following two fourteenth-century passages on idleness in *Cato Major*, published in *The Minor Poems of the Vernon MS*, ed. F. J. Furnivall, EETS, OS 117, vol. 2 (London: Kegan Paul, Trench, Trübner, 1901) 562-609:

> (1) Plus uigila semper: ne sompno deditus esto:
>   Nam diuturna quies uicijs alimenta ministrat.
>
>   …
>   Loke þou wake more þen sleple,
>   And god in alle þing drede;
>   Long rest and luitel swynk
>   To vices hit wol þe lede. [p. 562, lines 117-20 (I.2)]
>
> (2) Segniciem fugito, que uite ignauia fertur;
>   Nam cum animus languet, consumit inercia corpus.
>
>   …
>   3if þou ne wolt sleuþe forsake

condensed rendering of a distich, that is, to a *generalis sententia*, a device recommended by authors of the medieval *artes poetriae* as one of the possible ways of beginning a poetical work.[14] Well-known to the educated listener or reader and the Scottish poet, the maxim introduces the author's main concern of idleness and helps to establish a common bond between him and the addressee of his hagiographic collection.

But what is then the function of the narrator's reference to the *Roman de la Rose*, whose composers, Guillaume de Lorris and Jean de Meun, remain unmentioned? For an answer to the question, it is necessary to turn to the French work itself and to consider some aspects of its medieval reception.

According to the Scottish poet, the *Roman de la Rose* points out that those who want to live a virtuous life should flee from idleness. In the French work, Idleness (*Oiseuse*) is a lady of leisure who opens the gate to the garden of Pleasure (*Deduit*). She introduces herself to the narrator (*Amant*) as follows:

> 'Je me faz, fet ele, Oiseuse
> apeler a mes conoissanz.
> *Rice* fame sui et *poissanz*,
> s'ai d'une chose mout bon tens
> que a nule rien je n'entens
> qu'a moi jouer et solacier
> et a moi pigner et trecier.
> Privee sui mout et acointe
> de Deduit le mignot, le cointe:
> ce est cil qui est cist jardins, ... [I.580-89[15]]

['Those who know me call me Idleness,' she said. 'I am a *rich and powerful* lady, happy especially in one thing, that I have *no care* but to enjoy and amuse myself, and to comb and braid my hair. I am the most intimate friend of Pleasure, the charming and elegant owner of this garden ... (p. 11[16])]

> Wiþ ful gret bisynesse,
> Þi lyf is badde, þi bodi sone
> Schal falle in seknesse. [p. 588, lines 425-28 (III.5)]

A brief discussion of medieval English translations of the *Disticha Catonis* is, for example, provided by Karl Reichl, 'Disticha Catonis,' *Lexikon des Mittelalters*, vol. 3 (Munich: Artemis, 1995) 1125-26. Cf. also Long, 'Corpora and Manuscripts,' 53.

[14] Cf. Hennig Brinkmann, 'Der Prolog im Mittelalter als literarische Erscheinung: Bau und Aussage,' *Wirkendes Wort* 14 (1964): 6; James A. Schultz, 'Classical Rhetoric, Medieval Poetics, and the Medieval Vernacular Prologue,' *Speculum* 59 (1984): 8, 10.

[15] Guillaume de Lorris and Jean de Meun, *Le Roman de la Rose*, ed. Félix Lecoy, 3 vols. (Paris: Champion, 1983). All italics used for emphasis in the citations of the French work and its English translation are mine.

[16] This and all subsequent translations of the *Roman de la Rose* are based on Guillaume de Lorris and Jean de Meun, *The Romance of the Rose*, trans. Frances Horgan, World's Classics (Oxford: Oxford University Press, 1994).

When wandering about in the garden of Pleasure, *Amant* is wounded by the arrows of the God of Love (*Amor*). To ease the pain of the love-sick narrator, Reason (*Reson*) addresses him as follows:

> 'Biaus amis, *folie* et enfance
> t'ont mis em poine et en esmoi.
> Mar veïs le bel tens de moi
> qui fist ton *cuer* trop agueer;
> mar t'alas onques ombreer
> ou vergier dont *Oiseuse* porte
> la clef, dont el t'ovri la porte.
> *Fox* est qui s'acointe d'*Oiseuse*;
> s'acointance est trop perilleuse.
> El t'a traï et *deceü*;
> Amors ne t'eüst ja veü,
> s'*Oiseuse* ne t'eüst conduit
> ou biau vergier qui est Deduit.
> Se tu as *folement* ovré,
> or fai tant qu'il soit recovré
> et garde bien que plus ne croies
> le conseil por quoi tu *foloies*.
> Buer *folie* qui se chastie;
> et quant *joines hom fet folie*,
> l'en ne s'en doit pas merveillier.
> Or te veil dire et conseillier
> que l'amor metes en oubli
> dont je te voi si afoibli
> et si conquis et tormenté.
> Je ne voi mie ta santé
> ne ta garison autrement,
> …
> Hons qui aime ne puet bien fere
> …
> La poine en est desmesuree,
> et *la joie a corte duree*.
> Qui joie en a, petit li dure,
> et de l'avoir est aventure,
> car je voi que maint s'en travaillent
> qui en la fin dou tot i faillent.
> Onques *mon conseil n'atendis*
> quant au dieu d'Amors te rendis.
> Le *cuer*, que tu as trop volage,

> te fist entrer en tel *folage*.
> La *folie* fu tost emprise,
> mes a l'issir a grant mestrise.
> Or met l'amor en nonchaloir,
> qui te fait vivre, et non valoir,
> que *la folie adés engraigne,*
> *qui ne fet tant qu'ele remaigne.*
> Pren durement au denz le frain,
> si dente to *cuer* et refrain.
> Tu doiz metre *force* et desfense
> encontre ce que tes *cuers* pense.
> Qui totes eures son *cuer* croit
> ne puet estre qu'il *ne foloit.*' [2982-3007, 3028, 3035-56]

['Fair friend, *folly* and childishness have caused you this pain and trouble. It was an unlucky day when you saw the beauty of May that so gladdened your *heart*, and unfortunate that you ever sought the shade of the garden where *Idleness* keeps the key with which she opened the door for you. It is *foolish* to make a friend of *Idleness*, for hers is dangerous company. She has betrayed and *deceived* you; Love would never have seen you if *Idleness* had not led you to the beautiful garden of Pleasure. If you have behaved *foolishly*, now do what is necessary to retrieve the situation and take care no longer to believe the advice that led you into *folly*. Happy is the man who learns from his *folly*, and we should not be surprised when *a young man acts foolishly*. Now I would like to tell you and advise you to forget that love, which I can see has greatly weakened, subdued, and tormented you. I see no other prospect of health or recovery …

… A man in love can do nothing well … The pain is immeasurable, and *the joy lasts only a short time*. If there is joy, it does not last long and it depends on chance, for I see many who strive for it and fail completely to obtain it in the end. *You never heeded my advice* when you surrendered to the God of Love. Your too-fickle *heart* led you into this *folly*, *folly* that you were quick to undertake but will require much skill to abandon. Now forget love, which makes your life valueless, for *this folly will constantly increase if you do not stop it*. Take the bit firmly between your teeth, subdue your *heart* and master it. You must use your *strength* to protect yourself against the thoughts of your *heart*, for the man who always believes his *heart* cannot avoid *folly*.' (pp. 46, 47)]

Reason clearly links idleness to folly and guile, two of the three vices of idleness which are also named by the Scottish narrator (line 8); and the fact that *Amant* rejects Reason's advice in favour of being a true follower of the God of Love suggests an arrogant rejection of reason in favour of will, hence rendering him into nothing more than an animal, which is solely driven by its passions:[17]

---

[17]   Cf., for instance, Geoffrey Chaucer's *Knight's Tale* I (A) 1316-20:

Quant j'oï tel chastiement,
je respondi ireement:
'Dame, je vos veil maut prier
que me lessiez a chastier.
Vos me dites que je refraigne
mon cuer, qu'Amors plus nou soupraigne.
Cuidez vos don't qu'Amors consente
que je refraigne et que je dente
le cuer qui est siens trestoz quites?
Ce ne puet estre que vos dites,
ançois a si mon cuer denté
qu'i n'est fors qu'a sa volenté;
il le justice si forment
qu'il a fete clef fermant.
Or *me lessiez tot quoi ester,*
que *vos poriez bien gaster*
en oiseuse vostre françois.
Je vosdroie morirençois
qu'Amors m'eüst de fauseté
ne de traïson aresté.
Je me veil loer ou blasmer
au daerrain de bien amer,
si m'anuie qui me chastie,' [3057-79]

[When I heard these rebukes, I replied angrily: 'My lady, I would ask you to refrain from rebuking me. You tell me to subdue my heart so that Love may no longer have the mastery over it. Do you imagine, then, that Love would allow me to quell and subdue the heart that belongs to him absolutely? What you say is impossible, rather has Love so subdued my heart that it is entirely at his mercy; his power over it is so great that he has made a key to lock it. Now *leave me in peace,* for *you are wasting your words to no purpose.* I would rather die than that Love should have accused me of falseness or treachery. In the end, I wish to be praised or blamed according as I have been a true lover, and it is vexing to be rebuked.' (pp. 47-48)]

… man is bounden to his observaunce,
For Goddes sake, to letten of his wille,
There as a beest may al his lust fulfille.

All references are to Geoffrey Chaucer, *The Riverside Chaucer*, ed. Larry D. Benson (Oxford: Oxford University Press, 1987). Note also *The Cloud of Unknowing and the Book of Privy Counselling*, ed. Phyllis Hodgson, EETS, OS 218 (Oxford: Oxford University Press, 1944, repr. 1981) 116/17-19: 'Wille is a myȝt þorou þe whiche we chese good, after þat it be determinid wiþ reson; & þorow þe whiche we loue God, we desire God, & resten us wiþ ful likyng & consent eendli in God.'

Amant's arrogant rejection of reason recalls *vantones* in line eight of the Scottish prologue. *DOST* glosses the word with 'undisciplined or unruly behaviour, esp. immoral behaviour', but also gives the meaning of 'pride, haughtiness, insolence, arrogance' for other Older Scots passages.[18] According to the Dominican friar William Peraldus (or Guillaume Peyraut),

> Ratio est ut mater voluntatis, quia habet eam regere. Voluntas vero accidiosi in bonis non invenit saporem vel delectationem …[19]

> [Reason is like the mother of Will, because her function is to govern it. But the will of an *accidiosus* finds neither savor nor delight in the good …][20]

Peraldus's remark reflects 'the Scholastic notion that *acedia* [or *accidia*, 'sloth',] is a disease of man's affect or will', which is no longer under the control of reason.[21]

Reason's remark that it was the narrator's fickle heart which led him into folly and that folly can only be overcome by strength recalls lines eight to twelve of the Scottish prologue, lines which stress the difficulty of refraining from the three vices of idleness once they have gained access to one's mind.[22] From at least the times of John Cassian onwards, *fortitudo*, 'fortitude, strength, courage', was regarded as one of the three virtues which helped to fight the cardinal sin of *acedia*, the others being spiritual joy and diligence.[23]

---

[18] *DOST*, **Wanto(u)nes**, *n.*, 1. & 4; *Dictionary of the Scots Language*, available: http://www.dsl.ac.uk/ [last accessed 18 March 2010].

[19] *Sermo Qvartvs, Dominica III. in Quadragesima, Sermo LVI.*, in *Sermones*, in Guillaume d'Auvergne, *Opera omnia* (Orléans & Paris: F. Hotot, 1674) II, 227.

[20] Cited and translated by Wenzel, *Sin of Sloth* 103, 235, n. 23.

[21] *Ibid.*, 131.

[22] On the strong link between idleness and folly see also the late fourteenth-century *Of Shrifte and Penance: The Middle English Prose Translation of 'Le Manuel des péchés'*, ed. Klaus Bitterling, Middle English texts, vol. 29 (Heidelberg: C. Winter, 1998) 75-79.

[23] On the three traditional antidotes to sloth, cf. Wenzel, *Sin of Sloth* 89:

> Owing to the confusion of *acedia* with *tristitia*, the traditional remedy for the vice had been one of two virtues: fortitude or spiritual joy. … Either virtue occurs frequently in vernacular literature as the opposite of sloth, with fortitude ('prowesse' or 'strength') perhaps being more common because of its place in the traditional septenaries. But besides these two conventional virtues a third one appears as a new antagonist to sloth [in the early thirteenth century]: *busyness*. … It is fairly frequent in Middle English devotional literature and can also be found as a personified figure in allegorical works and medieval drama. Even Chaucer [*Gentilesse*, ll. 8-11] follows this trend: 'The firste stok was ful of rightwisnese … and loved besinesse, Ayeinst the vyce of slouthe, in honestee.'

To the modern reader, who tends to expect a strictly religious introduction to a hagiographic collection, it might be striking that the Scottish poet introduces his compilation with a favourable reference to the *Roman de la Rose*, the first part of which, some 4,000 lines in length and begun by Guillaume de Lorris between 1225 and 1245, so obviously focuses on aspects of worldly love.[24] A clue to a possible explanation might be found in Geoffrey Chaucer's *Legend of Good Women*. Here the God of Love is rebuking the narrator for having translated the French work into English:

> Thou maist yt nat denye,
> For in pleyn text, withouten nede of glose,
> Thou hast translated the Romaunce of the Rose,
> That is an heresye ayeins my lawe,
> And makest wise folk fro me withdrawe ... [F 327-31[25]]

For Chaucer's God of Love, the *Roman de la Rose* is a heretical work, a view which might have been triggered off by the second part of the French poem. In Jean de Meun's 18,000-line continuation of Lorris's work, completed between 1268 and 1285, the focus of the poem switches to a 'much less courtly view of love and ladies'.[26] Jean de Meun

---

See also *ibid.*, 231, n. 95 and *Dictionary of the Scots Language, DOST, besines, besynes*, n., and *bissines, bys(s)ynes*, n., and essed Hans Kurath, Robert E. Lewis and Mary Jane Williams, *Middle English Dictionary*, 1952-2001, University of Michigan Press, available: http://quod.lib.umich.edu/m/med/ [last accessed 18 March 2010]. On the Thomists regarding *caritas* as an antidote for *acedia*, see p. 11 below.

[24] N. D. Guynn, 'Le Roman de la Rose,' *The Cambridge Companion to Medieval French Literature*, eds. Simon Gaunt and Sarah Kay (Cambridge: Cambridge University Press, 2008) 54, but cf. also 52-53.

[25] *LGW* G 254 reads '... it nedeth nat to glose, / ...', a passage which has already been referred to by Metcalfe; see *Legends of the Saints in the Scottish Dialect of the Fourteenth Century*, III, 5, n. 6. Like the Scottish poet, Geoffrey Chaucer uses the noun *glose* in connection with the *Roman de la Rose*. Cf. also Chaucer's *Book of the Duchess* 331-34: 'And alle the walles with colours fyne / Were peynted, bothe text and glose, / Of al the Romaunce of the Rose'. Colin Wilcockson suggesty that the use of the two rhyme words in the *Book of the Duchess* might account for 'glose/Rose' (cf. *LGW*, F 328-29), but he also notes that the two rhyme words occur in the scribal *explicit* to one of the manuscripts of the *Roman de la Rose*; Chaucer, *Riverside Chaucer* note to *BD* 333-34. It is interesting that the plural form of OF *glose* also occurs towards the end of the *Roman de la Rose*. The Scottish poet was probably aware of this passage, and it might have contributed to the Scottish poet's decision to refer to the *Roman de la Rose*, with worldly love helping to define the otherness of divine love as illustrated in the ensuing saints' legends. Aristotle is mentioned twice in the *Legends of the Saints*, though in different contexts; see *Legends of the Saints in the Scottish Dialect of the Fourteenth Century*, II, 'Eugenia' (XXXI) 127/126, and 'Katerine' (L) 454/433.

[26] Douglas Gray, '*Roman de la Rose*,' *The Oxford Companion to Chaucer*, ed. Douglas Gray (Oxford: Oxford University Press, 2003) 420; Guynn, '*Roman*,' 54.

does not see women as the idealized creatures of courtly poetry, and sometimes treats them with marked irreverence. This caused some literary controversy, and he is accused by some taking part (e.g. Christine de Pisan) of anti-feminism. … This … is the background to the episode in the Prologue to *The Legend of Good Women* in which the god of love condemns Chaucer for having translated the work.[27]

According to Douglas Gray, Chaucer is alluding to an 'intense discussion and debate [of the *Roman de la Rose*] in French literary circles',[28] a discussion which might have been known to the Scottish poet and which found its culmination in the well-known *Querrelle de la Rose*,

> a late medieval polemic in which Christine de Pizan and Jean Gerson disputed the moral status of the *Rose* with Pierre and Gontier Col and Jean de Montreuil … The former object to Jean's *Rose* as an offence against public morality, with Christine objecting in particular to passages that are libellous to women. The latter echo Jean himself, countering that characters speak for themselves, not the author, and that their words must conform to their natures, whether upright or dissolute.[29]

So instead of drawing the reader's or listener's attention to penitential works, such as Peraldus's popular *Summa de vitiis* (*c.* 1236), or Biblical passages on idleness, such as Ecclesiasticus 33:29 ('multam enim malitiam docuit otiositas', 'for idleness is a great teacher of mischief'),[30] the Scottish hagiographer attracts the reader's/listener's attention by referring to passages in two well-known, non-devotional works. With his reference to the *Roman de la Rose*, he also alludes to a difference between worldly and divine love, a reference which is central to the concept of saints' legends in general and to that of the sin of idleness or sloth in particular. According to the Scholastic rationale, followed, for instance, by Peraldus in his aforementioned work, all the seven deadly sins are the result of misdirected love, but misdirected love resulting from sloth was regarded as a particularly severe offence. By following the Gregorian concept of *tristitia*, and by accepting its eventual fusion with Cassian's *acedia*, scholastics apprehended *acedia*

> as inappetence, as lack of desire for God and cheerlessness in activities that relate to Him directly (prayer, meditation, and the like), a consequence of the fact that after the Fall man's spirit is burdened by his flesh.[31]

---

[27] Gray, '*Jean de Meun*,' 257-58; see also 419-20 of the same publication.
[28] Gray, '*Roman*,' 420.
[29] Guynn, '*Roman*,' 60.
[30] Cf. Wenzel, *Sin of Sloth* 101, 129.
[31] *Ibid.*, 50.

For scholastics like Thomas Aquinas (1224/5-74),

> … *acedia* … refers directly to man's relation to God, not to himself or his neighbor or society at large. The object of this vice, so to speak, is the love of God, not the pursuit of virtue, let alone the quest for fame, wealth, or a better society.[32]

Hence, Thomas and his followers regard *acedia* as aversion

> against the divine good itself. Because of the dignity of its object (the *bonum divinum*), *acedia* actually occupies a very high rank among the chief vices. This exalted position … is also reflected in the virtue to which, according to the Schoolmen, it is opposed: the joy which man should experience in loving God and serving Him. *Acedia* is the negation of *caritas*, the greatest Christian virtue. This opposition, common among the Schoolmen, deviates somewhat from earlier, traditional views. The Egyptian desert monks had opposed *acedia* with the virtue of patience or endurance … Cassian, on the other hand, considered the opposite of *acedia* to be strength, *fortitudo* … and this view remained standard in Western theology until the Scholastic period, whereas in popular catechetical teaching it continued to be the favorite one to the end of the Middle Ages. The rival of *acedia*, however — Gregory's *tristitia* — had always been the vice opposed to spiritual joy (*gaudium* or *spiritualis laetitia*).[33]

And it is fortitude, spiritual joy and charity, as well as aforementioned diligence, which are emphasized in hagiographical writings.

The work's implied emphasis on the superiority of divine love and on the unwillingness of the slothful to offer their love in return, which results from a lack of fortitude, suggests that the Scottish poet took the term 'idleness' (*otiositas*) to be synonymous with sloth, a phenomenon which we already encounter in book ten of Cassian's *De Institutis Coenobiorum et De Octo Principalium Remediis* (c. 425). In Cassian's work, which was of substantial influence right up to the end of the Middle Ages, *acedia* and *otiositas* were treated as synonyms. Siegfried Wenzel also notes that the equation frequently occurred in the *libri poenitentiales* and in moral instructions for laymen written in the eighth and ninth centuries. Between 1200 and 1450, *acedia* was still frequently equated with idleness, although longer treatises, such as Peraldus's *Summa de vitiis* and Frère Laurent's *Somme le Roi* (1279-80), generally treat idleness as an offspring of sloth.[34]

By referring to the *Roman de la Rose*, the Scottish poet is making the listener/reader not just realize that idleness is affecting man's all important operative forces of will and

---

32 *Ibid.*, 66.
33 *Ibid.*, 55.
34 *Ibid.*, 173.

reason, resulting in a rejection of divine love, and that idleness can be overcome by *fortitude*, a common property of saints, but he is also suggesting that idleness is particularly a sin of the affluent, which finds its confirmation in the next few lines of his work.

The *Disticha Catonis* and the *Roman de la Rose* are works which would have been known to the literate ruling class, to whom the poet refers in lines thirteen to twenty-six of his prologue:

> þar-for þo lordis suld nocht [sa] wirke,
> þat steris landis & haly kirke;
> ʒit, quhene þai hafe þare thing done,
> þat afferis þare stat, alsone
> þai suld dresse þare deuocione,
> in prayere & in oracione,
> or thingis þat þare hart mycht stere
> tyl wyne hewine, tyl þai are here.
> & þe next way þare-to, I trew,
> Is for to red ore here now
> storysse of sere haly men,
> þat to plesß god vs ma kene,
> þat as merroure ar vs to,
> to kene ws how we suld do. [13-26]

Secular and ecclesiastical lords should flee from idleness after their daily work of ruling those divinely entrusted to them. They should repel the vice by praying, by pursuing (unspecified) devotional activities, by reading saints' legends or by listening to them, and by meditating on the saints' lives, activities which were repeatedly recommended in medieval texts discussing idleness or sloth.[35]

Wenzel has summarized the many effects of sloth mentioned in medieval texts, and several of these are specifically linked to the clergy and nobility. Among the facets of slothful behaviour linked to religious observances were the unwillingness to go to church, an overall lack of attention during the church service, the ignorance of the Lord's Prayer and the Creed, the delaying of confession, and the unwillingness to accept adequate punishment for one's sinful deeds. The courts were particularly known for their reluctance to practise mortification. The slothful would rather play chess, or other games and sports, than honour God. Further evidence of their spiritual negligence would be their reluctance to fulfil vows and to care for the poor. Slothful priests

---

[35] See, for instance, Alcuin Blamires, *Chaucer, Ethics, and Gender* (Oxford: Oxford University Press, 2006) 208; the author is referring to Chaucer's *Second Nun's Prologue* VIII (G) 22-28 cited below.

may perform their religious duties without devotion. On the whole, sloth was perceived as hindering men from fulfilling their spiritual duties.[36]

Thomas Heffernan points out that 'hagiographic collections ... could easily ... be the vehicle for political commentary',[37] and Sherry L. Reames notes that saints' legends may provide not just religious, but also 'a surprisingly wide array of ... sociopolitical teaching'.[38] Thus it is not surprising that the Scottish hagiographer is subtly criticising Scottish secular and religious leaders for their idleness during their spare time, but he refrains from criticising the quality of their occupational activities; had he done so, he would have drifted away from his attempt to establish a common devotional ground for himself and his listeners or readers. Alasdair A. MacDonald suggests that 'one may imagine them [*sc. The Scottish Legends of the Saints*] as being

---

[36] Wenzel, *Sin of Sloth* 84-87. A list of neglected religious duties is also provided in Sloth's confession scene in William Langland's *Piers Plowman*; see William Langland, *Piers Plowman: the B version*, eds. George Kane and E. T. Donaldson (London: Athlone Press, 1975) V, 400-447. Wenzel observes that William Langland refers to

> a series of faults that are proper to parish priests, and the change is indicated by Sleuthe's words, 'I haue be prest and parsoun.' The faults are those of ignorance: he cannot sing, read saints' lives and the canon law, or explain the Psalms to his parishioners ... Finally, Sleuthe mentions a longer series of non-clerical faults, and although no shift of identity is explicitly marked, the speaker now seems once more to be a layman. This section comprises faults of negligence in the realm of social obligations, of justice between landlord and servant and vice versa. Sleuthe forgets to pay or to return borrowed goods ... he is unkind toward benefactors and forgets favors received from his 'even-Christians' ... he spoils his master's goods by carelessness ... he wasted his youth in idleness instead of learning a craft, and he is now a beggar ... [Wenzel, *Sin of Sloth* 138]

Langland's sloth is also related to fourteenth-century popular handbooks which link *acedia* to worldly or social faults; cf. *ibid.*, 141:

> Neglect of social obligations between lord and servant or family head and household usually took up some space in manuals of confession. Such faults appear in *Piers Plowman* as the third section of Sleuthe's confession [V.423-41]. But in contrast to manuals, they occupy a proportionately much larger space ... and are neatly set off against strictly religious faults.

Similar complaints about a neglect of religious and worldly duties are supplied elsewhere; cf. *Of Shrifte and Penance*, 75-80. For a long list of games, sports and entertainments discussed in connection with sloth see *Jacob's Well, an Englisht Treatise on the Cleansing of Man's Conscience. Part I*, ed. Arthur Brandeis, EETS, OS 115 (London: Kegan Paul, Trench, Trübner, 1900) 105/23-106/2.

[37] Thomas J. Heffernan, 'Dangerous Sympathies: Political Commentary in the *South English Legendary*,' *The South English Legendary: A Critical Assessment*, ed. Klaus P. Jankofsky (Tübingen: A. Francke, 1992) 2-3. Heffernan aptly states that '[c]ontemporary scholarship's focus on the exemplary characteristics of the hagiographic legends in collections of *libri festivales*, like the SEL, tend to blunt the social and political edge of this genre' (*ibid.* 3).

[38] Sherry L. Reames, 'Artistry, Decorum and Purpose in Three Middle English Retellings of the Cecilia Legend,' *The Endless Knot: Essays on Old and Middle English in Honor of Marie Borroff*, eds. M. Teresa Tavormina and Robert F. Yeager (Cambridge: D. S. Brewer, 1995) 177-78 and 198.

read aloud by a churchman in the king's hall or chapel', which could explain the narrator's moderate criticism of members of the secular as well as clerical ruling class.[39] The Scottish audience and readership would have been aware of references to social and occupational misconduct in discussions on *acedia* and the value of saints' lives.

> Hagiography taught daily conduct and obedience to prevailing social values more often than it taught heroic virtue: best documented is the use of legends of the virgin saints as examples for girls, who were thought likely to identify with narratives of other girls like themselves. ... [Katherine J.] Lewis argues that the virginity of Edmund of East Anglia was held up as a model to Henry VI in the expectation that he would imitate it in the less inconvenient form of sexual moderation. [Alexander] Barclay's message to the 'englysshe youth' he envisaged as readers of his *Life of St George* was that they should imitate the saint's 'manly doughtynes' by eschewing 'thriftles game', a moral to which much of the action-packed narrative is quite irrelevant.[40]

Neglect of 'the obligations of one's *status* or profession'[41] is also an issue in a sermon by Thomas Brinton, bishop of Rochester (1373-89):

> Since man is by nature born to work, the army of Christians, which chiefly consists of three degrees, namely of prelates, religious, and workers, must in hope of the kingdom of God be constantly occupied: either in the works of active life (which are the works of mercy, such as feeding the poor, clothing the naked, visiting the sick and similar things), or in the works of contemplative life (which are praying, keeping vigil, preaching, hearing divine matters, etc.), or in the works of human servitude (such as digging, plowing, sowing, reaping, and working with one's own hands). In consequence, those miserable idlers who are not usefully occupied in any of these three degrees and hence are unfruitful, deprive themselves by divine justice of the kingdom of God.[42]

According to Wenzel, the 'appraisal of human or worldly activity ... seems to have come somewhat into the foreground during the fourteenth century' and 'is often expressed in works of instruction from the fourteenth and fifteenth centuries'.[43]

---

[39] A. A. MacDonald, 'Religious Poetry in Middle Scots,' *The History of Scottish Literature Volume 1: Origins to 1660*, ed. R. D. S. Jack (Aberdeen: Aberdeen University Press, 1988) 93.

[40] Sarah Salih, 'Introduction: Saints, Cults and Lives in Late Medieval England,' *A Companion to Middle English Hagiography*, ed. Sarah Salih (Woodbridge: D.S. Brewer, 2006) 18.

[41] Wenzel, *Sin of Sloth* 90.

[42] *Ibid.* 91-92, 232, 104n, and Thomas Brinton, '*Sermo* 20', in Thomas Brinton, *The Sermons of Thomas Brinton, Bishop of Rochester, 1373-1389*, ed. Sister Mary Aquinas Devlin, Camden Third Series, 2 vols. (London: Royal Historical Society, 1954) I, 83; cf. also '*Sermo* 56' and '*Sermo* 59', II, 259, 269.

[43] Wenzel, *Sin of Sloth* 92, 93, 232, 105n.

Although worldly faults, 'such as neglect of professional duties, failure to learn a trade and earn one's bread honestly, misspent youth, and so on', came to be included in the discussion of idleness, Wenzel stresses that in the theological literature between 1200 and 1450, the period of our concern,

> these are by far outnumbered by strictly spiritual or religious faults. … in the popular image the sin of sloth remained sloth in God's service, with 'God's service' being occasionally extended to include obligations in this world and to society.[44]

In contrast to the slothful, saints are characterized by their perfection in the exercise of religious devotion. Hence their *vitae* were used as a didactic tool to correct the spiritually negligent. Like the Scottish poet, the anonymous author of the *Gilte Legende* (1438), 'a close translation, with a few additions and omissions, of Jean de Vignay's *Légend Dorée* …, which in turn is a close translation of Jacobus de Voragine's *Legenda Aurea*',[45] begins his compilation by calling his hagiographic collection a 'mirror':

> Here biginnyth the meroure and the liuynge of holie martres and of seintis that suffriden here in her liuis grete peyne and passioune in encreysinge her ioie in the blisse of heuen, to excite and stere symple lettrid men and women to encrese in vertue bi the offten redinge and hiringe of this boke. For bi hiringe mannes bileuinge is mooste stablid and istrengthid. [1-6[46]]

The English author of the *Gilte Legende* and the Scottish compiler are not the only hagiographers who regard their collections of saints' lives as guidebooks on religious behaviour:

---

[44] *Ibid.*, 96.

[45] Richard Hamer, 'Editorial Procedures', in *Gilte Legende*, eds. Richard Hamer and Vida Russell, EETS, OS 327, 328 (Oxford: Oxford University Press, 2006-07) I, ix.

[46] *Ibid.*, I, 3. *MED* records the meaning of *merroure* & variants as 'a book which guides a person's conduct or spiritual well-being' as early as *c.* 1330, possibly even *c.* 1300; Kurath, Lewis and Williams, *Middle English Dictionary*, s.v. *mirour* (n.), 3. (c). William Caxton also refers to idleness in the Prologue to his French translation of Jacobus de Voragine's *Legenda aurea*; see 'The Golden Legende, 1483, [Prologue 2]', in William Caxton, *The Prologues and Epilogues of William Caxton*, ed. W. J. B. Crotch, EETS, OS 176 (London: Oxford University Press, 1928) 71-72 (I owe this information to Prof. Dr. Luuk Houwen). Caxton as well as de Vignay (*ibid.*. 71-73 (71-72)) claim that they wrote their previous works in order to avoid committing the sin of idleness. Both name St Jerome, St Augustine, Cassiodorus and Bernard of St Clairvaux as authorities warning against the sin of idleness. On account of the relatively wide word field of *acedia* and the occasional misinterpretation of Latin words by medieval writers, the identification of relevant passages proves to be problematical; cf. Wenzel, *Sin of Sloth* 31, 34, 92, 184-85. The fact that the Scottish prologue and de Vignay's prologue both emphasize idleness suggests that the Scottish author might have been aware of the French work, composed after 1330.

As holy examples of Christian perfection, saints were frequently treated or promoted as patterns for ideal behaviour — either for male or female religious, but also for lay audiences in late medieval England.[47]

As a result,

[t]he prologue … often affords the hagiographer a good opportunity to speculate on the educational value of saints' lives … hagiography is defined as religion-teaching by example, for the virtuous life of the saint is meant as an example to all Christians. As an anonymous hagiographer of Longpont remarks, in antiquity it had been customary to memorialize the heroic deeds of noble warriors in order to stir courage in the hearts of one's readers; the lives of the saints will in a similar way encourage Christian virtue.[48]

But the slothful ignore the mirrors of holy life. In William Langland's *Piers Plowman*, *Versio* B, *passus* V, line 417, we learn that the 'sleuthe' is unable to read 'seintes lyves', and in *passus* XIII, lines 418-19, we are informed that the slothful hate to listen to 'the passion of seintes' and that they despise all those who tell them.[49]

Like the medieval preachers, the Scottish narrator thus saw 'in *acedia* one of the gravest and most diabolical temptations, as the desert fathers had done before';[50] and on the basis of the traditional perception that saints' legends should function as guidebooks on religious as well as secular behaviour, the Scottish prologue would have made the reader or listener aware of the necessity to proceed with the collection proper.[51]

The fact that the poet is hoping for a clerical as well as a secular audience/readership also agrees with Anke Bernau's remark that 'vernacular hagiography, unlike Latin hagiography, was not just produced within clerical circles for clerical audiences. … vernacular hagiography therefore cannot be read simply as an expression of either clerical *or* lay values, but as a complex blend of the two'.[52] Hence, the Scottish prologue lends

---

[47]   Anke Bernau, 'Gender and Sexuality,' *A Companion to Middle English Hagiography*, ed. Sarah Salih (Woodbridge: D.S. Brewer, 2006) 104. Cf. also Brinkmann, 'Der Prolog im Mittelalter,' 19, 20, and Wolpers, *Die englische Heiligenlegende* 289-79.

[48]   Goodich, 'Note on Sainthood,' 171.

[49]   Cf. also Wenzel, *Sin of Sloth* 138-39.

[50]   *Ibid.*, 102.

[51]   Unfortunately, G. H. Gerould was unaware of the relevance of the Scottish prologue when he remarks that the author 'had his mind fixed, I should say, less on the public for which he was writing and more on the legends themselves than the makers of the English collections': G. H. Gerould, *Saints' Legends* (Boston: Houghton Mifflin Company, 1916) 182-83.

[52]   Bernau, 'Gender and Sexuality,' 106-07. Cf. also Simon Gaunt, *Gender and Genre in Medieval French Literature*, Cambridge Studies in French (Cambridge: Cambridge University Press, 1995) 181-82.

support to Sarah Salih's statement that the '[s]aint-cult was a continual dialogue of lay and clerical interests, and successful cults needed to satisfy both'.[53]

In contrast to the anonymous English narrator of the *Gilte Legende*, the Scottish narrator is intensifying the already established bond between the addresser and addressee by employing a didactic *us* (25, 26), and by doing so he enhances the role which is frequently ascribed to the narrators of medieval saints' lives:

> The hagiographic narrator typically takes the position of mediator, both between the saint and the audience and between textual tradition and his own present day; hagiographic texts often address their audience directly, prescribing their response.[54]

Following ancient rhetoricians, medieval authors occasionally expressed the notion that a prologue should render the listener or reader attentive (*attentus*), well-disposed (*docilis*), and willing to learn (*benevolus*), and all these intentions are reflected in the Scottish prologue.[55] The ancient rhetorical term *attentio* refers to the composer's attempt to catch the listener's or reader's attention by promising information important for his or her life as well as for that of the narrator.[56] *Docilitas* can be achieved by a brief summary or announcement of the work or matter to be discussed.[57] The Scottish hagiographer is blending the two devices of *attentio* and *docilitas*. He attracts the listener's/reader's attention by referring to two largely secular works, the well-known *Disticha Catonis* and the *Roman de la Rose*, by indirectly criticizing those in power and by referring to the originally secular tradition of the mirrors for princes and of courtesy. Thus, he tricks the foolish listeners/readers into believing that he will instruct them in secular behaviour.[58] In his attempt to gain the listener's/reader's *docilitas*, he states his intention

---

[53] Salih, 'Introduction,' 3.

[54] *Ibid.*, 11.

[55] Cf., for instance, Conrad of Hirsau, '*Dialogue on the Authors*: Extracts', 'Bernard Silvester', 'Commentary on the *Aeneid*, Books I-VI', and Dante Alighieri (?), '*Epistle to Can Grande della Scala*: Extract', in A. J. Minnis and A. B. Scott, eds., *Medieval Literary Theory and Criticism c.1100-c.1375* (Oxford: Clarendon Press, 1991) 150-54 (152), 39-64 (43), 458-69 (463), and see Schultz, 'Medieval Vernacular Prologue,' 4, 5, 11. Note also the introduction to the *Disticha Catonis* in the twelfth-century MS Munich, Clm 19475: And so the writer prefaces his work with a prologue in which his aim is to make us attentive, receptive to his teaching, and well disposed. For when he says SERIOUSLY he makes us attentive; when he tells us where he has detected that error, namely IN THE PATH OF BEHAVIOUR, in bringing morals under his scrutiny he makes us receptive to his teaching; and when he calls us sons, saying MY DEAREST SON, he makes us well disposed. [Minnis and Scott, eds., *Medieval Literary Theory* 16]

[56] Cf., for instance, Brinkmann, 'Der Prolog im Mittelalter,' 4, who on the same page also observes that another way of catching the listener's or reader's attention is the promise that something new will follow.

[57] *Ibid.*, 4.

[58] See also note 26 above.

to retell the lives of saints so that his audience/readership might learn how to serve God properly (lines 27-30), and he concludes with a subtle warning to those who will not heed the examples set by the saints (31-32):

> þare-fore, in lytil space here,
> I wryt þe lyf of sanctis sere,
> how þat men ma ensample ta
> for to serwe god, as did þai.
> & quha-sa wil nocht, sal haf blam,
> quhen he sal cume til his lang ham. [ll. 27-32]

The hagiographer then proceeds to achieve the *benevolentia* of the reader or listener, traditionally gained by the speaker's emphasis of his past achievements or/and weaknesses (lines 31-42):[59]

> þar-for, sene I ma nocht wirk
> as mynistere of haly kirke,
> fore gret eld & febilnes,
> ʒet, for til eschew ydilnes,
> I hafe translatit symply
> sume part, as I fand in story,
> of mary & hir sone Ihesu,
> þat, as I tre[w], is notyt now
> in syndry placis in wryt,
> to gere deuot men think on It: [ll. 33-42]

By referring to his old age and frailty, which can be contrasted with the young age of the protagonists in the *Roman de la Rose*,[60] and by alluding to his professional experience as a priest and the fact that he himself had been tempted by idleness in the past, the narrator is subtly stressing his authority on the subject matter.[61] Furthermore, the

---

[59] Brinkmann, 'Der Prolog im Mittelalter,' 4. Conrad of Hirsau in his *Accessus ad auctores*, for instance, remarks: 'Every prologue is either apologetic or else commendatory. For the writer either excuses himself, or tries to commend himself [to his readers]' (Minnis and Scott, eds., *Medieval Literary Theory* 43).

[60] Note again the introduction to the *Disticha Catonis* in the twelfth-century MS Munich, Clm 19475: 'When Cato the censor saw that young men and girls were living very wicked lives he wrote this book to his son, showing him the proper way to live, and through him teaching all men to live just and moral lives' (Minnis and Scott, eds., *Medieval Literary Theory* 15). See also the reference to Alexander Barclay's message in his *Life of St George*, referred to above on p. 14.

[61] Long, 'Corpora and Manuscripts,' 58, aptly notes that '[t]he author of (at least) the prologue and the legends of the apostles describes himself as a priest of "gret eld and febilnes", which may be a literary topos and does not enable him to be identified.'

listener's/reader's *benevolentia* is enhanced by the narrator's reference to Jesus Christ and the Virgin Mary. Since both are believed to have lived a life free from sin and in utter dedication to God,[62] it was only appropriate that the poet should have translated Latin renderings of their lives into his mother tongue before embarking on a translation of the lives of the apostles, evangelists and other saints, presented in the preserved collection. As already noted by Wenzel, '[t]he lives and deeds of the patriarchs and saints, of the Blessed Virgin and, of course, of Christ Himself, were in general held up by the preacher as "examples that will help to detest *acedia*."'[63]

In Geoffrey Chaucer's 'Prologe' to the *Second Nun's Tale*, contemporary to the *Scottish Legends of the Saints*, advice against idleness precedes the legend of St Cecilia, a legend which is also part of the Scottish collection:[64]

> The ministre and the norice unto vices,
> Which that men clepe in Englissh Ydelnesse,
> That porter of the gate is of delices,
> To eschue, and by hire contrarie hire opresse —
> That is to seyn, by leveful bisynesse —
> Wel oghten we to doon al oure entente,
> Lest that the feend thurgh ydelnesse us hente. [VIII (G) 1-7]

Chaucer refers to Idleness's role as keeper of the gate to the garden of Pleasure, without, however, mentioning the *Roman de la Rose* itself, a work which he himself had

---

[62] On 'the ideal of the *imitatio Christi*' see, for example, Goodich, 'Note on Sainthood,' 172.

[63] Wenzel, *Sin of Sloth* 103. Cf. also the following remarks by Wenzel (pp. 103-04):
Haste and eagerness in God's service are also shown in the life of the Blessed Virgin, who 'abiit in montana cum festinatione' (Luke 1:39) to visit Elizabeth upon a mere suggestion made by the Angel. To Mary are applied the words from the praise of the good housewife, 'Panem otiosa non comedit' (Prov. 31:27), and Conrad of Saxony says that, 'against *acedia* Mary was most indefatigable through her zeal [*sedulitas*]. … And since Mary was not *acediosa*, she also was not idle, but kept not only her mind busy in holy meditations and her tongue in devout prayers, but also her hands in good works' (pp. 45, 52). But the prime example of zeal and fervent devotion is Christ, who 'was not lazy but rejoiced as a giant running his way' (Peraldus, *Summa*, 3.5; cf. Ps. 19:5). As an illustration of the weariness and exhaustion He willingly suffered during His life, Peraldus cites John 4:6, 'Jesus ergo fatigatus ex itinere sedebat sic supra fontem' (1.142). Of the seven words Christ spoke on the cross, the fourth was especially directed against *acedia*: 'The fourthe word that Crist spak here, was when he criede Eloy; and bi this word he puttid out slouthe, whanne he preiede his God now, and confessid in a manere that God dide thus for his good. … And sith God lefte Crist in his enemyes hondis, to good of him and his Chirche, what art thou that grutchist aȝens God, to suffre peyne and flee slouthe?'
Elsewhere (130) Wenzel also refers to Dante's *Purgatory*, canto xviii, where two voices of the Slothful 'proclaim *exempla* against the vice of sloth. The first praises the zeal of the Blessed Virgin … The second *anti-exemplum* recalls the eagerness of Julius Caesar …'

[64] See 'Cecile' (XLIII), in *Legends of the Saints in the Scottish Dialect of the Fourteenth Century*, II, 368-86.

rendered into Middle English.[65] In the following stanza (VIII (G) 8-14), the Second Nun stresses that the devil can easily get hold of 'us' when he sees man in idleness; so Chaucer is employing a didactic 'us' as well. In stanza three of the prologue, the English poet is emphasising the role of reason in making man realize that idleness is 'roten slogardye' (VIII (G) 15-21):

> And though men dradden nevere for to dye,
> Yet seen men wel by resoun, doutelees,
> That ydelnesse is roten slogardye,
> Of which ther nevere comth no good n'encrees;
> And syn that slouthe hire holdeth in a lees
> Oonly to slepe, and for to ete and drynke,
> And to devouren al that othere swynke. [VIII (G) 15-21]

But in contrast to the Scottish narrator, Chaucer's Second Nun clearly regards idleness as a branch of sloth and not as a synonym of *acedia*; and to keep 'us' from falling victim to idleness, she will exercise diligence by telling the story of St Cecilia:

> And for to putte us fro swich ydelnesse,
> That cause is of so greet confusioun,
> I have heer doon my feithful bisynesse
> After the legende in translacioun
> Right of thy glorious lif and passioun,
> Thou with thy gerland wroght with rose and lilie —
> Thee meene I, mayde and martyr, Seinte Cecilie. [VIII (G) 22-28]

So whereas the Second Nun favours 'bisynesse' (5) and 'charite' (118) as a remedy against idleness, the Scottish poet alludes to fortitude as its antidote. On account of its secular connotations, fortitude would surely have been a more attractive virtue for a courtly ruling class interested in romances and historiographical writings and their depictions of prowess.[66] The introductory four stanzas of the *Second Nun's Prologue* are followed by an invocation to the Virgin Mary (VIII (G) 29-84), recalling the praise of the Virgin in the Scottish legend.[67] We do not know whether the Scottish poet

---

[65] Cf. also the reference to Idleness in the description of the murals of the temple of Venus in Chaucer's *Knight's Tale* I (A) 1940.

[66] Note here, for instance, Salih's remark that '[d]evotion could mimic heterosexual romance' (Salih, 'Introduction,' 19), and Goodich emphasizes that the saint was regarded 'as a divine instrument of the Church Militant' (Goodich, 'Note on Sainthood,' 168). In *Of Shrifte and Penance: The Middle English Prose Translation of 'Le Manuel des péchés'*, 76-77, sloth is linked to the pastime of holding tournaments. Too much hunting and hawking are, for example, also given as symptoms of idleness in *Jacob's Well*, 105/12-15, 23-24, 29-31. Finally, cf. Bernau, 'Gender and Sexuality,' 109.

[67] According to Ridley in the introduction to *The Second Nun's Prologue and Tale*, the invocation is 'based mainly on Dante (Par. 33.1-39)'; Chaucer, *Riverside Chaucer* 942.

was aware of Chaucer's prologue, and Florence H. Ridley notes that 'such a prologue is conventional'.[68]

Like Geoffrey Chaucer, the Scottish composer links his collection to a specific moral concern,[69] a device which Goodich ascribes to the more learned hagiographers.[70] He renders his collection more appealing to his audience/readership, secular as well as religious, by combining the courtly tradition of idleness with penitential teachings on sloth, criticizing the affluent, but, at the same time, aiming at a wider audience/readership. With its moral instruction, embedded in the literary and devotional context of the Middle Ages and presented in the traditional tripartite division of medieval prologues, the Scottish prologue suggests a compilation of some quality, which surely deserves a more comprehensive analysis than it has received so far.

---

[68] *Ibid.*, 942, and the note to lines 1-28 on p. 943. Cf. also Geoffrey Chaucer, *The Canterbury Tales*, ed. Jill Mann, Penguin Classics (London: Penguin, 2005) 1055. According to Ridley, Chaucer's lines on idleness 'may have come from the introduction to the French translation of the *Legenda aurea* by Jean de Vignay (1282/85-1348)' (*ibid.*).

[69] See also Wolpers, *Die englische Heiligenlegende* 279.

[70] Goodich, 'Note on Sainthood,' 172; cf. also 168, 174 and Wolpers, *Die englische Heiligenlegende* 279.

Looking at Mary: The Mother of Christ in Kennedy's 'Ballat of Our Lady' and 'Passioun of Crist'

Nicole Meier

The Blessed Virgin features twice in Walter Kennedy's *oeuvre*: in a praise and petition poem addressed to her (Incipit: 'Closter of Crist, riche, Recent flour delyß'; Title: 'Ane ballat of our lady'; IMEV 636; Meier 2008, poem III) and in a long Passion narrative (Incipit: 'Hail, Cristin knycht, haill, etern confortour'; Title 'þe passioun of Crist'; IMEV 1040; Meier 2008, poem IV).

It is not unlikely that Kennedy may have composed more poems to the Blessed Virgin, especially praise poems, since he is remembered for his aureate verse by David Lyndsay in his *Testament of the Papyngo*: 'Or quho can, now, the workis cuntrafait / Of Kennedie, with termes aureait?' (ll. 15-16).[1] The fact that the canon of extant poems is small (only six poems have come down to us) may partly be due to the effects of the Reformation — on Marian poetry in particular. Since after the Reformation 'plainness of style came to be prized more highly than traditional colours of rhetoric',[2] this resulted in the loss of many texts, such as of vernacular religious drama in Scotland, and in Protestant expurgations of poems which were included in Post-Reformation anthologies (and in manipulation of literary categories, such as the lyrics of Our Lady which are called 'ballatis of the nativitie of Christie' in the post-Reformation Bannatyne MS).[3]

The poems by Kennedy which have a Marian focus are extant in pre-Reformation manuscripts only: the Asloan MS (Edinburgh, NLS 16500) and London, BL MS Arundel 285. Arundel 285 owes 'its survival to the fact that it was acquired by the English recusant scholar, collector and antiquary, Lord William Howard'[4] and contains,

---

[1]   Sir David Lyndsay, *Sir David Lyndsay. Selected Poems*, ed. Janet Hadley Williams (Glasgow: Association for Scottish Literary Studies, 2000) 58.

[2]   A. A. MacDonald, 'Religious Poetry in Middle Scots,' *The History of Scottish Literature Volume 1: Origins to 1660*, ed. R. D. S. Jack (Aberdeen: Aberdeen University Press, 1988) 92.

[3]   A. A. MacDonald, 'Poetry, Politics, and Reformation Censorship in Sixteenth-Century Scotland,' *English Studies* 64 (1983); Nicole Meier, 'Protestant Censorship in 16th-Century Scottish Manuscripts: The Case of Walter Kennedy's "Leif luve, my luve, no langar it lyk",' *Anglistentag 2008 Tübingen: Proceedings*, eds. Lars Eckstein and Christoph Reinfandt (Trier: WVT, 2009).

[4]   A. A. MacDonald, 'Passion Devotion in Late-Medieval Scotland,' *The Broken Body. Passion Devotion in Late-Medieval Culture*, eds. A. A. MacDonald, H. N. B. Ridderbos and R. M. Schlusemann (Groningen: Forsten, 1998) 109.

besides Kennedy's long *Passioun*, items related to or dealing with the Passion; the Asloan MS is a verse and prose miscellany.

This article will be 'looking at Mary' in Kennedy's Marian and Passion lyrics in at least two ways. First, it will examine how devotees turn their eyes towards the Blessed Virgin in prayer and ask for intercession. Second, it will look at Mary as a witness to Christ's death on the Cross, where she herself is the beholder.

The Blessed Virgin Mary was a central figure in medieval devotion and the most-revered of the Christian saints, although she only plays a secondary or marginal role in the gospels. Apocryphal legends supplied missing details by describing Mary's parents, her birth, and her youth. The apocryphal book which exerted the greatest influence upon the cult of the Virgin in the East was the *Protoevangelium Jacobi Minoris* (The Book of James), and the apocryphal gospel to influence the cult in the West was the Pseudo-Matthew, an elaboration of the Book of James and a source for the birth of Mary, which in turn found its way into the *Legenda Aurea*. The Pseudo-Matthew also mentions one of Mary's most prominent qualities, her power of intercession. The embellishments of the biblical narrative led to the establishment of new liturgical feasts and a steady growth in Marian devotion, which also had an impact on literature and liturgy: innumerable hymns were written in praise of Mary and then found their way into the Office of the Blessed Virgin and into Books of Hours. But it was not only the apocryphal legends that shaped the way in which Mary was perceived and character-ised. Typological readings of the Old Testament, and the Song of Songs in particular, also played their part here: Mary is described as lily or rose; she is the enclosed garden or sealed fountain; she is compared to Old Testament figures (the *sponsa*, Judith, or Esther) and also contrasted with them, and with Eve in particular: Mary's obedience was opposed to Eve's disobedience.

The perception of Mary, and hence her portrayal in literature and art, changed over the centuries. Whereas early representations show Mary and Jesus both royally crowned, the image of Mary as queen gave way gradually to an emphasis on Mary as mother of the child Jesus. Especially the mendicant orders placed stress on the humanity of both Christ and the Blessed Virgin, who was now seen as the gentle, protective and merciful mother (*mater misericordiae*) who shows herself more approachable and kind than the enthroned and awe-inspiring queen of heaven. From the twelfth century onwards the title of *mediatrix* spread. One catalyst was the rapid spread of the Black Death through Europe, which caused Christians to turn anxiously to Mary for assistance trusting her to intercede for them with her son. The cult of Mary as the sorrowful mother began to flourish in England, Scotland and the Continent, reaching its full flowering from the fourteenth century onward. The humanisation of the suffering of Christ and meditations on the sorrows of the Virgin (the prophecy of Simeon, the flight to Egypt, the loss of Jesus in the temple, the meeting with Jesus on the road to Calvary, the crucifixion, deposition and entombment) were deeply rooted in affective piety and placed Mary centre stage. She is seen as co-sufferer and mediatory figure; her sorrows and suffering at the sight of her son's Passion enhance the emotional impact. She is 'represented as a model of suffering and compassion…to promote emotional responses to the sufferings of Christ.'[5]

Representations of Mary in art and literature mirror these developments, and her different roles as (suffering) mother, intercessor and heavenly queen are also present in Kennedy's poems. His Marian poem combines praise and petition. In the first stanzas, Kennedy names the main functions, positions, and attributes of the Blessed Virgin. The speaker addresses her as bearer of Christ, as 'closter' (l. 1),[6] and thus compares her to a vessel or an enclosure containing Christ.[7] A similar image occurs again in l. 39, where Mary's womb is chosen as Christ's 'houß & hant' (dwelling place). In the first line, she is then seen as 'flour delyß' (lily), underlining her beauty and purity, but also her regal status and power as queen of heaven, since the iris is also a royal emblem. These are two different aspects which are frequently evoked in Marian poetry and Kennedy calls her 'princes of hevyn, hell, erd and paradyß' in l. 3, which recalls the 'queene of hevene […] emperesse of helle' in the Primer and many other poems.[8] When the reference is to her nobility, the speaker is looking up to Mary in awe and honours her just like the 'orders of heaven'.[9] Her exalted position, power and beauty make it difficult for the poet to adequately describe her 'honouris Infinite' (l. 31): even if the sea

---

[5]   Thomas H. Bestul, *Texts of the Passion: Latin Devotional Literature and Medieval Society*, Middle Ages Series (Philadelphia, PA: University of Pennsylvania Press, 1996) 124.

[6]   Quotations and references are taken from my edition of Kennedy's poems: Walter Kennedy, *The Poems of Walter Kennedy*, ed. Nicole Meier, STS 5th ser. 6 (Woodbridge: Scottish Text Society, 2008).

[7]   This is a popular comparison. Mary is 'clo(y)ster' (enclosure) in 'Regina celi and Lady, letare' (*A New Index of Middle English Verse*, eds. Julia Boffey, A. S. G. Edwards and Rossell Hope Robbins (London: British Library, 2005) 2800 [*NIMEV*]; *Religious Lyrics of the XVth Century*, ed. Carleton Brown (Oxford: OUP, 1952) poem no. 28/56); 'The infinite power essenciall' (*NIMEV*, 3391, *Religious Lyrics of the XVth Century*, 38/31); 'Honour be euere, withowtyn ende' (*NIMEV*, 3297, *The Early English Carols*, ed. Richard Leighton Greene, 2nd ed. (Oxford: Oxford University Press, 1977) no. 181, stanza 3); Lydgate's 'Quen of heuene, of helle, eeke emperesse' (*NIMEV*, 2791; John Lydgate, *The Minor Poems of John Lydgate*, ed. Henry N. MacCracken, EETS, ES 107; OS 192, 2 vols. (London: Oxford University Press, 1911, 1934) I, no. 54/21), and the Prologue to Chaucer's 'Second Nun's Tale' (*CT* VIII.43) in Geoffrey Chaucer, *The Riverside Chaucer*, ed. Larry D. Benson (Oxford: Oxford University Press, 1987).

[8]   *Monumenta Ritualia Ecclesiae Anglicanae. The Occasional Offices of the Church of England according to the Old Use of Salisbury the Prymer in English and Other Prayers and Forms with Dissertations and Notes*, ed. William Maskell, 3 vols. (Oxford: Clarendon Press, 1846) II, 78; another example — among many others — of Mary as queen of heaven and hell can be found in a poem preceding Kennedy's in the Asloan MS, fol. 301[r].

[9]   Cf. Lydgate: 'The Ordris Nyne of Angellis with gladnesse, / As to there queen, to the doun obeisaunce' (*NIMEV*, 2565; Lydgate, *Minor Poems* I, no. 61/5-6).

and lakes were ink, the heavenly bodies, hills, and mountains were parchment, and everything was as Virgil's poetry, even if woods, forests, groves, gardens, and trees were pens, words would not suffice to describe the Virgin's innumerable glories. Kennedy makes use of the inexpressibility topos in stanza four, which was typically employed in panegyrics to claim the poet's inability to describe the excellence of the eulogised person. The formula used here goes back to Sanskrit literature but was also current in Western medieval literature.[10]

Yet, although Kennedy directs the reader to look up to Mary as exalted queen and royal beauty, whose merits are not always easy to put into words, he mainly addresses Mary as intercessor. She is full of mercy, has healing powers and 'bathis our blak syn with this balmis schouris' (l. 4), is comparable to a physician (l. 6) and is a protectress (l. 9) interceding on the sinner's behalf by exposing her breasts to Christ (ll. 11—12).[11] Mary's ears are always open to the sinner's request, even if 'all sanctis our synfull prayere contempne' (ll. 43). The power she has been eulogised for is employed to help the sinner (she overcame the devil, she brings the petitioner to eternal joy [iii.47] and saves the souls from hell [iii.61]). Whenever her regal status or beauty are acclaimed — as in stanza seven where she is praised from top to toe, this is always done in relationship with her son (her breast which appeased her son, her hands which embraced him, her womb which relates mankind to Christ). Mary is approachable as mother of Christ, and this is what Kennedy calls her in the last stanza of the poem, when the worshipper asks the Blessed Virgin for protection and intercession so that the speaker may be granted remission of sins and a place in heaven. In the last stanza, there is also a shift from 'ws' and 'our' to 'me' and 'my' when the petitioner entreats Mary to remember him ('mater dei memento mei', l. 72),[12] a popular plea found in breviaries and prayers.

Although in Kennedy's poem the Blessed Virgin is revered for her position, beauty and purity, she is approachable only when viewed in her humanity, addressed as mother, and implored as intercessor and *mediatrix*. This is also the reason why Kennedy's poem is less aureate than Dunbar's 'Hale, sterne superne', which is mainly a praise poem and prayer to the Blessed Virgin, and does not end with or involve any sort of petition. Kennedy's poem rather resembles other lyrics preceding it in the Asloan MS. Although it contains expository and celebratory aspects, it culminates in the speaker's petition at the end of the poem. In its essence, it is a petition, with the

---

[10] For the topos see Irving Linn, 'If All the Sky Were Parchment,' *PMLA* 53 (1938).

[11] The *ostentatio mammarum* was a popular theme in the iconography of Last Judgement scenes. See also Lk 11:27 where Jesus is reminded by a woman of the breasts that he sucked: 'beatus venter qui te portavit et ubera quae suxisti'.

[12] The singular form 'nescio', in the macaronic line at the end of stanza iii, is hardly an exception.

speaker imagining Mary as a powerful royal lady who can intercede on the devotee's behalf, and as a merciful mother who can be approached and asked for help. That the poem merges praise, petition and prayer is also underlined by the Latin lines concluding each stanza. They are mainly culled from the Office of the Blessed Virgin, and bear some relationship to the preceding and sometimes also to the following stanza. It is important to note that the Office of the Blessed Virgin was an integral part of many a Book of Hours, used by lay people who wished to structure their devotional life. They also frequently contained images, and were hence devotional tools. Kennedy's poem can thus be understood as the expression of the praise and prayer of a meditator with a Book of Hours or a painting (some sort of *Andachtsbild*) in front of him or her, looking at the Blessed Virgin, and finally asking her to intercede on his or her behalf.

That Kennedy's Marian poem therefore belongs to the realm of 'poems of meditation',[13] does not come as a surprise, since it is a devotional exercise 'by which the soul of the meditator may be brought into a better condition'.[14] This is also certainly true of the other lyric by Kennedy which features the Blessed Virgin, his *Passioun of Crist*. This is a long narrative of the life of Christ firmly rooted in the tradition of affective piety (and of the Pseudo-Bonaventuran *Meditationes Vitae Christi*), having Ludolph of Saxony's *Vita Christi* as it main source of inspiration.[15] These Latin meditations and narratives on the Passion of Christ had an impact on the lyrics of affective devotion, and the divine could now be approached 'through intimate knowledge and emphatic experience of Christ's humanity and Passion'.[16]

Mary appears five times in Kennedy's *Passioun*: at the Annunciation and nativity (ll. 120-147), at the foot of the Cross (ll. 1079-1162), when holding the dead body of Christ in her arms after the deposition (ll. 1240-1288), at the burial of Christ (ll. 1321-1351) and when Christ appears to her after his resurrection (ll. 1426-1449).

Since the focus of Kennedy's narrative of the life of Christ is clearly on the Passion, the annunciation, the visit to Elizabeth and the nativity are described only briefly. At the annunciation, Mary is portrayed in similar terms to those seen in the *Ballat*: she is virgin and royal queen ('angelicall regin', l. 123), while at the same time showing meekness and humility. In Luke's Annunciation episode (Lk 1: 26-38), Mary asks the angel 'How will this be … since I am a virgin?' and then voices her consent: 'Ecce

---

[13] The classification is that of MacDonald, 'Religious Poetry in Middle Scots,' 97.

[14] *Ibid.*

[15] The standard editions are Saint Bonaventure, *Bonaventuræ… Opera omnia*, ed. Adolphe Charles Peltier, 15 vols. (Paris: 1864-71) and Ludolphus de Saxonia, *Vita Jesu Christi: ex Evangelio et approbatis ab Ecclesia Catholica doctoribus sedule collecta*, ed. L. M. Rigollot, 4 vols. (Paris: Apud Victorem Palme, 1878). In the following, references to Ludolph's *Vita Christi* are by part (pars), chapter, sub-chapter.

[16] James Marrow, 'Circumdederunt Me Canes Multi: Christ's Tormentors in Northern European Art of the Late Middle Ages and Early Renaissance,' *Art Bulletin* 59 (1977): 167.

ancilla Domini, fiat mihi secundum verbum tuum.' That Mary's words are missing in Kennedy' *Passioun* (in Ludolph's *Vita Christi* she remains silent and her consent is merely acknowledged in stanza xix by 'scho concentit', l. 127) may be a deliberate condensation on the part of the author, but it could also be that a stanza is missing between stanzas xviii and xix. There is no doubt, however, that Kennedy intended to present the reader with a concise version of Christ's life up to the Passion, which is at the core of his narrative.

When Mary appears again, it is at the foot of the Cross. The Gospels, however, afford no material for her reaction to her son's suffering. John 19:25 only says: 'stabant autem iuxta crucem Iesu mater eius et soror matris eius Maria Cleopae et Maria Magdalene' and the other evangelists do not mention the Blessed Virgin at all, Mt 27:56 lists Mary Magdalene, Mary Jacoby, and 'the mother of Zebedee's children', Mk 15:40 Mary Magdalene, Salome, and Mary Jacoby, and in Lk 23:49 the 'women' are standing afar off. In Kennedy's *Passioun*, the Blessed Virgin, Mary Magdalene, Salome, Mary Jacoby and St John are witnesses of the crucifixion (ll. 1080-1082) and 'vthir ma'. Their immediate response to the crucifixion is that Mary is dying 'for dule of his grete wo & pane' (l. 1085). The narrator stresses the pain Mary experiences at her son's death: '[q]hen scho hir sone <u>saw</u> de apon þe tre' (l. 1087, my emphasis). The reader sees the events of the Passion through the eyes of Mary. She is looking at the Cross, watching her son die on the 'tree', and the reader is invited to share this perspective. She is hardly able to stand upright: 'On ground to stand þat sche had na powstie' (l. 1089). Whereas crucifixion scenes from before the thirteenth century typically show Mary standing upright at the foot of the cross with sorrowful but restrained gestures (her hands are clasped with fingers interlaced), later images depict Mary swooning, very often with eyes closed and legs faltering. It has been suggested that since the Virgin did not suffer labour pains at the birth of Christ, being exempt from the curse that condemned Eve to bear children in pain, she experiences this pain when she becomes a mother again on Calvary.[17] Jesus is recurrently described as 'sone' (ll. 1087, ll. 1092, 1094) rather than 'Crist', which reinforces the maternal aspect of her experience of the crucifixion. Mary's pain and her swoon express her compassion, her maternity, and her sacrifice — she shares Christ's Passion, which is literally her compassion. Her grief is compared to the sword of Simeon's prophecy, piercing her heart (Lk 2:35: 'et tuam ipsius animam pertransiet gladius ut revelentur ex multis cordibus cogitationes'). She is thus able to help in Christ's work of redemption. The *mediatrix* as addressee of petitions is also a *co-redemptrix*.

---

[17]   Amy Neff, 'The Pain of *Compassio*: Mary's Labor at the Foot of the Cross,' *Art Bulletin* 80 (1998): 255.

Mary is described as looking with 'E and hert' to the cross (l. 1093). This recalls the narrator's frequent appeals elsewhere in the narrative to the reader to behold a particular scene.[18] The 'hert' is also taken to be an inward eye, as in the narrator's exhortation to the reader at sext to 'luke with þi Inwart sycht' (l. 645). Like the Blessed Virgin, the reader is to look at the cross with his or her eyes and heart: 'With hert and E luke to þe tre' (l. 793), thus envisioning the Passion through the eyes of the mother of Christ. Effective meditation works through visualisation, and very often illustrations accompany texts on the Passion: in Arundel 285 woodcuts from early 16th century devotional works ornament the manuscript; on fol. 5ᵛ, at the beginning of Kennedy's *Passioun*, there is a coloured woodcut of the flagellation of Christ. Since visualisation is basically the reconstruction and experiencing of a scene in the mind's eye, the narrator's exhortations to see, behold or think on place the reader in a creative role. Additionally, since the eye was traditionally regarded as the most powerful sensory organ, the process of visualisation was credited with great power. Such a recreation of the Passion through the imagination was aimed at stimulating the emotions and moving the reader to apt responses of pity and compassion and at the 'imprinting of a religious topic upon the mind'.[19] Taking the perspective of an eyewitness of the Passion, and of Christ's mother in particular, draws the reader into a response which ideally led to or encouraged repentance and moral improvement. In her study, Bartlett identifies two strategies used by narrators: '(1) graphic appeals to the senses that allow the reader not only to visualize but also to imagine hearing, feeling, and even tasting aspects of the crucifixion; and (2) the use of narrators within the text (especially the Virgin Mary), who spur the reader on to a closer identification with the Passion, greater expressions of fervor, and ultimately to a contemplative transcendence of her sensory and cognitive processes.'[20]

In Kennedy's *Passioun*, although the events of the Passion are presented from Mary's perspective and her reaction is described by the narrator, the passages in which she herself speaks make the strongest impression upon the reader. After her son's death, Mary addresses the cross and complains that it has slain her son and holds him unlawfully (ll. 1095-1099). Mary is the rightful bearer of Christ, whereas the cross as 'tree' is bearing fruit which does not belong to it. Since the cross is a punishment fit for 'wile personis' (l. 1107), it should have rejected Christ, who was innocent, but it did not make a distinction between good and bad people and hence contrived to requite love,

---

[18]   Examples of the imperative of *behald* in the *Passioun*: ll. 281, 465, 617, 974, 1193, 1289, 1611; of *luke*: ll. 645, 778, 793.

[19]   MacDonald, 'Passion Devotion in Scotland,' 121.

[20]   Anne Clark Bartlett, *Male Authors, Female Readers. Representation and Subjectivity in Middle English Devotional Literature* (Ithaca: Cornell University Press, 1995) 123. Although Bartlett focuses on devotional texts written with a female audience in mind, her findings are applicable to a much wider range of texts.

charity, and honour with pain and shame (ll. 1116-1117). Mary cannot comprehend why the cross is functioning as servant of death (l. 1119) and why the son of God is crucified among thieves (l. 1120). Her complaint is followed by a reply from the cross itself, which addresses Mary as virgin, lady and heavenly queen and honours her. It explains that the 'frute of the richt mychty' (l. 1122) makes the cross, i.e. the tree, blossom; it is medicine to dead people, and it was born to the world (l. 1130) for the redemption of mankind. Thus, the tree of Paradise is contrasted with the tree of the Cross freeing mankind. The sweet fruit conquers bitter death, and the Blessed Virgin should therefore rejoice and understand the function of the cross, since it is a day-star spreading the news to the fathers in limbo (l. 1147-1148) and a wine stock which supports the vine's branches (although it did not bring it forth as Mary did) and since it bears the fruit ordained to die for mankind. The cross received Christ as mortal man and returned him immortal (ll. 1162-1163).

Mary's debate with the cross in Kennedy's *Passioun* belongs to the tradition of the *planctus Mariae*, with its roots in Byzantine Marian laments, and is indebted to poems influenced by the Latin tradition of the thirteenth-century pseudo-Bernardian *Liber de Passione Christi et doloribus et planctibus Matris ejus* (or *Tractatus de planctu Beatae Mariae*) beginning 'Quis dabit capiti meo aquam'.[21]

The *planctus* emerging from the cult of the *mater dolorosa* are laments in which the Virgin directly communicates her inner tribulation; they occur in both lyric and dramatic form, in monologue and dialogue. The *planctus* is already dramatic in its conception and could easily have been inserted into Passion plays, without necessarily being their source.[22]

Kennedy's direct source is a Latin poem by Philip de Greve ('Crux, de te volo conqueri').[23] There is no *planctus* in Ludolph's *Vita Christi*, which deals with the sufferings of Mary quite briefly, and the next chapter is concerned with the breaking of the criminals' legs and does not contain a Marian lament. It appears that Kennedy deliberately had Mary engage in a debate with the cross in order to help the reader to

---

[21] PL 182.1133a-42a.

[22] In his seminal study, Sticca refutes the traditional view that the *planctus Mariae* is the germinal point of the Latin Passion Play and maintains that the *planctus* developed alongside the Passion plays. See Sandro Sticca, *The Planctus Mariae in the Dramatic Tradition of the Middle Ages*, trans. Joseph R. Berrigan (Athens GA: University of Georgia Press, 1988). See also George R. Keiser, 'The Middle English *Planctus Mariae* and the Rhetoric of Pathos,' *The Popular Literature of Medieval England*, ed. Thomas J. Heffernan (Knoxville, TN: University of Tennessee Press, 1985), and John Rennell Secor, '*Planctus Mariae*: The Laments of Mary as Influenced by Courtly Literature,' Ph.D. dissertation, The University of North Carolina at Chapel Hill, 1985.

[23] *Analecta Hymnica Medii Aevi*, eds. Clemens Blume and Guido Maria Dreves, 30 vols. (Leipzig: Fues, 1886) XXI, no. 14, 20-21.

commiserate with Mary and furthermore to see the death of Christ through her eyes on the one hand, and to understand the divine plan of salvation on the other, which is explained by the cross to Mary and the reader. Kennedy merges arboreal and maternal imagery, and since the cross and Mary were linked through parallel imagery, they were frequently chosen as interlocutors. In iconography and exegesis they are both represented as fruit-bearing trees and thus 'linked as mothers or bearers of Christ.'[24]

The *planctus Mariae* achieves its effects on the reader (heightening of emotion, eliciting responses of compassion and empathy, moral reform) by a combination of dramatisation with an invitation to the reader to identify with the perspective of Mary. Since Kennedy makes use of the *planctus* twice in his *Passioun*, engaging the reader in affective experience through Mary must have been important to Kennedy. The second *planctus* is placed after the deposition of Christ: a wealthy disciple named Joseph of Arimathea, who had obtained permission to take Jesus' body and prepare it for interment, takes down Christ's body. Mary receives the body: she takes the dead body of Christ in her arms and sits down near the cross to 'price his pane' (l. 1241). The motif of the *pietà* (the Virgin Mary cradling the dead body of Christ) had no immediate scriptural basis, but developed from the theme of the lamentation over Christ's body and was influenced by the cross-cultural topic of the mother's grief for her dead son, and saw its heyday in the figurative art of fifteenth-century Europe. Kennedy uses the *pietà* scene here to prepare the reader for another Marian complaint.[25] When the mother of Christ holds her dead son in her arms, she sees and beholds ('saw' l. 1244; 'beheld' l. 1247) his mutilated, bloody body and his wounds, and kisses and embraces him. Again, the 'swerd of dule' (l. 1250) pierces her heart and she 'fights' with Death and the Jews. Many *planctus* contain addresses to the Jews[26] and to death, and the first direct addressee of her second *planctus* in Kennedy's *Passioun* is Death, which has spared her but taken her son. Mary's grief is mirrored by the tears she sheds, which are bloody and blur her vision: 'Scho couth nocht ceis þat blissit corps to brace / Thoucht bludy teris leit hir [for] to se (ll. 1265-66).[27] Mary also addresses her dead son, opposing his former beauty

---

[24] Peter Yeager, 'Dispute Between Mary and the Cross: Debate Poems of the Passion,' *Christianity & Literature* 30 (1981): 59.

[25] In several mystery plays, Mary is given a lament when she holds the dead body of her son in her lap.

[26] 'Wy haue ȝe no reuthe on my child' (*NIMEV*, 4159; *Religious Lyrics of the XIVth Century*, eds. Carleton F. Brown and G. V. Smithers, 2nd ed. (Oxford: Clarendon Press, 1952) no. 60) is a Marian appeal to the Jews; other apostrophes to the Jews can be found in 'As Reson Rywlyde my Recyles mynde' ('Filius regis mortuus est'; *NIMEV*, 404; *Religious Lyrics of the XVth Century*, no. 6) and in 'Lysteneth, lordynges, to my tale' (*NIMEV*, 1899; *Religious Lyrics of the XVth Century*, no. 10).

[27] Since the second *planctus* is based on Ludolph's account in his *Vita Christi*, the weeping of the Blessed Virgin is also mentioned in Kennedy's source: 'Flebat illa lacrymis irremediabilibus' (PII, LXV 5) — in Kennedy's *planctus*, however, Mary's tears are bloody.

and present deformity by comparing every trait of the living Jesus with the miserable look of the dead Christ: his crystal eyes are dim, his beautiful lips bluish. This is a popular stylistic device of many *planctus*, the contrast is based on the opposition of Ps 44:3 and Is 53:2.[28] Mary's view here is, of course, entirely maternal — and at the beginning and the end of her *planctus* she is duly called 'moder' (l. 1240, l. 1282). The last addressee of her second *planctus* is Jerusalem (l. 1275), echoing Christ's words of Mt 23:37: 'Hierusalem Hierusalem quae occidis prophetas et lapidas eos qui ad te missi sunt.' Unlike the first *planctus* in Kennedy's *Passioun*, the second lament is a monologue and every stanza closes with the Blessed Virgin's exclamation: 'full wa is me' (ll. 1246, 1253, 1260, 1267, 1274, 1281) which by repetition serves to alert the reader to Mary's grief and emotionally engage the reader to share Mary's sorrows. Kennedy must have been fully aware of the potential of the *planctus* to move the reader to compassion since although Ludolph describes the tears and lament of the Blessed Virgin in a separate subchapter (PII, LXV 5), Ludolph's account is a third-person narrative and not a monologue spoken by the Virgin herself.

That this form of complaint was an important device for Kennedy in his *Passioun* is underlined by the fact that he also has the narrator himself utter some sort of *planctus*: taking the meditation for none on the death of Christ as a starting point, Kennedy marks off thirteen stanzas from the main narrative by the repetition of the exclamation 'allace' at the end of each stanza (ll. 1002-1064).[29] Like the two Marian *planctus*, the narrator's lament is in effect an admonition to the reader to remember the pain and suffering Christ endured for man's sake, to call to mind the injustice of Christ's death, and to move the reader to penitence.

After the 'lamentacioun' (l. 1282) by the Virgin, the narrator describes her continuing grief. At the burial of Christ, we are again offered her view of the events when 'scho þe graif *saw* with a stane cloiß laid' (l. 1232, my emphasis) and she almost expires. It is 'hir sueit thing' (l. 1340) to which she bids goodbye when she embraces the sepulchre and before she leaves for the city.[30] She then spends three days in 'hir closit' (l. 1345), her heart torn 'betuix pyne and faith' (l. 1351) since on the one hand she cannot stop grieving at her son's death, while on the other hand she is confident that he will soon

---

[28] For similar antitheses, see also the 'Quis dabit' (Bestul, *Texts of the Passion: Latin Devotional Literature and Medieval Society* 170) and *The Towneley Plays*, eds. A. C. Cawley and Martin Stevens, EETS, SS 13, 14, 2 vols. (Oxford: Oxford University Press, 1994) I, 297/329-30 (Crucifixion): 'Thi face with blode is red, / Was fare as floure in feylde'; and 367-72: 'Alas, thyn een as cristall clere, / That shoyn as son in sight, / That lufly were in lyere, / Lost thay haue thare light, / And wax all faed in fere — / all dym then ar thay dight!'.

[29] The whole passage neither corresponds to the *Meditationes* nor to the *Vita Christi*.

[30] The burial is one of the sorrows of the Blessed Virgin (see above). It is a popular addition: in the Bible the mother of Christ is not present at his burial. It is described in detail by Ludolph (PII, LXVI 2).

rise from the dead. This episode is absent from the Gospels. The addition that Mary returns home after the burial is found in pseudo-Bonaventure and in Ludolph of Saxony (P II LXVI, 13). In the *Vita Christi*, however, the Blessed Virgin only sheds tears, whereas in the *Meditationes*, although she weeps, she retains her composure since she has hope of the resurrection of her son. Mary's behaviour guides the reader to an ideal reaction to the death and burial of Christ: following Mary's example, he or she is encouraged to feel compassion and grief, but also to have confidence in the resurrection of Christ.

In Kennedy's *Passioun* we encounter the mother of Christ one last time: after the resurrection. She is the first person Christ appears to since 'scho for his ded / Wes maist in pane' (ll. 1427-8). This is another addition, since in none of the Gospels Christ does appear to his mother. Seemingly a popular element in Passion narratives, it is mentioned in the Pseudo-Bonaventuran *Meditationes* and Ludolph's *Vita Christi*, where Christ's first appearance is to his mother, rather than to Mary Magdalene, as recorded in the Gospel of John. This invention also serves Kennedy's aim of letting the reader share Mary's perspective of the Passion: as the mother of Christ and the person grieving most, it is only natural that Christ appears to her first. When he addresses her as 'berar of þe king' (l. 1433), Mary rejoices and finally embraces her son, and they enter into a conversation.

In Kennedy's *Passioun*, various techniques — such as the use of affective details to conjure up images in the reader's mind, a discernible meditative structure (the apportioning of the events of the Passion to the canonical hours), apostrophes, repetition and enumeration — facilitate and provoke imaginative emotional participation which leads to moral reform, to repentance and to devout and virtuous action. Since drawing the reader into a joint and active participation is essential for Kennedy (as for many authors of devotional texts), this can be achieved particularly successfully by using the mother of Christ as a familiar point of contact and conduit for the reader's sympathy. Shared gaze engenders shared feeling and, as Sarah Stanbury has put it, the gaze on Christ's body 'takes on an increasingly strategic role in the meditative process.'[31] Moreover, looking at the events of the Passion through Mary's eyes encourages not only active emotional participation but also imitation. Mary is a model and identification figure for the meditator in Kennedy's *Passioun*, showing compassion and yet also having faith in the resurrection and the divine plan of redemption, just as in his praise and petition poem she is a paragon of faith, humility and purity; in short, a model of virtues to imitate.

---

[31] Sarah Stanbury, 'The Virgin's Gaze: Spectacle and Transgression in Middle English Lyrics of the Passion,' *PMLA* 106 (1991): 1085. Stanbury interprets the gaze as 'violation of boundaries' (1086) and 'assertiveness socially legitimized as a gesture of mourning or grief' (1087).

The Sedentary Swallow in Henryson's
The Preaching of the Swallow
Natural History, Genre Problems and
the Battle between the Body and the Soul

Luuk Houwen

In *The Preaching of the Swallow* Henryson turns a migratory bird into a sedentary protagonist who is always at hand to advise the other birds, even in winter (1832[1]). This
raises several questions about Henryson's swallow and in what follows I would like to
examine three hypotheses in somewhat greater detail. The first of these considers the
possibility that Henryson is not talking about a swallow at all, but about a completely
different bird. The second examines whether Henryson may not have known that swallows were migratory birds, and the last considers the possibility that the migratory
nature of the swallow was irrelevant because the exemplary character of the tale out-
weighed this detail from natural history. I shall argue that this last hypothesis is the
most likely one and that it resulted from the transformation of an aetiological fable
into an exemplum in which the debate between the body and soul plays a central role.

The source of Henryson's *Preaching of the Swallow* is generally held to be Walter of
England's fable *De seminatore lini et yrundinibus*,[2] although Robert Kindrick in his edition is a little less certain about it than Fox was in his.[3] The latter's hesitancy is hardly
surprising for if Henryson indeed followed Gualterius he certainly adapted his source
freely. The most striking difference with Walter's version is its length. Henryson
expands Walter's fourteen lines to well over two hundred and sixty, and that excludes
the *moralitas*. Even if we disregard the first eight Boethian stanzas this still leaves over

---

[1]   All references are to Robert Henryson, *The Poems of Robert Henryson*, ed. Denton Fox (Oxford: Clarendon Press, 1981).
[2]   Walter of England, *The Fables of 'Walter of England'. Edited from Wolfenbüttel, Herzog August Bibliothek,
Codex Gualferbytanus 185 Helmstadiensis*, ed. A. E. Wright (Toronto: Pontifical Institute, 1997) no. 20
(pp. 63-65).
[3]   Robert Henryson, *The Poems of Robert Henryson*, ed. Robert L. Kindrick, Middle English Texts
(Kalamazoo: Medieval Institute Publications, 1997) 136; Henryson, *Poems (Fox)* xlv, 274.

two hundred lines. More important to our present discussion is that Henryson also abandoned the aetiological message and in this he is apparently unique.[4]

The early history of this fable is a complex one, both with respect to its main protagonists and the nature of the aetiological message. In its earliest known form the fable was told about the owl,[5] although it has also been argued that this may have been an innovation rather than a starting point.[6] When the mistletoe starts to grow in the oaks the owl warns the other birds either to dig up all the oaks or, when that proves to be impractical, to become suppliants to men so as to avoid falling prey to the bird-lime which is made from mistletoe. The fable also explains why the other birds admire the owl for his wisdom and foresight. Analogous to this fable a second tradition developed which eventually took over, in which the swallow first takes the place of the owl and then the mistletoe is replaced by flax. The aetiological message of this fable explains why swallows make their nests in the houses of men where they enjoy their protection.[7]

The moralisation that accompanies the fable in Henryson is a common and obvious one: the fowler represents the devil, the swallow the preacher and the birds wretches who have fallen prey to the temptations of the world. Wheatley notes that the Latin commentary tradition for this particular fable is unusually uniform across Europe.[8]

---

4   Henryson, *Poems (Fox)* 274. For a medieval aetiological version of the tale compare Jacques de Vitry, *The Exempla or Illustrative Stories from the Sermones vulgares of Jacques de Vitry*, ed. T. F. Crane (London: 1890) CI (176). In the *Dialogus creaturarum moralizatus* the aetiological message is at best hinted at when the close connection between swallows and humans is mentioned; see *Dialogus creaturarum moralisatus. Dialog der Kreaturen über moralisches Handeln. Lateinisch-Deutsch*, eds. Birgit Esser and Hans-Jürgen Blanke (Würzburg: Königshausen & Neumann, 2008) 119 (pp. 328-31), and for the English version *The Dialoges of Creatures Moralysed*, eds. Gregory Kratzmann and Elizabeth Gee (Leiden: Brill, 1988) 119 (pp. 236-37).
5   B. E. Perry, 'Demetrius of Phalerum and the Aesopic Fables,' *Transactions and Proceedings of the American Philological Association* 93 (1962): 315-18. See also Francisco Rodríguez Adrados, *History of the Graeco-Latin Fable*, trans. Leslie A. Ray, rev. Gert-Jan van Dijk. Mnemosyne: Bibliotheca Classica Batava, 2 vols. (Leiden: Brill, 1999-2003) I, 55, 71. Adrados notes that we may have not just two (early) traditions of this fable, but as many as three or four, although he acknowledges that the version with the owl is the oldest (I, 477; II, 110-14).
6   Adrados, *History of the Graeco-Latin Fable* II, 89.
7   The Augustana version of the fable is summarised in *Babrius and Phaedrus,* ed. & tr. Ben Edwin Perry (Cambridge: Harvard University Press, 1965) Appendix no. 39 (p. 428).
8   Edward Wheatley, 'Scholastic Commentary and Robert Henryson's *Moral Fabillis*,' *Studies in Philology* 91 (1994): 89-91. For a discussion of Henryson's use of the fable commentary tradition see also Douglas Gray, *Robert Henryson*, Medieval and Renaissance Authors (Leiden: Brill, 1979) 125-27. See also *ibid.*, 127.

We do not need to waste too much time on the notion that Henryson's swallow may not be the same bird that we now call by this name, although this idea is not as odd as it may at first sight appear. In its early history the English word was not only restricted to the swallow (*hirundo*) but was in extended use also applied to other birds of the swallow kind. Albertus Magnus in his chapter on the swallow differentiates between four species, which its most recent translators identify as 'the chimney swallow, *hirundo rustica*; the house martin, *delicion urbica*; the sandmartin, *riparia riparia*; and either the cliff swallow, *hirundo rupestris*, or the common tern, *sterna hirundo*'.[9] This extended use has a long tradition, with both *sæswalwe* 'sea-swallow' and *stæpswealwe* 'shore-swallow' being used in Old English for the sandmartin, whereas the *heoruswealwe*, or 'sword-swallow', was a kenning for a hawk.[10] There is even a poisonous serpent called *irundo* which is discussed by Albertus Magnus, among others.[11] None of this is of much help in solving the mystery, however, since we can dismiss the serpent and the hawk, and all of the remaining candidates are migratory birds.

MIGRATION HYPOTHESIS

At first sight it would appear that there is overwhelming evidence to support the proposition that in the Middle Ages swallows were known to be migratory birds, if only because their vernal return was often celebrated. Classical authors regularly refer to the arrival time of swallows. Pliny and others passed this knowledge on to the Middle Ages.[12] Isidore refers to it on several occasions in the *Etymologiae* when he says about birds in general that 'some are indigenous and always stay in the same location, like [the sparrow], while others are migratory and return at certain seasons, like the stork

---

[9] Albertus Magnus, *De animalibus libri XXVI nach der Cölner Urschrift*, ed. Hermann Stadler, 2 vols. (Münster: Aschendorff, 1916-1920) 23.122. For the commentary and translations see Albertus Magnus, *Albertus Magnus On Animals. A Medieval Summa Zoologica*, trans. Kenneth F. Kitchell Jr and Irven Michael Resnick, 2 vols. (Baltimore: Johns Hopkins UP, 1999) 1633, n. 392.

[10] Jane Roberts, Christian Kay and Lynne Grundy, eds., *A Thesaurus of Old English*, 2 vols. (London: King's College, 1995) 02.06.08.06 (p. 93). The *heoruswealwe*, lit. 'sword-swallow', however, referred to the falcon (*ibid*, 02.06.08.04, p. 91). Cf. also *The Oxford English Dictionary*, ed. J. A. H. Murray, 2 ed. (Oxford: Oxford University Press, 1994) swallow n. 2.

[11] Albertus Magnus, *De animalibus* 25.31.

[12] *Historia naturalis* X.xii.28 & xiv.30, xxxiv.70. In X.xxxiv.70 Pliny adds that although swallows migrate in the winter months, they do not go very far away. All references are to Pliny the Elder, *Natural History III Books VIII-XI*, ed. H. Rackham (London: Heinemann, 1983).

and the swallow'. In the chapter devoted to the swallow he specifies that '[i]t flies across the sea and remains there for the winter.'[13] Isidore's observations are repeated in many later bestiaries[14] as well as in the encyclopaedias. Bartholomaeus Anglicus, for example, notes that it 'fleeþ ouere þe see to hote cuntreys in þe whiche he is in wintir, as me troweþ, and he kepiþ certeyne tymes of his comynge and goynge.'[15] Some authors even speculated about the swallow's destination. Caesarius of Heisterbach in, of all places, his *Dialogue on Miracles* gives a wonderful account of very effective empirical research in this matter:

> [Of Miracles: That swallows always return to their wonted dwellings] I have been told by a certain priest, that the father of a family had very many swallows' nests in his house, and wishing to find out that very point about which you ask me [where do migrating birds go?], he took one of them and fastening a piece of parchment to its foot containing these words: 'O swallow, where do you live in winter?' he let it go; for he knew by experience that they always return to their wonted haunts and dwellings. The swallow coming to Asia with the rest, // built its nest in the house of a certain Peter. Seeing on its foot in its daily coming and going that parchment, and wishing to know what it was, he caught the bird, read and removed the parchment tying on another which thus answered the question: 'In Asia in the house of Peter.' When the said householder learnt this on the return of the swallow, he told the story to me as a remarkable fact [X.59].[16]

Nevertheless, knowledge about the migration of birds is not self-evident. Brunsdon Yapp expresses his amazement at the medieval knowledge about migration when he notes that 'it is interesting to find migration of the swallow so firmly stated in the English Middle Ages, when later it was so often doubted or denied, for example by

---

[13] 'aliae *enc*horiae, quae manent in locis semper, ut struthio; aliae aduenticiae, quae propriis temporibus reuertuntur, ut ciconiae, erundines;' (XII.7.1) and 'Maria transuolat ibique hieme commoratur' (XII.7.70) in Isidore of Seville, *Etymologiae XII / Etymologies Livre XII Des Animaux*, ed. Jacques André (Paris: Belles lettres, 1986). The translations are based on Saint Isidore of Seville, *The Etymologies of Isidore of Seville*, trans. Stephen A. Barney, W. J. Lewis, J. A. Beach and Oliver Berghof (Cambridge: Cambridge University Press, 2006).

[14] For an example of a Second Family bestiary see *A Medieval Book of Beasts: The Second-Family Bestiary. Commentary, Art, Text and Translation*, ed. Willene B. Clark (Woodbridge: Boydell, 2006) 186 and n. 314.

[15] Bartholomaeus Anglicus, *On the Properties of Things: John Trevisa's Translation of Bartholomaeus Anglicus De Proprietatibus Rerum. A Critical Text*, ed. M. C. Seymour, 3 vols. (Oxford: Oxford University Press, 1975) XII.22 (p. 631).

[16] Caesarius of Heisterbach, *The Dialogue on Miracles*, trans. H. von E. Scott and C. C. Swinton Bland, 2 vols. (London: Routledge, 1929) II, 219-20. The tale is repeated in *An Alphabet of Tales: An English 15th Century Translation of the Alphabetum narrationum of Étienne de Besançon. From Additional MS. 25,719 of the British Museum*, ed. Mary Macleod Banks, EETS, OS 126, 127, 2 vols. (London: Kegan Paul, Trench, Trübner, 1904) no. 355.

Dr Johnson and Gilbert White.'[17] Indeed, among those who lived more towards the north and west and who therefore were not witness to the great bird migrations taking place between Europe and Africa across the Mediterranean the notion that birds travelled thousands of miles in search of warmer climes might have appeared somewhat far-fetched, particularly when such birds were observed to be so house-bound when they were around. The alternative school of thought that Yapp alluded to held that swallows and other birds entered some sort of torpid state in winter only to re-emerge from that in spring. Some thought they hid themselves in the mud under water, others that they favoured holes and caves like bats. In his *The Natural History and Antiquities of Selborne* (1789) the eighteenth century ornithologist Gilbert White addresses the lawyer and naturalist Daines Barrington along these lines (Letter IX, 1771):

> You are, I know, no great friend to migration: and the well-attested accounts from various parts of the kingdom seem to justify you in your suspicions, that at least many of the swallow kind do not leave us in the winter, but lay themselves up like insects and bats, in a torpid state, and slumber away the more uncomfortable months till the return of the sun and fine weather awakes them.

In a later letter he returns to the subject and adds:

> I am more and more induced to believe that many of the swallow kind do not depart from this island, but lay themselves up in holes and caverns; and do, insect-like and bat-like, come forth at mild times, and then retire again to their *latebræ*. [Letter XII, 1772][18]

The notion that swallows and other birds like the turtle-dove hibernate rather than migrate is an old one, even if it is not as well attested as the other. Aristotle refers to it in the *Historia animalium*:

> A great number of birds also go into hiding; they do not all migrate, as is generally supposed, to warmer countries. Thus, certain birds [as the kite and the swallow] when they are not far off from places of this kind, in which they have their permanent abode, betake themselves thither; others, that are at a distance from such places, do not migrate but hide themselves. Swallows, for instance, have been often found in holes, quite denuded of their feathers, and the kite on its first appearance has been seen to fly from out some such hiding-place [VIII.16.600a].[19]

---

[17] Wilma George and Brunsdon Yapp, *The Naming of the Beasts: Natural History in the Medieval Bestiary* (London: Duckworth, 1991) 174.

[18] Gilbert White, *The Natural History of Selborne*, eds. James Fisher and Claire Oldham (London: Cresset Press, 1960) 124, 131. These letters also show that White does not entirely reject the idea of migration. See also P. R. Kitson, 'Swans and Geese in Old English Riddles,' *Anglo-Saxon Studies in Archaeology and History* 7 (1994): n. 23 (pp. 82-83), where the same passages are cited.

[19] Aristotle, *The Complete Works of Aristotle. The Revised Oxford Translation*, trans. Jonathan Barnes, vol. 1, 2 vols. (Princeton, NJ: Princeton University Press, 1995).

Pliny may well have had this in mind when he tentatively suggests that swallows migrate but do not go very far.[20] That the idea that birds can go into hibernation was known in the Middle Ages as well is shown by Bede who refers to it in his commentary on Genesis:

> 'Be fruitful, and multiply, and fill the waters in the seas' (Gen. 1.22). This applies to either kind of living things created from the waters, that is to fishes and to birds, because just as all fishes cannot live except in the waters, so there are very many birds who, even if they sometimes rest on land and breed their young, live not so much off the land as off the sea, and more freely use marine than terrestrial habitations. What then is added, 'And let fowl multiply in the earth', applies to either kind of bird, that is to those who live on the waters and those who live on land, because even those birds which are unable to live without water, *so that for much the greater part of the year they lie hidden like fishes beneath the depth of the waters*, are accustomed sometimes to come out upon dry land, especially when they breed and rear their chicks.[21] [my emphasis]

Like Bede, Adelard of Bath does not mention the swallow directly but he does refer to the 'death' of many an animal 'both of the earth and the air' in winter in his *Questiones naturalis*:

> Another point: if their action is the cause of the death and life of lower animals, what should be thought about these stars? When the Sun withdraws from Cancer and from our region, first the greenness of the grass fades; then the delightful blooms of the flowers droop; soon not even the distinction of leaves remains on their branches; finally it is well known that *there are not a few animals — both of the earth and of the air — who naturally die in winter and come to life again in the summer*. What then should be said? To believe that what provides the effect of life for others is itself without life, can only be the belief of a frivolous jester.[22] [my emphasis]

---

[20] See note 12.

[21] Bede, *In Genesim* in Beda Venerabilis, *Opera exegetica 1. Libri quatuor in principium Genesis usque ad nativitatem Isaac et eiectionem Ismahelis adnotationum*, ed. C. W. Jones, CCSL 118A (Turnhout: Brepols, 1967) lines 653-667: 'Quod dixit, *Crescite et multiplicamini et replete aquas maris*, ad utrumque genus animantium de aquis factorum, hoc est ad pisces pertinent et ad aues, quia sicut pisces omnes non nisi in aquis uiuere possunt, ita sunt pleraeque aues quae, etsi in terris aliquando requiescunt, foetusque propagant, non tantum de terra sed de mari escuntur marinisque sedibus libentius quam utuntur terrestribus. Quod uero subiungit, *auesque multiplicentur super terram,* ad utrumque genus auium, hoc est et earum quae de aquis et earum quae uescuntur de terra, respicit, quia uidelicet etiam illae quae sine aquis uiuere nesciunt aues, ita ut multo saepe anni tempore sub profundo aquarum quomodo pisces lateant, non-numquam egredi super terras solent, maxime cum foetant et nutriunt pullos.' For the translation see Kitson, 'Swans and Geese,' p. 80 & n. 30.

[22] Adelard of Bath, *Conversations with his Nephew. On the Same and the Different, Questions on Natural Science and On Birds*, ed. & tr. Charles Burnett, et al. (Cambridge: Cambridge University Press, 1998) 222-23.

Early in his commentary on Aristotle's *De animalibus* (Michael Scot's translation) Albertus Magnus also alludes to this when, after stating that '[other animals] *hide* themselves for some period out of the year, after which they return to their territories' (my emphasis), he lists a few examples of such animals: they comprise the swallow, the bear, the stork, and the dormouse.[23] By mentioning migratory birds and hibernating mammals in one breath Albertus shows once again that these two concepts used to be closely related, and this is hardly surprising since they both explain the absence of some animals at certain times of the year. In book seven Albert demonstrates that migration and hibernation are two sides of the same coin when he reduces both to different manifestations of the same phenomenon:

> The things that have been said about the migration of animals need to be set in order and reduced to two types. For some animals go entirely into hiding, as if they were asleep and unmoving, and do not even feed. Others, however, pass from one place to another to find more temperate air.[24]

He then proceeds to explain the phenomenon with reference to Aristotelian humoral theory.[25]

These examples show that in the Middle Ages the swallow's absence could be explained in different ways. Which of these two explanations was favoured by Henryson is a moot point, but there may actually be some evidence that suggests that our schoolmaster was familiar with the hibernation theory. In the introductory passing-of-the-seasons section of the *Preaching of the Swallow* Henryson has 'wild animals' go into hibernation in winter[26] only to note that in spring small birds emerge from their hiding places:

> The mauis and the merle beginnis to mell;
> The lark on loft, with vther birdis smale,
> Than drawis furth fra derne[27], ouer doun and daill. [1710-12]

However, just like in the previous hypothesis on the identification of the bird, ultimately this does not really help us very much. To be sure, it demonstrates that we should not make rash assumptions about migratory swallows, but even if Henryson

---

[23] Albertus Magnus, *On Animals* 1.40.

[24] *Ibid.*, 7.154. Migration is discussed in 7.61-72 and further in 7.155-64.

[25] For a discussion of Albertus's innovative approach see Miguel J. C. de Asúa, 'The Organization of Discourse on Animals in the Thirteenth Century: Peter of Spain, Albert the Great, and the Commentaries on *De animalibus*,' Ph.D. thesis, University of Notre Dame, 1991: 145-47.

[26] 'All wyld beistis than from the bentis bair / Drawis for dreid vnto thair dennis deip, / Coucheand for cauld in coins thame to keip' (1703-05).

[27] *DOST*, *dern(e* n. b 'a secret place, hiding' [last accessed 27 January, 2011].

believes that swallows hide in warm holes in winter this still does not explain why his swallow chose to stay around for this time of year to admonish the other birds. The pervasiveness of references to either migration or hibernation in medieval literature makes it less likely, however, that Henryson would not have been aware of either one of these theories.

The anthropomorphised swallow

If Henryson knew that swallows were absent in Winter it corroborates my third hypothesis, namely that he had good grounds to either make some fundamental changes to the basic fable or accept such changes in his exemplar. One approach might be to examine the various characteristics attributed to swallows to see if they might shed some light on this. Indeed, Thomas Hill singled out the fact that the swallow was said to be able to foretell events to argue that this might have made it the ideal candidate for the *Preaching*.[28] There is no denying that within the narrative framework of the fable this foresight plays an important part, especially when compared to the blindness of the other birds, but in the non-narrative, 'secondary' literature on the natural world the foresight of the swallow is generally limited to knowing whether or not it is safe to build a nest in a particular house. Moreover, there are many other prophetic birds in addition to the swallow. A similar observation might be made about the swallow as a preacher. It is true that the *Aviarium* likens the swallow to a wise teacher, but this really adds little to what Henryson already said when he compares the bird to a preacher (2924).[29] Having gone through the many different characteristics attributed by a whole range of classical and medieval authorities to the swallow myself, I do not think any of these will be of much help in trying to understand why Henryson chose to ignore the one characteristic that would otherwise have interfered with the logical progression of the fable. Instead, I think we should have a look at what else Henryson left out and whether such elisions might shed further light on what motivates Henryson's swallow.

At the beginning of this article I noted that, compared with many other versions of this fable, including the one by Walter of England, Henryson's fable lacks the aetiological element that helps to explain why swallows nestle so close to human beings. It is not easy to determine why this is the case. He may have simply overlooked it; after all,

---

[28]   Thomas D. Hill, '"Hirundines habent quidem prescium": Why Henryson's *Preaching of a Swallow* is Preached by a Swallow,' *Scottish Literary Journal* 26 (Supplement) (1987): 30.

[29]   For the *Aviarium* reference see Hugh of Fouilloy, *The Medieval Book of Birds: Hugh of Fouilloy's Aviarium*, ed. & tr. Willene B. Clark (Binghamton: MRTS, 1992) 210-11.

it does not fulfil any function in *The Preaching of the Swallow*. In the allegorical interpretations of Walter's fable his aetiology — 'Hominem placat irundo sibi, / Cunque
viris habitans cantu blanditur amico' — is ignored,[30] and this is not that unusual since
even in the classical fable tradition aetiologies are sometimes relegated to secondary
importance.[31] On the other hand, Henryson may just be rationalising his source(s): it
would, after all, be very odd for a preacher to seek shelter in the house of the fowler
who in the *moralitas* is allegorised as the fiend.[32] In fact, Henryson does not only
remove the aetiological basis of the fable, he inverts the original plot in that he has the
other birds, driven by hunger in winter, 'hasten' to take up their habitat in houses and
barns (1838). Unlike the swallow in the traditional fable, once they have taken up
residence there they do not enjoy man's protection but on the contrary arouse the
wrath of the fowler, who traps them with his nets (1841-45). Disgusted by their
obtuseness the swallow then takes her leave, never to return: 'Scho tuke hir flicht, bot
I hir saw no moir' (1887).

Compared to such other fables as *The Two Mice* — which are rooted in the animal
world but in which Henryson deftly juggles both human and beastly elements,[33] and
by juxtaposing them subtly reminds his readers and listeners of the human dimension
of the fable — the *Preaching* is quite different. Characteristics commonly associated
with swallows or the fable genre are either transformed beyond recognition or omitted
altogether.[34] The end result is that we tend to forget completely that we are dealing
with a swallow rather than a preacher (or teacher) here and are only reminded of this
fact at the very end of the narrative when it flies away. The swallow's audience is a different matter. As Pittock points out, their behaviour, apart from when they answer the

---

[30] Cf. Wheatley, 'Scholastic Commentary,' 89-91. For the text see Walter of England, *Fables* no. 20,
ll. 8-9.
[31] For examples of this see Gert-Jan van Dijk, *ΑΙΝΟΙ, ΛΟΓΟΙ, ΜΥΘΟΙ: Fables in Archaic, Classical, and
Hellenistic Greek Literature: with a Study of the Theory and Terminology of the Genre*, Mnemosyne, Bibliotheca Classica Batava 166 (Supplementum) (Leiden: Brill, 1997) 17F5 (p. 196), 17F6, 17A2, 49F2, and
the conclusions reached on pp. 227-28, 286.
[32] Also commented on by Ian Robert Carruthers, 'A Critical Commentary on Robert Henryson's *Morall
Fabillis*,' Ph.D. thesis, University of British Columbia, 1977: 305.
[33] What Pittock calls the animal and the human poles, which represent minimal and almost complete
anthropomorphism: Malcolm Pittock, 'Animals as People — People as Animals: The Beast Story with
Reference to Henryson's *The Two Mice* and *The Preaching of the Swallow*,' *Critical Studies: Language and
the Subject*, ed. Karl Simms (Amsterdam: Rodopi, 1994) 165-66.
[34] J. A. Burrow, 'Henryson: The Preaching of the Swallow,' *Essays in Criticism* 25 (1975) also notes that
its point of view is 'distinctly human' (25) and '[t]his human point of view prevails, inevitably, at the
expense of the autonomy of the animal world in the poem. The individual birds are not very interesting,
by comparison with the town and country mice, or the fox, or the wolf' (26).

swallow, is consistent with their animal nature,[35] and this is confirmed when they are caught and savagely killed by the fowler. Nevertheless, I would argue that they too fall very firmly in the almost completely anthropomorphised category. One indication for this is the company they keep. With all the other major characters being either human (fowler and observer) or almost human (swallow), it becomes very difficult to still regard the lark and the others as mere birds who just follow their animal inclinations. The fact that they speak back and obstinately refuse to pay heed to the swallow only serves to underscore their humanity even more. Moreover, if we take Henryson's moralisations seriously at all, as I think we must, then we have been primed from the start of the *Morall Fabillis* to look for ulterior meanings in the fables themselves and this cannot but colour our reading of individual fables. It is good to remind ourselves that Henryson's moralisations are only the beginning of an interpretative process, as Gerke pointed out:

> the interpretation given in the *moralitas* may be only the starting point, of varying explic-itness, of the allegory contained in the fable. Essentially the *moralitas* … presents the theme which guides the reader into the, proper areas of thought whereby he can think about the allegorical significance of the details. The *moralitas* is only the beginning of the interpretative activity.[36]

This process not only urges the reader to look ahead but also to look back and it is when we look back to the introductory stanzas and the tale itself that we realise that the interpretation of *The Preaching of the Swallow* did not commence with the *morali-tas* but started with the theme of the body and the soul with which the tale opens.

By stripping the swallow of virtually all of its avian characteristics and the fable of its aetiological *raison d'être* Henryson rewrites the traditional fable and reduces it to something more akin to an *exemplum* rather than a fable.[37]

Henryson is not the only one to turn this aetiological fable into an *exemplum*. The inclu-sion of this fable in the *exemplum* collection generally known as the *Dialogus creaturarum*

---

[35] Pittock, 'Animals as People,' 171.

[36] Robert S. Gerke, 'Studies in the Tradition and Morality of Henryson's *Fables*,' Ph.D. thesis, University of Notre Dame, 1968, 10-11. See also Carruthers, 'A Critical Commentary on Robert Henryson's *Morall Fabillis*,' 146-47.

[37] That Henryson is stretching the limits of the genre has not gone unnoticed; in a discussion of the elegiac triad at the centre of the *Morall Fabillis* of which *The Preaching of the Swallow* is the last, one critic states that here 'Henryson is clearly concerned to push the genre to its limits, and in the process to raise the level of theological (and sociopolitical) discourse of which it is capable': R. J. Lyall, 'Henryson's *Mor-all Fabillis*: Structure and Meaning,' *A Companion to Medieval Scottish Poetry*, eds. Priscilla J. Bawcutt and Janet Hadley Williams (Cambridge: D.S. Brewer, 2006) 99.

moralisatus testifies to that. Here similar methods to those used by Henryson are employed, so that in the end almost nothing of the fable remains, apart from its animal protagonists.[38] Dialogue 119, *De quinque agnis et lupo*, actually recounts three *exempla*, linked together by moral-didactic observations. The title story tells of five lambs who had been abandoned by their parents. When a wolf offers to teach one of them reading and writing[39] provided the others come and confirm the arrangement, they are warned by their instructors against such teachers, but they disregard the advice of their elders and are subsequently devoured by the wolf and his whelps. The ensuing moral in the early sixteenth-century English *Dialoges of Creatures Moralysed* — 'He walkyth euyl and oftyn offendith / That to sadde counsell neuir attendith' — is equally applicable to the exemplum of the swallow that follows. The English version is brief enough to be quoted in full:

> A swalowe that was olde and wise, seynge that, callyd all othir byrdes togider and sayde: 'This feelde and this seede thretnyth vs soore, for in tyme comynge hereof shal be made many a comberows nette. Therfore go we all togider and spurn it a broode, or euir it growe or come vp.' But all other byrdes wolde not consente, but repreuyd the swalowe and sayde she was full of folyssh drede. Vppe grewe this erbe, and the swalowe warnyd them agayne that great parell that approchid and drew nere. The byrdes deryded the swalowe and sayde: 'This swalowe pleasith men and flaterith them with his songe.' This hempe was full growyn and mowe downe and dyuers nettis were made of it and cawght many a byrde. Then all the birdes knewe ther fawte and repentyd them whan ther was no remedye. Therfore he that despisith profitable cownsell oftyntymes takith vnprofitable, and he that thinkith him self to sure fallith oftyntymes in to snarys.[40]

Like Henryson the author of the *Dialogus* anthropomorphises his protagonist more than is generally expected or warranted in a fable. His swallow does not just talk but is 'olde and wise' to boot. In fact, if one were to replace 'swalowe' and 'byrdes' by 'person' and 'people' respectively, very little if anything would be lost. The *Dialogus* also dispenses with the aetiological element and concentrates exclusively on the theme of

---

[38] I strongly disagree with Esser and Blanke who place the *Dialogus* in the fable genre: *Dialogus creaturarum moralisatus. Dialog der Kreaturen über moralisches Handeln. Lateinisch-Deutsch*, 21. Kratzmann and Gee would concur. In their introduction to the genre in the *Dialoges* ('1. *The Dialoges of Creatures Moralysed* and the Exemplum Tradition') the *Dialoges* is assigned to the 'venerable traditions of the sermon exemplum handbook': *Dialoges of Creatures Moralysed*, 3, see also 10.

[39] The English texts differs slightly from the Latin text because it interprets the Latin 'litteras' in 'litteras insinuare' ('teach the ABC') as 'lettirs of proteccyon'; Colard Mansion's 1482 version has 'unes lettres par lesquelles tu puisses prouffiter' (3396-97). For the French text see *Le dialogue des créatures. Traduction par Colart Mansion (1482) du Dialogus creaturarum (XIVe siècle)*, ed. Pierre Ruelle (Brussels: Palais des Académies, 1985) 267-69.

[40] *Dialoges of Creatures Moralysed*, 237-37.

the importance of heeding good advice, a theme that is reiterated in the third *exemplum* of the eagle that caught a tortoise which it was unable to eat because it withdrew into its shell. A crow then remarks that the eagle may be the king of birds but it is not omniscient. It suggests to the eagle that it should drop the tortoise[41] from on high to break open the hard shell, which advice is followed and the eagle has its desired meal. The mere fact that the *Dialogus* uses three examples to hammer home a simple message distinguishes it from Henryson's much more elaborate account, but both anthropomorphise the tale more than one would expect in a traditional fable and both ignore its aetiological function. Both also share a similar theme, that of wisdom and prudence.

Immediately at the end of the example of the swallow and the birds the *Dialogus* draws a double moral. First it stresses that the advice of even a humble person can carry a lot of weight ('Et nota, quod quandoque consilium vilis personae tilissimum'[42]), a useful reminder that the swallow does not rank very highly among the birds, which may help to explain why its advice is so lightly disregarded. The text then adds a second adage, namely that reason is more important than strength ('ingenium plus valet virtute'[43]). That this is indeed the main moral is revealed in the Latin text by a repetition of the same message but now in verse: 'Ingenium superat vires et summa prudentia est prudenti'[44] ('the mind surpasses strength and the highest wisdom resides in a wise man'). It is this sentiment, I would suggest, that characterises the swallow in Henryson's tale. But it is not just in the tale proper that Henryson touches upon this theme; the notion of wisdom is also discussed in the introductory stanzas where the limitations of the (rational part of the) soul are shown. Thus reason (or wisdom) provides a thematic connection between the prologue and the tale that follows. This is not new, Fox had also noted this when he observes that

> [t]he basic contrast in the introductory section is between God the Creator and the diverse and mutable natural world, or more particularly, between the perfect wisdom of God and the blind and weak understanding of man. This of course matches the contrast in the fable between the foresight of the swallow and the blindness of the other birds.[45]

---

[41] L. *testudo*; the English text has *snayle* which does not only cover modern snails but indeed a turtle or tortoise; see *MED*, *snail* n. (d) [last consulted 27 January, 2011].

[42] *Dialogus creaturarum moralisatus. Dialog der Kreaturen über moralisches Handeln. Lateinisch-Deutsch*, 330.

[43] *Ibid.*

[44] The source of this line has not been traced but the editors of the Colard Mansion translation of the *Dialogus* refer to Hans Walther, ed., *Proverbia sententiaeque latinitatis medii aevi. Lateinische Sprichwörter und Sentenzen des Mittelalters in alphabetischer Anordnung*, 6 vols. (Göttingen: Vandenhoeck & Ruprecht, 1963-67) 12383 for the first, and 22802C for the second part; *Dialogue des créatures* 343. The line is omitted in the English text.

[45] Henryson, *Poems (Fox)* 275.

BODY & SOUL

The connection between prologue and text proper is, I think, even more intimate than Fox (and others) would allow for. In the prologue Henryson introduces the popular medieval theme of the conflict between the body and the soul. Having introduced God's 'hie prudence and wirking meruelous' (1622) in a somewhat confusing opening stanza in which the Boethian notion of God's existence beyond time is tagged on to his perfection and omnipotence, he explains that humankind is unable to fully appreciate His nature because they are bogged down in a 'presoun corporall':

> Thairfoir our saull with sensualitie
> So fetterit is in presoun corporall,
> We may not cleirlie vnderstand nor se
> God as he is, nor thingis celestiall;
> Our mirk and deidlie corps materiale
> Blindis the spirituall operatioun,
> Lyke as ane man wer bundin in presoun. [1629-35]

Man's soul, he continues in the next stanza, is like a bat's eye that is so weak it cannot face the sun and has to wait until dusk before it can fly out. It is so oppressed by 'fantasie' that it cannot know 'the thingis in nature manifest' (1642), which is quite similar to Theseus's words in the *Midsummer Night's Dream* that fantasy apprehends 'more than cool reason ever comprehends' (Act 5, Sc. 1). The next stanza reiterates the same sentiments and concludes with the commonplace that no one should attempt to understand the secrets of the Trinity by means of natural reason but, as a popular song has it, 'to let the mystery be':

> Nane suld presume be ressoun naturall
> To seirche the secreitis off the Trinitie,
> Bot trow fermelie and lat all ressoun be. [1647-49]

This is followed up in the next two lines with another commonplace, namely that we may yet have (some) knowledge of God through his creation ('3it neuertheles we may haif knawlegeing / Off God almychtie be his creatouris').[46] However, I would suggest

---

[46] In a fourteenth-century manuscript from the Benedictine abbey of Ramsey, for instance, a moralised version of Aristotle's *De animalibus* opens with a very similar sentiment 'Quia secundum apostolum invisibilia Dei per ea que facta sunt intellecta conspiciuntur, hoc est Deus invisibilis per creaturas corporales sensui exteriori obiectas ac per species suas intellectu conceptas illarum creator intuetur'; see Baudouin van den Abeele, 'Une version moralisée du De animalibus d'Aristote (XIVe siècle),' *Aristotle's Animals in the Middle Ages and Renaissance*, ed. Carlos Steel (Leuven: Leuven UP, 1999) 353. The same line is found at the start of the Prologue (A) to the *Lumen animae*; see Mary A. Rouse and Richard H. Rouse, 'The Texts Called *Lumen Anime*,' *Archivum Fratrum Praedicatorum* 41 (1971): 73.

that Henryson's variant on St Paul's 'invisibilia enim ipsius a creatura mundi per ea quae facta sunt intellecta conspiciuntur' (Rom 1.20) may here be understood in a different way as well. Apart from drawing attention to the macrocosm of the creation, it also serves as an invitation to 'read' the following tale in the light of the microcosm that is man, and more specifically the reflection in man of the macrocosmic conflict: the struggle between the soul and the body.[47] Man may not be able to understand God directly, but he may just gain some limited insight into his own condition when he — in the form of the observer-narrator contemplating the birds under the hawthorn — observes that same creation act out the need for wisdom and reason, and the perils that result if they are cast aside. Just as the *moralitas* 'reads' the tale tropologically, so the tale itself strongly suggests the body and soul theme introduced in the prologue. The swallow, birds and the churl together exemplify the human condition in which the unwise soul is unable to act according to reason because it allows itself to be imprisoned by the body or, as Henryson reminds us in the *moralitas*, when the soul gives in to sensual pleasure 'ressoun is blindit with affectioun':

> And quhen the saull, as seid in to the eird,
> Geuis consent in delectatioun,
> The wickit thocht beginnis for to breird
> In deidlie sin, quhilk is dampnatioun;
> Ressoun is blindit with affectioun,
> And carnall lust grouis full grene and gay,
> Throw consuetude hantit from day to day. [1902-08]

It may be the soul's natural inclination to reach for the sky, but the body with its earthly desires holds it back.

Echoes of the body and soul theme reverberate in the tale itself. The one warning that is repeated time and again by the swallow is to look ahead and not live in the present.[48] This comes to a head in the swallow's third and last warning not to eat from the chaff because the nets made from the flax are hidden nearby (under the snow?):

> 'Grit fule is he that puttis in dangeir
> His lyfe, his honour, for ane thing off nocht.

---

[47]   The conflict features prominently in the works of such twelfth-century writers as Bernardus Silvestris and Alanus de Insulis. In book VI, prose 3 of *De planctu naturae*, for example, the goddess Natura explains to the poet that 'Just as any army of planets fight against the accepted revolution of the heavens by going in a different direction, so in man there is found to be continual hostility between sensuousness and reason'; Alan of Lille, *Plaint of Nature / De planctu naturae*, trans. J. J. Sheridan (Toronto: Pontifical Institute, 1980) 119.

[48]   This warning is at the heart of almost everything the swallow says; cf. for example 1739-40, 1754, 1755-61, 1789, 1809-10, 1818-19.

> Grit fule is he that will not glaidlie heir
> Counsall in tyme, quhill it auaill him mocht.
> Grit fule is he that hes na thing in thocht
> Bot thing present, and efter quhat may fall
> Nor off the end hes na memoriall.' [1860-66]

The sentiments expressed in this stanza are highly suggestive and would not be out of place in any of the surviving debates between the body and the soul or related works that dwell on death and the afterlife, like *Everyman*.[49] In the Middle English *A Debate between the Body and the Soul* the soul accuses the body in similar terms, claiming that it only lived in the present and would not heed its advice:

> Þou was warned her bifore
> Ȝwat we boþe scholden haue;
> Idel tale held tou þat þore
> Þouȝ þou sauȝ fele bidun in graue.
> Þou dist al þat þe werld þe bad
> And þat þi fleys þe wolde craue;
> I þolede þe and dide as mad,
> To be maister and I þi cnaue.[50] [329-336]

Viewed from this perspective the swallow's warning may be interpreted as a call upon the readers to use the present to prepare for the life hereafter. But we need not search so far afield for a parallel. In the last of the *Morall Fabillis* Henryson returns to the conflict between the body and the soul in the *moralitas* to *The Paddock and the Mouse*.[51] Here the identification of the two animal-protagonists as the body and the soul respectively is made explicit and their 'debait' (2907) signals the ceaseless struggle between them. The paddock, instead of helping the mouse cross the river so she can reach the 'ryip aitis … barlie, peis, and quheit' (2792) on the other side, tries to drown her.

---

[49] This stanza also appears on its own with some variants as item 117 on f. 76v of the Bannatyne manuscript in the section devoted to poems of wisdom and morality. It is surrounded by two stanzas taken from the *De Regimine Principum* of the *Liber Pluscardensis* (items 116 and 119; item 118 has not been identified). They deal with poverty (116) and nobility and honour (118, 119) respectively. For the identification, see *The Bannatyne Manuscript. National Library of Scotland, Advocates' Library MS.1.1.6.* Introduced by Denton Fox and William A. Ringler (Aldershot: Scolar, 1980) xxv, and Henryson, *Poems (Fox)* 285. As Fox explains in a note to lines 1862-63 and 1864-66, the sentiments expressed here are proverbial.

[50] *Middle English Debate Poetry*, ed. J. W. Conlee (East Lansing: Colleagues Press, 1991) 36. Similar sentiments are voiced by the soul in lines 217-40 of the same poem.

[51] In general terms the need to look ahead and be prepared for death is also echoed in Henryson's *The Ressoning betuix Deth and Man* (e.g. lines 1-2) but in this brief poem Henryson is more concerned with man's transition from arrogance and pride to humility.

The resulting struggle is noticed by a kite who swoops down on both animals and kills them. That the tale is open to more than one interpretation Henryson's *moralitas* shows when it first provides the traditional *epimythium* also found in Walter of England which warns against 'ane fals intent vnder ane fair pretence' (2918), but once this reading has been expounded Henryson introduces a new interpretation, not found in any of his sources and consequently thought to be of his own making.[52] Starting in the fourth stanza he interprets the paddock as the human body and the mouse as the human soul:

> This hald in mynd; rycht more I sall the tell
> Quhair by thir beistis may be figurate:
> The paddok, vsand in the flude to duell,
> Is mannis bodie, swymand air and late
> In to this warld, with cairis implicate:
> Now hie, now law, quhylis plungit vp, quhylis doun,
> Ay in perrell, and reddie for to droun;
> …
> This lytill mous, heir knit thus be the schyn,
> The saull of man betakin may in deid—
> Bundin, and fra the bodie may not twyn,
> Quhill cruell deith cum brek of lyfe the threid—
> The quhilk to droun suld euer stand in dreid
> Of carnall lust be the suggestioun,
> Quhilk drawis ay the saull and druggis doun. [2934-54]

The water is the world (2955) and the kite is death which comes suddenly, wherefore one should 'be vigilant … and ay reddie' (2964). As Rosemary Greentree observed 'the incongruous journey of the two creatures offers Henryson's most disturbing comments on human life'.[53] However, as we have seen, this bleak view of the vain struggle between the body and the soul is not without precedent. Like *The Paddock and the Mouse The Preaching of the Swallow* stresses the need to look ahead and act upon good advice, but that is not where the parallels stop. Just as the mouse tries to swim up while the paddock tries to drown it by swimming down, so the swallow is situated 'hie in the croip [top of a tree]' (1735) while the other birds are at first perched on the branches below. One should not underestimate the power of this positioning which harks back to the conceptual metaphor of UP-IS-GOOD and DOWN-IS-BAD. An upright posture

---

52 Henryson, *Poems (Fox)* 325.
53 Rosemary Greentree, 'The Debate of the Paddock and the Mouse,' *Studies in Scottish Literature* 26 (1991): 482.

aimed at the heavens was concomitant with being a rational human being, whereas irrational animals always face the earth.[54]

The way the animals meet their sticky end is also quite instructive. In both cases this is particularly gruesome. The paddock and mouse are disembowelled by the kite:

> Syne to the land he flew with thame gude speid,
> Fane off that fang, pyipand with mony pew;
> Syne lowsit thame, and baith but pietie slew.
> Syne bowellit thame, that boucheour with his bill,
> And bellieflaucht full fettislie thame fled,
> Bot all thair flesche wald scant be half ane fill,
> And guttis als, vnto that gredie gled. [2900-06]

A similar horrific end befalls the birds, who are beaten without mercy with a stick, and have their heads and backs broken before being put into a bag:

> Allace, it wes grit hart sair for to se
> That bludie bowcheour beit thay birdis doun,
> And for till heir, quhen thay wist weill to de,
> Thair cairfull sang and lamentatioun.
> Sum with ane staf he straik to eirth on swoun,
> Off sum the heid, off sum he brak the crag,
> Sum half on lyfe he stoppit in his bag. [1874-80]

Although in *The Paddock and the Mouse* the kite is interpreted as death who 'cummis suddandlie / As dois ane theif' (2962-63), whereas the fowler represents the devil in *The Preaching of the Swallow*, their close similarity is brought to the fore by describing them both as butchers (2903, 1875).

CONCLUSION

In conclusion, it looks as if Henryson has not only stripped his fable almost wholly of animal characteristics, but that he has also used the resulting *exemplum* to reinforce the body and soul theme established in the introductory stanzas. This he accomplishes by having the anthropomorphised protagonists re-enact the conflict in a dialogue form

---

[54] This concept features in Boethius's *De cconsolatione philosophiae* where it eventually becomes a fully fledged simile that occupies all of the fifth *metrum* of the last book; see L. A. J. R. Houwen, 'The Beast Within. The Animal-Man Dichotomy in the *Consolation of Philosophy*,' *Boethius Christianus? Transformationen der Consolatio Philosophiae in Mittelalter und Früher Neuzeit*, eds. Reinhold F. Glei, Nicola Kaminski and Franz Lebsanft (Berlin: Walter de Gruyter, 2010) 254-59.

reminiscent of the medieval debate genre. Their re-enactment sheds a dramatic light on the body-soul conflict to which (medieval) Christians were thought to be particularly prone, and serves as a direct warning to his audience to act prudently and consider the end of things before embarking on thoughtless actions. In the following *moralitas* Henryson at first steers a difficult course between the external and the internal dangers humankind faces. It is almost as if he still has the conflict between the body and the soul in mind. The fowler is the devil, but he sows wicked thoughts in man's soul that blind his reason and prepare the field for sin (1895-1915). The hungry birds, on the other hand, are just wretches intent on vain pleasure; and the swallow is the preacher who manages to escape from the snare.[55] This last fact comes as a bit of a relief in this otherwise bleak meditation on human frailty. In the tale she had flown away and the narrator had seen her 'no moir' (1887), which in concrete terms might suggest she finally migrates, but symbolically might hint at the soul's escape. Thus Henryson ends his tale with a glimmer of hope.[56]

---

[55]   It is interesting to note that although the swallow symbolises the preacher and is addressed by the lark as 'Schir Swallow' (1741), it is otherwise referred to as 'scho'. This use of 'Schir' to address females is not that unusual; the mouse in *The Paddock and the Mouse* is also addressed as such (2790). Douglas Gray notes it is used ironically here and MacQueen points out that the lark's laughter signals its moral failings; see Gray, *Robert Henryson* 111, and John MacQueen, *Complete and Full with Numbers: The Narrative Poetry of Robert Henryson*, Scottish Cultural Review of Language and Literature (Amsterdam: Rodopi, 2006) 140-41. Latin *hirundo* is feminine, but perhaps Henryson also has the swallow (and the mouse) in mind as abstractions, which are also feminine.

[56]   Not everyone takes this view. For Gopen it 'demonstrates by contrast what happens in a God-forsaken world when we do not listen to reason, when we abandon righteous teachings'; George D. Gopen, 'The Essential Seriousness of Robert Henryson's *Moral Fables*: A Study in Structure,' *Studies in Philology* 82.1 (1985): 54.

The Manuscript of Adam Abell's Chronicle

Janet Hadley Williams and Kenneth Dunn

Adam Abell's 'Roit' or 'Quheill of Tyme' (Edinburgh, National Library of Scotland, MS 1746) is one of only a small number of early sixteenth-century prose works in Scots. Among them the 'Roit' is worth particular attention, because Abell has set out in his 'prologus' the reasons for his translation of the original Latin 'Rota Temporum'. In structure and much of its content the 'Roit' resembles the many other universal histories popular at this time and earlier; less commonly, however, this chronicle also includes near-contemporary and contemporary material not found elsewhere. As chronicler, Abell is individualized by his Franciscan emphases, range of reading, personal opinions and writing purposes.[1] Yet MS 1746 is also remarkable as a book, a rare surviving example of a work of the early 1500s in its original, possibly Scottish, binding. Neither the bibliography nor the provenance of the manuscript has been examined fully. We will consider these two aspects here.

BINDING

MS 1746 is pleasant to handle, the covers measuring approximately 160 mm x 200 mm. The sheepskin leather is dark brown, possibly burnished, the grain more visible on the turn-ins, which have tongued corners, now loose. There are four alum-tawed goatskin ties (actually two continuous ties, at the front appearing 34 mm from the top

---

[1] A native of Prestonpans, Abell professed the Augustinian Rule in 1495 at Inchaffray, and in the early 1500s moved to the more rigorous Observantine Franciscan discipline at Jedburgh ('Roit', folios 113^r and 82^v). See A. M. Stewart, 'Adam Abell's "Roit or Quheill of Tyme",' *Aberdeen University Review* 44 (1971): 126-29 (reprinted, with a transcript of folios 116^r–126^v, in Janet Hadley Williams, ed., *Stewart Style 1513-1542. Essays on the Court of James V* (East Linton: Tuckwell Press, 1996) 227-53); A. M. Stewart, 'Adam Abell, Martin of Valencia, Pedro de Gante, Andrea da Spoleto: or Jedburgh, Mexico, Yucatan and Fez in 1532,' *Bulletin of the Scottish Institute of Missionary Studies* 11 (1972); A. M. Stewart, 'Neues zum Macbeth-Stoff,' *Anglia* 92.3/4 (1974); A. M. Stewart, 'Sapiens, Dominabitur Astris: Wedderburn, Abell, Luther,' *Aberdeen University Review* 46.1 (1975); A. M. Stewart, 'The Tale of King Lear in Scots,' *Aberdeen University Review* 46.2 (1975) See also Stephanie M. Thorson, 'Abell, Adam (1475x80?–1537?),' *Oxford Dictionary of National Biography* (Oxford: Oxford University Press, 2004). Professor Stewart is warmly thanked for his scholarly generosity and encouragement.

and 40 mm from the bottom of the volume; at the back appearing 41 mm from the top and 35 mm from the bottom), their triangular stubs visible on both the outside covers at the foredges and inside under the pastedowns, the upper stub 22 mm x 20 mm and the lower 32 mm x 20 mm at the front; the upper stub 43 mm x 30 mm and the lower 15 mm x 29 mm at the back. The boards are made from a section of parchment, with a pulpy card, itself folded in the middle, with four pieces of vellum (on which a Latin text in two columns is written) doubled over.

The simple decoration on front and back, possibly Scottish, is of two-line fillets (the lines approx. 5 mm apart) placed as a frame around the outer edges of the covers and as a diagonally intersecting pattern, not quite symmetrical, across them. The compartments created by the lozenge pattern contain, centrally, twelve roundels of about 13 mm in diameter. These roundels contain fine hatching, not always in the same direction, possibly made by the same tool.[2]

There are worm holes on the front cover to the depth of the pastedown, and on the back across the leather only.[3] In addition, there are a few cracks in the leather, and one hole, which could have been made by a skewer, or a sharp, rounded but thin tool, has pierced the binding and all leaves, to folio 87.

The torn spine reveals rows of kettle stitches, 5 mm from the top and 18 mm from the bottom. Along it are also four sewing stations with double bands (or raised cords), from the top, the kettle-stitch row to the first sewing station is 15 mm; from the first to the second sewing station is 43 mm; from the second to the third station is 47 mm and from the fourth to the lower kettle stitches, 20 mm.

CONTENTS

Folio i[r] provides an explanatory table of the numbering used in MS 1746. Folios ii[r] – xiv[r] contain a carefully prepared 'Taibil alphabeit', actually several lists, of important

---

[2]   William Smith Mitchell, *A History of Scottish Bookbinding: 1432 to 1650*, University of Aberdeen (Edinburgh: Oliver and Boyd for University of Aberdeen, 1955) 15, describes several early bindings as Scottish. He includes, very cautiously, that of St Andrews University Library TypSwB.B39BL, François Lambert, *Exegeseos* (Basel, 1539), because 'a portion of a manuscript from St Andrews Priory was bound in with it'. In this binding's 'frame of a two-line fillet intersecting, the panel being divided into small lozenges by diagonals of the same fillet', and in the similarly-sized roundels within them (here, however, with blind stamps of thistle, fleur-de-lys, rose, scallop shell), the binding of MS 1746 has similarities to it. Further evidence that MS 1746 retains the original binding is possibly provided by indentations of many roundel shapes on fol. xviii[v] at the back of the manuscript. These are the same size as the roundels on the binding.
[3]   We wish to thank David Kerr, Manager, Conservation Unit, National Library of Scotland, for his video microscope images of the worm damage and cracks.

topics and people, then popes, emperors, and kings. For each, the same setting out applies (the later lists in two columns to each page, but retaining the same arrangement): a folio number, written close to the left margin, is placed adjacent to each one-line alphabetized entry, followed in turn by an upper case letter (to locate the reference on the individual leaf) that is written close to the right margin.

The chronicle text begins on folio 1 with a 'prologus', followed on the second half of the verso with an 'ordo declaratinus', ending on folio 2. This short section explains how the page is ruled up and what the various marginal annotations mean; what has been done to distinguish references to popes, emperors and Scottish kings in the text; what other sources the reader might seek to extend his or her knowledge. The chronicle itself begins on folio 2^r, continuing until folio 126^v (correctly folio 127^v).[4]

PAPER

The leaves of MS 1746 are mostly paper, and measure *c.* 148 mm x *c.* 198 mm with no obvious evidence of trimming. Chain lines are horizontal, about 26 mm to 30 mm apart. The written area is ruled, the horizontal lines 20 mm to 21 mm from the tail edge and 13 mm to 14 mm from the top edge. Vertically a set of double guide lines has been drawn on both left and right margins 10 mm to 11 mm from the outer edges. There are approximately thirty-seven lines on each page.

WATERMARKS

Traces of two differently watermarked papers may be found in the centre of some inner margins of MS 1746 (implying that each original sheet was folded in half, turned ninety degrees, and folded again).

(a) Paper stock containing a hand with a central line from the top surmounted by a cinquefoil, and below, within the palm of the hand, a five-petalled flower on a stem. This resembles Briquet's 'Main', 11.345 (Northern France, 1537).[5]

(b) From quire IX, (a) is interspersed with paper stock containing a jug with a handle and a lid, on top of which is a five-knobbed (not trefoiled) crown, and having

---

[4] To avoid confusion we have referred to the original foliation throughout the article. See further, under 'Signatures', hereinafter.

[5] C. M. Briquet, *Les filigranes: dictionnaire historique des marques du papier dès leur apparition vers 1282 jusqu'en 1600. A Facsimile of the 1907 Edition with Supplementary Material [...]*, ed. Allan Henry Stevenson, 4 vols. (Amsterdam: The Paper Publications Society, 1968).

below, in the bowl, two sets of two parallel horizontal lines with vertical lines across them to form a chequered strip of each set. This second watermark closely resembles Briquet's 'Pot à une anse', 12.662 (Northern France, 1538).

SIGNATURES

The makeup of the manuscript is revealed in the surviving signatures (b to k at the lower right corner of the last verso of the gathering), and from the position of the vellum sewing guards. The text, folios 1–127, is [a] – e (12), f (12: –1), g – k (12), [l] (8); all except h have vellum sewing guards in the middle, as do folios ii–xiv, the 'taibil alphabeit' (12 + 1), and folios xv–xix at the end (6: –3, 4 + 1).[6]

The original foliation is amended, beginning at the centre of gathering e (modern folio 55). This out-of-alignment in the two sequences of foliation is fully apparent from the original folio 57, which in modern foliation is 58. Original folio 60, or 61 according to the amended number, has been torn out. (With the help of the table alphabet's notes of what would have appeared on the folio, it can be established that this leaf of the chronicle would have covered the period 778–840.) The next folio is numbered 62, but does not correct the foliation, but at folio 88 an error in foliation means that folio 89 follows 87. The subsequent foliation continues the error until folio 97, which is repeated, thereby correcting the foliation by folio 98. Original folio 120 is also repeated, so that by the final leaf of the chronicle, the original foliation should read 127, but reads 126, with the following leaf, which also has the original foliation, reading 127 when it should read 128.

COLLATION

Vellum paste-down
Paper fly-leaf, pasted down (conjugate with folio xiv, front sequence)
Vellum singleton (conjugate cropped)
Quire I: 1^{12}
Paper singleton (conjugate with front fly-leaf, folio xiv)
Vellum singleton (cropped; conjugate with the first front paste-down)
Quires II–VI: $2–6^{12}$
Quire VII: $7^{12(-1)}$
Quires VIII–XI: $8–11^{12}$

---

[6]   We are grateful to Ian Cunningham, formerly Keeper of Manuscripts, Maps and Music, National Library of Scotland, for checking this.

Quire XII: 12[8]
Paper singleton (folio xv, back sequence; conjugate with folio xix)
Quire XIII[10(-2,3,4,5,6,7,8)]
Paper singleton (folio xix; conjugate with fly-leaf, folio xv)
Vellum bi-folium (conjugate with back paste-down)

SCRIBES

MS 1746 is written by two scribes. The first hand, responsible for almost all of the text, is an upright early secretary with a noticeable attacking stroke on 'a', a curl above final 's', curve to the left below the line on 'h'; and an 'r' like an arabic 2. The second hand, a less cursive but neat and competent early secretary, has written the preliminary matter, the brief addition on (original) folio 126[v], and the corrections and annotations throughout.[7]

RUBRICATION

This second hand may be responsible for the rubrication (in two reds from the beginning, one more orange, the other more crimson), used for initial letters and the in-filling of others in the preliminaries and text; for complete headings within the preliminary lists; for paragraph marks, underlining within the text and for the alphabetical finding aids in the outer margins of the text. His outstanding decoration is the letter 'A' on folio ii[r] of the preliminaries, of seven text-lines high. It is written in the ink of the text, but decorated with an outline and tiny curls on all sides and within, using the two colours of red. Smaller decorated letters in the two colours, the 'S' at the begining of the 'prologus' (folio 1[r]) and 'B' at the beginning of the chronicle (folio 2[r]) are also worth noting.

PROVENANCE

The brief description of MS 1746 in the National Library of Scotland's *Catalogue of Manuscripts Acquired Since 1925* includes the historical note that it 'was apparently the property of Sir William Sinclair of Roslin 1565'.[8] This was a significant owner, but his

---

[7]   See, for example, the notes at the foot of folio 12[v], in the margins of folios 14[r] and 84[v] and at the foot and in the margin of folio 116[v], these additions noting the appearance of the 'apostat & heresyarche martyn lutheir' and the burning of Master Patrick Hamilton.
[8]   National Library of Scotland, *Catalogue of Manuscripts Acquired Since 1925*, 8 vols. (Edinburgh: H.M.S.O., 1938-92) I, 204.

marks of possession are neither the only nor the first known associations of the manu-script. Logically, they are with the brothers and the friary where Abell wrote his chron-icle.[9] Within the manuscript, the colophon that follows the text of the chronicle as it stood in the year 1533 confirms this. This states that the work was written by 'ane pure brothir of the brethir minoris of obseruance in our place of Iedwart' (folio 120ᵛ).[10] A comment immediately following, that 'the forsaid brothir Adam Abell continuand his proces of the forsaid rute' from 'quhair he lewit [left] in the yere of god 1534 yeris and sa procedand for his schort tyme' (folio 120ᵛ), shows that the manuscript remained at the friary. The way in which the chronicle is ended a few leaves later also supports this.

   Another hand has added this end, which has been called 'abrupt', cutting off 'in the middle of a sentence, with some events still unresolved'.[11] This is not quite correct — only the events could be so described — but the sense conveyed, that the chronicle is ongoing, forms a contrast with the smoothly resolved 'ending' in the hand of the main scribe of the manuscript. This notes the return from France of James V 'with his spous in Scotland' and the fact that he 'wes resaifit with gret blithnes' (fol. 126ʳ). If the happy return in May 1537 is an appropriate place to end, there is no evidence that it was chosen. There is no formal colophon with authorial attribution, nor is there space for it. The added twenty-one line passage begins as if taking up the narrative, with a para-graph mark and the words, 'This yeir', written on the same line as 'blithnes'. There has been some damage to the manuscript here, so that the next few words are illegible, but the readable narrative, first making the link with the text in the hand of the main scribe with the words that 'eftir grit prosperite' followed 'grit calamite', is continued by the second scribe, 'Abowt the natiuitie of sant ihon lurkand perducyon aganys the kyng wes propalit [moved forward]'. It then records the accusations against and punishment of the lady of Glamis and her son for treason, and the death of the princess Madeleine. The addition ends in the present, the second half of 1537, on the topic of the divorce between the queen dowager Margaret and Henry Stewart with, 'bot the sentens is yit suspendit'.[12]

---

[9]   See the short archaeological survey, J. Todd, 'Jedburgh Friary,' *Discovery and Excavation in Scotland 1985*, ed. Edwina Proudfoot (Edinburgh: Council for British Archaeology (Scotland), 1985) 2; Richard Fawcett, *Scottish Architecture from the Accession of the Stewarts to the Reformation, 1371-1560*, Architectural History of Scotland (Edinburgh: Edinburgh University Press in association with Historic Scotland, 1994) 130-31.

[10] Abbreviations in quotations from Abell's text are silently expanded where necessary; the long s with a curving loop attached is transcribed as 's'; the letter form thorn is transcribed as modern 'th' when this is distinguishable; the letter form yogh is written 'y' when consonantal.

[11] Thorson, 'Abell'.

[12] Margaret announced her intention to divorce Henry Stewart in June 1537; see also *State Papers of Henry VIII*, 11 vols. (London: His Majesty's Commission, 1830-52) V, pt. iv, no. cccxxvii, 103–04, 'Queen Margaret to Norfolk'.

When added to the main scribe's comment on folio 120[v], that Abell had briefly continued his chronicle, these details suggest that most of the 'Roit' was copied, probably at the friary,[13] before the second half of 1537. They also imply that the main scribe was by then in a position to fill in the details about a brother author who by then was dead.[14] The considerable work of the second scribe, also probably a brother, that followed (the addition of a few more sentences, the correction and annotation of the whole text, and the compilation of the meticulous lists at the beginning of the manuscript) would argue that the manuscript stayed at Jedburgh into the second half of 1537.

In the 'prologus' there is possibly a clue to the manuscript's next move. Abell states there (fol. 1[v]) the several reasons why he made the translation: that secular men and women 'may haif plesant and prophetable commonyng'; and religious men 'may fynd mair of prechin and be mair reddy to gife of diuers thingis inquirit solutioune', after the advice of the provincial commissar, 'Michaell de Lyra', that the brothers should have 'knawlegis of croniculis of thare land';[15] and that, 'nocht withstanding this roit or quheill quhilk first … I compilit in lattyne [now agan][16] to the honour of god the wirgin mary and … sanct francis my merit and alswa plesour to my lord setone I haif translatit at in yngligis'. Seton family patronage of Abell and the Jedburgh friary would not be unexpected, as parts of the land inherited by the Seton to which Abell refers, George, fourth Lord, were not far from Jedburgh.[17] Professor Alasdair Stewart has hypothesized plausibly that the manuscript was 'in Seton's possession at least initially … possibly from its [the chronicle's] conclusion about 1537 till Lord Seton's death in 1549',[18] but this possession is as yet unproven.

Within the chronicle, however, Abell's strong interest in the Seton family and the fourth Lord is evident. Abell presents the Setons as among the first families. He lists the Seton name with those given to 'scottis men' in the reign of Malcolm III (folio 77[v]). He depicts the current Lord Seton as active in the role of king's supporter, as one

---

[13]   R. J. Lyall, 'Books and Book Owners in Fifteenth-Century Scotland,' *Book Production and Publishing in Britain 1375-1475*, eds. J. Griffiths and Derek Pearsall (Cambridge: Cambridge University Press, 1989) 245, notes, however, instances of Scottish monastic institutions contracting out the copying of a manuscript.

[14]   It is unlikely that Abell wrote this of himself, yet 'schort tyme' is open to interpretation.

[15]   On this point see John Durkan, 'The Libraries of Sixteenth-Century Scotland' in *Scottish Libraries*, ed. John Higgitt, Corpus of British Medieval Library Catalogues 12 (London: British Library in association with the British Academy, 2006) lxxiv–lxxv.

[16]   The words in brackets, written in the second hand, are in the margins.

[17]   Richard D. Oram, 'Seton, George, fourth Lord Seton (c. 1508–1549),' *Oxford Dictionary of National Biography* (Oxford: Oxford University Press, 2004).
[http://www.oxforddnb.com.virtual.anu.edu.au/view/article/25120, accessed 15 January 2010].

[18]   A. M. Stewart, 'Think and Drink Tobacco,' *Aberdeen University Review* 47.3 (1978): 262.

who helped the king to capture the 'chiftanis of the borduris in the est partis of Scotland' when at Yetholm with his 'gude fadir [father-in-law] lord yester' (folio 121ᵛ).

In the most prominent reference, Abell draws Seton as an exemplar for other Scottish noblemen. This occurs in the account of the events of 1332–33 (folios 100ᵛ–101ᵛ), where Abell reports that, as captain of the besieged Berwick, the 'nobill knycht' Sir Alexander Seton 'nobly defendit' the town from King Edward's invasion as long as he could, then offered his eldest son 'in plege' of future truce. Later, Abell narrates, Edward took Seton's second son prisoner, and threatened that the two boys would be hanged unless the town was surrendered. Seton, 'woundit with naturall pete', was 'perplexit quhat he suld do', but Abell gives Seton's 'lady' the role of showing him the 'skaith' that would befall if he did not allow the hanging of their innocent sons 'for the defence of the realme and fidelite of thare fathir and modir for the comone weill standand stabill'. In Bellenden's equivalent account,[19] by contrast, the long courageous speech of Alexander's lady is at the centre of the narrative. Bellenden gives little space to the knight himself.[20]

Abell's following formal aside on Justice is without precedent. He has two sub-topics: the 'fals crudelite' of the tyrant in the slaying of the innocent, with reference to Genesis and Aquinas; and 'Fidelite', with quotations from Cicero and Isaiah. The lament Abell adds, that many lords 'ar infaithful to the realm', is also distinctive, as is his next comment: 'This hous of seton wes ewir fund traist and trew to the crown and I traist to god euir salbe'. The words arguably associate the writer with the family in a more particular way and, whether or not the manuscript was afterwards in the possession of George, fourth Lord Seton, give support to John Durkan's proposition (centred on the earlier activities of the Oliphant family) that there was 'a constructive association of Observant Franciscanism with the secular lords as much as with … the royal house'.[21]

Further clues to the manuscript's history are to be found in the incidental material that has been added to it. This includes annalistic and literary insertions as well as signatures of book owners, readers, or borrowers. We have gathered the findings from earlier work on aspects of this material and have contributed to them where we can in order to examine what they reveal as fully as presently possible. The material to be discussed is found on the pastedowns at front and back of the manuscript; on folios iᵛ

---

[19] John Bellenden, *The Chronicles of Scotland, Compiled by Hector Boece*, eds. R. W. Chambers, Edith C. Batho, Walter W. Seton and H. Winifred Husbands, STS 3rd ser. 10, 15, 2 vols. (Edinburgh: W. Blackwood, 1938-41) II, 303–05.

[20] The Seton details also differ from those in Walter Bower, *Scotichronicon*, ed. D. E. R. Watt, 9 vols. (Aberdeen: Aberdeen University Press, 1987-98) VII, 88-91 (bk. xiii, ch. 26).

[21] John Durkan, 'The Observant Franciscan Province in Scotland,' *Innes Review* Autumn (1984): 55.

and xiv^r of the preliminary series of roman-foliated leaves; on folios 1^r, 2^r, 62^r and 126^v of the chronicle, and on the leaves (with a second roman foliation) following the chronicle. Care is essential: there is little discernible order; the status of the material varies, from possible 'doodles' to much more deliberate efforts, and several hands are involved.

Some annotations may be associated, though never with certainty, with the friary and its inhabitants. The first four of these, possible to group together because one early secretary hand has almost certainly written them, are at both front and back of the manuscript. On folio xiv^v, preliminaries, are two annotations. The second duplicates the first, 'Sapientiam antiquorum exquiret sapiens et narrationem', with the addition of a translation into Scots ('befor all day four thingis to gither wes creat be god of na thing quher'). The words in Scots echo the text of the 'Roit' on folio 2^r. At the back of the manuscript, on the spare half-page below both the last of the chronicle text and the details of 'W Santclair' that follow it (folio 126^v), this pattern of duplicate annotations is repeated, again with the second note containing additional words. The latter annotations, in Scots only, refer to Albany, the longer note reading, 'In the yeir of god 1514 yeiris Duik of albany come in Scotland to dumbartane the secund tyme on the fyrst day of nouember'. Like the annotations at the front, these could have drawn on Abell's text,[22] but in this case do not closely copy the chronicle wording. Considering the four together, the Latin and Scots echo of Abell in the front annotations could imply a writer aware of the original 'Rota Temporum' as well as the Scots version; the choice of Albany as subject of the later notes suggests more than ordinary interest in him, which might fit an annotator based at Jedburgh, as will become more evident.

Two groups of annotations, in early secretary hands, the first more cursive than the second, fill folio 127^r. The notes appearing first on the page, to 'Palagius' and 'niniane', are excerpted from Abell's text, folio 38^v, on 'Pelage [monk]'[23] and 'sanct ringyan' (an alternative name for Ninian). Below them after a space of about a line, is a more detailed Albany passage, not found in Abell. This mentions the dates of Albany's comings to Scotland in 1514, 1521 and 1523, his departure the following year, and the appearance in Edinburgh in that same year of the king and his mother, when the young James made an entry 'in the tolbuithe with suord of honour scepter and crowne'. The notes following these, in the second hand, on 'ursula the nune' (daughter of Dioneth king of 'brytanis' and the sister of 'fergus king of scotland'), and on 'eugenii king of scottis', copy Abell's text (on folios 39^v and 40^r). Considering together the passages derived from Abell, those on Pelagius, 'with his arrace [heresy]', Ninian, and Ursula, are likely to have been of particular interest within Scotland or a Scottish religious community. The extra details of Albany are also relevant, and to the brothers at

---

[22] Cf. the references to Albany, 'Roit', folio 116^r.
[23] The word 'monk' is an interlinear insertion.

Jedburgh most nearly; in the 'Roit' Abell tells of the threat from England that Albany averted (fol. 116ᵛ):

> Bot in the tyme of his cumming fra france the erll of surre with the erme of ingland cust down our howsis of fens [defence] on the bordur abone the nowmer of 30 & birnt the towne of iedburgh and gret othir skaith had thai done & thai had nocht hard of the cuming of the gubernatour [governor].

Similarly, the additional detail of the young James V might be of special interest at the place he had visited in 1526, three years after the events recorded in the passage. James had then rewarded the friars for their gift of cherries, and shortly afterwards had given money 'to the reparation and bigging of thair place'.[24] In this context the selection of the Eugenius excerpt by a brother at lately-threatened Jedburgh would also be apt, since it records the more successful outcome of an earlier engagement across the border, and notes the tribute paid by the Britons after the Scottish king had defeated them.

The notes written on the two following leaves (folios xvᵛ, xviʳ) are more problematic in terms of manuscript history. They are written in a strong secretary hand using very black ink, and begin in annalistic style ('Anno domini 1001 …', 'Anno domini 1180 …'). Both, the first referring to the body of the giant, 'empreour pallas', reported found at Rome in 1001 'withowt rotting', the lantern near his head not extinguishable 'with wynd nor weit'; and the second, describing Arthur's grave and that of his queen 'guanara', with a record of the gravestone inscription, concentrate on the marvellous. That on Arthur contains details familiar from sources other than the 'Roit', such as the note that in the grave the 'womenis hair wes haill and sound with fresche colour bot ane monk tuicht it couetuslie so it fell in poulder'.[25] It is unclear whether this annotator of MS 1746 obtained his additional material in a secular or religious setting.[26]

On folios xviᵛ and xviiiʳ are annotations in another contemporary hand with a neat slight slope and more polished upper case opening letters. The dates and numbers linked to these passages differ from those in the 'Roit', but in wording several are close to that of Abell's chronicle (for instance, that to the giant, 'fynla makcule', is similar to the 'Roit', folio 40ᵛ; that on the 'sewin sleperis at ephesis' to 'Roit', folio 41ʳ; the beginning of that to 'king arthur' to 'Roit', folio 47ʳ, and that to 'sanct abba' to Abell's

---

[24] *Accounts of the Lord High Treasurer of Scotland*, eds. Sir James Balfour Paul and Thomas Dickson, 12 vols. (Edinburgh: H.M. General Register House, 1877) V, 277 and 306.

[25] Compare, for example, the account in Gerald of Wales, *Giraldi Cambrensis. Opera VIII: De principis instructione liber*, ed. George F. Warner, Rerum Britannicarum Medii Ævi scriptores (London: H.M.S.O., 1891) 126-29.

[26] See, however (on the library of the Augustinian Abbey of Holy Cross, B. V. M. and All Saints, Jedburgh), *Scottish Libraries*, 206-08.

sentence on folio 50ᵛ). The moralizing emphases of another passage on the same page of notes would not be unsuitable as a comment from either a religious institution such as a friary or a zealous member of the lay community:

> In the tyme of king kanutus in saxonia in sanct magnus the martyre kirk yaird xv men and thre wemen dansit on yule nycht and the priest wes miscontent and said God and sanct magnus nor thai dans all the yeir and so it wes.[27]

The annotations in the same competent contemporary hand grouped together on folio xviiiʳ begin with a brief definition of the word 'pharo', then follow with a list of the reigns of the pharaohs of Egypt, from 'Pharao nefres rang xiiii yeiris' to 'Pharao thoneris rang xvi yeiris drownit in the Reid se'. Some, but not all, of the information here might have been drawn from Abell (folio 5ʳ). The annotator appears to be trying to apply the same chronological approach to pharaohs as that applied to popes, emperors and kings in the chronicle preliminaries. There is also evidence in these notes of the annotator's interest in the Christian elements — 'amenoptes … ordanit to droun all knaif bairnis borne of the hebreus'; 'moyses wes borne and put in the flude in ane skep' in the twenty-sixth year of his reign; Amenoptes' 'stok image' each day 'gaif ane rair and ane rowt lyk ane bull' but 'stude quhill christ wes borne' — but the annotator's identity, and thus the place that these and the previous notes have in the manuscript's history, cannot be conclusively defined.

On folio xixᵛ are five further entries. There are four annalistic passages, written in a free secretary hand, on 'Sanct mungo', 'Sanct feacris', the 'venerabyll Beid', and 'pape jhon xxii'. There is a hint of haste or inattention in their setting down; above the reference to Mungo's mother as 'hecht [called] tuymeir', the scribe has had to insert 'or thameir' (a detail that could have been obtained from the 'Roit', folio 44ʳ), and has struck through a number inserted too soon in the entry on Bede. Two of the saints mentioned, Fiacre and Mungo, have strong Scottish links (recalling the choice of Ninian and Ursula in the notes added to MS 1746 on folio 127ʳ), Fiacre's as a Scottish king's son and holy man noted by Abell on folio 51. Bede, too, is mentioned by Abell as an instructor to the Scottish king 'Eugin' (folio 54ᵛ) and a long-time dweller with the holy men at Melrose (folio 55ᵛ). The annotator refers to the Pope's wealth, evidently a cliché of the day but one of some concern to Observants; Abell also refers to it ('He left the grettest hurd [hoard] behind him at euir we red in any kirkman the sowme wes ten hundreth thousand merkis and twenty-five thousand', 'Roit', folio 104ᵛ). These selections, although perhaps more appropriate to an excerptor in a religious community, do not provide definite facts about the manuscript's location when they were written.

---

[27] A word is inserted above 'thai' but is too faint to decipher.

The fifth annotation, of two lines close to the top edge of the same page (thus probably written after the other four), is in a different category. In a rounder secretary hand,
it reads, 'anno domini m cccxxxvi jhon manduell / knecht doctor in medycene florest'.[28]
The wording of the reference to Sir John Mandeville, the supposed author of the *Voy-
ages de Jehan de Mandeville chevalier*,[29] is close to Abell's ('Roit', folio 104ᵛ) in his
record of events of the 1330s to 1360s: 'Heir florist Iohne Manduell knycht doctour
in medecin born in ingland'. In the 'Roit', however, Abell has added that Sir John
went 'amaist our all the warld and wrait in 3 ledis [languages] the mervellis at he saw'.
It is worth noting that Abell continues, as if to provide a balance to these comments
about one of the most popular figures of the time,

> Als in this tyme florist oderik of our ordur of brethir minoris in asy and ind prechand
> and kithand miraculis. He translatit the bodeis of 4 martiris of our ordur … be myraculis
> and wrait his pilgrames.

That the annotator of folio xixᵛ at the back of the manuscript chose to reproduce in part
only the comment about Mandeville, and not also that on 'oderik of our ordur', could
imply that the manuscript had entered or was being read in a secular setting. The hand
of this annotator, identifiable as that of the 'W Santclair of roislin knecht' who also
wrote his name in this style, with a 1565 date, on folio 126ᵛ, upholds the suggestion.
He was the Sir William Sinclair, laird of Roslin, who succeeded to the estates in July
1554, was 'a lover of books and something of a scholar', and died *c.* 1580–85.[30]

Sir William's signature and the 1565 date are also found on folios iᵛ (where he has also
briefly referred to the beginning of the world and to the flood, 'diluuvio inchoato'); xivʳ
of the preliminary sequence (the 'knecht' in the latter instance appearing to be a later
addition); and near the top of folio 2ʳ of the main foliation, where his signature is written
between the conclusion of the opening prayer and the words, 'Before al day four thingis'.

---

[28]   A shape resembling an arabic 2 or z has been written, at the end of the line, perhaps to signify the
completion of the particular annotation, or more probably to fill the line to its end. This flourish is also
on folio xivʳ, preliminary sequence, after the signature of Sir William Sinclair.

[29]   Manuscripts of Mandeville's work survive in English, German, Italian, other languages, and perhaps
also Scots. For James III's request to his chaplain to make a copy in 1467: *The Exchequer Rolls of Scotland.
Rotuli Scaccarii Regum Scotorum*, eds. John Stuart, *et al.* 23 vols. (Edinburgh: H.M. General Register
House, 1878-1908) VII, 500.

[30]   See T. A. F. Cherry, 'The Library of Henry Sinclair, Bishop of Ross, 1560-1565,' *The Bibliotheck* 4.1
(1963): 17; J. H. Lawlor, 'Note on the Library of the Sinclairs of Rosslyn,' *Proceedings of the Society of
Antiquaries of Scotland* 32 (1897-1898): 94-95; Sally Mapstone, *Scots and Their Books in the Middle Ages
and the Renaissance. An Exhibition in the Bodleian Library, Oxford 10 June – 24 August 1996* (Oxford:
Bodleian Library, 1996) 3; Father Richard Augustine Hay, *Genealogie of the Sainteclaires of Rosslyn*, ed.
James Maidment (Edinburgh: T. G. Stevenson, 1835) 136. Here, too, Sir William has added a note, 'fra
the begyneng of the varld 5527 efter the gret flud iiiᵐ viiiᶜ lxxi'.

Sir William probably obtained the manuscript in about 1565, from Henry Sinclair (1507/8–1565), Dean of Glasgow and later President of the College of Justice, Bishop of Ross, and envoy for Mary.[31] The signature of 'Hen. Sinclar' is inserted at the beginning of the chronicle (folio 1[r]), in the space beside 'The roit or quheill of tyme heir begynnis…'.[32] When and how Henry himself acquired the 'Roit' is not known,[33] but Professor Stewart's conjecture about Seton family possession would suggest that it was after 1549.

On the same folio, Henry's signature is joined by the large and distinctive signature of 'D Sinclair of Roisling', written in the top margin. Lawlor has identified it as that of William, son of the previous William, who held the estates from 1582 until at least 1612.[34] MS 1746 thus probably remained with the Sinclairs of Roslin into the early seventeenth century.

To these signatures may be added the four sets of initials, followed in two instances by the word 'roslin', on folio xviii[v], back sequence. Their status and date are difficult to establish.[35] The letters are written with a broadness to the down-strokes that suggests the considerable pen-pressure of a confident writer (one whose hand does not resemble that of identified Sinclairs), yet might also be that of the doodle. There is little material on which to base an argument, but it is possible that the hand involved is the same as that of a signature at the front of the manuscript (folio i[v]), where again there is some doubt about status. This signature repeats that of 'Mark Ker' written above it, and appears to be an attempt to copy it. It succeeds only as far as the distinctive

---

[31] On the links between Henry and William as book owners see John Durkan and Julian Russell, 'Further Additions (Including Manuscripts) to J. Durkan and A. Ross, *Early Scottish Libraries*, at the National Library of Scotland,' *The Bibliotheck* 12.4 (1985), *s.v.* 'Henry Sinclair' and 'William Sinclair'. On Henry, see further Robert Keith, *An Historical Catalogue of the Scottish Bishops, Down to the Year 1688* (Edinburgh: Bell & Bradfute, 1824) 193-94; Cherry, 'Library of Henry Sinclair,'; Mark Dilworth, 'Sinclair, Henry (1507/8–1565),' *Oxford Dictionary of National Biography* (Oxford: Oxford University Press, 2004) [http://www.oxfordnb.com.virtual.anu.edu.au/view/article.25621, accessed 30 Oct 2006].

[32] This is characteristic of him; see Lawlor, 'Library of the Sinclairs,' 96-97.

[33] For an earlier Seton-Sinclair connection, a bond made by the fourth Lord Seton's father to Oliver Sinclair of Roslin in 1480: NRS GD1/1192/1, Seton Papers; also in Hay, *Genealogie*, 110-11, (Bond by George Lord Seton to Roslyn, 1480.'

[34] Lawlor, 'Library of the Sinclairs,' 95-96, says: 'Apparently the signature should be read, "D [= Dominus] Sinclair of Roisling".'

[35] The hand does not resemble the two signatures of Oliver Sinclair we have seen: *The Works of Geoffrey Chaucer and The Kingis Quair: A Facsimile of Bodleian Library, Oxford, MS. Arch. Selden. B.24*, Introduced by Julia Boffey and A. S. G. Edwards, appendix by B. C. Barker Benfield (Cambridge: D.S. Brewer, 1997) fig. 2, p. 8, and Gilbert Hay, *Gilbert of the Hay's Prose Manuscript (A.D. 1456), vol. I, The Buke of the Law of Armys or Buke of Bataillis*, ed. J. H. Stevenson, STS 1st ser. 44 (Edinburgh: Blackwood, 1901) plate adjacent to p. xxii.

initial 'M',[36] and differs significantly in remaining letters. The 'r', for instance, is written like an arabic-2 rather than the open form of 'r' seen in the word above, which also has the added stroke to the right at the base. In the style of the letter 'K' of 'Ker, which has curls or loops at the base, the 'copied' signature resembles the second initial on folio xviii[v] (back sequence).

The bold signature of 'Mark Ker est huius libri' (folio i[v], preliminaries) itself may contribute to the discussion of the manuscript's history.[37] The Ker families of Cessford and of Ferniehurst were important land and property owners in the Jedburgh and Newbattle areas,[38] Mark Ker and his son, also Mark, first earl of Lothian (1606), in particular. As preceptor, the first Mark Ker held the benefice of the Maison Dieu hospital beside Jedburgh from 1536. Later, after the Reformation, he became a secular official, acquiring the extensive church property at Newbattle for his family.[39] These facts encourage speculation about a different path away from the friary for the manuscript, but there is as yet no direct evidence of such a move.

A group of almost exclusively 'Scott' signatures found among the manuscript's pen trials and marginal annotations underline the possibility that the manuscript remained in the Borders. On folio 62[r] in the top margin is the faint signature, 'Walterus Sco'. 'Walterus Scotus' and 'M[r] James S' are written on the front pastedown. On folio xvi[r], back sequence, 'M[r] James Scott' is written immediately after the last line in the black hand, and 'M[r] James Scot', twice, is written in another hand, below the first signature. On folio xix[r], back sequence, are 'Walte', 'Walt', and 'Walterus – Scotus est huius libri possesor'. Here, too, is an unidentified, non-Scott signature: 'Johne Cadre with my hand at the pen the yeir of god [?]291', the 'Johne' repeated below it in the same hand. A further Scott signature, 'Walter Scotus est meus herus', appears between, and at right angles to, the two columns of a Latin text on the manuscript's back pastedown. The relationship between Scotts and Kers, as both feuding enemies and co-operative neighbours and relatives, is well documented for this period, and the manuscript's possible circulation from one to the other seems highly likely.

---

[36] See the facsimile of the 1602 edition of Jean de Beau Chesne and John Baildon, *A Booke Containing Divers Sortes of Hands*, The English Experience (Amsterdam: Theatrum Orbis Terrarum, 1977) 'The Secretarie Alphabet', [p. 7], line 4, third upper case 'M'. The book was first published in 1571.

[37] The 'M' of this signature resembles the 'M' on the back pastedown, written c. 30 mm after the signature 'Walter – Scotus est meus herus'.

[38] See NRS records, GD40/1, 'Inventory of the Title Deeds, &c. of the Estates of the Marquess of Lothian embracing the Lordships of Jedburgh, Newbattle and others in Scotland'

[39] On Ker's Jedburgh connections see NRS GD40/1/167 and GD40/1/174; and Margaret H. B. Sanderson, 'Mark Ker 1517-18, Metamorphosis,' *Mary Stewart's People: Life in Mary Stewart's Scotland* (Edinburgh: J. Thin, 1987). A signature of Mark Ker, the preceptor, is appended to NRS GD40/3/51. It does not conclusively match that found on folio 1[v], preliminaries, MS 1746.

In his communication to the Society of Antiquaries of February 1846, David Laing gathered early seventeenth- and eighteenth-century references to Abell's 'Rota Temporum'.[40] William Nicolson, Laing noted, had referred to William Camden's allusion (*Britannia*, 1607 and Philemon Holland's translation, 1610) to Abell's 'Rota' as 'a good authority' for the explanation of the name, 'Graham's Dyke'.[41] Laing, who was hampered by the lack of the manuscript itself (in either Latin or Scots), expressed doubt about 'whether it actually was Friar Abell's work to which Camden refers'. On the contrary, the references in the 'Roit' (folio 39[r]), to 'ane chiftane callit gryme' and his valiant efforts to cast down the 'wall betwix abircorn and cliide', appear to confirm Nicolson's assertion. If Camden had seen the manuscript before 1607 there is no known record of the event, but his long trip to Carlisle and the north in 1600, accompanied by his friend and former student, the antiquary Robert Cotton, would have provided an opportunity.[42]

By 1624 the manuscript was in circulation, and perhaps also separated from the Sinclairs of Roslin.[43] On folio xiv[r], preliminaries, and on folio xix[r] at the back, are the annotations, in a careful later secretary, of James Tullo, including a signature, and (preliminaries only) a date of '14 of Maj 1624' with a 'musselbrugh' location. At the back there is 'James Tullo with my hand h[…]'.[44]

Tullo's hand resembles that of the scribe of the poem on folio xvii[v] at the back of the manuscript, a six-stanza work beginning, 'Why should any man dispise', with the refrain, 'Thus think and drink tobacco'.[45] This poetic addition to the manuscript has been studied by Professor Stewart, who suggested that the poem might have been

---

[40]   This was published as David Laing, 'Inquiries Respecting Some of the Early Historical Writers of Scotland (1846 and 1847),' *Proceedings of the Society of Antiquaries of Scotland* 12 (1878).

[41]   William Nicolson, *The Scottish Historical Library Containing a Short View and Character of Most of the Writers, Records, Registers, Law-books, &c. which may be Serviceable to the Undertakers of a General History of Scotland, Down to the Union of the Two Kingdomes in King James the VI* (London: T. Childe, 1702).

[42]   Kevin Sharpe, *Sir Robert Cotton, 1586-1631: History and Politics in Early Modern England*, Oxford Historical Monographs (Oxford: Oxford University Press, 1979) 20.

[43]   For another example of separation at that time, see Lawlor, 'Library of the Sinclairs,' 96-97.

[44]   On folio xix[r] at the back, Tullo has also written (upside down) a latinized version of his name. He also possibly wrote 'In my' and 'In my de' on the same page. On the popular phrase thus initiated ('In my Defens, God us Defend') see Priscilla Bawcutt, 'Dunbar's Use of the Symbolic Lion and Thistle,' *Cosmos* 2 (1986): 90-91.

[45]   Compare the decorative 'T', for example, in the poem, lines [5] and [13] (numbering including the refrain) and in Tullo's signature, folio xiv[r], front sequence. Another hand has added the line, 'Quhen thow behold the smock on hie / think' below the word 'finis'. A slightly different version of this poem has been added, some time in the seventeenth century, to NLS Adv. MS 1.1.6, folio 374[v]; see Priscilla Bawcutt, 'The Contents of the Bannatyne Manuscript: New Sources and Analogues,' *Journal of the Edinburgh Bibliographical Society* 3 (2008): 124.

copied into the manuscript at the time of the debate on tobacco, between about 1604 and 1626.[46] The hand, described as 'late XVI century' in the National Library of Scotland's *Catalogue* entry, equates even better with the later date Stewart's persuasive argument would require.[47]

The italic signature (struck through) of 'Johne Calderwode', which appears below Tullo's on folio xiv[r], preliminaries, may be instructive. It, too, records the location in the details written after the name, 'at musleburgh the 30 of maij 1624'.[48] Calderwode has also written below, in italic hand, 'cato / Legere et non et non [sic] Intelligere / est negligere.' Between the two signatures is another, of one word only, but in a careful italic, 'dougall', the three together creating a possible vestige of a literary circle of reader-borrowers, and indicating that the manuscript had moved northwards towards Edinburgh.

At some time later in the 1600s, as David Laing recorded, the manuscript of the 'Roit' came into the possession of George Mackenzie, Lord Tarbat (from 1703 first earl of Cromarty). Tarbat was Lord Clerk Register from 1681, that date in agreement with Father Hay's reference to him in this account of the attack in 1688 by 'the rabble' on Roslin Castle and Chapel (near Edinburgh), during which Hay lost 'several books of note, and amongst others, the original manuscript of Adam Abel, which I had of my Lord Tarbet, then Register'.[49] Hay speaks of the 'original manuscript', thus raising the possibility of two interwoven book histories, one about the Latin original, the other about the version in Scots now known as MS 1746. Laing's tantalizing addition, that after Cromarty's death in 1714 his library was sold in Edinburgh, and that in the catalogue of the sale in 1746 'the title occurs of apparently the MS. in question', suggests that what Hay lost was either returned to Cromarty, or was not the 'Roit' but the Latin 'Rota'.[50] If it was the Scots translation that was sold, a Cuninghame of Caprington possibly purchased it. The manuscript of Adam Abell's chronicle is not noticed again, as Professor Stewart has recorded,[51] until 1935, when Lt. Colonel W.W. Cuninghame of Caprington deposited it at the National Library of Scotland.[52]

---

[46] Stewart, 'Think and Drink Tobacco,' 263 and illustration.

[47] Cf. examples 24, 25, 26 and 27 in Grant G. Simpson, *Scottish Handwriting 1150-1650* (Aberdeen: Aberdeen University Press, 1986).

[48] Further proverbial annotations, in a small fluent secretary hand belonging to neither Tullo nor Calderwode, are written below.

[49] Hay, *Genealogie* 107.

[50] Laing, 'Inquiries,' 75. He also noted Thomas Hearne's 1731 allusion to the Earl of Pembroke's possession of the manuscript at Wilton House but, at least by the time of Professor Stewart's investigation (Stewart, 'Abell's 'Riot',' 392. n. 13.), this was incorrect.

[51] Stewart. 'Abbel's Roit',' 392. n. 13.

[52] Lt. Colonel Cuninghame's manuscript collection contained material contemporary to Abell's chronicle, including NRS GD149/234, known as the Caprington Letterbook; see *The Letters of James I Collected and Calendared by R. K. Hannay,* ed. Denys Hay (Edinburgh: H.M.S.O., 1954) xi-xiii.

Religious Elements in the Poetry of Gavin Douglas

Douglas Gray[1]

As well as being one of the most distinguished vernacular writers of later medieval Scotland, Gavin Douglas was also a distinguished 'kirkman', the Provost of St. Giles, and later Bishop of Dunkeld. Surprisingly, perhaps, criticism has found relatively little to say about any 'religious' elements in his extensive works, and the scholarly treatment of his biography has in general preferred to concentrate on his undoubted ambition for further ecclesiastical preferment. At first glance, the formal religious material may seem meagre. If the excellent mortality poem *King Hart* is to be removed from the canon of his works (as seems most likely) we are left (probably) with a single short explicitly moral poem *Conscience,* and the two apparently 'secular' poems, *The Palice of Honour* and the *Eneados.*[2] I will argue, however, that a careful reading of these will reveal some interesting 'overlaps' between the language, ideas and imagery of traditional religious writing and the predominantly 'secular' topics of his poetry, and will suggest that they are the product of an educated, intelligent and devout Christian mind — and will further suggest that we should be suspicious of attempts to establish an absolute boundary between the 'religious' and the 'secular' in the thought and writing of the period.

The little poem *Conscience* remains perhaps something of an oddity, in spite of its general similarity to other medieval moral verses and exempla dependent on wordplay (e.g. 'conscience' without 'science'), and its closer similarity to a poem in the Bannatyne MS.[3] But it is, however, a well-written satirical poem on decadence (from the old times 'quhen halie kirk first flurist in ʒouthheid' and 'prelatis wer chosen of all perfectioun') relating the stages by which Conscience's habit was cut down by 'schrewit correctioun' to 'science and na mair', and then to the single syllable *ens* ('being', here given an unu-

---

[1]   All quotations are taken from Gavin Douglas, *The Shorter Poems of Gavin Douglas*, ed. Priscilla J. Bawcutt, STS 5th series, 2, 2nd ed. (Edinburgh: Scottish Text Society, 2003), where I have cited the Edinburgh text and from Gavin Douglas, *Virgil's Aeneid Translated into Scottish Verse by Gavin Douglas, Bishop of Dunkeld*, ed. D. F. C. Coldwell, STS 3rd series 25, 27-28, 30, 4 vols. (Edinburgh: William Blackwood & Sons, 1957-64).
[2]   The lost poem 'of Lundeys Lufe the Remeid', whatever it was, does not sound like an overtly religious poem.
[3]   In Douglas, *The Shorter Poems of Gavin Douglas* 306, Bawcutt cites a closer parallel in a sermon of 1488.

sual interpretation[4] 'þat schrew,/Riches and geir'. The wordly goods that have corrupted 'science' and faithful conscience so that 'falset loukis in everie clerk*is* hude'). At the end Douglas moves in to 'flyting' mode, addressing the destructive creature directly

> O hungrie ens, cursit w*ith* caris calde! [22]

and dismissing him firmly and emphatically:

> Thow false ens, go hens, thow monsture p*er*alous!
> God send defence w*ith* conscience in till ws. [137/27-28]

The nearest parallel to this in Douglas's longer poems is the episode in the Prologue to Book 8 of the *Eneados,* where the poet in a dream is accosted by a strange person, who delivers a long complaint on the 'abuses of the age' –

> *Th*is cu*n*tre is full of Caymis kyn,
> *And* sik schire schrewis [viii.77-78]

— ending with the faults of the clergy.

The Palice of Honour (?1501) is a dream vision, and not without its nightmarish moments, but standing in the long courtly tradition of the allegorical dream vision, which reaches back to Chaucer's *House of Fame* and beyond. It also seems to have been influenced by the extensive tradition of visionary writing, Biblical (especially the Book of Revelation[5]) and medieval. In the Prologue of the poem, the poet-dreamer is already in the state of anxiety and perplexity commonly shown by such narrators in allegorical dream visions before they receive enlightenment (he asks May to 'comfort ȝour man that in this fanton steruis … / Quaiking for feir, baith pulsis, vane and neruis,' and curses his 'fatall weird' and 'febill wit'). However, Douglas's treatment differs in two important ways. Firstly, he sometimes deliberately and boldly heightens this anxiety, both here and later, throughout the various turns of the narrative, in a manner that is sometimes comical, creating a distinctive and original blend of the high serious and the comic.[6] Secondly, the anxiety is sometimes intensified in a way which suggests the deep fears and anxieties of visionaries and visitors to the other world. The sudden dazzling light or 'impressioun' that comes (here probably a 'fiery impression or exhalation' (Bawcutt), which is the precursor of other examples of dazzling and supernatural light,

---

[4]   Perhaps, as Bawcutt suggests (*ibid.* 215), the word may have developed additional senses in the way that *substantia* did.
[5]   *Ibid.* notes for Biblical references.
[6]   This combination of high seriousness and the comic is by no means unknown elsewhere in strictly religious writing in the Middle Ages. A well-known and extreme example is the juxtaposition of the sheep stealing scene and the Nativity in the Wakefield *Second Shepherds' Play.*

and is the occasion of the vision which he will go on to describe, produces an overwhelming physical effect, causing him to fall down 'in extasie or swoun.' His 'ravist
spreit' is now confronted by a hideous and terrifying landscape, with an 'vglie flude
horribill / Like till Cochyte the river Infernall', a 'wildernes abhominabill and waist'
and, later, 'maist gros and vile enpoysonit cludis clatterit, / Reikand like hellis smoke
sulfurious' (353-54). I would not wish to overstress the 'hellish' quality of this scene
— to a learned courtly writer hyperbolic expressions like 'hevinly' (already found in the
Prologue to the poem) or its opposites came easily (as well as other Christian terminology (cf. 'penance', 'predestinate', 'purgatorie', later), and probably came to form part
of traditional poetic diction. However, we shall see later in the poem cases where such
expressions are more obviously 'charged': even here they are clearly meaningful.

In this landscape he sees the procession of Minerva, containing 'Lords, Ladyis and
mony fair Prelait', and at the end two 'hangers-on', two notorious self-confessed trai-
tors (one Biblical, one classical), Achitophel and Synon (whose discussion with the
dreamer is a typically intriguing and original way of introducing the topic of Honour).
The fearful dreamer, hiding in a rotten stump of an oak tree, is partially comforted by
another 'schynand licht' and the sound of music, 'of Angellis as it had bene' (and later
the angelic beauty of the 'sound celestiall' is further elaborated — seeing the magnifi-
cent procession he exclaims 'Quhair sa thay went it semit nathing ellis / Bot Ierarchyes
of Angellis ordours nine'), but in his melancholy state the 'melodie' makes him sorrowful, and the sight of the goodly company moves him to sing a 'lay of inconstant love'.
The eloquent climax of this,

> Wo worth this deid that daylie dois me die!
> Wo worth Cupyd and wo worth fals Venus!
> Wo worth thame baith! Ay waryit mot thay be!
> Wo worth thair Court and cursit destenie! [633-36]

has unfortunate consequences — in a serio-comic scene of disaster the dreamer is
dragged before the offended goddess herself. In the trial scene that ensues the melancholy and fearfull poet finds courage to defend himself, objecting to the goddess acting
as judge ('For Ladyis may be Iudges in na place') and pointing out (with a nice touch
of self-conscious humour) that he is not a 'secular man' but 'a spiritual man'.[7] The
goddess is not amused, and launches into an anti-clerical tirade:

---

[7]   In a nice touch of humour directed at himself as 'kirkman', Douglas is perhaps reminding us that
'clerks' are not the normal members of Venus's admiring court. In the English *Court of Love* (where the
narrator is a Cambridge 'clerk') the plight of the friars and the religious provokes the comment: 'se how
they cry and wring their handes whyte, for they so sone went to religion.'

> ꝣit Clerkis bene in subtell wordis quent,
> And in the deid als schairp as ony snaillis.
>
> ꝣe bene the men bewrayis my commandis,
> ꝣe bene the men disturbis my seruandis,
> ꝣe bene the men with wickit wordis feill,
> Quhilk blasphemis fresche lustie ꝛoung gallandis
> That in my seruice and retinew standis. [716-22]

including

> Lat this Catiue kyith
> Gif our power may deming his misdeid. [728-29]

The unfortunate clerical dreamer is now in a parlous state ('I micht not say my creid
… /I micht not pray, forsuith, thocht I had neid') and is left fearing transformation
into some animal, and prey to 'terrible thoughts' and fantasies.

However, at the beginning of Part II the poet is rescued from his 'hard perplexitie'
by God's intervention:

> Lo thus amid this hard perplexitie,
> Awaitand euer quhat moment I suld die
> Or than sum new transfiguratioun,
> He that quhilk is eternall veritie,
> The glorious Lord ringand in persounis thre,
> Prouydit hes for my Saluatioun
> Be sum gude spreitis Reuelatioun,
> Quhilk Intercessioun maid, I traist, for me,
> I forꝛet all Imaginatioun. [772-80]

His spirits lighten and he forgets his dread and woe. He sees another 'heuinlie rout',
the muses and the poets crowned with laurel. Calliope intercedes on his behalf to
Venus, and delighted to have so great an advocate, he is inspired to write a lay, a more
joyful poem to 'Rander louingis for thy Saluatioun / Till Venus.' It pleases Calliope
and even Venus, who recognizes it as 'sum recompence' and that he is penitent. The
dreamer's words to Calliope

> My Protectour, my help and my supplie,
> My souerane Lady, my Redemptioun,
> My Mediatour quhen I was dampnit to die [1055-57]

are a good example of how Douglas can use religious language to achieve a half-courtly,
half-religious tone. And from this point on the religious diction, where it occurs, seems
to be more serious and significant. At the end of the dreamer's long aerial journey to the
fountain of the muses and the pavilion of the poets the visionary landscape is markedly

different from the earlier eerie desert and its monsters. Here, below the foot of a high mountain, the pleasant plain seems to have similarities with the earthly Paradise, with the ladies, playing, singing and dancing — 'full angellike and heuinlie was their soun …'

> The warld may not consider nor discriue
> The heuinlie Ioy, the blis I saw beliue … [1162-63]

But the final part of the journey is still to come, to the palace of Honour itself, set on a 'plesand Roche' amid a plain, at the end of Part II. Here the dreamer's language becomes very reminiscent of visionary writing:

> The hart may not think nor mannis toung say,
> The Eir nocht heir nor ʒit the Eye se may,
> It may not be Imaginit with men
> The heuinlie blis, the perfite Ioy to ken
> Quhilk now I saw … [1255-59]

whether he saw it in soul or in body. He is tempted to cease because of the sneers of backbiters, but decides to continue. In the third part the 'dream vision' becomes increasingly like a visionary experience, and the clear emergence of the idea of Honour will be seen to have a distinctly religious flavour. After the invocation to the muses the dreamer begins to climb up the hill, a rock of slippery hard marble stone, but as he climbs sees once again 'ane grislie sicht', which seems like a vision of hell:

> Ane terribill sewch birnand in flammis reid,
> Abhominabill and how as hell to se,
> All full of Brintstane, Pick and bulling Leid,
> Quhair mony wretchit creature lay deid
> And miserabill catiues ʒelland loude on hie,
> I saw … [1316-21]

His terror is soothed by his protecting nymph, who tells him that the victims are those wretches who gave up the quest for Honour because of sloth. Then, with a nice touch of comedy she carries the dreamer up by the hair (as Habbakuk was) to the top of the hill, and tells him to look down, and consider this wretched world. It is indeed a fearsome sight:

> Me thocht I saw birne in ane fyrie rage
> Of stormie sey quhilk micht na maner swage. [1349-50]

And this is followed by a vivid scene of a terrible shipwreck. (This is often admired: here perhaps it is worth drawing attention to the evident *pite* felt by the dreamer at the sight — 'It was ane pieteous thing, alaik, alaik, / To heir the dulefull cry quhen that scho straik; / Maist lamentabill the pereist folk to se …' *Pite*, that noble emotion celebrated by Chaucer and others, is not an exclusively religious one, but it often has deep religious undertones.) The nymph gives a further account of the scene's significance, in a much more directly Christian way, and with a certain 'clerkly' tone — the drowned are faithless folk, who 'misknawis God and followis their pleseir' who will be burnt in endless fire; and the ship is the 'Carwell of grace'. She urges 'all' to remain steadfastly in the ship of grace. (This may seem overly homiletic, but it may be suggested that in this section Douglas seems to be attempting to tap into the 'deep structures' of Christian allegory — the ideas of a psychomachia, a spiritual war between good and evil, or of the quest or perilous journey through life.) She now directs the dreamer's attention elsewhere ('consider wonders and be vigilant …'), and he has a moment of vision, in truth a 'heuinlie sicht', a landscape 'pleneist with plesance like to Paradice', and the great Palace itself, a 'heuinlie palice all of Cristall cleir'. The dreamer is brought in, and once again meets with Venus, who recognizes him.[8] In her mirror he sees universal history from the creation of the angels, through Biblical and ancient history to an ending which suggests the world's decadence and wickedness:

> I mycht behald in that Mirrour expres,
> The miserie, the crueltie, the dreid,
> Pane, sorrow, wo, baith wretchitnes and neid,
> The greit Inuy, couetous dowbilnes,
> Tuitchand warldlie vnfaithfull brukilnes[9] [1695-99]

and finally

> I saw the Feind fast folkis to vices tyst,
> And all the cumming of the Antechrist. [1700-01]

But we are also reminded of virtue. A watchman on the wall cries 'Out on falsheid, the Mother of euerie vice! / Away, invy and birnand coueticе!' He is called Lawtie, says the nymph, and she goes on to describe the court of Honour and its allegorical (and Scottish) officers, Discretioun as Comptroller, Temperance as Cook, Conscience as Chancelair, etc., in a nice passage which is moral and courtly as well as playful (and no doubt the idealisation might suggest some satiric thoughts on the actualities of court life).

The dreamer is brought in through the gate of burnished gold, and is overwhelmed by what he sees — his nymph rebukes him for being 'halflingis in ane farie'. He is overcome

---

8   With the words 'ye bene welcome, my presonar.' He replies to her question 'how plesis the our pastance and effeir' with the words 'Glaidlie … be God of heuin.' Is the oath here a simple example of the poet's 'automatic' Christian diction, or is it the rather cheeky response of a 'prisoner' now free and unencumbered (cf. his earlier attempt to question her role as judge)?

9   The 'abuses of the world' are brought back to our attention towards the end of the poem (cf. 2035ff.).

by the intense light: the walls shone 'like Phebus with fyrie bemis bricht', and their stones are those of the New Jerusalem in the book of Revelation (chap 21).[10] The interior is equally dazzling:

> The multitude of precious stanis seir
> Thairon sa schane my febill sicht but weir
> Micht not behald thair verteous gudlines. [1909-11]

Royal princes in 'plait and Armouris quent, / Of birneist gold couchit with precious stanis' are going to and fro in the hall, and the sicht of 'ane god omnipotent [or army-potent]' overwhelms him:

> On quhais glorious visage as I blent,
> In extasie be his brichtnes atanis
> He smote me doun and brissit all my banis [1922-24]

And he lies in a swoon 'with colour blaucht' until he is taken up by his nymph. The use of the imagery of light is widespread in medieval literature, but the intensity of it here is remarkable: it recalls some of the scenes in the Grail-romances, as that in the *Queste* when Lancelot approaches the Grail at Corbenic and sees a great light 'as if the sun had its abode within. The brightness that came pouring out of the room illumined the whole place till one would have thought that all the candles on earth were burning there'[11] — and he lies in ecstasy for twenty-four days. It is sometimes remarked that 'mystical' writing is found less in Scotland than in England in the Middle Ages. Perhaps this section of the *Palice of Honour* is almost an example of it.

However, as often in the poem, a moment of high seriousness is succeeded by comedy. The nymph takes the dreamer outside so that he can recover, and tells him that the worst is past — 'Get vp' she said, 'for schame be na Cowart.' To the taunt that he has 'ane wyifes hart' he responds with some anger. She then remarks (in a reply that may well be a mixture of the comic, the moral and the satirical) 'Soft ʒow … they ar not wise that stryifis, / For kirkmen war ay gentill to thair wyifis' before complimenting him on having at last shown some spirit.

She then gives him a gravely eloquent account of Honour:

---

[10] Already used in English by the author of *Pearl*; cf. Douglas Gray, '"Of sunne ne mone had they no need": Notes on the Imagery of Light in the Middle English Text,' *Essays in Honor of Edward B. King*, eds. Robert J. Benson and Eric W. Naylor (Sewanee, TN: The University of the South, 1991). See also Bawcutt's notes on this section of the *Palice* (Douglas, *The Shorter Poems of Gavin Douglas* 210).

[11] *The Quest of the Holy Grail*, trans. P. Matarasso (Harmondsworth: Penguin, 1979) 262. Interestingly, the vision of the grail that follows stresses the idea of the Trinity, which is important to Gavin Douglas (especially in the Prologue to Book 10 of the *Eneados*).

'Honour', quod scho, 'to this heuenlie King
Differris richt far fra warldlie gouerning,
Quhilk is bot Pompe of eirdlie dignitie,
Geuin for estait of blude, micht or sic thing.
And in this countrie Prince, Prelate or King
Allanerlie sall for vertew honourit be.
For eirdlie gloir is nocht bot vanitie
That as we se sa suddanlie will wend,
Bot verteous Honour neuer mair sall end. [1972-80]

She goes on to stress the inconstancy of the glory of this world — 'prosperitie in eird
is bot a dreme.' The 'hicht' of pope, prelates, emperors, kings and nobles is limited by
death, and nothing remains 'bot fame of thair Estaitis, / And nocht ellis bot verteous
warkis richt / Sall with thame wend, nouther thair Pompe nor micht.' But virtue has
no peer:

It makis folk perfite and glorious,
It makis Sanctis of pepill vitious,
It causis folk ay liue in lestand blis,
It is the way to hie Honour, I-wis. [2002-5]

She lists examples, ancient and modern (including Scotland's King Robert), and
rebukes those who nowadays transgress against it. Honour, it seems is divine, or quasi-
divine; as in ancient thought it comes through virtue. It is not an original idea — Bawcutt[12] appositely quotes *Le Temple d' Honneur et de Vertus* (1503) of the French poet
Jean Lemaire — 'c'est l'ediffice construict & fabricqué par la main des corps celestes,
habité & peuplé seulement des benoistes ames' — but Douglas gives it his own special
eloquence. And his mingling of humanism, chivalry and religion sometimes sounds
like a premonition of Spenserian noble chivalry.[13]

---

[12]   Douglas, *The Shorter Poems of Gavin Douglas* xxxvi.

[13]   It is often pointed out that the theme of Honour seems to have been a popular one in this period (see
ibid. xxxv-xxxvii). Two further parallels in England (though not sources) may be mentioned. At almost the
same time that Douglas was writing his poem, a most ambitious and elaborate set of pageants welcomed
the arrival of Catherine of Aragon to London (see Sydney Anglo, *Spectacle, Pageantry, and Early Tudor
Policy*, Oxford-Warburg studies (Oxford: Clarendon Press, 1969) 57-94). The royal procession passed
pageants such as the 'Castle of Policy, Noblesse and Virtue' and the 'Temple of God' to the 'Throne of
Honour', achievable only through virtue. From earlier in the period come the English versions of Chris-
tine de Pisan's *Epistre d'Othéa la deésse à Hector* (French text written *c.* 1400). See Christine de Pisan, *The
Epistle of Othea*, trans. Scrope Stephen, ed. C. F. Bühler, EETS, OS 264 (Oxford: Oxford University
Press, 1970). Cf. Douglas Gray, '"A Fulle Wyse Gentyl-Woman of France": *The Epistle of Othea* and later
Medieval English Literary Culture,' *Medieval Women: Texts and Contexts in Late Medieval Britain. Essays
for Felicity Riddy*, ed. Jocelyn Wogan-Browne (Turnhout: Brepols, 2000). The work consists of a series of

The ending of the *Palice of Honour* comes suddenly. The dreamer still yearning to see the torments of these who had transgressed, has to go to the garden outside, where a sudden awakening brings the vision to an abrupt end — to his extreme distress ('all eirdlie thing me thocht barrane and vile'). In his concluding verses in praise of 'hie honour' the religious imagery and diction predominate. He uses the language traditionally used in addresses to God and the Virgin Mary:[14]

> Hail rois, maist chois til clois thy fois greit micht!
> Haill stone, quhilk schone vpon the throne of licht!
> Vertew, quhais trew, sweit dew overthrew al vice … [2134-36]

Readers' opinions on the *Palice of Honour* differ widely. Some are repelled by the real excess of information, learning and rhetoric. Others, of whom I am one, admire it as a boldly experimental poem, which mingles high seriousness with 'game' and the language and ideas of the 'kirkman' with those of the learned courtly poet.

In the *Eneados* (1513), Douglas's brilliant translation of Virgil, we are struck by a careful, intellectual precision. He shares the concern of the newer humanism for exactitude — he is 'bound' to Virgil's text, and so will not normally resort to re-telling, rewriting or editorial censorship. The moments at which we sense that a specifically Christian view is being forcibly inserted into Virgil's text are very few: his version of *Veneris monumenta nefanda* in Book 6 as 'ane horribill takin of schrewit Venus wark' (taking 'Venus' firmly as the goddess rather than as a general expression for love) may suggest a clerkly view; or (more clearly perhaps) in Book 12:

> The kyng hym self, Latinus, for *the* affray,
> Fled to *the* cite, and tursyt with hym away
> Hys godd*is and* hys mawmontis, drevyn abak
> With a shamefull rebute *and* mekill lak [XII.v.163-66]

where 'gods and mawmontis' represents *pulsatos … divos*, the defeated gods of Latinus; or again in Book 4, '*the* serymonys of *th*ar payane gyß (in a passage (4.56ff) where Virgil remarks on the 'blind minds of prophets'). On the other hand, in his Prologues he is careful to emphasize the obvious differences between his Christianity and the ancient paganism found in the scenes and characters of the epic, and he will speak out

---

instructive *exempla*, each with a threefold structure — the story, a gloss applying it to the good knight, and an allegory giving its significance to the good spirit. It is a preparation for the good knight engaged in the tournament of life, and the advice sometimes has a distinctly 'Spenserian' quality (as was pointed out by Rosemond Tuve, *Allegorical Imagery: Some Mediaeval Books and Their Posterity* (Princeton: Princeton UP, 1966) 34-41.

[14] See Douglas, *The Shorter Poems of Gavin Douglas* 214 (notes).

loudly against those 'backbiters' who would criticize Virgil or his translator. It would obviously be rash to argue that Douglas was particularly avant-garde in his humanist admiration for Virgil, but it may well not have been a taste shared by all members of his audience[15]; perhaps this has something to do with the combination of aggressiveness and defensiveness in his denunciations of backbiters (although one sometimes suspects that Douglas was one of those writers who positively need 'backbiters' to attack). He sharply rebukes Caxton's *Eneydos* for its dismissal of the descent to Avernus; and speaks sharply to his own critics in the final 'Direction' to Lord Sinclair:

> Nane other thyng, *th*ai threpe, heir wro*ch*t haue I
> But fenӡeit fabillys of idolatry,
> With sik myscheif as aucht not namyt be,
> Oppy*nn*and *th*e gravis of smert iniquyte,
> And on *th*e bak half wryt*is* wyddyr sy*nn*ys
> Plente of lesyng*is*, and ald perversyt synnys. [XIII, 25-30]

before excusing himself: his work will pass the time pleasantly and avoid idleness; it will be useful for those who expound Virgil to children; and what he has translated is not the work of every 'bural ruyd' poet, but the 'flude' of eloquence itself[16].

Moreover, although in his Prologues he distances himself from the ancient religion, he often does not seem totally hostile to it, and indeed sometimes surprisingly sympathetic. In his translation he seems generally at ease with the old gods — Neptune with his 'gret mattock havand granys thre', and even Venus, 'schynyng ful cleir for al *th*e dyrk ny*ch*t / Confessyng hir tobe a godde β bry*ch*t' when she appears to her son in Book 2. And there is, of course, a very great deal of it — sacrifices, oracles, 'spamen and dyvynys', funeral ceremonies and prayers.[17] There is a certain amount of (more or

---

[15] Cf. the response of the nun Charitas Pirckheimer to the humanist Conrad Celtis (1459-1508): 'out of our singular friendship I admonish your worship to abandon the evil fables of Diana, Venus, Jupiter, and of other damned pagans who are now burning in hell fire, whose names and memory all true men who agree with the Christian profession must expunge, detest and deliver to complete oblivion.' (quoted by Lewis William Spitz, *Conrad Celtis: The German Arch-Humanist* (Cambridge, MA: Harvard University Press, 1957) 86.

[16] When Douglas is making an end, in the Prologue to Book 13, perhaps we sense a more defensive tone in the allusion to Jerome's story of his unease about the books of the gentiles: 'thus sair me dredis I sal thoill a heit / For the grave study I have so long forleit' — though 'my buke and Virgillis moral beyn, bath tway.' And, of course, in the 'conclusio' he declares 'my muse sal now be cleyn contemplatyve'.

[17] To be fair to Caxton, in spite of the rejection of the fables of Virgil's Book 6, elsewhere in the *Eneydos* he too seems at ease with much of the ancient religion — and even cites a parallel in England to the decorating of the altar with branches and boughs. (William Caxton, *Caxton's Eneydos, 1490: Englisht from the French Liure des Eneydes, 1483*, eds. Mathew Tewart Culley, Frederick James Furnivall and Jean Jacques Salverda de Grave, EETS, ES 57 (London: N. Trübner & Co., 1890) 17.

less) discreet 'medievalisation', like the nymphs and fauns 'quhilk fairfolk*is*, or *th*an elvys, clepying we' or the Sirens as 'marmadynnys'. In Book 4 Mercury 'gliding on thy wings' (*labere pennis*) has a 'feddyrame' (but a little later buckles his golden wings to his feet, and takes his wand 'as *th*at *th*ai tell / The pail sawlis he cachis furth of hell.'

More frequently Douglas will make use of a 'Christian' or 'semi-Christian' word like 'hell', 'purgatory' or 'heaven' as if 'to stress ideas he could reconcile with his own religion'.[18] So Orcus becomes 'hell' and Avernus 'the layk of hell' as in the *Palace of Honour*. This is sometimes eloquently done: the god smote Palinurus

> ...ba*th* his tymplis twane
> With a full sleipry and bedyit grane,
> Wet in *th*e myndles flude of hell, Lythe,
> And sowpit in Stix, the forcy hellis see; [IV.xiv.51-54]

('ecce deus ramum Lethaeo rore madentem / vique soporatum Stygia super utraque quassat / tempora')

Especially impressive is his description of the vale of Ampsanctus in Book 7 (ll. 565 ff.; where he discreetly simplifies Virgil's allusiveness and adds some 'explanatory' expansions):

> *The* vail Ansanctus hait, on athir hand
> Quha*m th*e syd*is* of thik wod of tre
> Closis full dern w*ith* skowgy bewys hie.
> A rowtand burn amydwart *th*ar*of* ry*n*nys,
> Rumland *and* soundand on *th*e craggy quhy*n*nys,
> And eik forgane *th*e brokkyn brow of *th*e mont
> Ane horribill cave wi*th* braid and large front
> *Th*ar may be sene, a thyrl or ayndyng sted
> Of terribill Pluto, fader of hell and ded;
> A ryft or swelch so grysly for to se,
> Till Acheron revin dovne, *th*at hellis see,
> Gapand w*ith* his pestiferus gowle full wide; [VII.ix.52-63]

Sometimes, almost of necessity, he uses words which (especially for modern readers) have a distinctly Christian ring, like the 'devout prayer' (*votibus precibusque*) of the Trojans when they are attacked by the Harpies in Book 3:

> Bot, w*ith* offerand*is and* eik devot prayer,
> *Th*ai wald we suld perdoun *and* pace requer,
> In cace gif *th*ai war goddess*is* or fowlis,
> Vengeabill wight*is* or ȝit laithly owlis. [III.iv.99-102]

---

[18] Priscilla Bawcutt, *Gavin Douglas: A Critical Study* (Edinburgh: Edinburgh University Press, 1976) 126.

Similar are the 'dyvyne seruys' (*divinis rebus*, 8. 306) or the 'oblacionys' that Helenus tells Aeneas to maintain (with 'every serimony of our religioun'; *morem sacrorum*, 3.408). More surprisingly, perhaps, 'purviance' is sometimes used. In the same prophecy of Helenus '*th*e purviance dyvyne wil so it be' (though the following lines sound more 'ancient': 'the kyng of godd*is* so distribut*is th*e fat*is*, / Rollyng *th*e chanc*is and* turnyng *th*ame *th*usgatis'). There are some oddities, but sometimes these seem mostly to be of our own making, like the 'pulpit of a ship' in Book 2 (but 'pulpit' is recorded in the sense of a stage or platform[19]), or the celebrated case of the 'nuns of Baccus' in Book 4, where Virgil describes Dido who rages (*bacchatur*) through the city like some Thyiad (a bacchante), and Douglas has

> myndles in hir rage
> Scho wysk*is* wild throw *th*e town of Cartage,
> Syk wyß as quhen *th*ir nu*n*nys of Bachus
> Ruschis and relis our bank*is*, brays and buß … [IV.vi.39-42]

where the modern reader has to make an effort not to visualise a group of nuns in wimples and habits. But, as Bawcutt pointed out 'nun' is often used for a female pagan *sacerdos*[20] (cf. the 'nun Sibilla' or 'the religyus nun').

Against such cases should be set those where the tactful use of 'semi-Christian' terms give a curious and impressive eloquence to be pagan characters. Thus in book 6, Anchises gives a fine account of creation:

> 'Fra the begynnyng, all thing leß *and* mar,
> *Th*e fyry regioun, the erth, *and* the ayr,
> The plane flowand bound*is* of the sey,
> The lyghtnyt monys lamp that lemys hie,
> The hevy*n*nys starnys [*Titaniaque astra*] *and* bright sonnys ball,
> Ane spreit *th*ar is within, sustenys all:
> In euery part *th*e hie wysdome dyvyne
> Diffundit movys *th*is warldis hail engyne,
> And by hys power mydlit is our all
> This mekil body clepit vniuersal. [VI.xii.]

And Evander's prayer in Book 8 has a simple dignity:

---

[19]   And *DOST* records it in the sense of a ship's poop, in 1512-13.

[20]   Bawcutt, *Douglas: Critical Study* 133. Caxton's *Eneydos* also seems to have had some trouble with (the not very common?) 'Thyiad', paraphrasing it as '[Dido] ra*n*ne thrugh þe citee of cartage as a mad woman, as thyas þe grete prestresse dyd in tyme passed' (Caxton, *Eneydos* 66/8-10).

> But O ȝe goddis abuf, and Ioue mast hie,
> The governour of hevynly wyghtis all,
> On ȝou I cry, on ȝou I clepe and call:
> Begyn to haue compaciens and piete
> Of your awin wofull kyng of Arcadye;
> Oppyn and inclyne ȝour dyvyne godly erys,
> To heir and resaue *the* faderis meik prayeris.
> Gyf it be so ȝour godhed *and* gret myghtis
> Be presciens provyd heß, and forsychtis,
> Pallas my son in salfty hail and feir,
> Gyf *the* fatis preservys hym of danger,
> So onys in my lyfe I may hym se,
> Agane togidder assemblyt I and he;
> I ȝow beseik my febill lyfe to respyte,
> *Th*at I mycht lyf and endur ȝyt a lyte
> All pane and labour *th*at ȝou list me send. [VIII.ix.66-81]

In the prologues some of these patterns and ideas recur, and there we find a fuller exposition of them. The prologue to Book 1 opens with an intense and eloquent invocation to Virgil the poet:

> Lawd, honour, praysyngis, thankis infynyte
> To the and thy dulce ornat fresch endyte,
> Maist reuerend Virgill of Latyn poetis prince … [I.Prol.1-3]

It reaches an almost religious intensity: 'Lantarn, laid stern, myrrour and A perse … /… thy wark sall endur in lawd and glory / But spot or falt condyng etern memory' — and indeed a little later (l. 148) he calls him 'the poet dyvyne'. It does seem that Douglas not only thinks of him as a profound philosopher but also almost as a semi-divine figure. Later in this prologue there is a striking juxtaposition of Virgil and God. Douglas moves directly from the Latin poet to God, who is his true inspiration, and although the passage is firmly Christian, its language is very similar to that which he uses to praise Virgil:

> Thou prynce of poetis, I the mercy cry,
> I meyn *th*ou Kyng of Kyngis, Lord Etern,
> *Th*ou be my muse, my gydar *and* laid stern,
> Remittyng my trespaß and euery myß
> Throu prayer of thy Moder, Queyn of Blyß.
> Afald godhed, ay lestyng but discrepans,
> In personys thre, equale, of a substans,
> On *th*e I call, and Mary Virgyn myld … [I.Prol.452-59]

— and not on Calliope 'nor payane godd*is* wild; — 'in Criste is all my traste, and hevy*n*-nys queyn' (who fostered that prince, that 'hevynly Orpheus … Our Saluyour Ihesus', words which clearly suggest that God is the prince and the patron of poets). He ends the Prologue with a warning and an appeal to would-be critics: 'beis not ourstudyus to spy a moyt in myne e, / *Th*at in ʒo*ur* awyn a ferry boyt can nocht se' — but before this, when he addresses his readers, asking for a careful and sympathetic reading before any reproof, he hints at some of the arguments he will use in the Prologue to Book 6 to show that Virgil was 'ane hie Philosophour': Juno and Venus never were goddesses, nor is it the case that souls 'hoppys fra body to body'; truthful matters are hidden in similitudes and 'vndir quent figur*is*' — 'all is nocht fals'. Who knows if Aeneas went to the underworld and saw and spoke with his father's soul 'by art magike, socery or enchantment' or in the likeness with some other spirit such as that of Samuel raised to King Saul by the 'Phi-tones'? 'I will no*ch*t say all Virgill beyn als trew / Bot at syk thyng*is* ar possibill …' Moreover, in the person of Aeneas Virgil describes 'eu*er*y vertu belangand a nobill man.'

The Prologue to Book 3 also has an example of an 'adjusted' invocation. It begins with an address to pale Cynthia, 'hornyt Lady', and the 'rewlare of passage *and* ways many one, / Maistres of stremys, *and* glaidar of *th*e nyc*h*t …', but in the final line of the stanza God is the inspiration: 'Thy strange went*is* to write God grant me slyc*h*t'.[21] And in the Prologue's final stanza he prays that the 'virgyne moder but maik' may be his 'laid star' (converting, as Bawcutt points out,[22] the traditional Marian image of *stella maris* to the voyagers' guiding star):

> *Thoch*t storm of temptacioun my schip oft schaik,
> Fra swelth of Sylla *and* dyrk Caribdis band*is*,
> I meyn from hell, salve al go not to wraik. [III.Prol.43-45]

Elsewhere in the Prologue his sympathetic humanism allows him to write gravely and solemnly, rather in the manner of the speeches of Anchises and Evander quoted above. And he often seems to share Virgil's deep melancholy. The Prologue to Book 2, for instance, has a kind of invocation to Saturn that is wholly appropriate:

> Saturn, *th*ou auld fader of malancholy,
> Thyne is *th*e cuyr my wofull pen to gy. [II.Prol.13-14]

and concludes with an equally appropriate proverbial truth:

---

[21] Similarly in the Prologue to Book 5, which also refers to Virgil as 'poete dyvyne', we find Douglas at the end refusing to call on Bacchus and 'funeral Proserpyne', and the goddess of triumph, 'clepyt Victorie', but appealing to God in words that are notably pious and devout.

[22] In Priscilla Bawcutt and Janet Hadley Williams, eds., *A Companion to Medieval Scottish Poetry* (Cambridge: D.S. Brewer, 2006) 129.

> Heir verifeit is *th*at proverbe teching so,
> 'All erdly glaidneß fynysith with wo.' [II.Prol.20-21]

And in the winter prologue (to Book 7) there occur some lines appropriately alluding to the preceding account of the descent to hell:

> Seir bittir bubbis and *th*e schowr*is* snell
> Semyt on *th*e sward a symylitude of hell,
> Reducyng to our mynd, in eu*er*y sted,
> Gousty schaddois of eild and grisly ded.[23] [VII.Prol.43-46]

Some other Prologues touch more directly — and extensively — on our theme. That to Book 4, for instance, much discussed, is a fervently moral piece on love, but is, I think, less narrowly didactic and homiletic than is sometimes claimed. Parts of it certainly sound like a sermon. The opening lines

> Wyth bemys scheyn *th*ou bricht Cytherea,
> Quhilk only schaddowist amang starr*is* lyte,
> And *th*i blyndyt weyngit son Cupyd, ȝe twa
> Fosterar*is* of byrnyng carnail, hait delyte,
> Ȝour ioly wo neidlyng*is* most I endyte,
> Begy*n*nyng with a fenȝeit faynt plesance,
> Continewit in lust, and endyt w*ith* pe*n*nance. [IV.Prol.1-7]

soon take on the urgent tones of the preacher:

> Quhat is ȝour forß bot feblyng of *th*e strenth?
> Ȝour curyus thocht*is* quhat but musardry?
> Ȝour fre*m*myt glaidnes lest*is* not ane howr*is* lenth …
> Ȝour sweit myrth*is* ar mixt w*ith* byttyrneß …
> O luf, quhiddir art *th*ou ioy or fulychneß,
> *Th*at mak*is* folk sa glaid of *th*ar distreß? [IV.Prol.15-28]

But love is by no means entirely destructive. Speaking of its awesome power, he is moved to exclaim on its role in Redemption:

> Thow cheyn of luf, ha benedicite,
> Quhou hard strenys *th*i band*is* eu*er*y wyght!
> The God abuf, from his hie maieste,
> With *th*e ybond, law in a maid dyd ly*ch*t:
> Thou ve*n*quyst *th*e strang gyant of gret my*ch*t;
> Thou art mair forcy *th*an *th*e ded sa fell,
> *Th*ou plenyst Paradice and *th*ou heryit hell. [IV.Prol.36-42]

---

[23] And he crosses himself before going to sleep (as he does on rising in the Prologue to Book 12).

And besides its destructive results, it infuses friendship and comradeship. Douglas seems concerned to establish its mysterious paradoxes; and when the fearsome power of human love becomes excessive and leads to tragedy, he shows a remarkable sense of *pite*. One of his examples is 'the reuthtfull smart and lame*n*tabill cace' of the young Leander, and he addresses Hero: 'quhou for *th*i luf, Hero, allace, allace! /In fervent flambe of hait desyre byrnyng' he came to his death ('Lo, quhou Venus kan hir *ser*-uandis acquyte!'). 'Lufe is a kyndly passioun, engendryt of heyt / Kyndlyt in *th*e hart': Douglas tries to distinguish love from lust, and from inordinate or imperfect love; he presents a moderate and pious pattern of behaviour:

> ... lufe God for his gudneß,
> With hart, hail mynde, trew *ser*vice, day *and* nyc*h*t;
> Nixt luf *th*i self, eschewand wykkytnes;
> Luf syne *th*i nychtburr*is*, and wyrk *th*ame nane onryc*h*t,
> Willyng at *th*ou and *th*ai may haue *th*e syc*h*t
> Of hevy*n*nys blyß ... [IV.Prol.135-40]

And urges young women to act chastely and young men to ground their love on 'char-ite al new'. Turning to the story of Dido, he expresses his *pite*, addressing her directly:

> Thy dowbill wound, Dido, to specify ...
> Quha may endyte, but teris, wi*th* eyn dry? [IV.Prol.215-17]

recalling that St. Augustine himself had wept, recording that love had indeed brought her and her achievements low, but also emphasizing his sorrow at her 'lame*n*tabill end mysfortunat', repeating the verse 'temporal ioy end*is* with wo and pane'.

His prologue to Book 6 is another extended study. It is in effect a justification for his work of translation, and is a fine example of his vigorous argumentative style. It begins with an appropriate invocation to Pluto and the Sybil:

> Pluto, *th*ou patron of *th*e deip Achiron,
> Fader of torment*is* in thyne infernal see ...
> Thyne now salbe my muse and drery sang:
> To follow Virgil in *th*is dyrk poyse
> Convoy me, Sybil, *th*at I ga noc*h*t wrang. [VI.Prol.1-8]

which is instantly followed by a vehement attack on those fools who think that the sixth book is 'bot iapis'; they should be silent, and read and reread, and think again, or else 'heich on ȝour hede set vp *th*e foly hat'.[24] However, a calmer style of disputation

---

[24]   He gives a good dramatic imitation of their jeering comments on supposed superstitions: 'All is bot gaistis and elrich fantasyis, / of browneis and of bogillis ful *th*is buke: / "owt on *th*ir wandrand speritis, wow!" thou cryis.'

also comes easily to him, as he goes on to argue that Virgil 'is ful of sentence our all quhare': his work describes the state of man, both life and death in the first five books, and in the sixth 'in quhat plyte saulis sal stand' after death. As befits a 'philosophour naturall' there are many statements in his poem which are in conformity with Christianity, which Douglas lists, before asking 'ar al sik sawis fantasy and invane?'

> He schawis *the* way, evir patent, down to hell,
> And ry*ch*t difficil *th*e gait to hevin agane,
> With ma gude wordis *th*an *th*ou or I kan tell. [VI.Prol.46-48]

And there are 'notabil histories, *and* diuerß *pr*overbis wyce' (later, he quotes Ascensius's saying that many of Virgil's words are like those of the apostles). Of course, he admits, our faith does not need authorisation from pagan books, but much of what Virgil says strengthens our faith. He notes the frequency with which Augustine quotes him, and alludes to Virgil's remark in his 'Bucolykis' concerning 'the maide cu*mm*yth bring*is* new ly*n*nage fra hevyn.' Virgil is 'ane hie theolog sentencyus' and 'maste *pr*ofound philosopho*ur*.' Of course, being a pagan, he is sometimes in error (as with the transmigration of souls and the belief that there are many gods — though he has one mover, one creator of the world), but a succinct statement of Christian belief (ll.81 ff.) is used to demonstrate that Virgil shares much of it, notably the place of torment and the divisions within it, and 'quhou iust pepil, in welthis monyfald, / Raiosys, syngand sang*is* of hevynly glory …' Virgil also gives sound advice to princes — 'quhat Cristyn clerk' could have counselled the emperor better?

Finally, Douglas sets about putting Pluto and the Cumanean Sybil into their proper Christian place:

> Quha bettir may Sibilla namyt be
> Than may *th*e gloryus moder *and* maydyn fre …
> Thow art our Sibill, Crystis moder deir,
> Prechit by prophet*is* and Sibilla Cumane …
> Moder of God, ay virgyne doith remane,
> Restoring wß *th*e goldin world agane. [VI.Prol.140-49]

As for Pluto, 'to name the God, *th*at war a manifest le'. He is but Jove's smith. He created nothing, but made himself a devil (and '*th*at was not to mak, bot rather fail3e / For Austyne says syn, myscheif or evill / Is no*ch*t at all' and he is now dismissed summarily (and rather skittishly):

> Help me, Mare; for certis, vail que vail3e,
> War at Pluto, I sall hym hunt of sty. [VI.Prol.167-68]

For all its special pleading, this Prologue is a remarkable piece of argumentation, combining intelligence with wit.

In two prologues (to Books 9 and 11) Douglas returns to the question of Honour that had preoccupied him in the *Palice of Honour*. The brief prologue to book 9 (a prelude to a narrative of battles and war) combines a statement of the idea central to the *Palice*

> Honeste is *th*e way to worthyneß,
> Vertu, doutleß, *th*e p*er*fyte gait to blyß; [IX.Prol.7-8]

with advice on behaviour:

> *Th*ou do na myß, *and* eschew idilneß,
> Persew prowes …
> Do tyll ilk wight as *th*ou done to waldbe;
> Be nevir sle *and* doubill, nor ȝit our light; [IX.Prol.9-14]

before it rather abruptly turns aside ('eneuch of *th*is, ws ned*is* prech na mor') to the well-known lines on the appropriate style, 'the ryall style, clepyt heroycall, / Full of wirschip *and* nobilnes our all.'

The prologue to Book 11 is much fuller. From its opening

> Thow hie renown of Martis chevalry,
> Quhilk glad*is* eu*er*y gentill wight to heir [XI.Prol.1-2]

it urges nobles to follow the example of their ancestors 'tyll hie curage, all hono*ur* till ensew.' Pure 'prowes' is shown in holy scripture, in Machabeus, Josua, David and Michael and the angels

> *Th*at can *th*e dragon furth of hevy*n*nys chace
> With vailȝeand dynt*is* of ferm mynd*is* contrar,
> Nane o*ther* strok*is* nor wapy*n*nys had *th*ai *th*ar
> No*ther* speir, buge, polax, swerd, knyfe nor mace; [XI.Prol.13-16]

(a clear example of 'spiritual chivalry'; and one which shows that in 'chivalry or battle' our minds should have a 'iust ententioun', grounds for the battle founded on 'rycht'; to redress wrong not for 'conquest, reif, skat, nor pensioun' — sentiments similar to these are found in his Scottish predecessor, Gilbert Hay, and other authors of medieval 'arts of war'). The religious tone is very marked: Douglas says his intention is to speak of 'moral vertuus hardyme*n*t / Or rathar of dyuyne', 'for warldly strenth is febill and impotent / In Godd*is* sight, and insufficient'. He gives us a definition of fortitude: 'Strang fortitud, quhilk hardyment cleip we, / Abuf *th*e quhilk *th*e vertu souerane / Accordyng prync*is*, hecht magnanymyte' is a good set between two clearly differentiated evils — 'fuyl hardynes' and 'schamefull cowardyce.' He goes on to speak of other 'chevalry', again in a rather Spenserian manner:

> Gyf Cryst*is* faithful knycht*is* lyst ws be,
> So as we aucht, and promyst heß at font,
> Than mon we byd baldly, and neu*er* fle,
> Nowd*er* be abasyt, tepyt, nor ȝit blunt,
> Nor as cowart*is* to eschew *th*e first dunt. [XI.Prol.57-61]

St Paul says that only he who stands 'wightly' and fights in the forefront will win the crown of everlasting bliss — whoever does not, must of necessity fear the fire eternal. We should follow the apostle's words on 'the armo*u*r of our chevalry', which is not corporal but spiritual, our 'conquyst haill, our vassellage *and* prowes' is against 'spret*is* and pryncis of myrknes', not against man, our own brother, nor against the creator.

The flesh contends with the spirit: 'the spreit wald vp, *th*e corpß ay down list draw.' Our second foe is the world, which fiercely attacks with 'covatys and estait':

> Lyff in thy flesch as mast*er* of thy corps,
> Lyf in *th*is warld as no*ch*t ay to remane;
> Resist *th*e fend*is* slych*t* wi*th* all thy forß,
> He is thy ancyent e*n*nemy, werst of ane; [XI.Prol.89-92]

with a thousand wiles and temptations. Stand firm against him using the whole armour of God (not described in the allegorical detail of Ramon Lull[25], but stirringly emphasized: 'Rayß hie *th*e targe of faith vp in thy hand, / On hed *th*e halsum helm of hoip onlace, / In cheryte thy body all embrace, / And of devoit oryson mak thy brand'). In this spiritual crusade think on the holy martyrs, on hell's pain and on endless glory, and on Christ's sacrifice for man ('thynk all *th*ou suffer*is* ontyll hys paynis nocht is')

> Feill beyn thy fays, fers and full of sly*ch*t,
> Bot be *th*ou stalwart compioun *and* knych*t*
> In feild of grace with forsaid armo*u*r brych*t*. [IX.Prol.113-15]

Be steadfast

> And quha so perseuer*is* to *th*e end
> Ane conquero*u*r and campioun eu*er* is kend,
> With palm of triu*m*phe, hono*u*r and glory. [IX.Prol.142-44]

Finally, take example from Aeneas

> *Th*at, for hys fatale cuntre of behest,
> Sa feill danger*is* sustenyt on land *and* see,
> Syk stryfe in stour sa oft with spear in rest,
> Quhill he hys realm conquest ba*th* west *and* est … [IX.Prol.178-81]

---

25 Rámon Llull, *The Book of the Ordre of Chyualry*, trans. William Caxton, ed. A. T. P. Byles, EETS, OS 168 (London: Oxford University Press, 1926).

He did it all for a temporal realm: let us press on to win the 'kynryk ay lestyng':

> Than lat ws stryve *th*at realm forto posseid,
> *Th*e quhilk was hecht till Abraham *and* hys seyd;
> Lord, at ws wrocht *and* bocht, grant ws *th*at hald! [IX.Prol.198-200]

A fervent ending to an accomplished exposition.

The prologue to Book 10 is the most clearly religious of all the prologues. Douglas is rarely linked with or compared with Dunbar as a writer of religious poetry, but if it is rare for him to reach the intensity of Dunbar's shorter religious lyrics, it is arguable that this prologue can match Dunbar's longer moral and 'expository' poems. As Alasdair MacDonald, one of the very few scholars to have done justice to it, rightly said:[26]

> As an exposition of the teaching of the church, it would be hard to better the grave, latinate dignity of Bishop Gavin Douglas, whose Prologue to the tenth book of *The Eneados* is incorporated as a religious 'lyric' by George Bannatyne.

Its opening address to God makes use of traditional and philosophical diction:

> He plasmato*ur*[27] of thyng*is* vniuersall,
> *Th*ou renewar of kynd *th*at creat all,
> Incomprehensibill thy wark*is* ar to consave … [X.Prol.1-3]

and praises the creator for the marvellous 'diuisions of thy grac*is*' – how He 'for diuerß causys schupe seir sessonys *and* spac*is*':

> Fresch veir to burgioun herbys and sweit flowr*is*,
> The hait symmyr to nuryß corn all howr*is*
> And breid all kynd of fowlys, fysch and beste,
> Hervist to rendir hys frut*is* maste and leste,
> Wyntir to snyb *th*e erth with frosty schowr*is*. [X.Prol.11-15]

Douglas moves on to his central emphasis in his account of the Deity ('thy maist supreme and indiuisibill substans' — another line which illustrates the ease with which he uses learned diction), that it is one God in three persons. (And already we notice how before he formally introduces 'similitudes' of the Trinity he has begun, consciously or unconsciously, to use a number of 'threefold' patterns of speech — 'fowlys, fysch

---

[26] Alasdair A. MacDonald, 'Religious Poetry in Middle Scots,' *The History of Scottish Literature Volume 1: Origins to 1660*, ed. R. D. S. Jack (Aberdeen: Aberdeen University Press, 1988) 101.
[27] A word from Christian Latin, found also in the York Plays (*OED*); for similar rare 'clerkly' words cf. *incommyxt* and *investigabill* later.

and beste', or, later (ll. 24-25) that God is, was, and ever shall be.) He stresses the indissoluble unity of the Godhead:

> Hys Godhed inco*mm*ixt remanys perfyte,
> The Son of God havand verray natur*is* twane
> In a person, and thre personys all ane
> In deite, natur, maieste and delyte …
> Ar, war, and be sall, eu*er* of ane age,
> Om*n*ipotent, a Lord, equale in blyß … [X.Prol.27-35]

Powerfully emphasizing the co-existence of 'threefold' and 'unitary' patterns, and once again showing a remarkable mastery of abstract language and thought.

> Quhilk souerane substans, in gre sup*er*latyve,
> Na cu*n*nyng comprehend may nor discryve;
> Now*ther* gener*is*, gen*er*at is, nor doith proceid,
> Allane begy*n*nar of eu*er*y thing, but dreid,
> And in *th*e self remanys etern on lyve. [X.Prol.36-40]

Notable is the sheer precision of expression: the father, 'of nane generat, creat ne boir', engenders his only son — 'not mak*is*, creat*is*, bot engendr*is* all way / Of hys substans.' The father 'knawys hym self' and spreads knowledge by eternal generation, engendering 'hys Son, hys word *and* wysdom et*er*nall' while between them is 'luf p*er*petuall,' which is the Holy Ghost. Whatever he gives to his son, he remains without diminuation:

> The ilk thing he hym gevis, *th*at he remanys:
> Thys syngill substans indifferently *th*us ganys
> To thre in ane, *and* ilkane of *th*a thre
> *Th*e sa*mm*yn thing is in a maieste,
> *Th*ocht thir personys be seuerall in thre granys … [X.Prol.61-65]

He illustrates this by two 'trinitarian' similitudes (of a traditional kind, found in Robert Grosseteste[28] and other earlier writers): the soul of man has three powers, distinct and separate — understanding or intelligence, reason and memory — and they are all knit together in one substance. Similarly, fire contains flame, light and heat —

> *Th*us rude exemplys *and* figur*is* may we geif;
> *Th*och*t*, God by hys awin creatur*is* to preif,
> War mair onlikneß *th*an liknes to discern. [X.Prol.83-85]

---

28 Cf. Servus Gieben, 'Traces of God in Nature according to Robert Grosseteste, with the Text of the Dictum "Omnis creatura speculum est",' *Franciscan Studies* 24 (1964).

Here he addresses the reader ('frend, farly nocht'), reassuring him that human reason is too feeble and 'light' to be able to comprehend God. Then, with an address to God the tone becomes more personal and emotional:

> O Lord, the ways beyn investigabill …
> I can write nocht bot wondris of thy mycht … [X.Prol.101-2]

being born as man in an ox's stable (where he uses another 'threefold' expression — 'angellis, scheiphyrdis and kyngis thy Godheid kend, / Set thou in cryb betwixt twa bestis was laid') and his creation of man ('that tynt him self throu hys fulych dotage') and his redemption through Christ's death. The emotion rises to an exclamation:

> O thyne inestimabill luf and cheryte
> Becam a thrall to mak ws bondis fre,
> To quykkyn thy sclavys tholyt schamful ded maste fell!
> And pait the pryce of the forbodin tre! [X.Prol.126-30]

In this more 'devotional' mood we find some very impressive lines:

> Thocht thou large stremys sched apon the rude,
> A drop had bene sufficient of thy blude
> A thousand warldis to haue redemyt … [X.Prol.131-33]

And the tone becomes more intensely personal:

> Quhat thankis dew or ganʒeld, Lord benyng,
> May I, maist wrachit synfull catyve indyng,
> Rendir for this souerane peirles hie bonte? [X.Prol.141-43]

he asks. And exclaims

> My makar, my redemar and support,
> Fra quham all grace and gudnes cumis at schort,
> Grant me that grace my mysdedis til amend,
> Of this and all my warkis to mak gud end … [X.Prol.146-49]

It is at this point that he dissociates himself from the pagan gods: 'God shall be my muse',

> All other Ioue and Phebus I refuß.
> Lat Virgill hald hys mawmentis to him self;
> I wirschip nowder ydoll, stok nor elf,
> Thocht furth I write so as myne autour dois. [X.Prol.152-55]

In his vehement denial he drops into the colloquial register:

> I compt not of thir paygane goddis a fudder

> Quhais power may no*ch*t help a haltand hen[29] [X.Prol.159-60]

The poem ends with a prayer to God the Father:

> Mak ws thy sonnys in cherite, but discord.
> Thow hald*is* court our cristall heuy*n*nys cleir,
> With angellis sanct*is* and hevynly spret*is* seir ...
> Concord for ever, myrth, rest and endless blyß,
> Na feir of hell, nor dreid of ded, *th*ar is
> In thy sweit realm, nor na kind of e*n*noy,
> But all wilfair, eyß and eu*er*lastand ioy;
> Quhais hi plesance, Lord, lat ws never myß! [X.Prol.165-75]

This prologue is an impressive and remarkable poem in many ways. In particular one must admire the sheer distinction and intellectual power of its thought. It is unusual to find this in a religious poem in this period. It seems in some ways to belong to the older, wider tradition of clerkly thought and writing rather than to the affective and devotional tradition so pervasive in its time. It would be hard to find many English writings of the period similar to it (perhaps Bishop Pecock might be a contender). In Scotland perhaps it is less surprising, since the older scholasticism seems to have had a continuing influence: perhaps we might set Douglas's poem against the prose of John Ireland as another example of vernacular theology.

In conclusion, it may be said that Douglas deserves to be taken seriously as a 'religious' poet. He shows some skill in a number of the styles of religious poetry, as well as being able to combine it with secular and courtly tradition. He can write piously and earnestly, can make the literature of antiquity alive for his contemporaries, and can balance earnest and 'game', intelligence and wit. He emerges as an interesting and intelligent 'kirkman' as well as a kind of early sixteenth century Christian humanist.

---

[29] This is in essence the same attitude that he has expressed before. Possibly the vehemence of its expression here is due not only to the emotional movement of the Prologue, but also may be encouraged by the fact that in Book 10 he will be going on to describe how Jupiter summoned the court of the gods (note the reference to God holding court (peacefully) in heaven in the final prayer). For an even more striking, and less subtle, linking of an interest in the pagan gods with a firm dismissal of them, cf. the fifteenth-century English poem *The Assembly of Gods*, formerly attributed to Lydgate in *The Assembly of Gods or the Accord of Reason and Sensuality in the Fear of Death*, ed. O. L. Triggs, EETS, ES 69 (London: Oxford University Press, 1896).

Pastoral Encyclopedism in *The Complaynt of Scotland*'s 'Monologue Recreative'

Michael W. Twomey

In this essay I propose to examine the encyclopedic composition of a text that falls on the cusp of the Reformation: the *Complaynt of Scotland* (STC 22009) attributed to Robert Wedderburn (*c.* 1510-*c.* 1553).[1] Specifically I will discuss the *Complaynt*'s puzzling 'Monologue Recreative,' which occurs in its pastoral middle section. Wedderburn is best known as one of three Wedderburn brothers who compiled the hymn collection *Gude and Godlie Ballatis* (Edinburgh, 1567). All three brothers were educated at St. Leonard's college of the University of St. Andrews. At the Reformation, Robert, vicar of Dundee, remained in the old religion while his brothers James and John embraced the new.[2] The *Complaynt* has been called Scottish literature's 'first sixteenth-century prose work of interest' because unlike earlier prose works such as Murdoch Nisbet's Scots version of Wyclif's New Testament, or John Bellenden's Scots version of Livy, the *Complaynt* is an original work.[3]

OVERVIEW OF THE COMPLAYNT OF SCOTLAND

Wedderburn seems to have composed *The Complaynt of Scotland* while serving as Chamberlain to the Knights of St. John at Torpichen from sometime in 1549 to about

---

[1] For the text of the *Complaynt*, plus biography of and attribution to Robert Wedderburn, see *The Complaynt of Scotland, c. 1550*, ed. A. M. Stewart, STS 4th ser. 11 (Edinburgh: Scottish Text Society, 1979) xi-xx. Four copies of the first printed edition of the *Complaynt* survive: Edinburgh, National Library of Scotland, H.34.a.19 and Ry II.h.27, and London, British Library, G.5438 and C.21.a.56. All of these lack a title folio; only BL G.5438 is not missing other folios as well.

[2] Biographical information from A. M. Stewart, 'Die europäische Wissensgemeinschaft um 1550 im Spiegel von Wedderburns *The Complaynt of Scotland*,' *Geschichtlichkeit und Neuanfang im sprachlichen Kunstwerk: Studien zur englischen Philologie zu Ehren von Fritz W. Schulze*, eds. Peter Erlebach, Wolfgang G. Muller and Klaus Reuter (Tübingen: Narr, 1981) 91, n. 1, and *The Complaynt of Scotland, c. 1550*, xi-xvi. Although I will take issue with one point in Stewart's Introduction below, this essay would not have been possible without Stewart's ground-breaking research and elegant analysis of the *Complaynt*. Stewart's Introduction and notes, the necessary starting-point for all study of the *Complaynt*, provide a thorough and illuminating discussion, together with what amounts to an exhaustive bibliographical survey.

[3] Maurice Lindsay, *History of Scottish Literature*, rev. ed. (London: Robert Hale, 1992).

mid-1550; he held this position from his friend Sir James Sandilands of Calder, whose efforts towards obtaining French assistance against the English via a marriage between Mary Queen of Scots and the French Dauphin Henry II must at least indirectly have included Wedderburn.[4] The *Complaynt* opens with a dedication to the Queen Mother, Mary of Guise, wife of James V, whom Wedderburn hails as 'the excellent, ande illvstir Marie queen of Scotlande, the margareit ande perle of princessis.' Since the *Complaynt* was published in France (Paris, 1550), it is presumed also to have been composed during Wedderburn's French sojourn. French influence on Wedderburn is immediately apparent: the *Complaynt* was modelled (without acknowledgement) on Alain Chartier's *Quadrilogue Invectif* (1422; various MSS and sixteenth-century editions).[5] Both Chartier and Wedderburn personify the nation as the *vox clamans* against the English; both mingle this voice with other voices, one of which is identified as the author's; both employ the dream-vision form as a vehicle for numerous moral and political *exempla*; and both level criticisms at the three estates for the moral failures that have occasioned the suffering of the nation at the hands of the English.

Wedderburn needed to update Chartier in order to articulate his own charges against the English. Written during the Hundred Years' War, the *Quadrilogue* indicts the English for a history of treachery, including the deposition of their own Richard II; and, alluding to the recent French defeat at Agincourt (1415), it calls on the French to resist 'ceulx qui voz peres et vox predecesseurs ont souvent guerroiez, ars et degastez voz champs et vos villes et qui de tele ligne sont issuz que naturelment convoitent anyentir du tout vostre generacion' ['those who have often warred against your fathers and your ancestors, burned and wasted your fields and towns, and who issue from a lineage that desires the annihilation of all your race'].[6] In a parallel passage, Wedderburn, alluding to the recent Scottish defeat at Pinkie Cleugh (1547) as 'the grite afflictione quhilk

---

[4]   *The Complaynt of Scotland, c. 1550*, xiv-xv.

[5]   See the analysis by Stewart in *ibid.*, xxi-xxiv. Generally on Chartier's influence, see William Calin, *The French Tradition and the Literature of Medieval England* (Toronto: University of Toronto Press, 1994) 250-61; Julia Boffey, 'The Early Reception of Chartier's Works in England and Scotland,' *Chartier in Europe*, eds. Emma J. Cayley and Ashby Kinch (Cambridge: D. S. Brewer, 2008); Catherine Nall, 'William Worcester Reads Alain Chartier: *Le Quadrilogue invectif* and Its English Readers,' *op. cit.*; unfortunately, each of these studies stops before 1500.

[6]   Alain Chartier, *Le Quadrilogue invectif*, ed. Eugénie Droz, Les classiques français du Moyen Âge, 2 ed. (Paris: H. Champion, 1950) 18/5-9. Further on Wedderburn's debt to the *Quadrilogue*, see A.M. Stewart, 'Alain Chartier et l'Écosse,' *Actes du 2e Colloque de langue et de littérature écossaises (Moyen Âge et Renaissance): Université de Strasbourg, 5-11 juillet 1978*, ed. Jean-Jacques Blanchot (Strasbourg: Institut d'études anglaises de Strasbourg et l'Association des médiévistes anglicistes de l'enseignement superieur, 1979); Margaret S. Blayney and Glenn H. Blayney, 'Alain Chartier and *The Complaynt of Scotlande*,' *Review of English Studies* 9 (1958).

occurrit on oure realme in september. m v.xlvii ȝeris on the feildis besyde mussilburgh,'[7]
lists a similar catalogue of English outrages as the occasion of the *Complaynt*:

> the cruel dolouris distructione of oure nobil barrons, & of mony vthirs of the thre estaitis,
> be cruel ande onmercyful slauthyr, ande alse be maist extreme violent spulȝee ande
> hairschip of ther mouabil gudis in grite quantite, ande alse oure ald enemeis be traisona-
> bil seditione, takkand violent possessione of ane part of the strynthis ande castellis of the
> bordours of oure realme, ande alse remanent vitht in the plane mane landis far vitht in
> oure cuntre, ande violentlye possessand ane certan of our burghis villagis ande castellis,
> to ther auen vse but contradictione: ande the remanent of the pepil beand lyik dantit
> venquist slauis in maist extreme vile subiectione: rather nor lyik prudent cristin pepil,
> quhilkis suld lyue in ciuilite policie & be iustice vndir the gouernance of ane christin
> prince. [p. 18; fols. 18v-19r]

The *Complaynt* is framed by its dedication to Mary of Guise and by a prologue to the
reader (1-14; fols. 2r-15v). The dedication explains that the occasion of the *Complaynt*
is the three 'vehement plagis' afflicting Scotland: English oppression, 'the vniuersal pes-
tilens and mortalite,' and ruinous internal conflicts among the three estates (1; fol. 2v).
The *Complaynt* is dedicated to Mary because God 'of his diuyne bounte' (2; fol. 3r) has
called on her to lead Scotland out of this oppression, just as illustrious rulers of the past
led their people out of tyranny. The prologue to the reader defends the moral, philosophical, and social value of authors, who, Wedderburn argues (anticipating his invocation of the estates model in part three) have as much to do with the patriotic defence of
the nation as any ruler or captain. It also defends Wedderburn's use of Scottish, as well
as his occasional employment of Latin when Scottish lacks the proper vocabulary — 'be
rason that oure scottis tong is nocht sa copeus as is the lateen tong' (13; fol. 14v). With
its insistence on the vernacular and its apology for aureate language weighing equally
with its denunciation of Latinate excess, the prologue to the reader thus enters the *Complaynt* in the sixteenth-century debate about 'inkhorn' terms and linguistic copiousness.[8]

Following the dedication to Mary and the prologue to the reader, the *Complaynt*
proper falls into three parts. The first (Chapters I-V) examines the rise and fall of kings
and the punishments of God visited on sinful peoples, concluding that English oppression of the Scots is God's punishment 'for the mysknaulage of his magestie' (21; fol.
22r). Marginal glosses citing biblical and classical sources enforce the encyclopedic
dimension of the argument here and throughout the *Complaynt*. In stark biblical terms,
this part warns that the world itself is hastening to its end on account of the sins of the
(Scottish) people.

---

[7]   *The Complaynt of Scotland, c. 1550*, here citing page 17, fol. 18v.

[8]   Further see *ibid.*, xli-xlvii, and Klaus Bitterling, 'Language and Style in *The Complaynt of Scotland*,'
Scottish Language 20 (2001).

Part two, beginning at the so-called 'Monologue Recreative' (Chapter VI), initiates a pastoral interlude of sorts. It is Wedderburn's original insertion into the framing political complaint adapted from the *Quadrilogue*. In it, the 'Actor' (a variant of Latin *auctor*), exhausted from his writing, seeks rest in 'greene hoilsum feildis' (29; fol. 30r). Fatigued though he may be, his attention remains keen. He lists the floral and ornithological delights of the fields in copious detail; then, entering a green forest, he notes the precise position of the setting sun. Not surprisingly after such hyper-stimulation, he sleeps through the night. Waking to a red dawn, the Actor now notes the precise positions of sun and morning stars in distinctly aureate prose. Marginal glosses anchor his observations in the *Aeneid* ('Iamque rubescat stellis aurora fugatis'; 3.521) and the *Metamorphoses* (Echo, lib. 3). All the animals of farm, field, and forest are making their morning noises, each of which the Actor not only catalogues but renders onomatopoetically (30-31; fols. 31r-31v). Continuing his walk 'throucht mony grene dail' and still 'sopit in sadnes' (31; fol. 32r), the Actor comes to a shore where he espies a galley being prepared for war. Just as he had reported every animal sound, he now reports the 'crying' and 'cals' of the mariners at their work, followed by the sounds of battle when the galley engages another ship (31-33; fols. 32r-34r). Unable to see for the smoke of the cannon, the Actor returns inland to the fields, this time encountering a group of shepherds and their flocks. He watches as they breakfast, and listens as the 'prencipal scheiphirde' speaks an 'orisone tyl all the laif of his conpangʒons' (34; fol. 34v)[9] which Wedderburn then quotes in its entirety — until the shepherd's wife begs him to halt his 'tideus melancolic orison' (49; fol. 50r) and take up something closer to his ken: tale-telling. It is the oration for which the 'Monologue' is titled. We shall return to it shortly.

The 'Monologue' is followed by a catalogue of the tales shared by the shepherds and their wives; this is followed by a list of the songs they sung and the dances they performed (50-53; fols. 50v-53r). The shepherd's artistry, says the Actor as he marvels at the dancing, could not be surpassed by any classical author or mythological figure. All told, Wedderburn names over 40 tales, about half of which cannot be identified. Of those that can, prominent are literary productions dear to the Scots, such as Chaucer's *Canterbury Tales* (cited as one tale), Blind Harry's *Wallace*, Barbour's *Bruce*, Dunbar's *Goldyn Targe*, and Douglas's *Palice of Honour*. There are also Arthurian texts such as Merlin's prophecies, 'the tayl of syr euan arthours knycht' (i.e., *Ywain and Gawain*), *Lancelot du lac*, 'Arthour knycht he raid on nycht vitht gyltin spur and candil lycht' (unknown), *Arthur of Little Britain*. The list includes Ovidiana such as the tales of

---

9   OED *orison*, n., 2: 'A speech, oration, (*Sc.* in later use),' quoting a passage from the 'Monologue' in the *Complaynt* as an illustration; the Scottish use preserves the etymology of *orison*, which is from Latin *oratio* via French.

Actaeon and of Pyramus and Thisbe, plus romances such as *Eger and Grime*, and even *Mandeville's Travels*. Together with the tales, Wedderburn's list of some 40 songs (most given by first line) and some 30 dances offers an epitome of literary and popular culture *c.* 1550. It also includes early attestation of some of the ballads collected by Frederick Child e.g., 'robene hude and litil ihone' (?Child 125), 'the battle of the hayrlau' (?Child 163), and 'thom of lyn' (?Child 39), among others.[10]

After this long rehearsal, somehow it is still the same day. The Actor abandons this pastoral scene for an unmown meadow whose flora he describes via their medicinal properties. Only then — after seeing these and 'mony vthir eirbis on thai fresche fragrant feildis' and 'mony landuart grumis pas to the corne lande to laubir there rustical occupatione' — is the Actor finally 'contentit' with his 'pleysand nychtis [*sic*] recreatione,' determined now to return to town in order to resume his complaint and complete his book; however, he is again overtaken by weariness and falls asleep on the earth, whereupon he dreams 'ane hauy melancolius dreyme' (53-54; fols. 53v-54r).

Part three (Chapters VII-XX) is that dream. In it, Dame Scotia appears to the Actor as a nationalist version of Boethius's Lady Philosophy, right down to her ragged attire, except that she is the victim of fortune rather than a teacher about its seductions. She upbraids the three estates, here represented as her three sons, for the vices, disagreements, and internecine strife that have made Scotland vulnerable to English oppression. She exhorts them to follow the example of Old Testament figures such as Abraham, Gideon, and Judas Maccabeus, and the modern example of the French in the Hundred Years' War. She reminds her sons of the history of English oppression of Scotland, and she cites precedents from ancient history by which she implies that divine justice will punish the English for their wrongs. Chapter X she devotes to the foolish belief of the English in the prophecies of Merlin; and Chapter XI she devotes to the illegality of English claims on Scotland, Wales and Ireland, in both cases citing numerous ancient analogues to the present situation. She accuses Scotland of weakening itself by doing business with England along the border, and she accuses the nobility of hypocritically punishing double agents from whose dealings they themselves profit. Hearing all this, Dame Scotia's third son, the commons, blames his two older brothers for their selfishness, cruelty, and indifference to him; for their taxes, their injustices, and their idleness. In short, he makes the case that the nobility and clergy have exploited and degraded Scotland as badly as the English. Dame Scotia imperiously rejects his excuses: the common people are blind to their own faults, and moreover they behave bestially, living by their appetites alone, incapable of self-discipline and any kind of

---

[10] Mary Ellen Brown, 'Balladry: A Vernacular Poetic Resource,' *The Edinburgh History of Scottish Literature. Volume One: From Columba to the Union (until 1707)*, eds. Thomas Owen Clancy and Murray Pittock (Edinburgh: Edinburgh University Press, 2007) 267-70.

improvement unless they are forced to it by the other estates. She then turns on the nobility and clergy, accusing them more through classical *exempla* than by contemporary history of the same vices alleged of them by the commons. She concludes by summoning Scotland to unite against the English and by rehearsing once more the suffering of the Scots at English hands.

The *Complaynt* has been unjustly neglected. It succeeds not only as a moral, political, and literary tour-de-force, but also as an implicit manifesto about the equality of Scots language and culture with that of England, France, and Rome. Wedderburn wrote the *Complaynt* to counter English propaganda advocating for a united Britain under English suzerainty, in support of which the English drew their evidence from fictionalizing medieval histories such as Geoffrey of Monmouth's *Historia Regum Brittaniae*. Dame Scotia is not only clearly modelled on Chartier's France, she also answers the figure of Dame Britain in contemporary English political pamphlets, through which the English advanced their claims on Scotland.[11] However, rather than blame Scotland's troubles solely on the English or the collective offenses of the three estates, Wedderburn locates the root of Scotland's predicament in failures of individual morality, which he seeks to correct via *exempla* from sacred and secular history throughout the *Complaynt*. For this reason, Stewart labels the *Complaynt* 'a sermon on the topic "the cause and occasione of the onmersiful afflictione of the desolate realme of Scotland"' (Stewart, xxxvii, quoting from fol. 6v). The cause of that unmerciful affliction is ultimately stated to be the 'rancor and discentione that ringis among' the Scots (133; fol. 133r), and for this collective suffering, nothing less than individual repentance is the remedy.

PASTORALISM AND ENCYCLOPEDISM IN THE 'MONOLOGUE RECREATIVE'

The problem that the rest of this essay will address is the role of the encyclopedic 'Monologue Recreative' within the larger purpose that the *Complaynt* expresses in its more obviously moral, political, and historical sections. In Chartier's *Quadrilogue* we have a model for the *Complaynt* as a whole, but we lack a model for the 'Monologue.' Given the broad scope of the *Complaynt*, is there a comparable encyclopedic text that might have inspired Wedderburn's pastoral interlude in the 'Monologue'? According

---

[11] *The Complaynt of Scotland, c. 1550*, xxxiii and n. 93 (p. lix); four of these pamphlets are printed in Robert Wedderburn, *The Complaynt of Scotlande, wyth ane Exortatione to the Thre Estaits to be vigilante in the Deffens of their Public Veil. A.D. 1549. With an Appendix of Contemporary English Tracts, viz.: The Just Declaration of Henry of Henry VIII; the Exhortacion of James Harrysone, Scottisheman (1547); the Epistle of the Lord Protector Somerset (1548); the Epitome of Nicholas Bodrugan, alias Adams (1548)*, ed. J. A. H. Murray, EETS, ES 17, 18, 2 vols. (London: N. Trübner, 1872-73). Being secular, none of the ballads in the 'Monologue' appear in *Gude and Godlie Ballatis*.

to the *Complaynt*'s Scottish Text Society editor, A. M. Stewart, in writing the 'Monologue,' Wedderburn translated the cosmographical and meteorological parts from Pliny's *Naturalis historia*:

> [the 'Monologue'] contains an encyclopedic tour conducted by the 'pastor' with disquisitions on astronomy, and meteorology and the expanding universe of cosmography (with Pliny's guidance): technical terms of artillery and sea-warfare enrich the vernacular; catalogues of herbs and their medicinal uses, catalogues of tales and romances, songs, dances and instruments, add to the copiousness; technical terms of musical intervals, add, to the seven liberal arts, material from beyond the 'trivium'; bird and animal cries add Rabelaisian literary virtuosity. The Monologue complements the rest of *The Complaynt* making the work all-encompassing.[12]

More specifically, by 'Pliny's guidance,' Stewart means that Wedderburn 'translates ten folios (folios 39r to 49v) from the Elder Pliny's *Natural History*. This is the Renaissance recovery of Classical scientific authors as a prelude to new discovery.'[13] By this argument, Pliny's *Naturalis historia* is the encyclopedic source and model for the 'Monologue.'

This is a large claim, but Stewart does not support it with source-passages from Pliny. Indeed, close inspection reveals that in fact the cosmography of the 'Monologue' not only is not translated from Pliny's *Naturalis historia*, only small bits of the 'Monologue' can be matched with Pliny at all. To be sure, there are enough slight resemblances between the *Naturalis historia* and the 'Monologue' to affirm Wedderburn's acquaintance with Pliny, but against these are very many glaring differences that indicate Wedderburn's use of other sources and his accomplished integration of those sources into a new encyclopedic text. Both Wedderburn and Pliny cover three large topics in their consideration of the heavens: the planets, celestial phenomena, and atmospheric phenomena. Only in the third of these is Pliny's *Naturalis historia* clearly a source. In the other two sections, Wedderburn resembles Pliny mainly in the most commonly-accepted astronomical facts, standard in the ancient and medieval world. For example, both Wedderburn and Pliny consider the heavens to be spherical;[14] the

---

[12] *The Complaynt of Scotland, c. 1550*, xxxix-xl. Punctuation is Stewart's. Stewart also applies the adjective 'encyclopedic' to the 'Monologue' in Stewart, 'Europäische Wissensgemeinschaft,' 92.

[13] *The Complaynt of Scotland, c. 1550*, xxvii.

[14] Wedderburn: 'Nou fyrst to speik of the mouyng of the spere and of the diuisione of the hauynis, ȝe sal knau that the varld is diuidit in tua partis …' (37; fol. 38r). Pliny: 'Formam eius [i.e., mundus, the subject of Book III] in speciem orbis absoluti … argumenta rerum docent' (II. ii.5). All citations to the *Naturalis historia* are to Pliny the Elder, *Naturalis historiae libri XXXVIII*, ed. Karl Friedrich Theodor Mayhoff, Bibliotheca Scriptorum Graecorum et Romanorum Teubneriana, 6 in 7 vols. (Leipzig: Teubner, 1870-1880). I have compared Book II in the Leipzig edition with that in the Paris 1532 edition (publ. Galeotus à Prato) as representative of printed texts available to Wedderburn, but I have found no significant difference.

heavens rotate every 24 hours,[15] and the planetary spheres rotate west to east, whereas the *primum mobile* rotates east to west.[16] Pliny covers each cosmographical topic more extensively than Wedderburn; and this is true also of the section on atmospheric phenomena—rain, dew, thunder, lightning, and wind (46-49; fols. 47r-49v). In Pliny these topics not only receive much lengthier coverage, the meteorological phenomena are given different causes (II.xxxviii.102-II.lvi.146); moreover, they are complemented by weather portents such as blood rain, armies in the sky, sunstones, and rainbows (II.lvii.147-II.lxii.153) that Wedderburn — who surely knew at least rainbows first-hand — ignores.

Wedderburn's Plinian borrowing is in fact limited to atmospheric phenomena. For instance, both Wedderburn and Pliny refer to three suns being seen in the sky in the time of Marc Antony and three moons in the consulship of a certain Domitius. But they disagree on some of the specifics. Wedderburn's three suns occurred 'befoir the ciuil veyris that occurrit betuix anthonius and agustus cesar' (45; fol. 46v), whereas Pliny's occurred during the consulship of Marc Antony (II.xxxi.99). Wedderburn's three moons occurred 'quhen domitius caius and flauius lucius var consulis of rome' (45-46; fol. 46v), whereas Pliny's occurred 'Cn. Domitio C. Fannio consulibus' ('when Gnaeus Domitius and Caius Fannius were consuls'; II.xxxii.99).[17]

Another example would be what Wedderburn and Pliny have to say about the appearance of a comet. Wedderburn writes: 'sum tyme it vil apeir lyik lang bludy hayr sum tyme lyik ane dart sum tyme lyik ane bludy speyr' (46; fol. 46v); to which we may compare Pliny: 'Cometas Graeci vocant, nostri crinitas horrentis crine sanguineo et

---

[15] Wedderburn: 'All thir nyne speris or hauynis ar inclosit vitht in the tent spere quhilk is callit the fyrst mobil the quhilk makkis reuolutione and course on the tua polis fra day to daye in the space of xxiiij houris fra orient til occident and returnis agane to the orient' (38; fol. 38v). Pliny: 'Hanc ergo formam eius aeterno et inrequieto ambitu, inerrabili celeritate, viginti quattuor horarum spatio circumagi solis exortus et occasus haut dubium reliquere' (II.iii.6).

[16] Wedderburn: 'ilk ane of thir speris hes bot ane sterne or planete that mouis in the zodiac, contrar the muuyng of the fyrst mobil that ve val [call] the tent spere … the fyrst mobil … makkis reuolutione and course on the tua polis fra day to daye in the space of xxiiij houris fra orient til occident and returnis agane to the orient. bot the mouyng of the tothir nyne hauynis is fra the occident to the orient, quhilk is contrar to the mouyng of the tent spere callit the fyrst mobil. 3it nochtheles the mouyng of the fyrst mobil is of sic violens that it constren3eis the tothir nyne speris or hauynis to pas vitht it fra orient tyl occident quhilk is contrar to there auen natural mouyng there for the compulsit retrograid mouyng is callit be astronomours motus raptus accessus, & resessus [sic] stellarum fixarum' (37-38; fols. 38v-39r). Pliny: 'omnium autem errantium siderum meatus, interque ea solis et lunae, contrarium mundo agere cursum, id est laevum, illo semper in dextra praecipiti; et quamvis adsidua conversione inmensae celeritatis attollantur ab eo rapianturque in occasum, adverso tamen ire motu per suos quaeque passus' (II.vi.32).

[17] It is Pliny who has the names correctly: Gnaeus Domitius Ahenobarbus and Caius Fannius were consuls together in 122 BC. Translations from Latin into English are my own.

comarum modo in vertice hispidas' ('The Greeks call them *comets*; we call them *shaggy-hairs* because at the top is a manner of blood-red hair'; II.xxii.89). Again, the difference is telling, as Wedderburn describes three ways comets may appear, Pliny only one. Both mention the rain of blood during the consulship of Marcus Actilius and Caius Portius, but in Wedderburn this rain followed a rain of milk (46; fol. 47r), whereas in Pliny it fell simultaneously with a rain of milk (II.lv.147). Both mention the rain of flesh during the consulship of Volumnius and Sulpitius (46; fol. 47r), but Pliny adds that none of the flesh untouched by carrion birds spoiled (II.lv.147). Pliny has much to say on the topic of thunder and lightning that Wedderburn omits. Pliny and Wedderburn especially disagree as to the origin of thunder and lightning; Pliny's remarks on thunder and lightning precede his remarks on portentous rain (in II. lv. 142-147), but the order of these topics is reversed in Wedderburn (46-48; 47v-48v). Loose similarities are also found in the sections on rain, frost, hail, snow, thunder and lightning. But no matter where Wedderburn seems to follow Pliny, there is more evidence that he takes another path.

The vast differences between Wedderburn and Pliny are not simply matters of which facts each considers important, or their order. Wedderburn's science is decidedly not Pliny's. For example, in discussing the causes of wind, Wedderburn admits only one cause: 'the vynd is no vthir thyng bot ane vapour or exalatione heyt and dry generit in the concauiteis and in the bouellis of the eird. the quhilk ascendis and discendis vp and doune betuix the eird and the sycond region of the ayr' (48; fol. 48v). Pliny, by contrast, admits several: 'Simili modo ventos vel potius flatus posse et arido siccoque anhelitu terrae gigni non negaverim, posse et aquis aera exspirantibus qui neque in nebulam densetur nec crassescat in nubes, posse et solis inpulsu agi, quoniam ventus haut aliud intellegatur quam fluctus aeris, pluribusque etiam modis' ('likewise I will not deny that winds or rather gusts can be produced by a dry and arid exhalation of the earth; and they can also be created when airs breathed out by bodies of water neither condense into a fog nor solidify into clouds; and it is also possible that they are created by the influence of the sun—because wind is understood to be nothing else than flowing air—and it can even be produced in other ways'; II.xliv.114).

PLINY AT ST. ANDREWS

It is of course possible that Wedderburn worked with a copy of Pliny that varied considerably from the manuscripts and printed texts used in modern editions.[18] Pliny had

---

[18]   The Plinian tradition is surveyed in Trevor Murphy, *Pliny the Elder's Natural History: The Empire in the Encyclopaedia* (Oxford: Oxford University Press, 2004) (early modern period); Marjorie Chibnall,

been read continuously through the Middle Ages and enjoyed renewed popularity in early modern Scotland. The *Historia* was printed in Venice, 1496, by Johannes Spira. Before 1500, Italy alone produced 39 editions. No English translation was produced until 1565, and that translated the partial French version by Pierre du Changy titled *Sommaire des singularitez de Pline* (Paris: A et C. Les Angeliers, 1542).[19] Wedderburn could have encountered this French version after his arrival in 1548 with the Knights of St. John at Torpichon. It is also possible that Wedderburn encountered Pliny in his studies at St. Andrews in the years 1526-30.[20] During Wedderburn's lifetime, a copy of the Parma, 1480, edition of Pliny was at King's College, Aberdeen, in the possession of Hector Boece, who served Aberdeen in different capacities from 1497 until his death in 1536. This book is still in the library.[21]

We have no record of the books at St. Leonard's college until a list made probably in 1597 or 1599 that is now in SAUL Special Collections, UY152/2, p. 172. Although this list is after Wedderburn's lifetime, in the estimation of John Higgitt, most books on the list before the main group of books — which was donated in the late 1550's and 1560's by James Stewart (1531-70, illegitimate son of James V), who matriculated at St. Leonard's in 1545 — were already present in the medieval library.[22] On the basis of this record, there was one possible copy of Pliny in the St. Leonard's library during or before Wedderburn's time as a student. This book is identified clearly as 'Plin' naturalis histor" in the booklist. Because it is listed amongst books printed earlier in the sixteenth century, and because it is listed well before the books donated by James Stewart, there is a distinct possibility that the booklist's 'Plin' naturalis histor" was a manuscript or an earlier printed book that Wedderburn could well have seen at St. Leonard's while he was a student.[23] Indeed, what is unusual is that the St. Leonard's

---

'Pliny's *Natural History* and the Middle Ages,' *Empire and Aftermath: Silver Latin II*, ed. T. A. Dorey (London: Routledge & Kegan Paul, 1975) (Middle Ages); Aude Doody, 'Pliny's *Natural History*: *Enkuklios Paideia* and the Ancient Encyclopedia,' *Journal of the History of Ideas* 70.1 (2009) (Plinian encyclopedism in the Classical period and Enlightenment); E. W. Gudger, 'Pliny's *Historia naturalis*. The Most Popular Natural History Ever Published,' *Isis* 6.3 (1924) (publication history of the *Naturalis historia*). Aude Doody, *Pliny's Encyclopedia: The Reception of the Natural History* (Cambridge: Cambridge University Press, 2010) was unavailable to me during the writing of this essay.

[19] Gudger, 'Pliny's *Historia naturalis*,' 273; ibid., 276, 277-78.

[20] Dates from *The Complaynt of Scotland, c. 1550*, xii-xiii.

[21] John Durkan and Anthony Ross, *Early Scottish Libraries* (Glasgow: John S. Burns & Sons, 1961) 77 (Section II, Individual Owners).

[22] *Scottish Libraries*, ed. John Higgitt, Corpus of British Medieval Library Catalogues 12 (London: British Library in association with the British Academy, 2006) 259, 264.

[23] This copy of Pliny is *ibid.*, S21.96, which Higgitt (see 260-61), regards as being in 'The earlier part of the inventory up to [item number] 111 and perhaps beyond, where particular editions can be suggested, [and which] seems to be composed largely of books printed in the later 15th and earlier 16th cents.' This

copy is the *only* copy of Pliny now known to have been in any institution in the city
of St. Andrews before the Reformation.

The likelihood that Wedderburn read Pliny at St. Andrews increases if we consider
that his cited sources for the 'Monologue' were also in St. Andrews libraries. Book
ownership in St. Andrews is the best-attested in late medieval and early modern Scotland. Records remain for the St. Andrews cathedral priory; the Dominican convent (of
the Assumption and Coronation of the Virgin Mary), in particular books owned by
John Grierson that were inventoried ca. 1522, shortly before Wedderburn's studies in
1526-30; the colleges of St. Leonard, St. Mary (New College), and St. Salvator; plus
the Faculty of Arts, college of St. John the Evangelist, and the Pedagogy at St. Andrews
University.[24] From these records, we can ascertain that the following of Wedderburn's
cited sources for the 'Monologue'—excluding biblical sources, which need no explanation—were available to Wedderburn before he departed for France in 1548:[25]

> Vergil, *Aeneid* (marginal gloss, 30; fol. 30v): S21.139; S30.1.
> Ovid, *Metamorphoses* (marginal gloss and text, 30; fol. 31r): S20.67.
> Josephus, *Antiquitates Iudaeorum* (36; fol. 37r): S20.75.
> Augustine, *De civitate dei* (40; fol. 41r): S21.6x.
> Augustine, *Opera*: S21.1, 3, 7, 9; S22.33-35, 37 = S23.19-21, 71.

As Stewart has observed, Wedderburn does not cite his major sources[26] — thus neither his framing narrative from Chartier's *Quadrilogue*, nor his cosmographical information, nor even his historical catalogue of shepherd-kings (i.e., 34-35; fols. 35r-36r) is
cited. But Wedderburn does pay tribute to his minor sources. For example, as mentioned above, one them is Josephus, whose *Antiquitates Iudaeorum* offers the ontological
explanation that astronomy was invented by the sons of Seth, the third son of Adam
and Eve.[27] Wedderburn does not specify that Seth's sons were shepherds, and although
it may be inferred that they were (since herding was the distinctive occupation of Old
Testament figures), classical, medieval, and early modern pastoral writing does not seem

---

assessment puts the St. Leonard's Pliny amidst holdings available to Wedderburn, but Higgitt inexplicably
contradicts himself by saying (at S21.96) that the book is 'probably' SAUL Special Collections, PA6611.
A2B49, which is *ex dono* James Stewart, i.e., the edition printed in Basel by Hieronymus Froben and
Nicolaus Episcopius in 1549 — too late for Wedderburn to have seen it. Other early editions now in the
St. Andrews library (Paris: Laigue, 1530; Basel: Ziegler, 1531; Basel: Froben, 1537 and 1539) were also
printed after Wedderburn's years as a student. These may be searched online at the St. Andrews library
catalogue, SAULCAT; URL: http://138.251.116.3/.

[24] Listed in *ibid.*, 238-385, booklists S20-S30.

[25] All citations are to *ibid.*

[26] Stewart, 'Europäische Wissensgemeinschaft,' 96.

[27] 36-37; fols. 37r-v; cf. Josephus 1.2 in Flavius Josephus, *The Latin Josephus*, ed. Franz Blatt, Acta Jutlandica 30.I, Humanistisk Serie 44 (Aarhus: Universitetsforlaget, 1958).

to include Seth and his sons.[28] But Wedderburn's reference to Josephus is a miniature of his encyclopedic compositional practice — borrowing information from here and there, assembling it into an expandable framework, and citing sufficiently to lend an aura of authority, but not so much that the narrative is bogged down. By the same token, we should not assume that all of Wedderburn's citations are accurate, or meant to be. References to arguments against the existence of the antipodes in Lactantius 'in his thrid beuk in the xxiiij cheptor' and Augustine 'de ciuitate dei in the ix cheptour of his seuynt beuk' (40; fol. 41r) are straight-faced falsehoods. The list of names in the Actor's exclamation about the wondrous learning of the shepherd — Ptolomey, Averroes, Aristotle, Galen, Hippocrates, Cicero — is as reliable as the footnotes of a desperate undergraduate's term paper. They are names meant to suggest only that the *kind* of information imparted by the shepherd can be found somewhere in the works of these authors. Dear reader — he strongly implies — you will have to find the originals yourself. In that regard, Wedderburn resembles the great medieval encyclopedist Bartholomaeus Anglicus — whose *De proprietatibus rerum* could still be found at St. Leonard's College of St. Andrews University at the end of the sixteenth century — tossing off commonplaces and alluding to his sources with a wave of the professorial hand.[29]

A POSSIBLE SOURCE OF WEDDERBURN'S COSMOGRAPHY

The *Complaynt* is a tour-de-force of sixteenth century learning.[30] In the 'Monologue' alone Wedderburn combines cosmography, weather, literature, history, agriculture, herding, amusements, seafaring, warfare, and medicinal plants. Its coverage of human intellectual, scientific, political, artistic, and social life is all-embracing. Scottish civilization at all levels is summoned to Wedderburn's project. More broadly, the *Complaynt*'s vision of Scottish political life is as all-embracing as the 'Monologue's' vision of Scottish civilization, involving all three estates in the revival of the nation. Finally,

---

[28] Seth appears in none of the texts surveyed in Helen Cooper, *Pastoral: Mediaeval into Renaissance* (Ipswich: D.S. Brewer, 1977), which I take to be an exhaustive survey.

[29] Bartholomaeus at St. Leonard's College: *Scottish Libraries*, S21.178. Bartholomaeus's citational practices: Baudouin van den Abeele, Heinz Meyer, Michael W. Twomey, Bernd Roling and R. James Long, eds., *Bartholomaeus Anglicus, De Proprietatibus Rerum I* (Turnhout: Brepols, 2007) Introduction to Book I, 'De Deo,' 60-63; and Michael Twomey, 'Editing *De proprietatibus rerum*, Book XIV, from the Sources,' *Bartholomaeus Anglicus, De proprietatibus rerum. Texte latin et réception vernaculaire / Lateinischer Text und volkssprachige Rezeption*, eds. Baudouin van den Abeele and Heinz Meyer (Turnhout: Brepols, 2005) *passim*.

[30] As is evident from *The Complaynt of Scotland, c. 1550*, Introduction, and Stewart, 'Europäische Wissensgemeinschaft,' *passim*.

its language suits its encyclopedic scope, ranging from aureate terms at one end of the scale down to onomatopoetic animal sounds at the other, with sprinklings of Latin in the text and the marginal glosses. We should therefore expect that whatever the source of Wedderburn's cosmography, Wedderburn did not copy it verbatim but re-worked it into a new form. I wish to propose that although the shepherd's mastery of astronomy does not appear to derive from Pliny, it can be matched in important respects with the cosmography described in the popular sixteenth-century genre known as the shepherd's calendar. Shepherds' calendars are, like Wedderburn's *Complaynt*, moral treatises touching on an encyclopedic variety of topics surrounding a cosmographical centre. They are presented in the voice of a 'master shepherd' like the one who delivers Wedderburn's 'Monologue'; they refer to the author as *Auctor*, as does Wedderburn; and like Wedderburn their cosmography covers the stars, planets, heavenly manifestations, and weather.[31]

Shepherds' calendars cannot be considered direct verbal sources of Wedderburn's 'Monologue' because there are no verbal parallels between them; but in subject-matter there is such striking agreement that they are likely to have been a model in the same way that the *Quadrilogue* was a model. The most relevant for our purposes is the popular group of shepherd's calendars that translate the French *Le compost et kalendrier des bergiers* (Paris: Guyot Marchant, 1493). These attained nine editions before 1500; a Scottish translation by Alexander Barclay, *The Kalendayr of the Shyppars* (Paris: [A. Vérard], 1503; STC 22407); and an anonymous English translation, *The Kalendar of the Shepherdes* (London: R. Pynson, 1506; STC 22408), six versions of which are listed as STC 22409, 22409.3, 22409.4, 22409.7, 22410, and 22411.[32] As almanacs, the shepherds' calendars contain a wealth of practical information about diet and health, planting seasons, medicinal plants, and so on. They also contain moral and religious instruction both in prose and verse. Whereas Wedderburn's 'Monologue' lists ballads among the literary productions of Scotland, some of the verse selections towards the front of the calendars are labelled 'ballads' in the table of contents.[33] The readership of the shepherd's calendars were educated readers like Wedderburn for whom pastoral life represented a Vergilian literary ideal. The calendars' encyclopedic concatenation of knowledge both moral and scientific also characterizes Wedderburn's 'Monologue.'

---

[31] The *Complaynt*'s employment of materials from the shepherd's calendars is indicated by Cooper, *Pastoral*, 49, 51, 54, 56, 71, 78-9, 160. Here my purpose is to focus on the astronomical material, which Cooper scarcely acknowledges.

[32] It is not possible to specify which of the shepherds' calendars Wedderburn knew.

[33] For example, chapter xx in the table of contents to de Worde's 1528 *Kalender*: 'A balade how p27nces & states shold gouerneth the*m*, Ca. xx.' Other ballads are Chapters xv, xvi, xvii, xix.

The shepherds' calendars immediately explain why the shepherd in Wedderburn's 'Monologue' attributes the discovery of astronomy to shepherds:

> the riche and opulent potestatis that dueillis in citeis and burroustounis, reputis vs that ar scheiph*ird*is, to be ignora*n*t inciuil & rude of ingyne zit nochtheles al the sciencis and knaulage that thai ascribe and proffessis to be dotit in them hes fyrst procedit fra our faculte, nocht alanerly in the inuentione of natural mecanyc consaitis. bot as veil the speculatione of supernatural thingis as of the firmament and of the planetis, the quhilk knaulage ve hef prettikyt throucht the lang contemplene of the motions and reuolutions of the nyne hauynis. [36; fols. 36v-37r].

In de Worde's 1528 *Kalender*, from which I will quote as a typical example,[34] both the Author's Prologue and Chapter xxxi begin with a woodcut depicting the master shepherd studying the stars, which is followed by an account of the discovery of moral and practical knowledge, including astronomy, by a shepherd:

> As here before tyme there was a Shepeherde kepynge shepe in ye feldes / whiche was no clerke / nor had no vnderstandy*n*ge of ye letterall sence / nor of no maner of scrypture nor wryty*n*ge / but of his naturall wytte and vnderstandynge sayd. How be it that lyuynge and dyenge be at the pleasure of almyghty god … Thus he trauayled his vnderstandynge / and made grete dylygence to knowe and to do thy*n*ges possyble and requysyte for to lyue longe / hole / and ioyfully / which this present compost and kalender of Shepeherdes sheweth and techeth. ¶ Wherfore we wyll shewe you of the bodyes celestyall / and of theyr nature and moeuynges… [Author's Prologue, n.p.]

> Those that wyll as Shepeheherdes [sic] that kepe shepe in ye felde / without knowynge one letter / sawe onely by some fygures that they make in lytell tables of woode / haue knowlege of ye mouynges and propryetes of the heuens And dyuers other thynges co*n*teyned in this present compost and kalender of Shepeherdes … Fyrst one ought to knowe what the figure is / the dysposycyon of the worlde / the no*m*bre and ordre of the elementes / & the mouynges of the skyes apperteyneth to be knowen of euery man of fre condycyon and noble wytte. [Ch. xxxi, n.p.]

The general content of the *Kalender*'s Chapter xxxi, on cosmography, is close to key aspects of the shepherd's discourse on cosmography in the 'Monologue.' Both valorize astrology.[35] Indeed, the 'Monologue' closes with a warning to resist the evil influences

---

[34] In the following discussion I will cite the 1528 de Worde edition because the facsimile in Early English Books Online, where I have consulted it, is clearer and more legible than other editions, including the Scottish *Kalendayr* (1503; STC 22407); and because it corrects the errors of Pynson's first English edition (1506).

[35] Wedderburn: 'for throucht the lang studie and contemplene of the sternis, ve can gyf ane iugement of diuerse futur accedentis, that ar gude or euyl, necessair or domageabil for man or beyst for it is manifest that scheiphirdis hes discriuit and definit the cir(c)lis and the mouyng of the speris as i sal reherse to зоu

of the stars that is paradoxically glossed in the margin: 'Sapiens dominabitur astris' (49; fol. 49v). Both the 'Monologue' and the shepherds' calendars describe the universe as twofold — a lower, corruptible part and a higher, incorruptible part,[36] with a series of spheres enclosing one another from largest to smallest, and with the earth at the centre and the seven planets and fixed stars circling it.[37] Above the eighth sphere of fixed stars is the sphere of the *primum mobile*, beyond which is a crystalline tenth sphere, the throne of God, which does not move.[38] This latter detail is crucial evidence of Wedderburn's reliance on a version of this particular shepherd's calendar, because even though Wedderburn and the *Kalender* switch the names and properties of the ninth and tenth spheres, at least they agree on the number of spheres. Pliny is altogether unclear about how many spheres there are *in toto*.[39]

that ar ʒong scheiphyrdis to that effect that ʒe may hef speculatione of the samyn' (36; fol. 37r). *Kalender*: 'it is a fayre thynge / delectable profytable / and honeste / and therwyth it is necessary to haue dyuers other knowleges / specyally the astrology of Shepeherdes / whiche sheweth how yᵉ worlde is rounde as a ball' (Ch. xxxi; n.p.).

[36] Wedderburn: 'Nou fyrst to speik of the mouyng of the spere and of the diuisione of the hauynis, ʒe sal knau that the varld is diuidit in tua partis that is to say. the fyrst part is the regione elementair quhilk is subiect til alteratione and to corruptione. the nyxt part of the varld is callit the regione celest (quhilk philosophours callis quinta essentia) vitht in the concauite of the quhilk, is closit the regione elementar this said regione celest is nothir variabil nor corruptabil' (37; fol. 38r). *Kalender*: 'and therefore the sterres and skyes ben of another nature than the elementes and the thynges of them composed / the whiche ben transmutable and corruptyble' (Ch. xxxi, n.p.).

[37] Wedderburn: 'the gritest spere quhilk is the outuart spere inclosis in it, the spere that is nyxt til it & sa be progressione and ordur euyrie spere inclosis the spere that is nerest tyl it. in the fyrst, the regione elementair is inclosit vitht in the spere of the mune and nyxt is the spere of mercurius,' Venus, Mars, Jupiter, and Saturn; after which comes 'the firmament quhilk is callit the hauyn or the spere of the sternis' (37-38; fol. 37r-38v). *Kalender*: 'The elementes and all thynges of them composed ben enclosed with the first skye…/ and yᵉ first skye is enclosed of the seconde / and the seconde in the thyrde / and the thyrde in the fourthe / and so of other. The fyrste skye nexte the elementes is the skye of the mone. Next it is the skye of Mercury,' Venus, Mars, Jupiter, and Saturn; after which the 'eight skye is of sterres fyxed / and they ben called so for that they moue more regulerly and after one guyse then the planettes do' (Ch. xxxi, n.p.).

[38] Wedderburn: 'and about it is the nynte spere callit the hauyn cristellyne, be cause that there can nocht be na sternis seen in it. All thir nyne speris or hauynis are inclosit vitht in the tent spere quhilk is callit the fyrst mobil' (38; fol. 38v) … al the thyng that circuitis this last tent hauyn or fyrst mobil is immobil and mouis nocht, there for it is callit the hauyn empire quhar the trone diuine standis' (38; fol. 39r). *Kalender*: 'Than aboue yᵗ is the first mobyle / in the whiche nothynge appereth yᵗ Shepeherdes may se. Some shepeherdes saye that aboue these .ix. skyes is one immobyle / for it tourneth not /and aboue that is one of crystall / ouer the whiche is yᵉ skye imperyall in yᵉ whiche is yᵉ throne of god' (Ch. xxxi, n.p.).

[39] Wedderburn: 'this said regione celest is nothir variabil nor corruptabil it is diuidit in ten speris, and the gritest spere quhilk is the outuart spere inclosis in it, the spere that is nyxt til it & sa be progressione and ordur euyrie spere inclosis the spere that is nerest tyl it' (37; fol. 38r). Pliny counts seven planets (II. iv.12) surrounded by the *mundus* ('world'), i.e., the sphere of the stars (II.i-ii.1-5), but he is no more specific than that.

There are further parallels with the shepherds' calendars. There are two heavenly motions: the east-west motion of the *primum mobile* and the west-east motion of the planets.[40] The course of the planets is given as follows: Saturn, 30 years; Jupiter, 12 years; Mars, two years; the sun, one year; Venus, 348 days; Mercury, 339 days; the moon, 27 days, eight hours.[41] The equinoctial divides the sphere of the heavens into two parts equally from the poles, and the zodiac divides the equinoctial into two parts.[42] The signs of the zodiac, their measurement (30 degrees), the colures, the solstices, the arctic and antarctic circles are also common topics.[43] Likewise, both treat the length of the days and nights in various parts of the word in various seasons.[44] Finally, both discuss the reasons for the moon's phases and for eclipses of the sun and the moon.[45]

It would be misleading, however, not to emphasize that the *Complaynt* and the shepherds' calendars differ significantly in some of their contents and emphases. For example, the *Kalender* explains how errors in calculations arise from using outdated charts; and it dwells on the meridian and horizon (Ch. xxxiii, n.p.); it discourses on the climates of the earth (Ch. xxxvii, n.p.) and on particular stars within the constellations (Ch.xxxviii, n.p.). Its coverage of astrological influence is extensive and aimed at the practical concerns of agriculture and herding (Ch. xxxviii-xliii, n.p.). In contrast, Wedderburn ignores the problem of outdated charts, and he treats the meridian and horizon briefly. Unlike the *Kalender*, he dwells on the roundness of the earth and the existence of the Antipodes, using the example of a ship whose mast disappears below

---

[40]   Wedderburn: 'the fyrst mobil … makkis reuolutione and course on the tua polis fra day to daye in the space of xxiiij houris fra orient til occident … bot the mouyng of the tothir nyne hauynis is fra the occident to the orient, quhilk is contrar to the mouyng of the tent spere callit the fyrst mobil' (38; fol. 38v). *Kalender*: 'the one is frome oryent in to the occydent aboue the erthe / and fro occydent in the oryent under it / that is called the dyurnall mouynge / that is to saye that it maketh frome daye to daye .xxiiij. houres / by the whiche mouynge the .ix. skye that is the fyrst mobyle draweth after and maketh the other skyes to tourne that ben vnder it. The other moment [*sic*] is of the .vii. planettes / and is from occydent to oryent aboue the erthe / and frome oryent in to the occydent under it / and is contrary to yᵉ fyrst' (Ch. xxxii, n.p.).

[41]   42-43; fols. 42v-43v; *Kalender* Ch. xxxii, n.p.

[42]   Wedderburn: 'There is ane vthir circle of the spere callit, the circle equinoctial the quhilk deuidis the spere in tua partis it is of ane lyik distance fra the tua polis … Ther is ane vthir grit circle in the spere callit the zodiac the quhilk deuidis the circle equinoctial *in* tua partis' (39; fols. 39v-40r). *Kalender*: 'In the concaue of the fyrst mobyle shepeherdes ymagineth to be the .ii. cyrcles / and they ben there royall / the one is as smal as a thred and it is called equynoccyall/ & the other is large in maner of a gyrdle /or as a garlande of floures / whiche they do call yᵉ zodyake.... [there are north and south celestial poles] in the myddes of the whiche poles *in* the first mobyle is cyrcle equynoccyall equally before in the partye as in the other of the sayd poles' (Ch. xxxiii, n.p.).

[43]   Wedderburn 39-40; fols. 40r-40v; *Kalender* Ch. xxxiii, n.p.

[44]   Wedderburn 40-41; fols. 41v-42v; *Kalender* Ch. xxxvii, n.p.

[45]   Wedderburn 43-44; fols. 44r-45r; *Kalender* Chs. vi and xlv, n.p.

the horizon as evidence (40; fol. 41r); he discusses the reasons for the moon's phases and for eclipses of the sun and the moon (43-44; fols. 44r-45r). Although like the *Kalender* he promotes the idea of stellar influence on earthly plants, creatures, and events, his treatment is cursory, even spotty, and he names different stars from the *Kalender* (44-46; fols. 45r-46v).

It would also be misleading not to point out that the cosmographical information in the shepherd's calendars is not unique to them, but rather is common to the sixteenth century, and that it was regarded as Ptolomean astronomy — for example, in *The Compost of Ptholomeus, Prince of Astronomye: Translated out of Frenche in to Englysshe* (London: Robert Wyer [1530?]; STC 20480), made of extracts from the Scottish *Kalendayr of the Shyppars* (1503; STC 22047), chapters xvi-xlix provide essentially the same astronomical and astrological information found in de Worde's *Kalender*, but under the name of Ptolemy. This may explain Wedderburn's remark that 'Quhen the scheiphird hed endit his prolixt oriso*n* … i meruellit nocht litel, quhen i herd ane rustic pastour of bestialite, distitut of vrbanite and of speculatione of natural philosophe, indoctryne his nychtbours as he hed studeit ptholome auerois aristotel galien ypocrites or Cicero' (49; fol. 50r) — all of which names are not to be regarded as Wedderburn's sources, but rather as authorities whose names are attached metonymically to the study of the heavens, weather, medicinal plants, and, one presumes in the case of Cicero, oration.

Wedderburn's citational practices therefore make the task of identifying verbal sources extremely challenging. His mode of composition is far closer to that of a modern author under obligation to be original than it is to a medieval author under obligation to reflect authority. This is easily observed via a comparison to a medieval encyclopedia. Again, Bartholomaeus's *De proprietatibus rerum* will serve. The medieval encyclopedist more carefully acknowledges authorities than does Wedderburn. For example, in his treatment of the heavenly sphere Bartholomaeus cites Isidore of Seville's *Etymologiae* (composed in 636), the *Liber de aggregationibus* or *Astronomia* of the Persian Alfraganus (al-Farghānī, 9th c.), (Pseudo-) Aristotle's *De proprietatibus elementorum*, and Macrobius's *In somnium Scipionis*, all standard sources of later medieval astronomy:

> Sphaera coeli, *vt dicit Isidorus*, est species quaedam in rotundam formata… Sphaera itaque *secundum Alphraganum* est orbicularus superficies coelestis corporis, in quo fixae stellae continentur…. Nam *sicut dicit Aristoteles in libro de proprietatibus elementorum*, ex ordinate spherae motu & contrario planetarum occursu, gignitur in orbe stridor, id est, harmonia. *Vnde Macrobius*, impulse & motu ipsorum efficitur sonus ille.[46]

---

[46] *De proprietatibus rerum* VIII.vi; Frankfurt 1601, 381-83. On the medieval sources of astronomical study, see J. D. North, *Chaucer's Universe* (Oxford: Oxford University Press, 1988) 7-37.

In contrast, on the same topic, Wedderburn cites no source:

> Nou fyrst to speik of the mouyng of the spere and of the diuisione of the hauynis, ze sal knau that the varld is diuidit in tua partis, that is to say. the fyrst part is the regione elementair quhilk is subiect til alteratione and to corruptione. the nyxt part of the varld is callit the regione celest (quhilk philosophours callis quinta essentia) vitht in the con-cauite of the quhilk, is closit the regione elementar this said regione celest is nothir vari-abil nor corruptabil it is diuidit in ten speris, and the gritest spere quhilk is the outuart spere inclosis in it, the spere that is nyxt til it & sa be progressione and ordur euyrie spere inclosis the spere that is nerest tyl it. in the first, the regione elementair is inclosit vitht in the spere of the mune and nyxt it is the spere of mercurius, and syne the spere of venus and nyxt it is the spere of the sone, and abufe and about it is the spere of mars. and syne the spere of Iupiter and than the spere of Saturnus…. nyxt thir speris, is the firmament quhilk is callit the hauyn or the spere of the sternis and about it is the nynte spere callit the hauyn cristellyne, be cause that there can nocht be na sternis seen in it' [37-38; fol. 38r-38v].

Nevertheless, this and other passages in the cosmographical section of the 'Monologue' can be traced to a source. They resemble parts of the thirteenth-century treatise by Johannes de Sacrobosco (John of Holywood), *De Sphaera*, which John North once called 'the staple university text in astronomy' in the Middle Ages.[47] *De Sphaera*'s roots are in William of Conches' *Philosophia*, Macrobius's *In somnium Scipionis*, and Ptolemy's *Almagest*, although more than any of these sources Sacrobosco cites the Persian astrologer Alfraganus (al-Farghānī), perhaps in order to appear up-to-date.[48] Sacrobosco's *De Sphaera* enjoyed wide distribution. The number of manuscripts is unknown, but it generated numerous medieval commentaries and glosses, it was printed first in 1472, and it received its last early-modern printing in 1673.[49] A copy of *De Sphaera* was in the Dominican convent of St. Andrews, where it was listed in c. 1522 as being one of 100 books in the possession of John Grierson, prior of the convent from 1517-23 and dean of the St. Andrews University theology faculty beginning in 1555.[50]

---

[47] *Ibid.*, 7; Joannes de Sacrobosco, *The Sphere of Sacrobosco and its Commentators*, trans. Lynn Thorndike (Chicago: University of Chicago Press, 1949) 42-46. Olaf Pedersen, 'In Search of Sacrobosco,' *Journal of the History of Astronomy* 16.3 (1985), reviews various hypotheses about Sacrobosco's origin, including the argument that he was from the monastery of St. Cross at Holywood in Nithsdale, but finds no satisfactory evidence for any of them, though he favours the possibility that Sacrobosco was English because he was in the 'English nation' at the University of Paris.

[48] Sacrobosco, *Sphere, ibid.*, 14-21.

[49] Pedersen, 'In Search of Sacrobosco,' 183-84.

[50] The list, item S20 in *Scottish Libraries*, was written into a copy of *Omnia Aristotelis opera cum commento Auerrois* (Venice 1489) that is now Bristol Central Library, Early Printed Books 191-2/SR45, sig. T6v.

Unlike the passages in Wedderburn traceable to Pliny, the few passages from Sacrobosco are nearly verbatim. For example, the passage on the motion of the spheres and the division of the heavens just quoted above is very close to the following passage in *De Sphaera*:

> Universalis autem mundi machina in duo dividitur: in etheream et elementarum regionem. Elementaris quidem, alterationi continue pervia, in quatuor dividitur ... Circa elementarem quidem regionem etherea lucida, a variatione omni sua immutabili essential immunis existens, motu continuo circulariter incedit. Et hec a philosophis quinta essentia nuncupatur, cuius novem sunt spere, sicut in proximo pretactum est, scilicet lune, Mercurii, Veneris, solis, Martis, Iovis, Saturni, stellarum fixarum, et celi ultimi. Istarum autem quelibet inferiorem sperice circumdat.

> ['The machine of the universe is divided into two, the ethereal and the elementary region. The elementary region, existing subject to continual alteration, is divided into four ... Around the elementary region revolves with continuous circular motion the ethereal, which is lucid and immune from all variation in its immutable essence. And it is called the 'Fifth Essence' by the philosophers. Of which there are nine spheres, as we have just said: namely, of the moon, Mercury, Venus, the sun, Mars, Jupiter, Saturn, the fixed stars, and the last heaven. Each of these spheres incloses its inferior spherically.']51

In his handling of cosmographical material and source citations, Wedderburn follows the Scottish precedent of writers such as David Lindsay in *Testament of the Papyngo* (1530), who, like Wedderburn in the 'Monologue' dates his text in clear astronomical terms, but without citing a source; in other words, presenting his astronomical knowledge as a fully assimilated and mastered body of knowledge that is an integral part of his literary craft.52

CONCLUSION

The 'Monologue Recreative' is a pastoral encyclopedia embedded within the *Complaynt of Scotland* as a reminder to Wedderburn's readers of the pastoral ontology of Scottish civilization in cosmography. Certainly, the *Complaynt* finds order in cosmography, implicitly promising that if there is order in the celestial spheres, then God will restore order to earth. Together with its positive examples of human behaviour and activity, the cosmography of the 'Monologue' offers the only examples of hope, necessary for defence against Fortune and the English, found in the *Complaynt*. Against the conflict that divides the estates in Dame Scotia's speech, in the 'Monologue,' as in the *Rota Vergilii*, the shepherd, farmer, and warrior are on a continuum blending into one

---

51 Sacrobosco, *Sphere* 78, 79, 119.
52 See the discussion of *Testament of the Papyngo* lines 113-35 in J. C. Eade, *The Forgotten Sky: A Guide to Astrology in English Literature* (Oxford: Clarendon Press, 1984) 157-59.

another, all manifestations of the same civic ideal.[53] For Wedderburn, Scots cannot isolate themselves within their estates—they must play multiple social roles, being as versatile as the mariners in the sea-battle towards the beginning of the 'Monologue,' who are both sailors and soldiers. The shepherd's role in the 'Monologue' is as a teacher, a repository of Scottish culture, a shepherd of souls,[54] in which role he is as vital as Dame Scotia, the personification of the nation. What the shepherd says in veiled terms about this need for unity and cooperation in the 'Monologue,' Dame Scotia expresses directly in her diatribe in the last part of the *Complaynt*.

The 'Monologue' is therefore pastoral in both the rustic (literary) and preaching (moral) senses of the term. Like Dame Scotia, the shepherd speaks both for and through the Actor, as a persona or mask. But in contrast to Dame Scotia's speech, a social and moral critique, the 'Monologue' presents an idealized picture of Scotland in harmony with the very spheres themselves. The shepherd presents what Scotland could and should be, against which parts one and three of the *Complaynt* present Scotland as it is. It is the 'Monologue' that makes the *Complaynt* more than a mere complaint, and takes it beyond the frame of Chartier's *Quadrilogue*. Chartier created a heteroglossic work of four voices—those of France and the three estates.[55] But whereas in titling his work a 'quadrilogue' Chartier pointedly limited the Actor's role to that of witness, Wedderburn's Actor is the voice of the dedication and prologue to the reader, both innovations in the *Complaynt*. Most significantly, however, to these four voices and this empowered author, Wedderburn has added a fifth voice, the shepherd's, whose position at the heart of the *Complaynt* calls Scotland back to its pastoral roots.

---

[53]   The *Rota Vergilii* was devised by the thirteenth-century rhetorician John of Garland to schematize literary style; see F. A. C. Mantello and A. G. Rigg, *Medieval Latin: An Introduction and Bibliographical Guide* (Washington, D.C.: Catholic University of America Press, 1996) 523.

[54]   On the *topos* of the shepherd as teacher see Cooper, *Pastoral* 71-79.

[55]   I borrow the concept of heteroglossia from Mikhail Bakhtin's essay, 'Discourse in the Novel,' which appears in M. M. Bakhtin, *The Dialogic Imagination: Four Essays*, trans. Michael Holquist and Caryl Emerson, ed. Michael Holquist, University of Texas Press Slavic Series (Austin: University of Texas Press, 1981).

James VI's Translations of the Psalms

J. Derrick McClure

King James VI's set of Psalm translations forms a not inconsiderable section of his poetic oeuvre, consisting as it does of no fewer than thirty of the Psalms rendered into verse.[1] That these have not attracted any substantial amount of critical attention in the context of the King's entire literary achievement, it must be acknowledged at the outset, is not wholly surprising; for the faults which can be found in the collection are all too readily visible. Although the Psalms are, as an essential part of their literary nature, designed to be sung, he has chosen to translate several of them in continuous sequences of rhyming pentameter couplets and in one case (Psalm 7) Poulter's metre: formats which obviously do not lend themselves to the kind of musical setting which untutored congregations could readily use. Short and intense lyrics such as Psalms 11 and 13 are rendered in stanzas of pentameter lines with interlacing rhymes: verse forms which lend themselves to imposing poetry, but in this context impart a methodical and even ponderous air to the poetic statements sadly out of harmony with their intrinsic nature. On an even more elementary level, the writing is at times frankly poor: distorted syntax, flagrantly padded lines, feeble and overused rhymes (*in any cace, into that cace* or the like is resorted to as a rhyme, often for *face* and/or *grace*, so regularly as to be virtually a hallmark of the entire collection), appear with disheartening frequency, sometimes marring otherwise fine poems. His free metrical treatment of the name *Iehoua*, which he sometimes stresses on the second syllable (*O mychtie God o great Iehova save* …: Ps.12), sometimes on the first and third (*O iehoua from boddume of my hairte I uill thee loue* …: Ps.18), and sometimes uses as a disyllable (*In tymes of straite mott iehoua giue thee eare* …: Ps.20), if hardly a major fault is at any rate a rather obvious shift. Craigie's account of the manuscript and the appearance of the Psalms as printed in his edition[2] suggest that not only the collection as a whole[3] but several, perhaps all, of the

---

[1]   Including one, number 150, of which the manuscript text is so badly damaged that the quality of the translation is impossible to assess.

[2]   *The Poems of James VI of Scotland*, ed. James Craigie, STS 3rd ser. 22, 26, 2 vols. (Edinburgh: Blackwood, 1955) II, xx. This edition is the one used throughout.

[3]   The fact that the set begins with Psalms 1-21 in continuous sequence, only Psalm 8 being omitted, before proceeding to ten more selected on no discernible principle, suggests that at some stage at least James's intention was to translate the entire book.

poems are in an uncorrected state, and James may certainly receive the benefit of the doubt that if he had revised and polished his translations they would be much better; but the collection as we have it cannot be said to contribute greatly to his reputation. Nonetheless, it would be short-sighted to dismiss the Psalms as unworthy of serious consideration from a literary point of view: not only do they reveal much about James's poetic assumptions and practices, but many of them are far from negligible as poems.

The most individual and most noteworthy feature of the *Psalms of His Majestie*, and the one which provides the clearest and perhaps most interesting demonstration of the skill James has brought to the task, is the metrical variety observable within the set. Indeed, the Psalms show a greater degree of metrical range and inventiveness than any, or all taken collectively, of his other poetic compositions: an unexpected demonstration of one aspect of the King's poetic talent. Some were undoubtedly suggested by particular tunes, James tailoring his translation to fit a specific tune in the manner of Montgomerie's 'The First Psalme to the tone of the Solsequium' and 'The 2 Psalm to the Tone of In throu the windows of myn ees':[4] Psalm 148 is a certain example, James using the same distinctive stanza form as the version of this Psalm by John Pullain in the 1564 Scottish Psalter;[5] and it is a perfectly likely supposition that this also applies to some of the more unusual stanzas at least. Many of the verse forms which he uses, however, appear to be his own invention. Craigie suggests that James, in choosing to employ a wide variety of metres instead of adhering to the ballad stanza form which had come to predominate in translations of the Psalms, may have been influenced by the metrical variety of the versions in the *Gude and Godlie Ballatis*: it is observable that of the five Psalms which appear in both the latter collection and James's work (numbers 2, 12, 13, 15 and 128)[6] none is in the same stanza form in both collections, which suggests (if it is weighty enough to suggest anything at all) that the influence of this source, if any, extended to the fact of using different metres but not to the metres used. Another possibly significant fact is that only four of James's Psalms, numbers 14, 17, 18 and 29, are in ballad metre,[7] a form which by then had come to be closely

---

[4]   See *Alexander Montgomerie, Poems*, ed. David J. Parkinson, STS 4th series 28, 29, 2 vols. (Edinburgh: Scottish Text Society, 2000) I, 3-5.

[5]   See Millar Patrick, *Four Centuries of Scottish Psalmody* (London: Oxford University Press, 1949) 32. I am most grateful to Dr Jamie Reid Baxter for this reference and other information used in the article. The same format is used for one of the two versions of this Psalm in the familiar Church of Scotland Psalter, 'The Lord of Heaven confess', suggesting that the rousing tune to which it is now sung is one of the few to have survived from the 1564 Psalter.

[6]   Numbering as in the Authorised Version, which, as James does, follows the ordering of the Hebrew text: some are numbered differently in the *Ballatis*.

[7]   The first three are printed in Craigie's edition as fourteeners, but the difference between these and ballad metre with unrhymed first and third lines is typographical only.

associated with Psalm translations;[8] suggesting a decision not to be bound by existing conventions.

That James was keenly interested in not only the nature of metre and metrical technique but in the propriety of fitting metre to subject matter and style is evident from his *Reulis and Cautelis*:[9] it is interesting and perhaps curious that he chose a set of translations, despite his remark in the same work[10] that translation restricts the poet's scope for exercising his *awin ingyne*, in which to give free reign to the choosing of both established and newly-devised stanza forms; and still more so that he did this in translating a set of sacred texts, reverence for which might have (and certainly did with other translators) acted as a damper on his free inventiveness. In this essay I propose to consider the literary effects of James's metrical ingenuity: to discuss what the various metres offer as poetic assets, and to what extent James has been successful in exploiting their potential to enhance his translations.[11]

The renderings of Psalm 1 by Alexander Scott, Alexander Montgomerie and King James provide a test case for the effects of a translator's choice of verse form. Scott's version has the metrical pattern of ballad stanza but, typically of a poet noted for a wide range of stanza forms and mastery of sound patterns, shows a distinctive elaboration of the basic pattern in the form of a quadruple rhyme in each verse, the tetrameter lines showing internal rhyme as well as end rhyme. Alliteration is also conspicuous; not indeed in every line but with sufficient frequency to be a definite feature of the poem. The combination of those features, and the opening trochee and grammatical inversion, impart an arresting brightness and vigour to the first stanza:[12]

> Happy is he has hald him free
> From folkis of defame;
> Always to flee iniquity
> And sait of sin and shame. [1-4]

The consistent maintaining of this pattern has of necessity entailed some additions to the original and departures from its literal sense: this is of course integral to the process of poetic translation, and here as always the issue is not the mere fact that such changes

---

[8]   A fact of which the recording *Psalms for the Regents of Scotland* by Edinburgh University Renaissance Singers (EURS 003) provides memorable illustrations.

[9]   See *Poems*, I, 65-83 and especially 79-83.

[10]   *Ibid.*, I, 79.

[11]   For an account of the religious and cultural background to James's translations, see Craigie's notes and references therein, and especially (for a convenient and readable summary) Patrick, *Four Centuries of Scottish Psalmody* chapter 8.

[12]   Alexander Scott, *The Poems of Alexander Scott*, ed. Alexander Scott (Edinburgh: Saltire Society, 1952) 89.

have been made but how skilfully they have been chosen to contribute to the poetic effect. In this stanza, the interpolated *always* and the rendering of the Septuagint *pestilentiae*[13] by the doublet *sin and shame* add emphasis to the original statement. A more notable alteration is that none of the three negatives (*non abiit ... non stetit ... non sedit*) has been literally translated, the first being rendered as *has hald him free* and the word *flee*, part of the same rhyme pattern, doing duty for the other two: this certainly contributes to the confident tone of the stanza. In several instances Scott fills out his lines by using a phrase with two lexical items to translate a single word (conceivably the presence of *die ac nocte* in the original, retained as *both day and nicht*, may have been seen as a sort of licence for a frequent re-use of the structure):[14] *command and law* (for *lege*),[15] *leaf and blade* (for *folium*), *dust and stro* (for *pulvis*). Once (*air and late*) a phrase of this form corresponds to nothing in the original; once (*To burge and shoot, and sall give fruit / In time, as God has grantit*) such a phrase forms part of a more extensive and elaborate expansion (the original is simply *quod fructum dabit in tempore suo*). Similar slight, unobtrusive, but perfectly fitting expansions of the original text appear at a few points: the last of them, *Sall perish out of ken* (for *peribit*), brings the psalm to a graceful and decisive conclusion. Scott's multiple rhymes occasionally, but only rarely, land on a semantically weak word (*until*) or a vacuous one (*still, ofsyiss*): more frequently (stanzas 3 and 4 providing good examples) the rhymes are skilfully placed on significant words. The simple vocabulary, totally lacking in the aureation which Scott uses in other poems, and equally simple grammatical structures accord well with the quiet, meditative tone of the lyric. This verse must be rated highly on all counts as a poetic translation.

Montgomerie's rendering of the same Psalm is metrically much more intricate, by the requirements of the tune for which it was written;[16] and it cannot be maintained that his choice of verse structure for his translation was a happy inspiration. In almost painful contrast to the dexterity with which he fits the argument of the poem to the

---

[13] The translation suggests this, at any rate, more than it does the Vulgate *derisorum* which is followed in the versions of Montgomerie, James and the modern Church of Scotland version.

[14] A much more far-reaching point is that the use of parallel phrases is (of course) a feature of the poetic style of the Psalms throughout; but on the scale of the present translation that is hardly a necessary consideration.

[15] I cite the Latin words in the form in which they appear in the Vulgate text, without raising the question, irrelevant in the immediate context, of *grammatical* equivalence between the Latin and the Scots versions.

[16] A transcription of the tune is found in *Montgomerie: Poems*, 300-01. *The Solsequium* is one of the items in the recorded album *The Songs of Alexander Montgomerie*, Paul Rendall (tenor) and Rob MacKillop (lute), ASV, Gaudeamus GAU 249. The subtle and complex tune is not an obvious choice for a Psalm setting, as it is surely beyond the capacity of an ordinary congregation.

metre and rhyme scheme in the *Solsequium* itself, his struggle to force the Psalm into the same mould has resulted in a sequence of feeble rhymes, ineptly positioned grammatical breaks and vacuous interpolations.[17] The tercets of two-beat rhyming lines are all marred either by semantic redundancy (*Weill is the man / 3ea blessed than ...*), rhymes on unimportant words (*in* and *begin* to rhyme with *sin*), uninformative padding (*day by day ... thairfor I say*), or awkward mismatches of metrical and grammatical units:

> His Actionis all
> Ay prosper sall
> Quhilk sall not fall
> To godless men bot as the chaffe or sand ... [1.17-20]

A competence more worthy of Montgomerie is shown in the rendering of verse 2 as

> Bot in Jehovahis lau   Delyts aricht
> And studies it to knau Both day and nicht; [1.9-10]

but the corresponding section of the second stanza is flawed by the placing of the conjunctive adverb in *vhair the just remanes* in a rhyming position: a venial fault, perhaps, since there is no break in the melody at this point; but a lapse nonetheless. This translation is a memorable illustration of the fact that even a poet of Montgomerie's technical skill can be ingloriously defeated when endeavouring to force a poetic statement into a mould which it simply does not fit.

The King's version is the least elaborate in respect of sound patternings, eschewing repeated rhymes and making little use of alliteration. The unusual stanza form, however (a quatrain in pentameters followed by one in ballad metre), makes its own contribution to the exposition of the argument. Notably, each quatrain is applied to the expression of a particular statement, and the second quatrain of each stanza is introduced by an overt marker of the transition to a new stage in the argument: most obtrusively in the second stanza with the clumsy interpolation *Now this is surely for to say ...,* most neatly in the third with a simple *For ....* It is tempting to see the poetic re-casting of this Psalm as a carefully constructed step-by-step argument, in contrast to Scott's dainty lyric and Montgomerie's misplaced display of rhyming fecundity, as characteristic of James's meticulous scholarly mind. The translation has other merits: the opportunity for *amplificatio* afforded by the pentameter lines and eight-line stanzas, if sometimes squandered by the inept use of a vacuous *we see* or *withoutin doute*, more often results in competently-wrought lines, in which the expansions to the original text avoid

---

[17]   As Parkinson's edition shows, the variations among the texts of this poem are very numerous; but though I will confine my comments to the text which he uses as his exemplum it does not appear that any of the variant readings produce a substantially better version.

the appearance of mere padding and are in some cases adorned with alliteration (*Bot as the caffe which be the wind is tost … Nor sittis in seatis of scornful men in talk … Whose pleasant leif doth neuer fade nor fal*). Montgomerie's rendering of *beatus vir* is a patent case of an author being mastered by his chosen format, but James's *That mortal man most happy is and blest* surmounts the same problem with confidence. The short final line of each stanza (*To think is neuer slaw … Most prosperously stand … Sall perish be his micht*) provides a forceful conclusion both semantically and prosodically, the necessary slight expansions of the original phrases being aptly devised for the purpose.

As is to be expected, therefore, James has endeavoured to link his chosen poetic form to the exposition of his material; and (in this case at least) succeeded to a creditable degree. The same is true of the next Psalm, which is even more straightforward metrically: eight-line stanzas of iambic tetrameters. The short lines have a markedly beneficial effect: unlike the pentameters of the version in the *Gude and Godlie Ballatis,* which in parts reads like an expanded paraphrase rather than a translation, they constrain him to avoid (for the most part at least) vacuous words or phrases and to express the thoughts of his original in concise and strictly-disciplined phrases. Several lines effectively combine a powerful statement with a punchily regular rhythm: *And sitt commanding every thing*[18] (an expansion with no exact equivalent in the original text) … *Thow art my sonne and cumd of me… Reioyse with trembling euermore.* The opening line *Quhy makis the gentils tumultes great?* at once conveys, by its word-order as well as its prosody, an urgent and forceful mood; though the second line *Quhy do the nations panse in vain?* is weaker by reason of the placing of *do* in a stress position.[19] Here as in several cases, James has shown fidelity to the original by translating parallel phrases precisely in pairs of successive lines: other examples are

> He lawchis that sitis in heawins impyre,
> yea euen the Lord doth mock at thame; [2b.9-10]
>
> Ye kings giue cairfull eare thairfore,
> And learne ilk iuge in earthlie throne, [2b.29-30]
>
> Lett ws brek all thair bondis, say thay,
> And cast thair strongest cordis away. [2b.7-8]

— the last being neatly positioned as the final rhyming couplet of a stanza. This is one occasion where James exploits the expressive potential of the unusual rhyme scheme he has chosen: *axabcbcc.* The final couplet calls for a decisive full close to the argument of

---

[18]   What Craigie categorises as the *b* text of this Psalm will be cited in the discussion except when a difference between it and the *a* text is relevant to the argument.

[19]   Making *Quhy do …* into a trochaic inversion improves the prosody, but semantically the line is still weaker than its predecessor.

each stanza; and this expectation is invariably fulfilled; even if once, in the final stanza, at the cost of a somewhat strained translation:

> Thay happy all[20] that from thair syn
> Takis vp, and vnto him do rin. [2b.39-40]

A more peculiar feature of the rhyme scheme, the lack of a rhyme for the second line, is also a potential poetic asset: the defeated expectation that line 4 will rhyme with line 2 ensures that the first half of each verse ends with a word which is thrown into high relief; and this could be exploited by ensuring that a semantically powerful word, or one conveying important information, is chosen for that position. In this, however, James is less successful. *& princes go to counsall all*, line 4 of the first stanza, ends with a word that is striking in neither sound nor import;[21] and given that the rhyme word in line 6 is the semantically feeble *uithall* the verdict must be that here James is guilty of very amateurish work. The other stanzas are better in this respect (possibly excepting number 4 with its redundant *sone*): *if once a kendling, thocht but small* (st. 5) highlights a potent qualification, and *And fray thame with his furious heat*[22] (st. 2) provides an impressive midstanza climax. James's choice of poetic format for this translation has allowed him definite opportunities, of which he has at least sometimes made effective use.

After this Psalm, it is observable that the only ones for which James has used tetrameter lines throughout are among the shortest and simplest in the book: Psalms 15, 125, 128 and 131 (the last three coming together in the collection as if conceived as a miniature set). In Psalm 15, which takes the form of five eight-line stanzas rhyming *ababbcbc*, James has again tailored the translation to ensure that each pair of successive lines represents a self-contained unit of thought. The two balanced clauses of the opening verse *Domine quis habitabit in tabernaculo tuo aut quis requiescet in monte sancto tuo* become a quatrain of two similarly balanced pairs:

> ô Iehoua quho shall abyde
> into thy tent[23] & holy place
> or quho shall duell all tyme & tyde
> into thy holy hill of grace [15.1-4]

---

20 The *are* of the *a* text is a better reading.

21 The *a*-text reading, *uith thaime consultis the reularis tall* is again better, *tall* still being regularly used in the sense of 'brave, valiant'.

22 This translates Tremellius's *cum aesto suo* instead of the Vulgate *in ira sua*: see Craigie, *Poems*, II, 219.

23 James regularly translates *tabernaculum* as *tent*, though *tabernacle* was already long established in English Biblical translations. *Tent* also appears in the works of other translators besides James, and in a verse with short lines the use of a monosyllable was no doubt a metrical convenience; but it is hard to escape the impression that in both its sound and its connotations the word lacks the dignity of its alternative: *And for the sunne a tent in thaim he maid* (Psalm 19) sounds particularly bathetic.

and throughout, the items in the description of a 'citizen of Zion'[24] are enumerated in a format in which the grammar, the metre and the content are matched, for the most part, with unfailing precision in the basic unit of a two-line sequence. Only in the last verse is a slight faltering visible, line 3 being unrelated to line 4 and the latter closely linked grammatically to its successor. The expansions are fitting and aptly chosen: even *in euery cace* has a precise applicability in its context and is not a mere tag. Psalm 125, metrically the simplest of the entire set (four-line tetrameter stanzas rhyming *abab*) is also one of the simplest in expression, embroideries or developments of the original being very inconspicuous: the interpolated qualification in … *his people compas **that abound*** if clearly rhyme-forced is at least in keeping with many Old Testament references. The rhyme scheme of Psalm 128, *ababcc*, invites a decisive conclusion to each stanza, and by achieving this James has produced what is surely as attractive a rendering of this Psalm as any in Scots or English (the version in the *Gude and Godlie Ballattis*, with its hopelessly irregular lines and infelicities such as an irrelevant *be not feird* to rhyme with *dreid*, is incompetent by comparison). Psalm 131 shows the same craftsmanship: curiously, its two stanzas are asymmetrical, the first having six lines (*ababcc*) and the second eight (*ababccdd*); but the last couplet, corresponding to the last verse of the original, is separate in thought from the body of the poem and suggests a detachable *envoi*.[25]

James's use of tetrameter lines appears to have been a definite asset, enabling him to render his models in an organised and structured fashion and to avoid an excessive amount of line-padding. For other Psalms he has in several cases used stanzas of pentameters: a stylistic choice which has not always proved unreservedly successful. The intuitively-recognised 'feel' of a pentameter line differs from that of a tetrameter much more than the issue of two syllables more or less might suggest. [26] Impressionistic terms like 'weightier' 'more dignified' or 'more imposing' reflect the fact that in physical reality a pentameter line is longer than a tetrameter by an inaudible, though perfectly perceptible, space of time in addition to the obviously longer time which its words take in the saying;[27] and therefore is also more isolated from its neighbours, inviting a greater

---

[24] The AV's heading to this Psalm, 'David describeth a citizen of Zion'.

[25] This argument cannot apply to Psalm 12, which is likewise asymmetrical and consists of a ten-line stanza rhyming *ababcdcdee* and a twelve-line rhyming *ababcdcdeeff*.

[26] The difference is *not* merely this, of course. A point made long ago by David Abercrombie, 'A Phonetician's View of Verse Structure,' *Linguistics* 6 (1964), rept. in David Abercrombie, *Studies in Phonetics and Linguistics*, Language and Language Learning (Oxford University Press: London, 1965) 26-34, is that whereas tetrameter lines run smoothly on from one to the next without a pause, pentameters invite a foot-length pause containing a silent stress at the end of each line.

[27] Note that I am saying 'pentameter' and 'tetrameter', of which the statement is by definition true, and not 'decasyllabic' and 'octosyllabic', of which it would often be true in practice but not of necessity.

degree of attention on the part of the hearer to its content as an individual unit. James's choice of an eight-line stanza in pentameters rhyming *ababbcbc* for his translation of Psalm 114, a majestic paean to the power and glory of God as manifested in all His works, is entirely successful: the rhetorical pageant unfolds in a poem as memorable as any in James's output. His use of the same verse form for the much shorter, more concentrated and more highly-wrought Psalm 19, however, gives rise to a poem of conspicuously variable quality.

Though the main focus of the present essay is not on accuracy of translation, the apparent radical misunderstanding, or at any rate misrepresentation, of verses 2-5 (James's first stanza) must be noted. James's lines

> day follouing day dois speiches utter uell
> euen so the nichtis do scyence make us knou [19.3-4]

not only loses the rhetorical figure in *dies diei eructat verbum et nox nocti indicat scientiam*, which is surprising in itself, but defies the clear implication of the Latin dative[28] to give a completely different — and much less imaginatively potent — sense to the words. Likewise,

> no uordis nor kyndlie speichis from thaim flou
> yett uithout thir thaire uoyce is understand [19.5-6]

though sound enough in itself both as thought and as poetry, is not what is implied by *non est sermo et non sunt verba quibus non audiatur vox eorum*. Even at the young age at which those translations were evidently made, James had of course a thorough knowledge of Latin; and the reason for his departure from the sense of his original can only be conjectured.

In itself, however, this stanza can certainly pass muster as a verse of poetry: the syntactic arrangement of the first line effectively places *michty godd* in its centre; *no uordis nor kyndlie speichis* and *throuch all the earth and habitable land* are decorous and fitting expansions; the strange *thaire beames and drauchtes* has at least an explanation in that it translates an idiosyncratic reading in James's model text.[29] In the second stanza too, the embellishments necessary to bring the lines to the statutory length are tactfully chosen (*glaid, steadfastly, in glancing braue array*), and the line *And nothing from his heate can lurke or fende* imparts a climactically decisive conclusion to the verse. The central rhetorical figure in the next sequence, the repeated *Domini*,[30] is maintained at

---

[28] Both the rhetorical pattern and the actual meaning are conveyed in the Authorised Version's 'Day unto day uttereth speech, and night unto night showeth knowledge'.

[29] *Delineatione eorum*: see *Poems*, II, 221.

[30] *Lex Domini … testimonium Domini … iustitia Domini … praeceptum Domini … timor Domini … iudicia Domini …*

least in part: each successive pair of lines begins with *Iehouais ... his ... his ... his ...*,
and in the first three pairs the second line corresponds to the participial clause in the
Latin. *And dois the soule from trublouse greif restore*,[31] if not precisely what the original
says, is expressive and not inappropriate; *And makis him uyse that foolish uas before*[32]
has an endearingly magisterial ring. James's sure touch, however, then begins to falter:
his beginning the translation of the fourth participial clause half-way through a line
instead of at the beginning of the next line may have been a deliberate ploy to mark
the end of the sequence and the stanza, but the adjective clause in *And cleir the eyes
that fixe on thaim thaire sicht* (for an unadorned *inluminans oculos*) is little more than
padding; and in the following stanza the vacuous line *And in like mainer are thay iuste
againe* and the inflation of *dulciora super mel et favum* to three full lines suggests a poet
approaching the end of his resources. Conversely however, in the last stanza, where
James's rendering of a single verse as an eight-line sequence has resulted in what is
undisguisedly an expanded paraphrase and the personal prayer with which the Psalm
ends has become the personal prayer of a sixteenth-century Scottish Protestant worshipper, the additions fulfil their purpose of re-locating the poem in its Christian
context. This translation illustrates the danger, but also the potential, of using a verse
form which calls for statements pronounced in a formal manner and organised in an
ordered sequence.

The various forms of *cuttit and brokin verse*[33] which James has employed for several
of the Psalms form an interesting variety. One, Psalm 100, is puzzlingly asymmetrical:
the first stanza, or section

> induellers of the earth reioce in god
> uith glaidnes him adore
> uith singing loude cum in his sicht abrod
> knou iehoua thairfore
> to be the god of glore
> quho creat us to be
> his people flok & store
> no uayes our selues maid ue [100.1-8]

uses the sequence of short lines to bring the section to a decisive conclusion; but the
second stanza, though beginning similarly with a quatrain of pentameter and trimeter
lines, proceeds not to a quatrain of trimeters but to a pentameter couplet, ending with
the woefully redundant *quhose mercy and treuth all ages laistis alluayes*. Psalm 6 combines
lines of different length in an interesting verse form: the eight lines rhyme *ababcccb*,

---

[31] *Convertens animam* in the Latin; *converting the soul* in the AV.
[32] *sapientiam praestans parvulis* in the Latin; *making wise the simple* in the AV.
[33] James's term for verse with lines of varying length: see *Reulis and Cautelis* in *Poems*, I, 82.

the quatrain being in tetrameters, the tercet trimeters and the final line a dimeter bob.[34] This form would be most satisfactorily utilised by ensuring that the lines of the tercet were mutually independent in grammar but closely linked in thought, and that the final bob by either summarising or countering the thought of the tercet provided a sword-stroke conclusion to the stanza. The first verse fails signally to achieve this:

> for that I languish sore
> then cure me lorde thairfore
> for bones & soule are more
> then trublit ay [6.5-8]

Here the first line of the tercet is more closely linked to the last line of the quatrain than to the lines which follow it, and the shift to which James has resorted to obtain the last rhyme, adding *more than* to *conturbata sunt ossa mea*, not only is virtually meaningless in itself but places the final line break right in the middle of a phrase. In the following stanza the structure is handled much more effectively, however; and at the end of the Psalm the semantically powerful rhyme words in the tercet and the placing of *feare*, in a slight and surely permissible elaboration of the original, as the last stress of the bob make for a strong conclusion[35]:

> quhom shame mott so confounde
> as at â suddaine stounde
> thay may out of this grounde
> turne bakke uith feare. [6.37-40]

The combination of tetrameter and trimeter lines presents no technical difficulty; but Psalm 47 shows a less satisfactory experiment: it is in seven-line stanzas of alternating pentameter and tetrameter lines — an unusual and inherently awkward arrangement, because of the tendency already mentioned for pentameter lines to be followed by a pause and tetrameters to run straight on,[36] and made even more idiosyncratic by the presence of two disyllabic bobs, rhyming with each other and with nothing else, preceding and following the final (pentameter) line. This detail has its possibilities: it highlights the final word *abydis*, especially by contrast with its vacuous rhyme-word

---

[34]   Psalm 4 has the same rhyme scheme and the same bob, but all its lines except the last are tetrameters.

[35]   Unlike *in graue that be* or *and pitteouse cace*.

[36]   The suggestion is made by Abercrombie (see n. 26) that lines of verse in stress-timed languages have a natural tendency to contain an even number of feet: a trimeter line thus, like a pentameter, invites a foot-length pause with a silent beat. For that reason a pattern of alternating tetrameter and trimeter lines flows with ready ease and fluency as each trimeter line with its final silent foot matches the length of a tetrameter; but as a pentameter in effect is not one but two feet longer than a tetrameter a sequence of alternating pentameters and tetrameters is extremely difficult to sustain with any degree of grace.

bisidis; and in the preceding stanza *then sing – oure king* likewise makes for a neat conclusion. (The multiple repetitions of *sing* in this stanza are not a sign of laxity on
James's part: the Latin is *canite Deo canite canite rege nostro canite*.) The oddity of
combining pentameters with tetrameters, however, has a deleterious effect on the
expression: each of the first two lines

> all people sing to god uith uoycis cleir
> & clapp youre handis youre ioye to shou [47.1-2]

is perfectly good in itself, but the failure of the tetrameter to proceed to a fifth foot
inevitably arouses a sense of incompleteness and stopping short; and this is worse still
in the next pair of lines where the last foot of the tetrameter is the vacuous rhyme-
forced *ye knou*. Here James's difficulties are of his own making: in Psalm 148, where he
has chosen to adopt an individual and tricky stanza form to fit a specific tune, his bold-
ness is at least in part rewarded. The opening stanza hardly arouses a reader's hopes:

> Sing laude vnto the lord
> Heavens Indwelleris, I say,
> To do the same accord
> In places hie & stay
> And so alwayse
> Ye angellis all
> Great hostes & tall
> Iehoua prayse. [148b.1-8]

Heavens Indwelleris, apart from the prosodic clumsiness of placing the word *indwelleris*
where the stress falls on its first and last syllables, sounds singularly inexpressive; the *I
say* is a mere rhyming tag; and *stay* (i.e. steep), though a perfectly common and familiar
word, seems out of place as a description of the heights of Heaven. James's version
cannot be rated as an improvement on that of Pullain in the 1564 Psalter:

> Giue laude vnto the Lord,
> From heauen that is so hie:
> Praise him in deed and worde
> Aboue the starrie skie.
> And also ye,
> His angells all,
> Armies Royall,
> Praise him with glee. [148.1-8][37]

---

[37]   This is also the version included in the Scottish Metrical Psalter of 1635, for which see http://www.
archive.org/stream/scottishmetrical00livi#page/215/mode/2up [accessed November 2010]. Unfortunately
this is not one of the Psalms for which a tune is included in this collection.

— and even it can hardly be described as distinguished. Soon, however, James appears to get into his stride, handling the short lines and interlacing rhymes with dexterity. Several of his trimeters — *and starres of shyning light, with stormy winds and shill, eche earthlie Iudge and King* — show more than basic competence; and the requirement set by the rhyme scheme to make a climactic conclusion out of each stanza's final line is generally fulfilled. Notably, every final line except one contains the word *praise* in some form: surely a deliberate attempt to replicate the effect of the repeated *laudate* of the Latin. The exception is the conclusion to stanza 3, *Whose iust decree / Can nowise be / by oght transgrest*; and that justifies itself by the added force imparted to *praeceptum dedit et non praeteribit*. The elaborations in the stanza corresponding to verses 7 and 8 are both appropriate and appealing:

> Praise him eche leving beast
> That on the earth dois go
> Thou deape with most and least
> Of fishe and whailes also
> Thou glanceing lowe
> Haill roundlie rolde
> Snow whyte and colde
> His praise furth showe. [148b.25-32]

Lapses notwithstanding, the challenge which James set himself by choosing this elaborate stanza form have surely been creditably surmounted.

Despite James's careful categorisation in his *Reulis and Cautelis* of the suitability of various metres to particular themes or subjects, I can see no evidence that the metrical diversity of his Psalm translations bears any relationship to the diverse tones of the individual Psalms — praise, lamentation, personal prayer and so on: his metrical experimentation appears on the face of it to have been simply for its own sake. In this and other respects, though the seriousness with which James approached the task of translating the Psalms cannot be doubted, the collection as we have it, in its hit-or-miss mixter-maxter of inspiration and plodding, expertise and clumsiness, suggests *essayes of a prentice in the divine art of poesie* fully as much as do the poems in the collection so named. Nonetheless, apart altogether from their historical interest as evidence of James's concern with the forms of worship in his realm, the *Psalmes of his Maiestie* show clear evidence of the young poet's developing skill and readiness to experiment with a range of poetic forms; and, as I hope to have shown, in a pespectable number of cases his experiments resulted in a creditable degree of success.

'Holy Words for Healing':
Some Early Scottish Charms and
their Ancient Religious Roots

Priscilla Bawcutt

Middle English charms in recent years have received growing attention from folklorists, students of religion, and literary historians. Those in verse have been indexed in *A New Index of Middle English Verse* (henceforth *NIMEV*);[1] some are included in anthologies, such as Rossell Hope Robbins's *Secular Lyrics* (1952) and Theodore Silverstein's *Medieval English Lyrics* (1971),[2] and several others are printed in scholarly journals.[3] A subtle and learned article on the topic was published by Douglas Gray in 1974, and Eamon Duffy devoted a substantial section of *The Stripping of the Altars* (1992) to 'Prayers and Spells'.[4] The position for Scotland is quite different: the charms known to survive from the early period are few in number, and so far little studied. The purpose of this essay is to make these Scottish charms better known, and to indicate their religious significance and wider cultural interest. Since they are not easily accessible and their sense has often been misunderstood, a text of each charm is also provided, freshly transcribed and edited from the manuscript.

One simple yet characteristic example is preserved in the Kirk Session Records of Perth. There it is recorded that on 21 May 1632 Laurence Boik and his wife Janet Black were accused of 'charming'. They confessed that 'they would sometime use some holy words for healing of shotts and sores, which words are these:

---

[1]   *A New Index of Middle English Verse*, eds. Julia Boffey and A. S. G. Edwards (London: British Library, 2005).

[2]   *Secular Lyrics of the XIVth and XVth Centuries*, ed. Rossell H. Robbins (Oxford: Clarendon Press, 1952); *Medieval English Lyrics*, ed. Theodore Silverstein, York Medieval Texts (London: Edward Arnold, 1971).

[3]   See, for instance, Curt Bühler, 'Prayers and Charms in Certain Middle English Rolls,' *Speculum* 39 (1964).

[4]   See Douglas Gray, 'Notes on Some Middle English Charms,' *Chaucer and Middle English Studies in Honour of Rossell Hope Robbins*, ed. Beryl Rowland (London: George Allen & Unwin, 1974); and Eamon Duffy, *The Stripping of the Altars: Traditional Religion in England, c.1400-c.1580* (New Haven: Yale University Press, 1992) 207-98.

> Thir sairis are risen thro' God's work,
> And must be laid thro' God's help;
> The mother Mary and her dear son,
> Lay thir sairis that are begun.'[5]

It is clear that the purpose of these charms was not black magic or the raising of spirits or the devil, but 'healing' — the alleviation of everyday ailments in men and beasts, in a period when both the causes and the cures of disease were mysterious. Many of the charms surviving from England had a similar purpose, being designed to heal wounds, reduce toothache, or staunch bleeding. One such, discussed below, has the title *Medicina pro morbo caduco & le fevre*. It is striking too that Robbins placed the Middle English specimens in the 'practical' section of his anthology, along with other useful verses, such as mnemonics for the length of months.

But it is the 'holy' rather than the medical aspect of charms that is the topic of this article. The words uttered by this Perthshire couple today appear innocuous and highly pious, a plea for God's help against disease. Indeed in many cases the dividing line between a medieval charm and a prayer seems very fine, and it is not surprising that they were sometimes termed 'orisons'. Charms, like prayers, turned for assistance to Jesus, and more particularly his Passion, and also (as in this case) to his mother the Virgin Mary. Often they also invoked the aid of the saints. Two Scottish charms that were added at some time in the fourteenth or early fifteenth century to fol. 2v of the Herdmanston Breviary (NLS, Adv. MS 18.2.13A) were designed to heal a virulent cattle-disease known as 'lung-socht'.[6] The first is largely in Latin:

> Coniuro te morbum qui dicitur lowngsocht per uirtutem quinque wlnerum Ihesu Christi et per preciosum sanguinem eius per quem redempti sumus et per quinque gaudia dulsis-sime matris sue Marie et per dulsissimum lac quod de uberibus sue suxit vt non habeas

---

Extracts from the Kirk Session Records, printed in *The Chronicle of Perth, a Register of Remarkable Occurrences, Chiefly Connected with that City, from the Year 1210 to 1668*, ed. James Maidment, Maitland Club (Edinburgh: s.n., 1831) 97; also William George Black, *Folk-Medicine: A Chapter in the History of Culture*, Publications of the Folklore Society (London: E. Stock, 1883) 74.

6   *DOST, lung-, lowngsocht*, on the circulation and meaning of this word. The Herdmanston Breviary is thought to have originated in the North of England, but came into the possession of the Sinclairs of Herdmanston some time in the fourteenth century. For further information, see *Kalendars of Scottish Saints with Personal Notices of Those of Alba, Laudonia, & Strathclyde, an Attempt to fix the Districts of their Several Missions and the Churches where they were Chiefly had in Remembrance*, ed. A. P. Forbes, Literature of Theology and Church History (Edinburgh: Edmonston and Douglas, 1872) liii, liv, and Catherine R. Borland, 'Catalogue of the Mediaeval Manuscripts in the Library of the Faculty of Advocates at Edinburgh.' Edinburgh: Department of Manuscripts, National Library of Scotland, 1906-08. For advice and assistance concerning this manuscript, I am much indebted to Dr Kenneth Dunn and Miss Elspeth Yeo.

plus potestatem inter ista animalia migrare aut amplius nocere contra mandatum regale nostri redemptoris ...

The second, entitled 'Carmen pro lonsoucht', opens in Latin but later switches to Scots:

In nomine patris et filij et spiritus sancti amen. Deus benedicat greges istos sicut bene-dixit greges in deserto et per uirtutem illorum uerborum quod nocet non nocebit morbo de lonsoucht nec aliquo alio morbo caduco in uirtute et per uirtutem sancte Brigide sicut Deus dedit potestatem ei benedicere omnia animalia in terra. amen.

Nov ye sal tak a best and mak a bor [hole] in the horne and thar in put this forsaid charm and tak a peny and bow [bend] in the bestis hevyd [head] and gar a voman gan to sant Brid and offer it in hir nam and tak holy vater and cast on tham as thai gan furth fra the charmyng. Non plus, etc.

St Bridget, or St Bride, was particularly popular in Scotland and, as Sir David Lindsay satirically noted, she was the saint to whom women regularly prayed 'to keip calf and koow'.[7]

Although the medieval Church did not approve of charms and conjurations, nonethe-less it seems to have permitted their use. Chaucer's Parson well conveys something of the ambivalence of medieval churchmen on this topic: trenchant disapproval of 'mal-efice of sorcerie' is combined with a grudging tolerance of 'charmes for woundes or maladie of men or of beestes'. Perhaps, he says, 'if they taken any effect, it may be peraventure that God suffreth it, for folk sholden yeve the moore feith and reverence to his name'.[8] In the sixteenth and seventeenth centuries, however, vehement attacks were made by Protestants, such as Conrad Platz and William Perkins, on charmers and 'blessers'. It was not simply that such charms alluded to beliefs and doctrines that were now regarded by the Reformers as papistical. What was offensive, as Stuart Clark has shown, was the inappropriate and devilish use of 'holy words':

To claim that holy words in particular had an inherent efficacy was an outright rejection of the second commandment. If success was obtained, if children and livestock in fact recovered, this was by demonic intervention and should not be taken as a gain but as a loss — as a *punishment* for lack of steadfastness in affliction ... It was one thing to say

---

[7]   The bending of pennies in this way was apparently common in medieval healing rituals. See Ronald C. Finucane, *Miracles and Pilgrims: Popular Beliefs in Medieval England* (London: J. M. Dent, 1977) 94, and Lindsay, *Dialog betuix Experience and ane Courteour,* 2382 and 2306, in Sir David Lindsay, *The Works of Sir David Lindsay of the Mount, 1490-1555,* ed. Douglas Hamer, STS 3rd ser. 1, 2, 6, 8, 4 vols. (Edin-burgh: Blackwood & Sons Ltd, 1931-36) I, 197-386.

[8]   See Geoffrey Chaucer, *The Riverside Chaucer,* ed. Larry D. Benson (Oxford: Oxford University Press, 1987) *Canterbury Tales,* X. 340; X. 603-6.

the words of blessing over the baptized child as part of a formal ceremony, and quite another to bless adults and cows in the home and in the fields; it was one thing to speak of the 'power' of prayers and sermons, but quite another to attribute to utterances a material efficacy.[9]

It was thus not merely superstitious but demonic, if one attempted to heal cattle by invoking St Bridget or by reciting the *Ave Maria* over them in their byres.

The latter accusation was laid against Agnes Sampson, a midwife, cunning woman, and diviner from Haddington, who is known to history as one of the alleged ringleaders of the North Berwick witches, accused of plotting with the devil to murder King James VI on his return from Denmark in 1590.[10] Their subsequent trial in Edinburgh in January 1591 is one of the most notorious episodes in Scottish history.[11] Agnes Sampson (also known by other names such as Annie Simpson) was eventually found guilty and sentenced to death. The many detailed charges against her were listed in the *dittay,* or indictment, preserved in the Books of Adjournal that record trials and court decisions of the sixteenth and seventeenth centuries, and now in the National Archives of Scotland (NRS, JC 2/2, fols. 201-206v). They contain two particularly interesting verse charms or conjurations that Agnes Sampson is said to have used for healing sick people or animals.[12] Since the witch trials were so sensational — in view of the king's involvement — there was enormous interest in England. The English ambassador, Robert Bowes, in a letter to Lord Burghley (23 February 1591), included an account of them compiled by a Scotsman; this account also contains copies of the two charms (National Archives, State Papers 52/47).[13]

---

[9]   Stuart Clark, 'Protestant Demonology: Sin, Superstition, and Society,' *Early Modern European Witchcraft: Centres and Peripheries*, eds. Bengt Ankarloo and Gustav Henningsen (Oxford: Clarendon Press, 1990) 66-67.

[10]   See Lawrence Normand and Gareth Roberts, eds., *Witchcraft in Early Modern Scotland: King James VI's Demonology and the North Berwick Witches* (Exeter: University of Exeter Press, 2000) 241-42 (item 46) [Henceforth Normand and Roberts].

[11]   There is a vast literature on this subject, but for an excellent general introduction, see Julian Goodare, *The Scottish Witch-Hunt in Context* (Manchester: Manchester University Press, 2002).

[12]   These were first printed by *Ancient Criminal Trials in Scotland Compiled from the Original Records and MSS*, ed. Robert Pitcairn, 3 vols. (Edinburgh: Bannatyne Club, 1833) I, 234-47 [Henceforth Pitcairn]. A modernized text is also printed in Normand and Roberts, 231-46. Unfortunately, neither text is wholly accurate.

[13]   The letter of Robert Bowes, together with the Scottish report, is printed in *Calendar of the State Papers Relating to Scotland*, eds. William Kenneth Boyd and Henry W. Meikle (Edinburgh: H.M. General Register House, 1936) X, item 526, pp. 462-67 [Henceforth *CSPS*]. There are some inaccuracies in the transcription.

The shorter charm, 'All kindis of illis that ewir may be', must have circulated in Edinburgh legal circles, because a third unpublished copy of it is preserved, along with other miscellaneous jottings by the Clerks of Chancery, on a formerly blank page in the Responds Book, Register of Signatures (NAS, E 30/ 13, fol. 61). Although most of the material in this volume of the Register of Signatures is dated 1580-81, the charm, which is here entitled 'Agnes Samsonis orisoun', was presumably entered much later, at a time when interest in the trial was at its height. The other entries on the page unfortunately do not aid the dating. One, written in the same hand as the charm, is a short untraced prose prophecy, here attributed to 'mr Iohne Capgraith [?Capgrave] Inglisman'; the other, in a different hand, is a verse riddle included in the Bannatyne Manuscript.[14]

Further light on this particular charm is shed by the existence of an earlier English text that appears to be its source. This is preserved in the Register of Missenden Abbey, Buckinghamshire (British Library, Sloane MS 747, fol. 57r). The work is a collection of Latin documents relating to the possessions of the abbey, compiled in the reign of Henry VII; the charm and many other miscellaneous items in English are thought to have been added c. 1501-1506.[15] These are mostly religious and didactic in character; the page on which the charm occurs also contains lists of the ten commandments and the seven deadly sins. Although the English charm cannot be precisely dated, it must have been circulating in England in the fifteenth century, and probably reached Scotland at least a century before it was recorded at the trial of Agnes Sampson.

I print here first the Scots version of the charm (based on NRS, JC 2/2, fol. 205), collated with the texts in E (Register of Signatures) and B (Bowes' letter); secondly the English version.

All kindis of illis that ewir may be,
In Crystis name I coniure the.
I coniure the, baith mair and les,
With all the vertewis of the mes.
And rycht sa be the naillis sa   5
That naillit Iesus, and na ma,
And rycht sa be the samin blude
That raikit owre the ruithfull rwid,
Furth of the flesch and of the bane
And in the eird and in the stane,   10
I coniure the, in Godis name.

---

14 For more information on the latter, see Priscilla Bawcutt, 'The Contents of the Bannatyne Manuscript: New Sources and Analogues,' *Journal of the Edinburgh Bibliographical Society* 3 (2008): 115-16.
15 For a brief account of the manuscript and its contents, see William A. Ringler Jr, *Bibliography and Index of English Verse in Manuscript, 1501–1558. Prepared and Completed by Michael Rudick and Susan J. Ringler* (London: Mansell, 1992) 33. Ringler classifies the piece (no. 1822) as 'Medical'.

Textual notes.
1. illis] euill E evils B
3. baith mair] both more B
6. Iesus] deir Iesus B
8. owre] on E over B ruithfull] michtefull E
9. Furth] Out E and of] and in E
10. Line missing in B

> Medicina pro morbo caduco & le fevre.
> In nomine patris et filii et spiritus sancti Amen.

> What manere of ivell thou be,
> In Goddes name I coungere the.
> I counger the with the holy crosse
> That Iesus was done on with fors.
> I con[g]ure the with nayles thre   5
> That Iesus was nayled vpon the tree.
> I coungere the with the crowne of thorne
> That on Iesus hede was done with skorne.
> I coungere the with the precious blode
> That Iesus shewyd vpon the rode.   10
> I coungere the with woundes five
> That Iesus suffred be his lyve.
> I coungere [the] with that holy spere
> That Longenus to Iesus hert can bere.
> I coungere the neuerthelesse   15
> With all the vertues of the masse,
> And all the holy prayeres of seynt Dorathe.[16]

Textual notes.
5. MS conure.
13. the] Not in MS.

How significant are the differences between these versions of the charm? The English text is longer, and much more overtly Catholic, invoking the instruments of the Passion with a reverence that resembles the tracts in the famous pre-Reformation Scottish devotional anthology, British Library, MS Arundel 285.[17] The Scottish version retains

---

[16]   This charm is also published in *Secular Lyrics*, no. 65; and *Lyrics*, no. 103. My readings occasionally differ.
[17]   *Devotional Pieces in Verse and Prose from MS. Arundel 285 and MS. Harleian 6919*, ed. J. A. W. Bennett, STS 3rd ser. 23 (Edinburgh: Scottish Text Society, 1955). On the background, see A. A. MacDonald, 'Passion Devotion in Late-Medieval Scotland,' *The Broken Body. Passion Devotion in Late-Medieval Culture*, eds. A. A. MacDonald, H. N. B. Ridderbos and R. M. Schlusemann (Groningen: Forsten, 1998).

some original rhymes (in lines 1-2, 3-4, 7-8), but is obviously abridged. It omits key references to the Crown of Thorns, the Five Wounds, and the Centurion Longinus and his spear, whom it was not uncommon to invoke in charms to staunch bleeding. The omission of St Dorothy is less surprising. Her cult was possibly less popular in medieval Scotland than England — she does not figure in the fourteenth-century Scottish *Legends of the Saints*, for instance, nor is she mentioned in Sir David Lindsay's satiric list of saints idolatrously worshipped in sixteenth-century Scotland.[18] Even in the English text Dorothy seems indeed something of an afterthought — one wonders if the scribe had a special devotion to that saint. Nonetheless the Scottish charm does keep the unambiguously Catholic appeal to 'the vertewis of the mes'.

Line five of the Scottish charm appears corrupt, although it is difficult to supply a satisfactory emendation. There is a clumsy repetition of *sa* within the line, and the phrase *na ma* (6) would imply that a definite number of nails had been mentioned, as in the English text. The devotional tradition of the Crucifixion was as specific concerning the Three Nails as the Five Wounds. In Walter Kennedy's *Passioun of Christ*, Thomas thus says that he would only believe in the risen Christ, when 'in his handis and his feit I see / All the taikynnis of the nalis thre' (1588-9). A graphic illustration of 'The Measure of the Nails', taken from Henry VIII's prayer roll, is provided by Eamon Duffy.[19]

Lines 9-10 of the Scottish charm are peculiarly interesting, since they have no equivalent in the English text. The 'illis' that are here addressed, may not be simply conjured away into thin air, but must be transferred to some other location:

> Furth of the flesch and of the bane
> And in the eird and in the stane.

In his *Discours des Sorciers* (c.1590), Henri Boguet (*c.* 1550-1619) remarked on cures performed by witches: 'the cure is only effective for a limited time, or else it is necessary for the sickness to be transferred to someone else'.[20] Such a belief might have alarming consequences, as is evident from the remarks of Robert Kirk, writing later in the seventeenth century, concerning charmers in the Highlands:

> There are words instituted for transferring of the soul or sickness on other Persons Beasts, Trees, Waters, Hills or Stones, according as the Charmer is pleased to name … which scares many sober persons among the Tramontanes from going in to see a sick person,

---

18 See Lindsay, *Dialog*, 2325-85.
19 See Walter Kennedy, *The Poems of Walter Kennedy*, ed. Nicole Meier, STS 5th ser. 6 (Woodbridge: Scottish Text Society, 2008); and Duffy, *Stripping of the Altars* plate no. 110.
20 For this citation, see Henry Boguet, *An Examen of Witches Drawn from Various Trials*, trans. E. Allen Ashwin, ed. A. J. A. M. Summers, 1971 ed. (London: John Rodker, 1929) 108.

till they put a dog in befor them or one that perteans to the house: For where charmers are cherished they transfer the sickness on the first living creature that enters after the charm is pronunced.[21]

The second charm attributed to Agnes Sampson is preserved in two witnesses: the *dittay* (fols 204r-v), and Robert Bowes' letter to Lord Burghley.

I trow in almychtie God that wrocht
Baith heavin and erth and all of nocht.
In to his deare sone Chryst Iesu,
In to that anaplie lord I trow,
Wes gottin of the haly gaist   5
Borne of the Virgin Marie.
Stoppit to heavin that all weill[dand]
And sittis att his faderis rycht hand.
He baid ws cum, and thair to [deme]
Baith quick and deid as he thocht [queme].   10
I trow als in the haly gaist,
In haly kirk my hoip is maist,
That haly schip quhair hallowaris winnis,
To ask forgevenes of my sinnis
And syne to ryis in flesch and bane   15
The lyffe that newir mair hes gane (?)
Thou sayis, lord, lovit mot ye be,
That formd and maid mankynd of me,
Thow coft me on the [h]aly croce,
And lent me body, saull and voce,   20
And ordanit me to heavinnis bliss,
Quhairefore I thank the lord of this.
And all your hallowaris lovit be,
To pray to thame to pray for me
And keep me fra that fellon fea   25
And from the syn that saull wald slay.
Thow lord, for thy bytter passioun,
To keip me frome syn and wardlie schame
And endles damnatioun,
Grant me the joy newir wilbe gane.
Sweit Iesus Cristus Amen.   30

---

[21]   Robert Kirk, *The Secret Common-Wealth & A Short Treatise of Charms and Spels*, ed. Stewart Sanderson, Mistletoe series (Cambridge: D.S. Brewer, 1976) 109.

Textual Notes: copy-text JC (the *dittay*); B (Bowes); *CSPS* transcript

1. in] intil B til CSPS
2. Baith] Both B
4. anaplie B aullholie CSPS
5. haly gaist] holie ghost B
7. Stoppit] Steppit B
    weilldand] ed. conj. weill yane JC wene than B went then *CSPS*
8. faderis] fathers B
9. deme] ed. conj. dome JC B
10. queme] ed. conj. conuene JC quhome B
16. hes] is B
25. fra] from B
28. and] not in B

Most later commentators have been struck by the Christian orthodoxy of this charm. Pitcairn described it as 'a doggerel version of the Apostles' Creed',[22] and Normand and Roberts called it 'impeccably orthodox'.[23] The charm does indeed contain the main outlines of the Creed, although it oddly omits one important clause concerning Jesus's crucifixion, death and descent into hell. Jesus, in Dunbar's succinct version of the Creed, was

> Off Mary borne, on croce deid and discendit,
> The thrid day rais, to the faderis rycht hand ascendit.[24]

There seems no obvious reason for this omission — perhaps it may be attributed to forgetfulness on the part of Agnes, or carelessness on the part of the scribe. Similar metrical versions of the Creed were common in Middle English, usually based on the Latin, but varying considerably in length and metrical form.[25] There also exists an interesting Scottish parallel, copied on a blank page of the Makculloch Manuscript (Edinburgh University Library, Laing III.149, fol. 87v).[26] This consists of twenty-one lines, arranged in slightly irregular rhyme royal stanzas. There is no close verbal resemblance, however, apart from the opening lines:

> I trow in god the fader almychty
> Makar of hewyne and erd and alkyne thing.

---

[22] Pitcairn, 234.

[23] Normand and Roberts, 208.

[24] 'The Tabill of Confessioun', in William Dunbar, *The Poems of William Dunbar*, ed. Priscilla Bawcutt, 2 vols. (Glasgow: Association for Scottish Literary Studies, 1998) no. 83/60-61.

[25] *NIMEV* lists 16 examples in its Index. For discussion, see R. H. Bower, 'Three Middle English Poems on the Apostles' Creed,' *PMLA* 70 (1955).

[26] The text is printed in *Pieces from the Makculloch and the Gray MSS together with the Chepman and Myllar Prints*, ed. George S. Stevenson, STS 1st ser. 65 (Edinburgh: W. Blackwood and Sons, 1918) 19.

The charm was termed a devilish prayer, however, despite its orthodoxy, because of the use to which it was put, which involved the practise of divination, a skill that Agnes was said to have learnt from her father. According to Robert Bowes' informant, Agnes Sampson 'understude be her said prayer gif the patient wald die or leive'; and in the *dittay* itself it is said that if she halted in its recitation over the sick person, she refused to visit him further, because she knew he would die.[27]

The language of sacred texts often preserves ancient words, idioms and formulaic expressions that with the passage of time have dropped out of common use. Charms are no exception to this, their literal sense sometimes being misunderstood by later users, copyists and even scholars. This is particularly evident in this charm, and may be a sign of its antiquity. The word *anaplie* (4), for instance, is likely to baffle many modern readers. Pitcairn commented: '"Anaplie" seems to be written for *aneplie*, "aefald", "afald", literally *one-fold*, "sincere, without guile, &c."'[28] The editors of *CSPS* could make no sense of the word either, and mistranscribed it as *aullholie*. The historical dictionaries, however, show that the word was current throughout the middle ages, that it derived from an OE word *anlepi3*, and that it had such senses as 'only, sole, single, unique'.[29] It is probable that the word was becoming archaic by the end of the fifteenth century, since the latest occurrence in *MED* is dated before 1450. What is also striking is that the word is most commonly used, as here, in vernacular versions of the Creed, of Jesus the 'only' begotten son of God.

Although Normand and Roberts gloss this rare word correctly as 'single, sole, unique', a few everyday words have, unfortunately, defeated them. *Coft* in 'Thow coft me on the haly croce' (19) is not only misprinted as *cost,* but rendered as 'made an exchange for'. Yet *coft* was a common Scots word, and makes good sense as 'bought, redeemed'. It was frequently used in a theological sense of the redemption of man effected by the Crucifixion. Henryson wrote of 'Chryst that deit on tre / And coft our synnis deir' in *The Bludy Serk* (102), and in *The Gude and Godlie Ballatis* a repentant sinner says:

> I was sauld, and thow me bocht,
> With thy blude thow hes me coft.[30]

---

[27] *CSPS*, 465; Normand and Roberts, 208 and 233.
[28] Pitcairn, 234.
[29] For discussion and copious illustration of the usage in Scots and Middle English, see *DOST, anelape; MED, onlepi;* and *OED, anlepi, onlepy, onelepi, lepi.*
[30] See Robert Henryson, *The Poems of Robert Henryson*, ed. Denton Fox (Oxford: Clarendon Press, 1981) 161; and *A Compendious Book of Godly and Spiritual Songs Commonly known as The Gude and Godlie Ballatis, Reprinted from the Edition of 1567*, ed. A. F. Mitchell, STS 1st ser. 39 (Edinburgh: William Blackwood and Sons, 1897) 220.

Fellon fea (25) has likewise received bizarre modern interpretations, being transcribed by one scholar as *sellon sea*,[31] and explained by Normand and Roberts as 'terrible inheritance, i.e. original sin'. But, as the rhyme with *slay* suggests, *fea* is a late sixteenth-century spelling for a word more commonly spelt *fa*, 'foe, enemy', and the reference is to man's ancient foe, the Devil. The same alliterative formula is found in Richard Holland's *Howlat* (746): 'The fende is our felloune fa'.[32]

Even in the sixteenth century some words in this text were already posing problems. Both scribes appear to have had difficulty with lines 9-10, which in the unemended text of the *dittay* read:

> He baid ws cum and thair to dome
> Baith quick and deid as he thocht conuene.

The rhyme here is clearly faulty, yet the sense is not obviously improved by B's reading *quhome* instead of *conuene*. As these lines refer to the Last Judgment, *dome* might at first seem highly appropriate. The sense of line 10, however, requires a verb — Christ will come to *judge* the living and the dead — and *deme* seems a better reading than *dome*. The puzzling last word of line 10 is likely to be an error for *queme*, a mostly northern and Scottish adjective, with a range of senses, of which the first in *DOST* — 'fit, proper, right' — provides excellent sense.[33] It is interesting that the usage here is remarkably close to that found in several passages in the fourteenth-century Scottish *Legends of the Saints*. These two lines resemble a passage that describes Jesus in heaven, sitting

> of god, his faddyr, one þe rycht hand,
> & sal cum thine, ȝe vndirstand,
> þe quek & ded bath to deme
> on domysday, as hym think queme.[34]

Other instances of this formulaic usage occur elsewhere in references to the Last Judgment in *The Legends of the Saints*, and also in *Cursor Mundi*.[35] It is possible to devise a palaeographical explanation for both misreadings of the word *queme*. The letter *q* was sometimes confused with *quh*, as was *e* with *o*; hence *queme > quhome*. In the case of

[31] P. G. Maxwell-Stuart, *Satan's Conspiracy: Magic and Witchcraft in Sixteenth-Century Scotland* (East Linton, Scotland: Tuckwell Press, 2001) 20.

[32] For the context, see *The Buke of the Howlat*, in *Longer Scottish Poems Volume One 1375-1650*, eds. Priscilla Bawcutt and Felicity J. Riddy (Edinburgh: Scottish Academic Press, 1987) 74. This alliterative phrase was often applied to the devil; cf. citations in *DOST, fa*.

[33] The word derives from OE. *gecweme*. On its later history and uses, see *DOST, queme; MED, queme; OED, queme*.

[34] *Legends of the Saints in the Scottish Dialect of the Fourteenth Century*, ed. W. M. Metcalfe, STS 1st ser. 13/18; 23/25; 35/37, 3 vols. (Edinburgh: Blackwood and Sons, 1888-96) I, 155/183-84.

[35] *Ibid.*, II, 207/95-96; 258/1235-36; citation from *Cursor Mundi*, in *MED, queme(e, 1 (a).*

conuene, it is likely that the scribe misunderstood a badly written *q* as the common contraction for the prefix *con-*.[36]

There remain other obscurities in the text that cannot be easily solved, such as the sense of *haly schip* (13). Normand and Roberts take it as 'holy ship', whereas *DOST* glosses as 'a holy place'. The line corresponds to that part of the Creed which speaks of the *Communio Sanctorum*, a late clause that has provoked much discussion but is usually interpreted as the fellowship of all holy persons.[37] Also puzzling is the second half of line 7 that in the *dittay* reads 'all weill thane'. The poor rhyme and dislocated syntax are ignored by Normand and Roberts, who explain as 'So that all was then well, i.e. after Christ's Ascension'. My emendation is based on the need to provide a rhyme with *hand* (8) and a subject for the verb *stoppit*, 'stepped, ascended'. I take it to be a compound noun: *all-weilldand*, signifying 'the all-ruling, the almighty', i.e. God. This word can be traced to Old English, and was employed in northern Middle English and Scots, usually as a participial adjective.[38] It was regularly applied to God, and occasionally, as here, specifically to the second person of the Trinity.

Other charms were associated with Agnes Sampson's name, long after her execution. George Sinclair, author of *Satan's Invisible World Discovered* (1685), commented on her use of 'Long Scriptural Prayers and Rhyms, containing the main points of Christianity so that she may seem not so much a white Witch as an holy Woman'.[39] He quotes one 'Nonsensical Rhym' that opens 'White Pater Noster, God was my foster'. A second is termed 'The Black *Pater Noster*':

> Four newks in this house for haly Angels,
> A post in the midst, that's Christ Jesus,
> Lucas, Marcus, Matthew, Joannes,
> God be into this house, and all that belangs us.[40]

The prayer, of which this is a Scottish version, has a very long history. As Iona and Peter Opie noted, 'its beginning lies centuries deep, and it is part of the living traditional matter in most European countries'.[41] In some form it was known to Chaucer, who alludes in 'The Miller's Tale' to what he terms the white *pater noster*:

---

[36] For illustrations, see Grant G. Simpson, *Scottish Handwriting 1150-1650* (Aberdeen: Aberdeen University Press, 1986) 44, item 6, plate 1. Also *The Sex Werkdays and Agis*, ed. L. A. J. R. Houwen (Groningen: Forsten, 1990) 24.

[37] See J. N. D. Kelly, *Early Christian Creeds*, 3rd ed. (Harlow: Longman, 1972) 388-97.

[38] See *DOST, all-weldand*; *MED, al-welding*.

[39] Quotations come from George Sinclair, *Satans Invisible World Discovered* (Edinburgh: T.G. Stevenson, 1871) 22.

[40] *Ibid.* 22-23.

[41] *The Oxford Dictionary of Nursery Rhymes*, eds. Iona Opie and Peter Opie (Oxford: Clarendon Press, 1952) 304.

Therwith the nyght-spel seyde he anon-rightes
On foure halves of the hous aboute,
And on the threshfold of the dore withoute:
'Jhesu Crist and Seinte Benedight,
Blesse this hous from every wikked wight,
For nyghtes verye, the white *pater noster*!'[42]

Thomas Ady, an English contemporary of Sinclair, recorded a version, very similar to that still familiar to English children, in *A Candle in the Dark: Or a Treatise concerning the Nature of Witches and Witchcraft* (1656). His source was 'an old woman in Essex who was living in my time'. She 'had learned many Popish charms, one whereof was this: every night when she lay down to sleep she charmed her Bed, saying:

Matthew, Mark, Luke and John,
The Bed be blest that I lye on.

This she claimed to have been taught 'by the Church-men of those times'.[43]

Another long-forgotten Scottish charm occurs in a fifteenth-century chartulary belonging to the Cistercian convent at Coldstream, founded in the twelfth century by Gospatric, Earl of Dunbar (British Library, MS Harley 6670). This collection of charters and other muniments was copied by John Lawrence, a notary public, who recorded its completion on 3 April 1434 (fol. 55).[44] The charm is recorded on a blank leaf (now foliated as 56r), and written in a different hand, probably of the late fifteenth or early sixteenth century. Although laid out as prose, it consists of three rough four-stress couplets, followed by a direction to utter the name of the person afflicted, then another couplet and directions for various prayers.

For blud stanchyn
Lord, as thow was don on rud,
Throw thi mychtfulnes stem this blud.
Fader and son and haly gast
Stem and stanch this blud in hast.
Suchtfast lord in personis thre   5
I nem this nam in nam of the

---

[42] Chaucer, *Riverside Chaucer, Canterbury Tales*, I. 3480-85.

[43] Thomas Ady, *A Candle in the Dark: or, A Treatise Concerning the Nature of Witches & Witchcraft* (London: printed for R.I. to be sold by Tho. Newberry, 1656) 58.

[44] See *Chartulary of the Cistercian Priory of Coldstream with Relative Documents*, ed. Rev. Charles Rogers, Grampian Club Publications (London: Grampian Club, 1879). For further information, and transcripts of the charters; also Ian B. Cowan, David Edward Easson and Richard Neville Hadcock, *Medieval Religious Houses: Scotland. With an Appendix on the Houses in the Isle of Man*, 2nd ed. (London: Longman, 1976) 145-46.

And than say the man or woman name and
That ilka forbyddyn (?) forbyd I the
That Ihesu partit land and se.
And than say v paternosteris and v awe maryas and a creid and say this oryson
thris and ilk tym wyth v paternostris and v awe maryas and a creid, and gif it
stanchis nocht quhen it is said thris, than say it ix tymis.[45]

Charms designed to stem the flow of blood are very common, and several Middle English examples survive. One, as yet unpublished, has a very similar incipit to this: 'Lord as thow hange vpon the rode'.[46] What appear to be vestiges of a Gaelic charm of this type exist, written in the late fourteenth or early fifteenth century on the Murthly Hours (NLS, MS 21000).[47] The Scots charm is simple, yet characteristic of the genre in its appeal to Christ, who shed his own blood on the cross, to 'Stem and stanch this blud in hast'. The devotional cult of the Holy Blood was then at the height of its popularity. No less traditional is the number symbolism, with the stress on three (explicitly mentioning the persons of the Trinity in line 5), and five (recalling though not mentioning the Five Wounds of Christ). Other charms are sometimes more explicit: 'sey thys Charme fyue times with fyue Paternosters, in the worschep of the fyue woundys'.[48] The sense of the last couplet is obscure, but seems to allude to the well-known legend that the River Jordan stood still on the day that Jesus was baptised. Many charms devised to staunch blood, known as the so-called *Flum Jordan* type, allude to this legend; in Middle English they commonly began with some version of the line 'Crist was born in Bethlehem' (see *NIMEV* 624, 993, 993.11, and 2451.77).[49]

Many other charms probably circulated in sixteenth-century Scotland. One such is recalled in a mysterious and haunting couplet recorded in *The Complaynt of Scotland* (printed *c.* 1550):

Arthour knycht he raid on nycht
Vitht gyltin spur and candil lycht.[50]

---

[45] The charm is printed, with some inaccuracies, in *Chartulary*, 44-45. It is followed by a note, in a different hand, on *dies mali*, 'unlucky days'.
[46] See *NIMEV*, 1946.5 (Rylands, Latin MS 228, fol. 74).
[47] Cf. the note by Ronald Black in John Higgitt, *The Murthly Hours. Devotion, Literacy and Luxury in Paris, England and the Gaelic West*, The British Library Studies in Medieval Culture (London: British Library, 2000) 339-40.
[48] Black, *Folk-Medicine* 76, 79-80.
[49] See the charm printed in *The Oxford Book of Late Medieval Verse and Prose*, ed. Douglas Gray (Oxford: Oxford University Press, 1989) 137; also Gray, 'Charms,' 62.
[50] *The Complaynt of Scotland, c. 1550*, ed. A. M. Stewart, STS 4th ser. 11 (Edinburgh: Scottish Text Society, 1979) 50. Many titles have long been unidentified; see Priscilla Bawcutt, 'A Song from *The Complaynt of Scotland*: 'My Hart is Leiuit on the Land',' *N&Q* 247 (2002).

This occurs, written as prose, in the famous pastoral interlude that describes how Scottish shepherds and their wives passed the time with songs, tales and dances. It is sandwiched between the titles of romances well-known in Scotland, some Arthurian — e.g. 'Lancelot du lac' and 'Gauen [Gawain] and gollogras'.[51] The closest analogy to these two lines, however, is found not in an Arthurian romance but in a charm recorded in the nineteenth century, and communicated by a Shetlander to the scholar and journalist Karl Blind, who printed it in 1879:[52]

> Arthur Knight
> He rade a' night,
> Wi' open swird
> An' candle light.
> He sought da mare;
> He fan' da mare;
> He bund da mare
> Wi' her ain hair.
> And made da mare
> To swear:
> 'At she should never
> Bide a' night
> Whar ever she heard
> O' Arthur Knight.

The 'mare' in this charm is the nightmare, which was believed to afflict both humans and animals. Another version was recorded by Mrs J. M. E. Saxby from the Shetlands at almost the same time, which differs chiefly in its opening phrase: 'De man o' meicht / he rod a' neicht'.[53]

Both these nineteenth-century Scottish charms correspond closely to a medieval English one, later versions of which survive from the sixteenth century. This English charm, however, invoked the protective powers not of 'Arthur Knight' or a mysterious unnamed man of might but St George:

---

[51] On these, see Rhiannon Purdie, 'Medieval Romance in Scotland,' *A Companion to Medieval Scottish Poetry*, eds. Priscilla J. Bawcutt and Janet Hadley Williams (Cambridge: D.S. Brewer, 2006).

[52] See Karl Blind, 'Discovery of Odinic Songs in Shetland,' *The Nineteenth Century* 5 (1879): 1106. I am much indebted to Jacqueline Simpson, for communicating to me her discoveries about these charms, later published as Jaqueline Simpson, 'The Nightmare Charm in *King Lear*,' *Charms, Charmers and Charming: International Research on Verbal Magic*, ed. Jonathan Roper (Basingstoke: Palgrave Macmillan, 2009).

[53] See Rev. Biot Edmondston and J. M. E. Saxby, *The Home of a Naturalist*, 2nd ed. (London: James Nisbet & Co., 1889) 186-87. Both of the Shetland versions are cited in *County Folklore. Printed Extracts No. 5: Examples of Printed Folklore Concerning the Orkney and Shetland Islands*, eds. G. F. Black and N. W. Thomas, Publications of the Folk-lore Society (London: David Nutt, 1903) 145.

Seynt Iorge, our lady kny3th,
He walked day, he walked ny3th,
Till that he fownde that fowle wy3th;
And whan that he here fownde,
He here bete and he here bownde,
Till trewly ther here trowthe sche ply3th
That sche sholde not come be ny3hte,
With-inne vij rode of londe space
Ther as Seynt Ieorge I-namyd was.[54]

This, the oldest English version, was particularly associated with the healing of horses: according to the rubric, it was to be written in a bill, and hung either over the stable door or in the horse's mane. A later but similar version was quoted by Thomas Blundevill in *Fower Chiefyst Offices of Horsemanshippe* (1566) in a section on horse diseases; rather defensively he claimed to have included it, in part to make the reader laugh, and said contemptuously that it was 'a fonde foolishe charme' invented by 'the false Fryers in times past' to extract money from the gullible.[55]

But what is the sense of 'Arthur Knight' or 'Arthour knycht'? Karl Blind asserted that 'Arthur Knight' was 'a substitution for the Germanic god of storms and battles', i.e. Odin, and also claimed that 'in half romantic, half boorish form, an Odinic myth is thus preserved in this Nightmare incantation'.[56] This assertion is wholly unconvincing. But should we then interpret the phrase as signifying King Arthur himself? This too seems mistaken. Grammatically, 'Arthur' in the phrase 'Arthur knight' is best interpreted as an example of the rare uninflected zero-genitive, which in Older Scots was commonly found with nouns of relationship ending in –r (examples are 'sister son' and 'brother dochter').[57] Such zero-genitives are said to occur occasionally with personal names, and the fact that *Arthur* ends in -r is probably significant. Indeed one can find other instances of this very construction in sixteenth-century Scottish verse: what we today call 'Arthur's Seat' in Edinburgh appears as 'Arthour Sait' in Bannatyne's text of

---

[54]   *NIMEV*, 2903; see *Secular Lyrics*, no. 66.

[55]   Thomas Blundeville, *The Fower Chiefyst Offices Belongyng to Horsemanshippe* (London: VVyllyam Seres dwellyng at the west ende of Paules churche, 1566) 17; Iona Opie and Moira Tatem, *A Dictionary of Superstitions* (Oxford: Oxford University Press, 1990) 378.

[56]   Blind, 'Discovery,' 1108 and 1113.

[57]   For discussion of the zero-genitive in Scots, see A. J. Aitken, 'Variation and Variety in Written Middle Scots,' *Edinburgh Studies in English and Scots*, eds. A. J. Aitken, Angus McIntosh and Hermann Pálsson (1971) 179 and note 13. Caroline Macafee, in *DOST*, XII, cvi; and Anne King, 'The Inflectional Morphology of Older Scots,' *The Edinburgh History of the Scots Language*, ed. Charles Jones (Edinburgh: Edinburgh University Press, 1997) 165.

The Flyting of Dunbar and Kennedie, and as 'Arthure Sait' in one of the satirical poems attributed to Robert Sempill.[58]

In the world of Arthurian myth it was surely more common for one of the knights to ride out in search of adventure than for King Arthur himself. Even so, how does one account for the metamorphosis of St George into 'Arthur's knight'? Jacqueline Simpson has suggested that St George was possibly discarded in Scotland, 'as too English and too Catholic (especially when called "Our Lady's Knight")'.[59] It is true that by the later Middle Ages St George had become the patron saint of England, and the phrase 'Our Lady's Knight' was so often linked with his name in carols and religious lyrics that R. L. Greene called it his 'most hackneyed epithet'.[60] But devotion to this saint was by no means confined to the English. St George was widely popular throughout Europe, and evidence exists for his veneration in late medieval Scotland.[61] There are many parallels between the activities of a military saint, such as St George, and the exploits of the knights of King Arthur. Indeed in the ceremonies of the Order of the Garter St George was closely associated with the Arthurian world.[62] Dr Simpson's hypothesis is highly plausible, yet it is arguable that simple confusion of protective warriors, rather than nationalistic sentiment or Protestant censorship, might have led to the substitution of 'Arthour knycht' for St George.

'Arthour knycht', with its vivid imagery, is hardly typical of the verse charms discussed in this article, which are examples of the simplest and most elementary kind of poetry. Yet they are not completely lacking in verbal art. The traditional poetic formulae, alliteration, octosyllabic couplets, and other simple repetitions — 'I conjure thee ... I conjure thee' — would have lifted them out of the language of everyday, contributed to their incantatory effect, and made them easily memorable.

---

[58] See *The Bannatyne Manuscript Writtin in Tyme of Pest 1568*, ed. W. Tod Ritchie, STS 2nd ser. 22, 23, 26; 3rd ser. 5, 4 vols. (Edinburgh: Scottish Text Society, 1928-34) III, 55/336; *Satirical Poems of the Time of the Reformation*, ed. James Cranstoun, STS 1st ser. 20/24, 28/30, 2 vols. (Edinburgh: W. Blackwood and Sons, 1891, 1893) I, 169/118.

[59] Simpson, 'Nightmare Charm,' 103.

[60] *The Early English Carols*, ed. Richard Leighton Greene, 2nd ed. (Oxford: Oxford University Press, 1977) note to no. 311.1. For Scottish familiarity with this phrase, see also *Legends of the Saints in the Scottish Dialect of the Fourteenth Century*, ed. W. M. Metcalfe, STS 1st ser. 13/18; 23/25; 35/37, 3 vols. (Edinburgh: Blackwood and Sons, 1888-96) II, 176/14.

[61] See the valuable study by Steve Boardman, 'The Cult of St George in Scotland,' *Saints' Cults in the Celtic World*, eds. Steve Boardman, John Reuben Davies and Eila Williamson (Woodbridge: Boydell Press, 2009). Cf. Lindsay, *Dialog*, 2304; John Higgitt, *'Imageis maid with mennis hand': Saints, Images, Belief and Identity in Later Medieval Scotland*, Whithorn Lecture (Whithorn: Friends of the Whithorn Trust, 2003) *passim*; and David Ditchburn, *Scotland and Europe: The Medieval Kingdom and Its Contacts with Christendom, 1215-1545* (East Linton: Tuckwell, 2001) 55-56.

[62] Cf. Jonathan Good, *The Cult of Saint George in Medieval England* (Woodbridge: Boydell Press, 2009).

James Anderson's Poem *The Winter Night*

Jamie Reid-Baxter

The brief manuscript *Collections upon the life of Mr James Anderson* made by Robert Wodrow (1679-1734) begin thus:

> 'I doe not [find] this learned and pretty considerable man, minister of the Gospel in the parish of *Bendochie* in the presbitery of *Meigle* in the shire of *Angus,* taken notice of in any of our historians in print, though in our Assembly registers and in Calderwoods MS I find him severall times mentioned as a person of weight [and] influence. I take him to be likewise the author of a little poem that hath been once and again printed'.[1]

Anderson died in 1603, and the earliest known edition of his 'little poem' is dated 1595.[2] It was indeed 'once and again printed'; an edition of 1614 is extant, but the only title-page currently known dates from as late as 1713, and reads 'Ane godly treatis, callit the first and second cumming of Christ, to the toone of the Winter Night, showing plainly the blindness wherein were [sic] misled of in Popery, and the clear light of the Gospel now manifested in our days to the glory of God, and the comfort of all them that hope for Salvation'. Hereinafter referred to as *The Winter Night,* the poem runs to 837 lines, and like its author, it has hardly been 'taken notice of by any our historians in print', although it received several pages of discussion in a 1987 PhD thesis.[3]

Consideration of this poem is peculiarly appropriate to a volume honouring Alasdair MacDonald. His extensive work on Scottish religious verse includes several key articles

---

[1]   Glasgow University Library, Special Collections, MS Gen 1211 (no foliation).

[2]   Robert Dickson and John P. Edmond, *Annals of Scottish Printing: From the Introduction of the Art in 1507 to the Beginning of the Seventeenth Century, with Analytical Descriptions of Books Printed and an Index of Names, Subjects and Titles* (Cambridge: Macmillan and Bowes, 1890) 486: 'Ane godly treatis, calit the first and second cumming of Christ, with the tone of the winters-nicht: shewing brieflie of our native blindness. Be James Anderson, minister of Christ his Evangell. Edinburgh, Printed be Robert Smyth, dwelling at the Nether Bow. 1595'. They note a further edition of 1599, with the comment that Smith 'had 1134 copies in stock at the time of his death in 1602. No copy is known to us'.

[3]   Reverend Frank D. Bardgett, 'Families and Factions: The Scottish Reformation in Angus and the Mearns,' Ph.D., University of Edinburgh, 1987, 2 vols. Anderson is discussed, and his poem quoted, in chapter 7, 'Theological Conflict after 1560', pp. 307-10, 314-15, 318-22. I am extremely grateful to Dr Bardgett for giving me access to this and other related material.

on the subject of the militantly protestant *Gude and Godlie Ballatis*, and Anderson's *Winter Night* has a great deal in common with the didactic and anti-Roman propaganda material in that famous collection. Indeed, as will be shown below, *The Winter Night* shows the direct influence of at least two poems found in all editions of the *Ballatis*. Anderson's 'Treatis', however, is much more ambitious than anything in the *Ballatis*. It begins with eleven stanzas of dedicatory epistle, using 'Troilus verse' (*ababbcc* pentameters; also known as 'rhyme royal'). The poem proper consists of 85 stanzas of *rime couée* (*aaabcccb*, tetrameters and trimeters) on the Second Coming, and ends 'This Winter night it endeth here,/ To God bee praise for ay'. There follows a closing prayer, voiced in a further ten stanzas of *rime couée*. While almost entirely devoid of literary merit, the poem is of considerable historical interest. This essay, arguing that it was written in 1581-82, examines the reasons for its prolonged success with the Scottish public.

JAMES ANDERSON

A former Cistercian monk of the great abbey at Coupar Angus,[4] Anderson appears to have begun his career in the reformed church in 1567,[5] at Bendochy and Kettins, near Coupar Angus. In his manuscript *Collections,* Wodrow notes that he first found Anderson mentioned in the records of the March 1573 General Assembly of the Kirk,[6] and comments 'that meeting began to look into the corruption of the tulchan[7] *Bishops* ... having declared their power not to exceed that of a superintendent', to which he adds that the Assembly appointed Anderson one of the commissioners who were 'to conveene before the end of the Assembly and report... This makes me think that at this time Mr *Anderson* was of some standing in this ministry and of a good skill in the constitution and discipline of the church'.[8] Anderson's early anti-episcopal activity on behalf of the Assembly is entirely of a piece with his later being found as a member of the commission for Angus, appointed by the April 1581 General Assembly to 'tak care,

---

[4]   See Fr. Mark Dilworth, 'Monks and Ministers after 1560,' *RSCHS* 18 (1974): 207-08. Dilworth says Anderson must have professed between 1553 and 1558, and, being young, may not have been ordained priest before he embraced the Reformation of 1560. Of the poem's purple-faced raging against the Roman Church, Dilworth comments mildly that the language is anti-Papist.

[5]   See Charles H. Haws, *Scottish Parish Clergy at the Reformation, 1540-1574*, Scottish Record Society (Edinburgh: printed for the Society by Smith and Ritchie, 1972) 24, 251.

[6]   David Calderwood, *The History of the Kirk of Scotland*, ed. Thomas Thomson, 8 vols. (Edinburgh: Wodrow Society, 1842-49) III, 272.

[7]   Essentially clerical placemen appointed by the Crown and other lay patrons, as a means of siphoning off the revenue of the bishoprics. The term is discussed on p. 159 below.

[8]   Glasgow UL, Special Collections, MS Gen 1211.

and travell' to see presbyteries constituted[9] — a directly anti-episcopal move by the Kirk. The 1581 commission was headed by John Erskine of Dun (1509-1590), Superintendent of Angus since 1561. It was to this distinguished 'father of the Reformation' — Anderson's ecclesiastical superior since 1567 — that *The Winter Night* was dedicated.

In the heading to the dedicatory poem, Anderson is described as 'Minister at Collace'. He was presented to this charge on 18 August 1573. Collace lies six miles southwest of Coupar Angus, and Anderson had almost certainly been responsible for the parish before his official presentation thereto,[10] along with nearby Bendochy, Ketttins and Cargill.[11] In mid-1582, Anderson was transferred from this rural setting to the burgh of Stirling, one of the most important towns in Scotland, to replace the disgraced and excommunicated Robert Montgomerie as incumbent. In the autumn of 1581, against the express wishes of the Kirk, the Crown had appointed this man[12] to the archbishopric of Glasgow, in order to secure the bulk of the archbishopric's revenues for Esmé Stuart, the king's French cousin and all-powerful favourite. Esmé had arrived in Scotland in September 1579, and his personal charm swept the adolescent king off his feet; James rapidly raised the Frenchman first to the earldom and then the dukedom of Lennox. The long-simmering disagreement between the Crown and the Kirk over the matter of Kirk-governance escalated sharply with Montgomerie's appointment to Glasgow. Considerable physical violence was used to intrude him, and the government overruled the Kirk's proceedings against Montgomerie, including his excommunication in June 1582. The Kirk's anger played no small part in bringing Esmé's rule to an abrupt end in September 1582: James VI was taken hostage in August by the Earl of Gowrie and other disgruntled noblemen, to the delight of the General Assembly. The king's escape in July 1583 led to a second round of resolutely anti-presbyterian rule by James Stewart, Earl of Arran, who in 1584 imposed the 'Black Acts', severely restricting the Kirk's autonomy and reinforcing episcopacy. While a significant number of leading presbyterian clerics fled into English exile,[13] the aged Erskine of Dun negotiated a compromise for his clergy in Angus, reaping presbyterian opprobrium in consequence. Most of the exiles returned after Arran's fall in October 1585. The following year, the General Assembly appointed James Anderson commissioner

---

[9] See Calderwood, *History of the Kirk* III, 524.

[10] This is stated to be the case by Haws, *Scottish Parish Clergy* 44.

[11] Bendochy lies two miles north-west of Coupar Angus, Kettins is one and a half miles south-east. Cargill is six miles west of Coupar Angus, towards Perth.

[12] Duncan Shaw, 'Montgomerie, Robert (d.1609x11),' *Oxford Dictionary of National Biography* (Oxford: Oxford University Press, 2004).

[13] See Gordon Donaldson, 'Scottish Presbyterian Exiles in England, 1584-8,' *RSCHS* 14 (1960-2), reprinted in Gordon Donaldson, *Scottish Church History* (Edinburgh: Scottish Academic Press, 1985) 178-90.

for Dunblane,[14] a responsibility he retained until 1602,[15] long after his 1589 translation from Stirling back to Kettins.[16] Wodrow's *Collections* tell us that the (now lost) Assembly Records for 1593 showed Anderson in controversy, over an issue unknown, with Mr Henry Guthrie, the man who had succeeded him at Collace in 1582 and who would, in his turn, be transferred to Anderson's former charge of Bendochy in 1595.[17] James Anderson died on 31 December 1603.[18]

Introduction

The only printed comments on the poem which run to any length were published in 1851 by the Rev. Andrew Bonar, the Free Church minister of Collace.[19] Bonar argued that *The Winter Night* was written as late as 1588-89, and that its apocalyptic message and strident anti-Papalism are connected with the Spanish Armada. In his unpublished doctoral thesis, Frank Bardgett argued much more plausibly for 'c. 1580'; the heavy focus on the Jesuits found in Anderson's anti-Papalist diatribe almost certainly reflects the presence in Angus of Fr John Hay, S.J., protected by the earls of Errol and Morton, from January to October 1579. However, as noted earlier, I believe that the poem has much wider resonances and was written in 1581 or early 1582. The Crown refused to take action against Hay, and indeed, he had not even departed for France when Esmé Stuart arrived, to the grave alarm of the Kirk. As early as December 1580[20] the battle

---

[14] The records of Anderson's first visitations are extant, see James Kirk, ed., *Visitation of the Diocese of Dunblane and Other Churches, 1586-1589* (Edinburgh: Scottish Record Society, 1984).

[15] Calderwood, *History of the Kirk* VI, 164.

[16] Hew Scott, *Fasti Ecclesiae Scoticanae: The Succession of Ministers in the Parish Churches of Scotland, from the Reformation, A.D. 1560, to the Present Time*, 10 vols. (Edinburgh: W. Paterson, 1866-) IV, 318; Anderson's successor at Stirling was the unflinching Presbyterian Patrick Simson (1556-1618), one of the several clerical sons of the Perth schoolmaster (and later grammarian) Andrew Simson (d. *c*.1590), who embraced the Reformation and in 1562-64 was minister at Cargill, a charge of which James Anderson had the oversight 1568-70; see Haws, *Scottish Parish Clergy* 37.

[17] Scott, *Fasti* IV, 159; V, 437.

[18] *Ibid*.V, 263. Bardgett, 'Families and Factions,' II, 145, citing Anderson's testament dative (National Archives of Scotland, Register of Testaments, CC8/8/42 f.28v) says '31 Jan.1603/4'. Anderson left £474 13s. 4d.

[19] James Anderson, *The Winter Night*, ed. Andrew Bonar (Edinburgh: John Greig, 1851). To this octavo pamphlet of forty pages Bonar (future editor of *Letters, Communion Sermons* and *Quaint Sermons* of the great Presbyterian Samuel Rutherford) provided an introduction of fourteen pages.

[20] See Calderwood, *History of the Kirk* III, 480, 577-85, 620-25, 633-34. The escalation is discussed on pp. 165-166 below.

lines were already drawn for a court-Kirk conflict which would long outlive the favourite's regime.[21] It is my contention that Anderson's poem was actually written in direct response to the Robert Montgomerie scandal and Esmé Stuart's interference in ecclesiastical matters. Its long-lived success with the public, however, is due to the fact that Anderson did not name names, thus allowing later readers to apply its warnings to their own time.

Precisely the opposite is true of the other major poetic response to the court-Kirk confrontation of the 1580s. Robert Sempill's *The Legend of the Bischop of St Androis Lyfe, callit Mr Patrik Adamsoune,* alias *Cousteane,* was written in the autumn of 1584. As David Parkinson has shown, the 1292 lines of this attractive and entertaining *ad hominem* satire have many riches to offer.[22] *The Legend* is the sparkling work of an accomplished professional poet. Yet there is no evidence that it ever saw print. The doggerel of James Anderson's *Winter Night,* on the other hand, would enjoy a long printed afterlife, continuing to speak to subsequent generations of presbyterian readers. Indeed, it elicited a deep-felt poetic meditation entitled 'The winter nicht' from the gifted Elizabeth Melville, Lady Culross (*fl.* 1598-1631).[23] Intensely inward-looking and personal, Melville's 'Winter nicht' makes an interesting contrast with Anderson's homiletic *Agitprop* work, but unlike her popular *Godlie Dreame* (1603), it was never published. The latest known early edition of Anderson's *Winter Night,* from Robert Sanders of Glasgow, dates from 1713,[24] almost a century later than any of the eminently comparable (if shorter) sixteenth-century anti-Catholic poems to be found in the *The Gude and Godlie Ballatis.*

After 1713, however, *The Winter Night* disappeared from view and has remained shrouded in almost total darkness ever since. When Enlightenment antiquarians like John Pinkerton started to take an interest in sixteenth-century Scots poetry in the late eighteenth and early nineteenth centuries, Anderson's muse had no hope whatever of appealing to the prevailing poetic aesthetic. Even the militantly Calvinist historian

---

[21] The conflict would lead directly to the National Covenant of 1638, the ensuing Wars of the Three Kingdoms, and the execution of Charles I. It ended only when William of Orange returned the Kirk of Scotland to Presbyterian obedience in 1689.

[22] D. J. Parkinson, '*The Legend of the Bishop of St Androis Lyfe* and the Survival of Scottish Poetry,' *Early Modern Literary Studies* 9.1 (May, 2003): 5.1-24<URL: http://purl.oclc.org/emls/09-1/parkscot.html> (2003) (8 January 2011).

[23] Copied on fols. 173v-74v of Robert Bruce, *Sermons on Hebrews XI,* New College Library, Edinburgh, MS Bru 2, it is, like Anderson's poem, written in *rime couée* and runs to 244 lines. The introspective, private tone of this long spiritual meditation results in a poem very different from Anderson's work. Melville's poem is discussed in Jamie Reid-Baxter, 'Elizabeth Melville, Calvinism and the Lyric Voice,' *James VI and I, Scotland and Literature: Tides of Change, 1567-1625,* ed. D. J. Parkinson (Leuven: Peeters, forthcoming).

[24] Interestingly, Sanders issued editions of Lady Culross's *Godlie Dream* in 1686, 1698 and 1727.

Thomas McCrie wrote in 1819 that 'the excellence of this small work certainly does not lie in the poetry'.[25] *The Winter Night* was ignored by the tireless scholar David Laing, whose sympathies were admirably wide: for example, when he republished Melville's *Godlie Dreame* in 1826, he defended it against Pinkerton's derision, calling it 'a poem of considerable beauty and imagination'.[26] In Andrew Bonar, *The Winter Night* did have an admirer, however.[27] His introduction ends: 'People of Collace, young and old, you see by this Poem that it is nearly three centuries since in this place the silver trumpet proclaimed the coming Jubilee … The same message comes to you still'.[28] Bonar describes Anderson as 'evidently a man of considerable information and learning, and a scribe well instructed for the kingdom of heaven'. However, James Cranstoun, when editing *Satirical Poems of the Reformation* for the Scottish Text Society (1891-93), passed over *The Winter Night,* even though he took a very broad view of what constituted satire. Frank Bardgett says that the poem's 'most attractive feature is its Christology', expressed in 'terse, ambitious and occasionally over-strained verse'. He notes that 'both Erskine of Dun and Anderson … denied the value of "good works" before God', but adds that Anderson 'displays a way with words which surpasses his superintendent', and may have had 'an effective, if repetitious, pulpit style'.[29] Scholarly interest in *The Winter Night* has not been helped by the fact that the earliest witness currently known is an incomplete single copy from 1614. Like the 1713 Glasgow edition, this edition contains numerous typographical errors, and eschews any consistent form of orthography — a fact which, thanks to things like the apparent rhyming of 'long/gang' or 'approued/ grieued', and the omission of final –*is*, makes Anderson's uncertain grasp of the basics of verse composition seem even poorer than it actually was.

Anderson's verse epistle dedicatory to Erskine of Dun

John Erskine, laird of Dun, is a well-known and important historical figure, a true 'father' of the Scottish Reformation.[30] The text of Anderson's verse dedication has

---

[25] Thomas McCrie, *The Life of Melville*, 2 vols. (Edinburgh: Blackwood, 1819) II, 21. McCrie quotes three stanzas from the 1614 edition of the poem, an edition unknown to Andrew Bonar.

[26] *Early Metrical Tales Including the History of Sir Egeir, Sir Gryme, and Sir Gray-Steill*, ed. David Laing (Edinburgh: W. & D. Laing, 1826) xxxiii.

[27] Bonar used the 1713 edition as his base-text, but inserted several sub-headings, and suggested various verbal emendations.

[28] Bonar rejected Anderson's sixteenth-century post-millennialism: 'In our day, we are only looking forward to the "thousand years" and we regard the *revealing* of the Man of Sin as the full development of the "Mystery of Iniquity"' (Anderson, *The Winter Night* 14).

[29] Bardgett, 'Families and Factions,' I, 307-10.

[30] See D. F. Wright, 'Erskine, John, of Dun (1509?1590),' *Oxford Dictionary of National Biography* (Oxford: Oxford University Press, 2004). See also Frank D. Bardgett, 'John Erskine of Dun: a Theologi-

survived complete only in the 1713 print.[31] It begins by praising Erskine's impeccable protestant credentials:

> Right ancient Professor of the Trueth
> Long time before it came to com*m*on sight,[32]
> Such perillous time thou passedst not with slouth
> But hardily didst hazard day and night
> To bring the Trueth to libertie and light. [1-5]

The first eight stanzas instance Erskine's godly achievements over the decades. Anderson notes, with a quotation from *The Gude and Godlie Ballatis,* that it pleased 'Christ Iesus King of grace'[33] to call Erskine 'to that dignitie/ To plant his Kirke in *Gowrie, Mernes, and Angus,*/ Which prudently thou hast planted among us'. Erskine has laboured 'faithfully,/ Till infirme age perforce constrained thee', so that he can 'not from thy Chamber journey farre'. Anderson then pays personal tribute to the Superintendent:

> Beside those fruits shown forth in general,
> As common comfort to all before exprest:
> I found thy favor my self in special
> Most kindly Kyth on me amongst the rest.
> Yea, undeserved, I gladlie will confest (*i.e. confess it*)
> Which I acknowledge, and shall do to end.
> In sign whereof, this Treatise I thee send. [57-63]

Anderson concludes his dedication with fully justified expressions of modesty: 'The Widows mites were measured by her heart' (70). He even tells Erskine that the poem 'is not worthy, that you one moment lose,/ To read or hear the matter therein meaned' (66-67). And indeed, Erskine would have nothing to learn from the very simple, basic

---

cal Reassessment,' *Scottish Journal of Theology* 43 (1990), and Frank D. Bardgett, *Scotland Reformed: The Reformation in Angus and the Mearns* (Edinburgh: John Donald, 1989) *passim.*

[31] It may not contain the whole text of the original publication, however. Anderson says to Erskine that 'this Treatise I thee send/ The sum whereof is pen'd before in prose,/ Showing shortly the heads therein contained', and there is no means of knowing whether this 'prose' is merely the lengthy full title of the poem.

[32] Erskine's earliest contacts with Protestantism are a mystery; it is not known whether he accompanied his eldest son to Germany in 1542, when the latter studied under Melanchthon. But in 1543 and 1545 Erskine was host to the preacher George Wishart, translator into Scots of the 1536 Helvetic Confession, martyred at St Andrews in 1546. Erskine was supportive of oppressed Protestants, but broke openly with Catholicism only in 1555, during Knox's preaching tour, when Knox celebrated the Lord's Supper at Dun.

[33] The phrase forms line 6 of the *Nunc dimittis* found in *A Compendious Book of Godly and Spiritual Songs Commonly known as The Gude and Godlie Ballatis, Reprinted from the Edition of 1567,* ed. A. F. Mitchell, STS 1st ser. 39 (Edinburgh: William Blackwood and Sons, 1897) 58.

Protestant catechetical material and endless anti-Roman commonplaces which make up the bulk of the poem. But Anderson had a conscious strategy in dedicating the work to the Superintendent of Angus, as opposed to anyone else. This strategy, as we shall see in our conclusions, only becomes apparent when the poem is read in the light of the prayer offered up in the final ten stanzas.

The poem proper, stanzas 1 to 85

In *Ane Satyre of the Thrie Estaitis*, Sir David Lyndsay had, like his English contemporaries, used *rime couée* mostly for comic speeches,[34] and it is deployed almost continuously in the later court comedy *Philotus, c.* 1567.[35] But *rime couée* was also used for serious religious verse: Alexander Scott used it for his metrical paraphrase of the *Miserere* (*c.* 1560), and in the 1580s, Alexander Montgomerie would use it for his equally serious 'Poets Dreme'. In terms of both content and style, however, Anderson's model was not Alexander Scot's polished psalm-paraphrase, but thirteen stanzas of *rime couée* beginning 'Remember man', included in *The Gude and Godlie Ballatis*.[36] In this 'ballad', Christ Himself denounces the Church of Rome and the Papal Antichrist in terms strikingly similar to those found in Anderson's stanzas.[37] The papists

> … hes set vp thair fals doctrine
> For couetice, in steid of myne,
> With fyre and sword defendis it syne,
> Contrair my word and me.
>
> The Antichrist is cumit but dot,
> And hes zow trappit round about,
> Furth of his gyrne, thairfoir, cum out,
> Gif ze wald sauit be. [200/17-24]
>
> Thay sell zow als the Sacramentis seuin
> Thay mycht haif maid as weill aleuin,
> Few or mony, od or euin
> Zour pursis for to pyke [202/49-52]

---

[34] This is a gross simplification; for a nuanced discussion, see John J. McGavin, 'The Dramatic Prosody of Sir David Lyndsay,' *Of Lion and of Unicorn. Essays on Anglo-Scottish Literary Relations in Honour of Professor John MacQueen* eds. R.D.S. Jack and Kevin J. McGinley (Edinburgh: Quadriga, 1993).

[35] For this early dating, see Jamie Reid-Baxter, '*Philotus*: The Transmission of a Delectable Treatise,' *Literature, Letters and the Canonical in Early Modern Scotland*, eds. Theo van Heijnsbergen and Nicola Royan (East Linton: Tuckwell Press, 2002).

[36] *Gude and Godlie Ballatis* 200-04.

[37] See inter alia lines 568-84, quoted on pp. 156-157 below.

> Mariage is ane blissit band,
> Quhilk I gaif man in my command
> To keip, bot thay my word withstand,
> Ane sacrament it maid. [202/57-60]

> And ze sall leue in rest and peace,
> Instructit with my word of grace
> For I the Antichrist deface
> Sall, and trew Preichouris send [203/89-92]

The title page of Anderson's poem tells us that the *Treatise* is 'to the toone of the Winter Night', clearly a popular song, now unfortunately lost. Anderson's first stanza hammers home the association with the original lyric:

> The Winter night, I thinke it long,
> Full long and teugh till it ouergang:
> The winters night I thinke so long,
>   Both long and dreigh till day.
> Full long thinke I the winters night,
> While daye breake up with beames so bright,
> And banish darknesse out of sight,
>   And workes of darknesse, Aa. *sic* [1-8]

That Anderson was inspired to make his *contrafactum* of the secular song by the example of the militantly protestant lyrics of the *The Gude and Godlie Ballatis*[38] can be shown by the textual evidence for Anderson's familiarity with 'O Christ quhilk art the lycht of day'.[39] This is a parody of the Lenten Compline hymn 'Christe qui lux es et dies'. Unsystematically, but repeatedly, the *contrafactum* calls Christ 'the licht' usually adding 'of day'. Anderson's stanzas 3-6 repeatedly describe Christ as the Day: 'The joyefull day is Jesus Christ'; Satan strives ceaselessly 'To draw vs from our Day'; 'We haue no Day but onlie one/ The Son of God, our Life alone', and He is 'that precious Day', and 'blessed Day'. Anderson, a former monk, will have known 'Christe qui lux es' as part of the Lenten liturgical journey towards the light of Easter, with its promise of the General Resurrection at the Last Trump. The *contrafactum* begins by stating that Christ, as light, drives away 'the clude of nycht', and explains

---

[38] See A. A. MacDonald, 'Contrafacta and the *Gude and Godlie Ballatis*,' *Sacred and Profane: Secular and Devotional Interplay in Early Modern British Literature*, eds. Helen Wilcox, Richard Todd and Alasdair A. MacDonald, Annual Bibliography of English Language and Literature (Amsterdam: VU University Press, 1996).

[39] *Gude and Godlie Ballatis* 173-74. Anderson seems also to have known the metrical paraphrase of *Christe qui lux es* printed on 144-45 — see note 70 below.

> This is na nycht as naturall
> Nor zit na clude materiall [173/5-6]

Anderson's second stanza clearly echoes this:

> The Winter night that I of mean
> Is not this naturall night I weine
> That lackes the light of the Sunne shine
>   And differs from the day. [9-12]

Much later, Anderson's 'Christ did abhore Idolatrie,/ So did hee vaine Hypocrisie' (513-14) again echoes the *contrafactum*:

> This nycht I call Idolatrie,
> The clude ouerspred, Hypocresie,
> Send from the Prince of all vnrycht,
> O Christ, for till obscure thy lycht. [173/9-12]

The anonymous 'O Christ, quhilk art the lycht' is a short, unsophisticated and unsystematic attack on specific Roman Catholic practices 'lang ledand to distructioun/ The maist part of this warld' (13-14). James Anderson's relentless denunciation of Rome and all its works is set out on a much larger canvas. He depicts the history of the cosmos from the Creation to the advent of the Heavenly Jerusalem after the Last Judgement.[40] Anderson explains what he means by 'winter night':

> … darknesse of our minde it is,
> Which hides from vs the Heauens blisse,
> Since Adam first did make the misse,
>   In Paradise that day.
> The joyefull day is Jesus Christ,[41]
> The Womans seede by God promist. [13-18]

And, says Anderson in line 41, this 'blessed Day must twise appeare':

> The first cumming is long fore-gane
> Sensyne fourescore of yeares and ninetane,
> Beyonde six hundreth and a thousand,[42]

---

[40] Anderson presumably knew Sir David Lyndsay's *Ane Dialog betwixt Experience and ane Courteour* (1554), which expounds cosmic history on a truly vast scale, and contains many attacks on superstitious late-mediaeval practices and ecclesiastical abuses.

[41] Cf. 'O Christ, quhilk art the lycht of day'; *Gude and Godlie Ballatis* 173/1.

[42] This date (1699), given in both extant editions, makes no sense whatever, not even prosodically. In 1851 Bonar (Anderson, *The Winter Night* 12-13) emended thus: 'Since syne of fourscore years and nine,/ Beyond five hundred and a thousand', inter alia because Calderwood recorded Erskine of Dun as being confined to his chamber in 1588 (Calderwood, *History of the Kirk* IV, 688). Bonar's knowledge (4-5) of the early prot-

> Not an houre lesse or maa.
> Since the first cumming is past
> Wee should be looking for the last [49-55]

The Old Testament's long wait for Christ is then very briefly evoked, 'lest wee ouer-long delay',[43] and eleven stanzas are devoted to a concise summary of the life of Christ and His saving work, from the Annunciation to Doomsday.

Which great day brings Anderson to the meat of his treatise: fifty-two stanzas devoted to the signs and tokens of the impending end. These tokens are six in number. The first, wars and rumours of wars, ignored by a world sunk in 'security', receive but two stanzas. The second, persecution of the professors of the truth, is quickly reviewed in five stanzas, which denounce Spain, the Duke of Alba, Catherine de Medicis, and Mary Tudor, and culminate in 'master Wishart and Walter Mill', two of Scotland's thin crop of Protestant martyrs.[44] The third token is the abounding of sin and the love of many growing cold, which again receive two perfunctory stanzas. But 'the fourth shall bee defection', and here, the first kind of apostates, namely Roman Catholics and above all, the diabolical Jesuits, are denounced for no fewer than fourteen stanzas, not least for their 'invasion' of Scotland and their insidious writings:

> Full many of our Nation, Scots,
> Spread daylie foorth of their foule spots:
> Who would bee glade to cut our throats,
>   If they might see their day. [401-04]
>
> Though they haue pleasure in despite,
> Which they spue out by word and write,[45]

---

estant clergy of Collace, far into the seventeenth century, was limited to the mere name of James Anderson; he did not know that in 1582, Anderson had become minister of Stirling, nor did he know that Anderson's successor at Collace in 1582, Henry Guthrie, was incumbent there until 1595. The '1699' date may hint that the original text read (with the correct number of syllables) 'fourscoir of yeirs and *ane*, / Beyonde *fyve* hundreth…', i.e. the eminently plausible 1581, which would have lasted until March 25 1582.

[43] Bardgett, 'Families and Factions,' 316: 'Both John Erskine and James Anderson appear to have been "New Testament men" — somewhat removed from John Knox's brand of Old Testament prophecy'.

[44] Wishart, so closely linked with Erskine of Dun, was tried and burned for heresy in March 1546. Walter Miln, who had earlier in life been a priest at Lunan in Angus, was burned in April 1558. See John Knox, *The Works of John Knox*, ed. David Laing, 6 vols. (Edinburgh: Wodrow Society, 1846-64) I, 550-55.

[45] For example, the Angus-born Jesuit James Tyrie, who published *Ane Refutation of an Answer made be Schir John Knox* in 1573 and debated with Andrew Melville in Paris in 1574. In April 1581, at Paris, the non-Jesuit John Hamilton published *Certane Orthodox and Catholik conclusions … in name of ye Catholikis, to the Caluinolatre ministeris*. He was commended in print by Nicol Burne, a former St Andrews lecturer, who had converted in 1579; the introduction to his prose work *The Disputation concerning the controvertit headdis of Religion* (Paris, October 1581), also commends the Jesuit Fr John Hay, from Fife.

> In such pastime wee not delite,
>   Neither in earnst or play. [409-12]

Only one stanza is dedicated to 'the other sort [of apostates] … Who will not mend, but stirre up strife/ Against the Kirke alway' (419-20), and whom therefore

> The pure Kirke from her companie
>   Doeth cut off euery day.[46]
> That is the true Catholicke Kirke,
> Of Gods owne word that doth not irke [423-26]

There ensue three stanzas of furious execration of the 'Romish Kirke that Babels Hoore', leading to the fifth token, namely that 'Antichrist shall be reuealed'. And Anderson reveals him in no uncertain terms —as the Pope, to whose boundless perversion of Christ's Gospel are devoted no fewer than twenty stanzas, loud with echoes of 'Remember man' from *The Gude and Godlie Ballatis,* as here:

> Christ into his New Testament,
> Ordained not a Sacrament,
> Safe Baptisme, and the Supper meant,
>   These two but any moe.
> The Pope to these hath added fiue,
> And Sacraments made seuen beliue,
> So as hee lists doth clamp and ryue,
>   Christs ordinances each day.
>
> Christ lawfull Marriage approued,
> To eate all meates all men lieued,
> That no mans conscience should bee grieued,
>   No state, no time, no day.
> The Pope forbiddeth Matrimonie,
> To all estates of his Clergie:
> And who eateth flesh, sinnes, deadly:
>   In Lent, or on Fryday. [568-84]

After his 1579 visit to Angus and points north, Hay published *Certaine Demandes … proposed to the Ministers of the new pretended kirk of Scotland* in 1580, These works are all reprinted in *Catholic Tractates of the Sixteenth Century, 1573-1600,* ed. Thomas Graves Law, STS 1st ser. 45 (Edinburgh: William Blackwood and Sons, 1901). Bound in with several copies of Burne's *Disputation* is a vigorous verse polemic published at Paris, 1581, 'Admonition to The Antichristian Ministers in the Deformit Kirk of Scotland' (*Satirical Poems of the Time of the Reformation,* ed. James Cranstoun, STS 1st ser. 20/24, 28/30, 2 vols. (Edinburgh: W. Blackwood and Sons, 1891, 1893) I, 333-45). It names and denounces many of the reformed clergy, including '[John] Davidson, your Poet', but not James Anderson, and presumably antedates *The Winter Night.*

46   In April 1582, the General Assembly stated its wish to excommunicate Robert Montgomerie.

The sixth and final token, the calling of the Jews, is again dealt with in two stanzas; the second demands quotation in full:

> For of that people rebellious,
> God hath now cald Tremellious,[47]
> A conuert most commodious,
>   Unto his Kirke this day.
> Most learned in the Hebrwe phrase, *sic*
> That was since the Apostles dayes,
> The Bible doth giue him that prayse
>   Which hee translated this day [617-24]

Anderson concludes his narrative with the endless joy that awaits the Faithful, evoked in four stanzas packed with Scriptural allusions, e.g. in the penultimate stanza, which also features a neat inversion of his poem's title:

> No sorrow shall bee in their spleine,
> And all teares wyped from their eine:[48]
> Both soule and body then shall shiene,
>   Like Sunne[49] in Summers day.
> When they shall get that Crowne of glore,[50]
> Preparde for them so long before:[51]
> Which they shall brooke for euermore,
>   Without change or delay. [665-72]

The poem proper is rounded off with an attempt at paradox and a very definite conclusion:

> Though this bee calde the Winters Night,
> It is a verie Lampe of Light,
> To guide us to the Heauen aright,
>   By Christ the onely way.
> Then meete it were wee did it cleare,
> And had the same in prompe perquiere,
> This Winter night it endeth here,
>   To God bee praise for ay. [673-680]

---

[47] Immanuel Tremellius (1510-80), a Jewish convert from Ferrara, lecturer in Hebrew at Cambridge 1547-53, then professor at Heidelberg till expelled in 1577; he died at Sedan. His scholarly Latin translation of the Syriac New Testament appeared in 1569 (ironically, in the context of this particular poem, it does not contain the Apocalypse) and his Old Testament, done jointly with Franciscus Junius, was published between 1575 and 1579.

[48] Rev. 21.4.

[49] Matt. 13.43.

[50] I Peter 5.4.

[51] II Tim. 4.8.

Stanzas 86 to 95: Anderson's concluding prayer

The ten stanzas which follow the end of 'this Winter night' are entirely different in nature from the preceding eighty-five. These stanzas, also couched in *rime couée*, constitute a litany-like prayer[52] beginning "Christ Prince of Pastors defend and keepe', a very clear echo of the end of the dedication to Erskine: 'Farewel in Christ … That Prince of Pastors thee comfort and defend'. The epithet is significant: while it obviously means that Christ is 'first' (*princeps*) of pastors, it presumably also implies that neither the king nor any bishop — including the Pope — is a 'prince' in an ecclesiastical context. It was the content of this litany (directly inspired by the Robert Montgomerie scandal) which kept Anderson's poem alive for so long, not his presumably tuneful but rudimentary Protestant history of the world from Adam to the Second Coming, nor its tedious reiteration of well-worn Protestant clichés about the Roman Antichrist. The reason for the poem's long publishing life are much the same as those adduced by Rebecca Laroche for Elizabeth Melville's *Godlie Dreame*,[53] namely the presence of certain key elements with a potential 'political' resonance amongst the godly. These elements would continue to speak to hardline presbyterians for well over a century.

The first stanza of the prayer ostentatiously quotes the translation (included in the metrical Psalter) of Luther's *Vater unser im Himmelreich* made by Richard Cox,[54] when it asks Christ to 'defend and keepe/ The little Flocke of thy poore sheepe' — not merely, as in Cox, from 'all errors',[55] but quite specifically from Sathan 'and from all earthly enmity' and, of course, from 'bloody Papists specially'. The Prince of Pastors is then asked to save 'the Kings Majestie', significantly in order 'that hee may know his duetie/ And do the same alswa', that duty being to 'purge this Realme of Papistrie./ And do doe justice equally/ Both to the great and smaa'. Much of this derives from *The Forme of Prayers,* but stanza 88 is entirely original. It asks God to purge the secular authorities — 'Court, Counsell, and Nobility' — of impiety, hypocrisy, and avarice. Revealingly, the deity is asked to 'reward them one and aa' in accordance with what

---

[52] Andrew Bonar actually prefaced these stanzas with the heading 'Concluding Prayer' in his 1851 edition. There are unequivocal verbal parallels with the prose 'Prayer for the whole Estate of Christs Church' in the Kirk's *Forme of Prayers,* but Bardgett, 'Families and Factions,' I, 314-15, argues strongly for the direct influence of the prayer 'for the whole estate of Christ's church militant here on earth' from Cranmer's 1552 Prayer Book, which he shows was known and used in Angus and the Mearns.

[53] Rebecca Laroche, 'Elizabeth Melville and Her Friends: Seeing "Ane Godlie Dreame" through Political Lenses,' *Clio* 34.3 (2005): 289.

[54] 'From all errours defend and keep the little flock of thy poore sheep'. 'Cox's Lord's Prayer' had first been published in the *Psalmes of Dauid in metre* (Wesel, 1556) STC 2426.8. It reappeared in *Psalmes of Dauid* in English metre (London, 1560), STC 2427 and all subsequent English editions of the metrical psalter, and from no later than 1575, it was printed in almost all Scottish psalters.

[55] Luther had written 'von falscher Lehr', i.e. theological errors, meaning Papistry.

'their heartes meane inwardly/ To thee, and to his Majestie/ To thy pure Kirke, and this Countrie' — a direct criticism, and not least a comment on Esmé Stuart's supposed protestant conversion and the Kirk's conviction that he had been sent by the Pope to restore Catholicism. Stanza 90 invokes God's blessing on 'thy Pastours Spirituall' in order to enable them 'Christs cause stoutly to debate/ Say contrare who will say', again a direct comment on Esmé's and James's contempt for the excommunication of Robert Montgomerie.

And then come the lines most important, perhaps, to the poem's continuing relevance to the concerns of generations of ordinary, increasingly egalitarian-minded Scottish presbyterians. Two stanzas, not one, demand that God purge the Kirk itself of

> Balaams priests that therein beene
> Who not thy glorie, but their owne meane
> And vantage all the way [722-24]

— that is, the 'tulchan' bishops brought in from 1571 onwards by the future Regent Morton to milk an already cash-starved Kirk,[56] and specifically, in the Scotland of 1581, Robert Montgomerie. Anderson goes so far as to ask God to 'make the king once vnderstand/ The great corruptiouns in that band' and reform them 'according to thy Laa'. Balaam, who 'loued the wages of vnrighteousnes' (II Peter 2.15), appears in Numbers 22 and 23, and is cited most disapprovingly in Jude 11 and Revelations 2.14. Anderson was not the first Scottish cleric to mention Balaam in connection with attempts to assert state control over the Kirk. In 1573, John Davidson, lamenting the death of fearless John Knox in November 1572, warned the General Assembly that

> … craftie heidis sall na mair hyde
> The hurde of thair Hypocrisie,
> Bot all sinceirnes set asyde,
> With policie will all things gyde,
> Thir Balamis birds sair may thou feir.[57]

Balaam had a long life ahead of him in the repertory of the anti-episcopal party: in the wake of the Black Acts of May 1584, the new episcopal order, firmly under royal control, was denounced by the minister James Melville in terms of 'Balaam, the false prophet',[58] while the poet Robert Sempill attacked the tulchan bishops as the sons and

---

[56]   James Melville explained the term thus: 'calfis skinnes stuffed with stra, to cause the cow giff milk; for everie lord gat a bischoprie, and sought and presented to the kirk sic a man as wald be content with least, and sett them maist of fewes, takes and pensiones': James Melville, *The Autobiography and Diary of Mr. James Melvill*, ed. Robert Pitcairn (Edinburgh: Wodrow Society, 1842) 31.

[57]   *Satirical Poems of the Time of the Reformation* I, 291/39-43.

[58]   Melville, *Autobiography and Diary* 201.

heirs of 'Bischop Balaam, brecking the law of God'.[59] Decades later, sometime after 1607, Andrew Melville commenced an epigram from the Tower of London 'Cum balamitarum sit tanta frequentia vatum' (Since Balaamitous prophets abound). His nephew James Melville, banished from Scotland, wrote a related sonnet against 'Balaams band' (Pitscottie MS, NLS, Crawford Collections, Acc. 9769, Personal Papers 84/1/1, f.154v); James's poem 'Bees for Bishops' (NLS, Adv. MS 19.2.7 f.9v) denounces the prelates 'Be Balaams wages and be Judas hyre'. In April 1619, Andrew Duncan, summoned before the bishops, told them to 'remember Balaam, who was eaten away by the deceate of the wages of unrighteousnes'.[60] As late as 1664, Balak and Balaam were cited — twice — as impediments to the Elect's crossing over Jordan in the vast and utterly forgotten poem *The Turtle Dove,* published in Edinburgh by John Fullartoun, the doughty old Covenanting laird of Carlton in Galloway.[61] By 1664, Fullartoun's coreligionists will automatically have associated these names with the idea that bishops constitute an obstacle to the practise of the true faith.

James Anderson's poem reflects the growing uproar in Kirk, and latterly in state, that raged from October 1581 onwards over the Balaam-like figure of Robert Montgomerie. Indeed, one of the Assembly's charges against Montgomerie in October 1581 was that in his preaching in Glasgow, 'he accused the ministers of pasquills' and of using 'fallacious arguments, and captious',[62] which might refer to *The Winter Night.* It is certainly striking that it was Anderson himself who was appointed as Montgomerie's replacement at Stirling, after James Melville had declined the town's call during the October 1582 General Assembly.[63] Robert Montgomerie was but the very last straw in the Kirk's prolonged struggle against tulchan bishops. In 1576, the Regent Morton nominated the infamous Patrick Adamson to the archbishopric of St Andrews. This appointment was to prove an endless source of problems to the Assembly, which in July 1580 decreed 'the office of a bishop, as it is now used and commountlie takin within this realme'[64] to be unlawful. That Assembly suspended all the bishops until they were readmitted as simple pastors by the Assembly. Patrick Adamson briefly complied, to the delight of those presbyterian stalwarts Robert Pont and James Lawson (who wrote Latin liminary epigrams lauding Adamson's Latin verse catechism of 1581), but James Boyd, archbishop of Glasgow, simply refused to bow to the Assembly's

---

[59] *Satirical Poems of the Time of the Reformation* I, 347/25.

[60] Calderwood, *History of the Kirk* VII, 378.

[61] Fullarton was a friend of Samuel Rutherford, and of Lady Culross; he is referred to in both their correspondences.

[62] Calderwood, *History of the Kirk* III, 579-80.

[63] Melville, *Autobiography and Diary* 135.

[64] Calderwood, *History of the Kirk* III, 469.

decrees; and on his death, all the Kirk's objections notwithstanding, the vacant see of Glasgow was awarded to Robert Montgomerie.

Anderson's second stanza (no. 92) on the tulchan bishops calls them 'dumbe dogs that cannot barke … wastefull Bees that make no warke/ Who neuer aime at the right marke', but 'To fill their ydle bellies fow / Bothe flocke and heard they plucke and pow'. This is terminology which had been used to attack the Church of Rome before and during the Reformation, for example in songs found in the *Gude and Godlie Ballatis*.[65] Anderson's antepenultimate stanza (no. 93) clearly echoes his own earlier charges against the Church of Rome and the Papacy:

> From Idolater and Hypocrite,
> From Athist, Papist and Jesuite,
> And from the vsurs of Sathans sprite,
>   By Witch-craft any way,[66]
> From oppression, Murder, and Mischiefe,
> From Bellie-gods, from Hoore and Thiefe,
> From Auarice, of others chiefe,
>   Lord, purge this Land this day. [736-44]

This stanza is a startling foreshadowing of James Melville's 2 August 1584 letter to the earl of Angus and the Master of Glamis, stating that the young King James VI had not been 'diligentlie gardit from pernitious flatterers, carnall Atheistes, seditius and bludie idolaters, licentius libertines, filthie harlotes, hellishe witches', and that as a result, the royal government's Black Acts had put the Kirk in the hands of 'belli-godes, fals preists of Baal … whure and witch mungars'.[67]

But Anderson, unlike James Melville, is not addressing himself exclusively to noblemen (despite his dedicatory epistle to Erskine of Dun), nor even to a select coterie of manuscript readers. He is aiming at a wide, general audience. After his various denunciations of the upper classes and the king's blindness to the wickedness of the tulchan bishops, his penultimate stanza bluntly opens 'Inspire the common Populare,/ Inspire their heart, and open their eare', and its second half evokes the close of Revelation: 'that blessed sight haste let vs see'.[68] Thus the poem's promise that the Second Coming is at hand culminates in a positively populist denunciation of prelacy in the Kirk. The epithets Anderson applies to the tulchan bishops had been applied to the Catholic

---

[65] *Gude and Godlie Ballatis*, 188: 'Thay gadderit vp baith woll and mylk/ And tuke na mair cure'.

[66] Bardgett, 'Families and Factions,' I, 300-02, discusses Erskine of Dun's active persecution of witchcraft (throughout his superintendency) in terms of the perceived need to eradicate 'the rural traditions and superstitions which… struggled against the new Biblical rationalism'.

[67] Melville, *Autobiography and Diary* 174, 176.

[68] Rev. 22:20 'Surely I come quickly, Amen. Euen so, come Lord Jesus' (Geneva Bible, 1560).

hierarchy by the original Scottish Reformers. They form part of a vocabulary of denunciation that would be repeated by the presbyterian dissenters from royal policy in the early seventeenth century, and by the Covenanters after 1637 and the Prayer-Book riot in St Giles. In sum, Anderson's final ten stanzas make all the enraged denunciation heard in the body of the poem directly applicable to the current state of Scotland. Whether or not Anderson wrote the last ten stanzas as an addition to an existing poem, his final stanzas firmly tie the litany into the 'winter night' and apocalyptic subject matter of the main poem. The last stanza, a Trinitarian doxology, is by far the most poetic in the entire work. It brings *The Winter Night* to an end in the eternal daylight of the radiance of the Triune Godhead, as evoked by St John the Divine in his description of the New Jerusalem in Revelation:[69]

> Glore to the Father full of might,
> Glore to the Sonne, our Day so bright: [70]
> Glore to the holy Ghost, that Light,
>   That lets us see our Day,
> One GOD equall in Majestie:
> And yet distinct in persons three.
> As was, is now, and aye shall bee,
>   Beyond all Night and Day

Conclusions

The long shelf-life of Anderson's *Winter Night* is a striking demonstration of the ready market that anti-prelatical verse was to find amongst Reform-minded Scots from the days of David Lyndsay down into the early eighteenth century. Reference was made earlier to Sempill's *The Legend of the Bischop of St Androis Lyfe* of autumn 1584. The subject (or rather victim) of Sempill's devastating satire is the corrupt, venal and very unspiritual Patrick Adamson, Archishop of St Andrews. *The Legend* appeared in the wake of the Black Acts of May 1584, and Sempill prefaces his relentless attack on Adamson with 16 ballad royal stanzas containing a detailed denunciation of the 'pestiferus prelatis' who make 'thair Gods of warldlie gudis and geir', and who 'be now Tulchin bischops stylit'. Although the scale of Sempill's attack (and its virtuosic deployment of

---

[69] Rev. 21:23-25, 22:5 – 'and there shalbe no night there … for the Lord God giueth them light' (Geneva Bible, 1560).

[70] The closing doxology of *Christe qui lux es* in the *Gude and Godlie Ballatis* begins 'Gloir be to God, Father of mycht,/And to Christ Jesu, his Sone sa brycht' (145).

literary Scots) are far removed from Anderson's stanzas 91 and 92, Sempill makes exactly the same points as the minister of Collace had done. Anderson's pedantic doggerel, however, went on being read for generations, precisely because the minister's relatively colourless, heavily watered-down Scots had been used to formulate generic criticisms that could be applied to successive historic situations. Apart from the anglicising of its orthography (though several of the Scots rhymes proved irreducible) and the clumsy interference with the date in line 50, Anderson's poem remained unaltered. In print, he remained 'minister of Collace' forever, and the dedicatory stanzas to the long-dead Erskine of Dun continued to hold the superintendent up as a model of what a Reformed Christian member of the upper classes ought to be.

It might be thought there is a contradiction here. The readership of this poem through to 1713 consisted of militant presbyterians, ferociously opposed to prelacy and hence, royal supremacy. But was not the dedicatee of Anderson's poem, the courtly aristocrat John Erskine of Dun, Superintendent of Angus, a bishop in all but name? Gordon Donaldson in his *Scottish Reformation* was at pains to point out that the superintendents were very similar indeed to bishops, and that they lived like bishops, earning vastly higher salaries than ministers.[71] He also notes that Erskine was basically conservative, not revolutionary. But, as Donaldson cannot but acknowledge, Erskine's own letter to the Regent Mar of 10 November 1571, after discussing exactly what St Paul meant by a bishop, explicitly states

> As to the questioun, If it be expedient a superintendent to be where a qualified bishop is, I understand a bishop or a superintendent to be but one office, and where the one is the other is. But having some respect to the cace whereupon the questioun is moved, I answere, the superintendents that are placed ought to continue in their offices, notwithstanding any others that intruse themselves, or are placed by suche as have no power in such offices. They may be called bishops, but are not bishops, but idols, (Zech.xi.17), sayeth the prophet. And, therefore, the superintendents which are called, and placed orderlie by the kirk, have the office and jurisdictioun; and the other bishops, so called, have no office nor jurisdictioun in the kirk of God; for they enter not by the doore, but by another way, and therefore are not pastors, sayeth Christ, but theeves and robbers. [...] Some counsellors now think now good time to conqueis from the kirk (being now, they judge, weake and poore) priviledges and benefites to the temporall authoritie [...] their unrighteous conqueist and spoile of the kirk sall never profite them, but rather be a caus to bring plague and destructioun both upon the head and counsellors of suche abominatioun.[72]

---

[71] Gordon Donaldson, *The Scottish Reformation*, Birkbeck Lectures (Cambridge: Cambridge University Press, 1960) 125-28.

[72] Calderwood, *History of the Kirk* III, 160-61.

Erskine was throughout his career regularly criticised by the General Assembly for failing to work miracles, but he was never accused of being a self-seeking, unspiritual time-server like Patrick Adamson, however large his superintendent's salary and however 'conservative' his views.

Nonetheless, Anderson's dedication to Erskine of a poem so critical of the tulchan bishops must have caused Erskine to wince. For in 1572, the Laird of Dun had been a leading architect of the infamous Concordat of Leith, of which the many unfortunate results included both Patrick Adamson's ascension to the archiepiscopal title of St Andrews, and, ultimately, Robert Montgomerie's appointment to the see of Glasgow. Erksine must have been used to wincing at criticism in verse from pastoral pens. He had been one of the commissioners who 'granted supply from the thirds [of benefices] for the support of the king's house and the regent's house and expenses' and 'organised his province during the 1570s firmly along the lines of the "platt" of 1574 whereby one minister was allocated four kirks'.[73] In January 1574, the young minister John Davidson had anonymously published his telling and detailed criticisms of precisely these policies in the workmanlike verse of *Ane Dialog or Mutuall talking betuix a Clerk and ane Courteour concerning foure Parische Kirks till ane Minister*.[74] By 1581, James Anderson appears to have felt that the corruption of the tulchan bishops under Esmé Stuart's regime was so blatant that it would be worth associating Erskine, however 'ancient' and 'warded, as it were/ From tedious travells', with the Kirk's alarm over Esmé Stuart's intentions. Erskine was, after all, the senior survivor of the glory days of the Reformation. Indeed, Anderson's stressing of Erskine's age and enfeeblement may even be a deliberate attempt to provoke the Grand Old Man into taking an active stance against the regime.

If we can find no trace of any action by Erskine in late 1581 or spring 1582, the Duke of Lennox was fiercely attacked as an abuser of the king by the Edinburgh minister John Durie, who was banished from the city on 30 May 1582. Undeterred, the presbytery of Edinburgh proceeded to excommunicate the deposed Robert Montgomerie on 9 June.[75] On 27 June, Andrew Melville, as moderator of the 'extraordinarie'

---

[73] Bardgett, *Scotland Reformed: The Reformation in Angus and the Mearns* 141. James Anderson himself appears, at least for some years after his presentation to Collace in 1573, to have been responsible for four kirks.

[74] Interestingly, the *Dialog*'s sharply specific critique got Davidson into so much trouble with the Regent Morton that the poet fled into exile, fearing for his life. Some years later, Robert Sempill's satirical publications landed him in prison under Esmé Stuart's regime, and in May 1584, criticism from the minister of Edinburgh, James Lawson, caused the Earl of Arran to make 'manie vowes, that if Mr James Lowson's head were as great as an hay stacke, he would cause it leap from his hawse'. (Calderwood, *History of the Kirk* IV, 65). James Anderson was well-advised to express his criticisms in broad generalities.

[75] *Ibid*.III, 620, 621.

General Assembly that had been called in Edinburgh, 'inveyghed against the bloodie gullie (so he termed it) of absolute authoritie, whereby men intended to pull the crown off Christ's head, and wring the scepter out of his hand'. The Assembly appointed a delegation of ministers, headed by Erskine of Dun,[76] to present a list of 'Greeves' (including much about Montgomerie and Glasgow) to the king and council; they 'gott no good countenance'.[77] However, Edinburgh's town council expelled Robert Montgomerie from the capital amid a near-riot on 25 July, and there were lairds and nobles prepared to take very decisive steps to end Esmé's absolutist regime. They did so by the simple expedient of kidnapping the king at Perth in the Ruthven Raid of 22 August 1582, and were loudly applauded by the Kirk for doing so.[78] On 4 September Edinburgh welcomed the returning John Durie to the thunderous singing of 'Now Israel may say, and that truly' — Whittingham's great metrical version of Ps. 124, written to fit the stirring French melody in Geneva in 1558, reputedly as a spontaneous reaction to the news of the death of Mary Tudor.

This brief triumph of the presbyterian party did not last. Under the regime quickly established by the new royal favourite, Esmé's former henchman the Earl of Arran, Archbishop Adamson's revived rule of the Kirk saw the position swing back so far that some twenty leading ministers, including Andrew and James Melville, fled into exile in England in the late spring and summer of 1584.[79] Arran's regime proved short-lived, and almost all the presbyterian exiles returned in triumph in November 1585. In 1587 Robert Montgomerie resigned the archbishopric of Glasgow, and Patrick Adamson was suspended from the ministry, to be deposed in 1589. The ensuing improvement of Crown-Kirk relations culminated in the 'Golden Acts' of 1592, which established a presbyterian polity. But the good relations quickly soured, and by autumn 1596 the Kirk was again at furious loggerheads with the Crown. The *coup d'état* attempted by the presbyterian party in mid-December 1596 failed miserably;[80] the king regained the upper hand and was soon re-establishing royal control — and by 1600, appointing bishops. The battle between presbytery and episcopacy would go on until 1688 — a situation which guaranteed that generations of unpoetic presbyterian readers, despairing of the state of their world, would find apocalyptic inspiration in the generic and therefore ageless critique set out by James Anderson in his *Winter Night*.

---

[76] *Ibid*.III, 622, 623, 627.

[77] *Ibid*.III, 631.

[78] They wrote to Erskine requesting his support: see Bardgett, 'Families and Factions,' I, 340, n.120.

[79] See note 13 above.

[80] See Julian Goodare, 'The Attempted Scottish *Coup* of 1596,' *Sixteenth-Century Scotland: Essays in Honour of Michael Lynch*, eds. Julian Goodare and A. A. MacDonald (Leiden: Brill, 2008), and Julian Goodare, 'How Archbishop Spottiswoode Became an Episcopalian,' *Renaissance and Reformation / Renaissance et Réforme* 30.4 (2006-7).

John Mair on Divine Creation and Conservation

Alexander Broadie

The question of the relation between God's creation of the world and his conservation of it held the attention of many philosophers and theologians during the Middle Ages and the early modern period. For example John Duns Scotus has a lengthy discussion whose conclusion is that there is no real distinction but only a distinction of reason between God's creation of the world and his conservation of it; or, more precisely, he demonstrates that the relation in which a creature stands to God as creator is really the same as that in which the creature stands to God as conserver, and that the distinction is one of reason only.[1] And Descartes famously argued that the distinction between God's creative act and his conservative act was a distinction of reason and not a real distinction.[2] The view that the distinction was one of reason only and was not real seems to have been very much the predominant view, and among those who are on the side of this predominant view is John Mair, a Scottish philosopher/theologian who was prominent in Paris during the first three decades of the sixteenth century and who had a lively interest in the theology of creation. Since the account of the relation between creation and conservation that is much the best known by modern philosophers is that penned by Descartes, I shall end by commenting, though briefly, on the relation between Mair and Descartes regarding the issue of this relation. It will become apparent that though Mair and Descartes are in agreement on the question whether the relation at issue is one of reason only, they are very much in disagreement on the details of their respective positions. My principal, though not sole source, as regards Mair, will be his Commentary on Book Two of the *Sentences* of Peter Lombard.[3] And my source, as regards Descartes, will be the third of his *Meditations*.

---

[1] See Question Twelve in *Quaestiones Quodlibetales*, in John Duns Scotus, *Opera Omnia*, ed. Luke Wadding, 26 vols. (Paris: Vivès, 1895) XXV. For secondary literature see Alexander Broadie, 'Scotus on God's Relation to the World,' *British Journal for the History of Philosophy* 7 (1999). See also Alexander Broadie, 'Scotistic Metaphysics and Creation *ex nihilo*,' *Creation and the God of Abraham*, eds. David B. Burrell, et al. (Cambridge: Cambridge University Press, 2010).

[2] *Meditations on First Philosophy*, Meditation III. See René Descartes, *Oeuvres de Descartes*, eds. Charles Adam and Paul Tannery, 13 vols. (Paris: Léopold Cerf, 1897-1913) VII, 48-49.

[3] John Mair, *In Secundum Sententiarum* (Paris: 1510). I shall be using the Paris 1519 reprint, printed by Jean Granjon (henceforth *In 2 Sent*). I shall also be using his John Mair, *In quartum Sententiarum questiones utilissimae* (Paris, 1516) (henceforth *In 4 Sent*).

The question Mair poses, 'whether creation and conservation are really different' (*an creatio et conservatio realiter differant*), draws in its wake the question of what creation and conservation are essentially, that is, what the qualities or attributes of an act are that make the act creative or conservative. As regards the concept of creation Mair's approach is crabwise. He turns first to the term 'creature' and notes that in ordinary speech a creature is 'every effect produced', with the implication that, since a creature is a product of an act of creating, in one sense to create is simply to produce an effect, whatever the effect may be. Mair does not dismiss out of hand this sense of 'creature' and in fact goes on to use the term with just that sense.

But he does not embrace in an unqualified way the concept of creation that seems implied, for he accepts that the verb 'create' is used equivocally. On the one hand it means 'produce an effect, of whatever kind', and his example as regards this broad sense of creation is the students at Paris 'creating' the university's rector,[4] a use of 'create' that fits well the sense of 'creature' that we have just noted. On the other hand there is a narrower sense of 'create', one of more interest to theologians: 'To create is to produce something *extra passum*, that is, where the *passum* is not presupposed in the productive act.'[5] As Mair uses the term 'passum' the distinctive feature of a *passum* is its passivity or receptivity. It is what an agent works on, forms, reforms or transforms, in producing an effect. The effect is what the agent has made out of what already had to be in place for him to work on. Creation in the narrow sense is an effecting that does not presuppose a *passum*, something already in place that is being transformed. Though the creativity of human beings is not to be gainsaid, it is not a creativity of the narrow kind, for not even a Michaelangelo can sculpt a statue without something to chisel. The position Mair here adopts, which is familiar in another guise as the doctrine of creation *ex nihilo*, is clearly stated by him later in his commentary on the *Sentences*.[6]

Mair affirms that an effect that a human being produces (without creating it since humans are not creators) can be created by God. He does not here give his reason for holding this but it is plain that his reason is that anything produced by a secondary cause (that is, by a created thing) can be created directly by God without the help of any secondary cause. But the fact that one and the same object can be produced by God and by creatures does not in the least imply that the acts would have much, if anything, in common. It is one thing for Michaelangelo to produce his Pietà from marble. It is a wholly different order of act to produce it from nothing.

---

[4]   Mair *In 4 Sent*, distinctio 1, quaestio 1 (fol. 9 recto).

[5]   '…capitur creare ut tantum valet sicut producere aliquid extra passum vel in sua actione non praesupponere passum.' *In 2 Sent*, d.1, q.6 (fol. 8 verso).

[6]   Mair *In 4 Sent*, d.1, q.1 (fol. 9 recto).

Conservation is in one sense the contrary of creation; though creation excludes the existence of an antecedent something for the agent to act on, conservation requires just such an antecedent for what is being conserved must already exist for the agent to be able to conserve it. Hence it might seem that God's first act cannot be conservative, and indeed it seems intuitively obvious that creation must precede conservation. Yet, as we shall observe, Mair does not accept this intuition, or at least does not accept it in an unqualified way, even if unqualified acceptance of it seems implicit in the first move he does make in regard to conservation, namely: 'Conservation, properly understood, bespeaks, beyond production and maintenance, the pre-existence of a thing; that is, the term 'conservation' connotes that the thing existed earlier. So that the thing in the first instant in which it is produced is not conserved, but always thereafter it is said to be conserved for as long as it remains in existence.'[7] Since creation implies a thing's being produced from nothing and conservation implies the thing's pre-existence creation must surely therefore precede conservation.

Mair's reason for rejecting this inference emerges from the following set of four theses (*conclusiones*): (1) God's active creating (*creatio dei activa*) is God; (2) God's active conserving (*conservatio dei activa*) with regard to creatures is God; (3) God's active creating is a conserving, though sometimes God would be the creating of something B and not the conserving of B; (4) Passive creating and likewise passive conserving is a creature created and conserved, and is nothing else. These four theses are termed '*conclusiones*' because they are presented as things to be drawn as conclusions and they do in fact figure as the conclusions in arguments that are thereupon produced. The first two theses rest on the assumption of the oneness of God, a oneness so tight that there is no real distinction between God and his powers, including his power of will, and that there is no real distinction between God's powers and the acts that he performs by the exercise of his powers, where by 'real distinction between A and B' is meant a distinction between A and B such that either can exist without the other, or, put otherwise, that God could annihilate one while conserving the other. Where there is a distinction, but not a real one, between A and B, then the distinction in question is one of reason only. Mair is affirming that God's will is not really distinct from his acts of will, and hence God himself is not really distinct from those acts. Hence neither God's acts of creating nor his acts of conserving, or (in alternative terminology) neither his active creating nor his active conserving, are really distinct from God. Hence God is really his active creating and his active conserving. And, moving now to the first part of the third thesis, since God's active creating and his active conserving are both really

---

7   Mair, *In 2 Sent*, d.1, q.6 (fol.8 verso): 'Conservatio proprie capiendo dicit ultra productionem et manutenentiam praeexistentiam ipsius rei, ita quod res in primo instanti quo producitur non conservatur, sed semper post hoc dicitur conservari quamdiu manet in rerum natura.'

indistinguishable from God they are really indistinguishable from each other; each, that is, is the other. They are the same thing, for they are both God.

The qualification that forms the second part of the third thesis draws us into new territory. Mair affirms: 'Suppose God first created an angel at instant A. Then as follows: At instant A it was true to say: "God is the creating of an angel", but at that instant there is no conserving of the angel.'[8] Suppose the angel is instantly annihilated. In that case there is God's active creating of the angel but not his active conserving. If it is conserved then it must have lasted for a time. But being for an instant only is not a way of lasting for a time — an instant does not last.

One might be doubtful that anything can exist for only an instant, since an instant takes no time. If it did take, or take up, or occupy time then that time would be composed of a plurality of instants. But even if nothing can exist for just an instant and then be instantly annihilated, we can still make sense of the idea of an instantaneous existence, for the instant can be conceived, as Mair appears to conceive it, as a terminus of a period of time, whether the beginning or the end. If a period exists then so does its beginning and its end. So we can conceive of the angel as existing by God's creative act at the first instant of the angel's existence, but not being conserved till thereafter, however soon thereafter it may be be. How long after the first instant? Not, according to Mair, at the next instant, for there is none. A next instant would imply that two instants are adjacent, that is, so close that there is no time between them. But this, he thinks, is impossible since, as I shall shortly demonstrate, he believes time to be continuous. One might in any case wonder what makes the difference between an instant and the next if neither of them lasts any time and if there is no time between the occurrence of the first and the second. How can the second instant be later if no time has lapsed in the earlier instant, no time lapses between the earlier and the later, and no time lapses in the later? It seems that the later must occur simultaneously with the earlier, in which case, of course, neither is earlier or later than the other. Let us say, then, following Mair, that the angel is created at the first instant of its existence and if the angel lasts more than an instant then at any subsequent instant of its existence God is actively conserving it. Hence the qualification that forms the second part of the third thesis. God would sometimes (*interdum*) be the creating of a thing B and not be its conserving. When is that 'sometime'? It is at the first instant of B's existence. If B is instantly annihilated, assuming instant annihilation to be possible, then B is never conserved; if B is not instantly annihilated then it is conserved, but only after instant A.

---

[8] 'Pono quod deus creaverit angelum primo in A instanti. Tunc sic: Deus fuit creatio angeli in A instanti. In A instanti verum erat dicere: Deus est creatio angeli. Et tamen in illo non est conservatio illius angeli.' *In 2 Sent*, d.1, q.6 (fol. 8 verso).

Regarding the fourth thesis, Mair deploys a distinction which is equally permissible in Latin and English. The English term 'creation' can be used to refer both to a productive act and also to the product of that act. Thus we speak of God's creation of the world, using 'creation' to refer to God's creative act, and we speak also of the natural features of God's glorious creation, using 'creation' to refer to the world that God had created. These are the active and passive voices of creation, the productive act and the product. The Latin 'creatio' has the same two voices. *Creatio* is something that God does, and *creatio* is also the product of that same act; in which case it is understandable that Mair should distinguish between an active creating (something God does) and a passive creating (the product of that act). Although it does not work so well in English, what he is saying is at least readily intelligible when he invokes two sorts of conservation, an active conserving (something God does) and a passive conserving (the product of that act). Just as there is an active creating and an active conserving and as they are the same as each other in that both are God, so also there is a passive creating and a passive conserving and they are the same as each other because they are both the product of that same act of creation and conservation, the product being the world that God made. It is the same world. There is not one world that God created and another that he has conserved, for of course it is the very same world that he both created and has thereafter conserved, a situation that parallels the sameness of the act by which God created the world and conserves it.

We can attend to the world in its first instant and consider the possibility that it does not survive the first instant. And we can think that if it had not survived it there would have been no conservation of the world because conserving connotes an earlier existence. But Mair regards us as inhabiting a world that God created and conserves, and in answer to the question what the relation is between these two acts, his answer is that in reality they are not two acts but one and the same. On an obvious interpretation of his words Mair is saying that by a single act God created a world that has a time span. He did not create a world and then have to do something in addition in order that the world continue to exist. It was the continually existing world that he created, continuity being a feature of the product of his creative act. How is it that after the first act of creation the world continues? Does the world have the power from within its own resources to keep going? Or does God, having created it, have to return to the task of recreating it in order that it keep going? Mair's answer, on my interpretation of him, is that to ask these questions is to miss the point of the creative act. It was to bring into existence a universe which has a temporal dimension. The universe at any instant of its existence is as much part of what God created as it is in the first instant in the temporal span of the universe. Since it lasts, we speak of it being conserved, but what we call its being conserved is in reality its having been, or its being, created. Hence Mair's answer to the question whether creation and conservation are really different, is that they are not.

The central feature of Mair's concept of creation is the concept of the total depend-
ance of the *creatum* on the creator, for by the creative act the world exists, and without
that act there is no world. This point, clear enough in *2 Sent*, d.1, q.6, on which I have
been focused up to this point, becomes yet clearer in q.7, where he asks whether God
is creator and conserver of everything, or, staying closer to the Latin idiom, whether
God has conservative and causally effective power in relation to all things.[9] His move
is via analogical language and he is as aware as anyone can be that his language is no
more than analogical. The first example is of a builder whose product comes into existence by the builder's efforts but thereafter remains in existence even though the builder
then leaves. In a broad sense of creator the builder creates the building, but once in
place the building has the resources to keep going without further input from its creator. Likewise, to take another of Mair's example's, a fire is the cause of the water being
hot, but if the fire is extinguished the water will not instantly cease to be hot. This is
not true of all created creators. As Mair points out, light depends on luminous bodies.
Blow out the candle and things that are visible for as long as it has been shedding light
cease on the instant to be visible. Here the created creator, which is what the lighted
candle is, must remain in place as a luminous body if its creatures, the surrounding
visible objects, are to remain visible.

Let us say then that their visibility is co-temporal with the candle's luminosity.
Comparison with God is therefore imperfect, as is immediately hinted by Mair: 'Every
creature depends much more upon God than light depends upon a luminous body or
[adds Mair] than an accident, according to Aristotle, depends upon its subject'.[10] But
how much more does a creature depend on God the creator than any product depends
upon a created being? One answer, the main point of this paper, concerns the relation
between creation and conservation. In the case of the candle, as soon as it is lit it sheds
light and in so doing it creates the visibility of the objects close by. As long as it stays
lit it conserves the visibility of those objects. The conservative act of the candle is really
different, because really at a different time, from its creative act, since the conserving is
later. And all this holds in a framework in which the act of the candle, whether creative
or conservative, is temporally co-terminus with the product (the visibility) of the surrounding objects. But this is not in the least like God's act of creation and conservation. As Mair puts the point, there is a distinction of reason, but not a real distinction,
between God's creating the world and conserving it; God's creating and conserving are
really one and the same act.

---

[9] 'Utrum deus habeat vim conservativam et effectivam respectu omnium.' *In 2 Sent*, d.1, q.7 (fol. 9
recto).
[10] 'Multo magis creatura quaelibet a deo dependet quam lumen a corpore luminoso vel accidens a
subiecto secundum Artistotelem.' *In 2 Sent*, d.1, q.7 (fol. 9 recto).

I should like now to take up a point made at the start, namely that Descartes argued that the distinction between God's creative act and his conservative act is a distinction of reason and not a real distinction, and to probe the issue of how far Mair and Descartes are in agreement on the matter of divine creating and conserving. It will be demonstrated that though there is some surface agreement, their positions are in fact mutually incompatible. Descartes's position is stated in the course of his arguments in his *Meditations on First Philosophy*, Meditation Three, for the existence of God: 'It is as a matter of fact perfectly clear and evident to all those who consider with attention the nature of time, that, in order to be conserved in each moment in which it endures, a substance has need of the same power and action as would be necessary to produce and create it anew, supposing it did not yet exist, so that the light of nature shows us clearly that the distinction between creation and conservation is solely a distinction of the reason.'[11] Though this looks like territory Mair himself occupied appearances are deceptive.

That Descartes's application of the distinction between creation and conservation has a dimension that is alien to Mair's thinking is signalled by the fact that Descartes broaches the question of the relation between creation and conservation in the course of a discussion of the nature of his own existence. He wonders whether, had he always existed, he must be uncreated, for creation implies a beginning whereas uncreated beings have no beginning. To which he responds that the assumption of his having always existed needs first to be spelled out, for the assumption that he is identically the same being that he always was is questionable. In fact it turns out that Descartes thinks that in a sense he has never been the same identical person that he had previously been. For his duration is infinitely divisible, or, as he puts it, 'my life may be divided into an infinite number of parts, none of which is in any way dependent on the other'. The dependence in question is a dependence for existence. For Descartes this is as true of the world as it is of Descartes, that is, the world's duration, or any period of the world's duration is divisible into parts none of which depends for its existence on any other. It follows that if to create is to cause the world to exist, the creative act must be followed by a conservative act, for without a new act the world would be annihilated in an instant. But from Descartes's perspective the conservative act must be another creative act since God has, so to say, to start again from scratch, and then again, so that God's conservative acts are constant repetitions of what he did the first time (if there had been a first time).

<hr />

[11] René Descartes, *The Philosophical Works of Descartes*, eds. Elizabeth S. Haldane and G. R. T. Ross, 2 vols. (New York: Dover, 1931) I, 168.

One might wonder why an infinitely creative God would be so repetitious, and Descartes's answer must be that since time is discrete each new instant is a new beginning and a world just like, or almost just like, the previous one must replace that previous one. But if that is Descartes's reason for holding that God has to be repetitious as a way of conserving the world, then it is reasonable to wonder why God should have willed the world to have a kind of temporality that would require him to be repetitious as the only way to conserve the world he had created, when he could instead have willed time to be of such a nature that, once the world is in existence, its continued existence does not require God the creator to be endlessly repetitious as a conserver.

Whatever be the explanation for Descartes's judgment that time is discrete it is at least clear why he thought the distinction between creation and conservation was only a distinction of reason and not a real distinction. For conservation is repetitious creation. It is creation *again*. But it is not the less creation. In so far as the distinction is one of reason only, Descartes's position resembles Mair's, but there can be no doubt that Mair would be almost totally hostile to Descartes on the relation between creation and conservation because, as hinted earlier, Mair does not accept the doctrine of time as a succession of discrete moments or instants. As is clear from his discussion of the terms *immediate* and *incipit*, Mair does not accept that there can be adjacent instants. And if there cannot, then something cannot cease to exist in one instant and be re-created in the next — there is no next.

This does not mean that Mair has no way of expounding the notion of something existing immediately after not existing, or of something now existing existing immediately before now; it means only that the exposition cannot take the form of saying that at one instant the thing does not exist and at the next it does, or that at one instant it existed and at the next instant it still exists. Instead Mair writes as follows: 'A proposition involving "immediately" is expounded in this way: "Immediately before this hour you existed" [is equivalent to] "Before this hour you existed and there was no namable instant before this hour but that between that instant [*sc* when you existed] and this hour you existed." "Immediately after this day you will exist" [is equivalent to] "After this day you will exist and there will be no namable instant after this day but that between that instant [*sc* when you will exist] and today you will exist."'[12] These expositions do not imply that there is a next instant, and they leave Mair free to accept, which he does, the concept of time as non-discrete. Some lines after the passage just quoted he argues that however soon after this instant there occurs instant A, 'A is not

12   John Mair, *Exponibilia* (Paris: 1503) fol. 27 recto col. 2; *ibid.* 'Et propositio de immediate sic exponitur: Immediate ante hanc horam tu fuisti et non fuit dabile instans ante hanc horam quin inter illud et hanc horam tu fuisti. Immediate post hunc diem tu eris post hunc diem tu eris et non erit dabile instans post hunc diem quin inter illud et hunc diem tu eris.'

the instant closest to the instant in which we now are. Indeed infinite instants are intermediate.'[13] He could hardly have stated his belief in the continuity of time with greater clarity.

To sum up, there is no logical pressure on Mair to wonder what God does to maintain in existence the world in the next instant after creating it. Mair's answer must be that God does nothing next because he has no need to. The very same act by which he creates the world is the act by which he conserves it. As Mair says, there is no real distinction between creation and conservation. Since, *pace* Descartes, God created the world as a something with a timespan, there is no need to invoke the concept of divine repetitiveness to explain how the world, once started, continues in existence.

---

[13] Mair, *Exponibilia*, fol. 27 verso col.1. 'A non est instans propinquissimum instanti in quo sumus. Immo mediant infinita instantia.'

Scotland's First Protestant Coronation: Revolutionaries, Sovereignty and the Culture of Nostalgia[1]

Michael Lynch

In 1567, the newly Protestant Scotland shed its Catholic monarch, Mary Queen of Scots (1542-67), and substituted a godly prince in her stead — her infant son, James (1567-1625). It was, in retrospect, a key moment in the history of both Protestantism and a fledgling Protestant nation. This coronation has never been subjected to detailed study yet much has been inferred from it, mostly as regards the path it laid down towards future conflicts between monarchical and resistance theories of government.

The coronation was undoubtedly a revolutionary act, complete with a full-blooded sermon by John Knox based on the second Book of Kings. Yet at this iconic moment — the crowning of a godly prince supervised by what Knox claimed to be the most perfect church in all the world — its organisers chose to indulge in a culture of nostalgia for the nation's medieval past. Almost all the standard ingredients of medieval coronations were present and the attention given to precedent was marked. Remarkably, the ceremony included the formal rite of anointing, a concession awarded to the Scots by the pope and used in every coronation since 1331. It was also an inauguration as well as an investiture and, as such, reminiscent of a much older ceremony going back to the ninth century or earlier.

There were, however, also key differences: some of the standard ingredients in medieval coronations were put in a different order, most were given a new twist and there were some outright novelties. Any attempt to reconstruct the ceremony staged in 1567 is bedeviled by two sets of difficulties. The first is that no detailed account of the coronation survives. The fullest account is that written into the record of the privy council, but it is heavily skewed, featuring the three deeds of demission signed by Queen Mary rather than the ceremony itself.[2] Otherwise, there is only a small handful of fairly laconic descriptions, all of them at second or even third hand. There are in addition fairly brief accounts in two contemporary sources, the anonymous *Diurnal of Occurents*

---

[1] I am grateful to Dr Julian Goodare and Professor Roger Mason for their advice and helpful comments on this chapter.
[2] *The Register of the Privy Council of Scotland*, eds. John Hill Burton, David Masson, Peter Hume Brown and Henry Paton, 36 vols. (Edinburgh: H.M. General Register House, 1877-1933) II, 531-44 [*RPC*].

and a second-hand report by an agent of Sir Nicholas Throckmorton, the English envoy, who declined to attend what many regarded as an illegal act. There are subsequent accounts in the anonymous *Historie of King James the Sext* and in other later histories.[3] These sources broadly agree as to the content, if with minor discrepancies, but they are sometimes vague as to the sequence of the ceremony or to key details within it.

There is a second set of difficulties. Knowledge of the detail of medieval investitures in Scotland is limited and is, to an extent, influenced by seventeenth-century sources preparatory to the Scottish coronation of Charles I (1625-49) in 1633.[4] Nonetheless a comparison of the ceremony of 1567 with those that went before it can shed some light on the shape, content and aspirations of Scotland's first Protestant coronation. Even so, a word of caution may be appropriate: the more one looks at this period, at the sequence of events which led up to the coronation and the ceremony itself, very little is as it first appears.

THE BACKGROUND

On 29 July 1567, a little before 2 o'clock in the afternoon, a small procession wound its way down the 400 metres from the royal palace of Stirling Castle to the Church of the Holy Rude, the parish church of the burgh of Stirling. The procession was headed by three members of the aristocracy carrying what have come to be called the 'Honours

---

[3]   *Calendar of State Papers Relating to Scotland and Many, Queen of Scots, 1547-1603,* ed. Joseph Bain *et. al.* (Edinburgh: H.M.S.O., 1898-1969) II, 370-71 [*CSP Scot*]; *Calendar of State Papers, Foreign Series, of the Reign of Elizabeth*, eds. Joseph Stevenson, Allan J. Crosby, Arthur James Butler, S. C. Lomas and R. B. Wernham, 25 vols. (London: Longman & Co., 1861-1950) VIII, 291-306 [*CSPF Eliz*]; *A Diurnal of Remarkable Occurrents that have passed within... Scotland since the Death of King James IV till the Year M.D.LXXV,* ed. Thomas Thomson (Edinburgh: Bannatyne Club, 1833) 118; *The Historie and Life of King James the Sext being an Account of the Affairs of Scotland, from the Year 1566, to the Year 1596; with a Short Continuation to the Year 1617,* ed. Thomas Thomson (Edinburgh: Bannatyne Club, 1825) 17; David Calderwood, *The History of the Kirk of Scotland,* ed. Thomas Thomson, 8 vols. (Edinburgh: Wodrow Society, 1842-49) II, 384; Robert Keith, John Parker Lawson and C. J. Lyon, *History of the Affairs of Church and State in Scotland from the Beginning of the Reformation to the Year 1568,* 3 vols. (Edinburgh: Spottiswoode Society, 1844) II, 719-23, 726-27n, 728-29; John Spottiswoode, Mark Napier and M. Right Russell, *History of the Church of Scotland, Beginning the Year of Our Lord 203 and Continuing to the End of the Reign of King James VI,* 3 vols. (Edinburgh: The Spottiswoode Society, 1847-51) II, 68.
[4]   See R. J. Lyall, 'The Medieval Scottish Coronation Service: Some Seventeenth-Century Evidence,' *The Innes Review* 28 (1977); Andrea Thomas, 'Crown Imperial: Coronation Ritual and Regalia in the Reign of James V,' *Sixteenth-Century Scotland: Essays in Honour of Michael Lynch,* eds. Julian Goodare and A. A. MacDonald (Leiden: Brill, 2008) 49-55.

of Scotland': the Earl of Morton carried the sceptre, the Earl of Glencairn had the sword of state and the Earl of Athol carried the closed imperial crown, commissioned by James V (1513-42) in 1540.[5] The Earl of Mar, hereditary Keeper of the Castle or perhaps his wife the Countess (accounts differ or are silent on the issue) carried the thirteen-month old infant, Prince James, son and heir of Mary, Queen of Scots. This was the first time that the coronation of a Scottish monarch had taken place in an ordinary parish church. It was one extraordinary feature of many in the coronation ritual of 1567. For those in attendance — or for those outside the church or well away from Stirling that day who diplomatically declined to be present at the ceremony itself — this remarkable occasion must have brought to mind two previous events which had taken place in recent times.

One was obvious. It would have been the coronation of the young Prince's mother twenty-four years before, when she too was an infant, nine months old. It also took place in Stirling, in September 1543, but in the Chapel Royal of the Castle rather than the Church of the Holy Rude.[6] It was probably the first time that the imperial crown had featured in a full coronation, raised above the infant Mary's head.[7] Centrally featured in 1543, as in 1567, were the sword and the sceptre. There was one possible added ingredient in 1543: that Mary was also confirmed during the ceremony, as would logically have to be given the standard terms of the coronation oath: 'I shall be loyal and true to God, and Holy Kirk, and to the three estates of my realm ...'.[8]

The other contrast that must have been in the minds of many that day was more immediate — the baptism of the infant prince. It had taken place just seven and a half months before, in December 1566, again in the Castle and Palace of Stirling. There, over the course of three days, the first born son of Mary, Queen of Scots had been fêted, celebrated and baptized according to full Catholic rites in the Chapel Royal. The baptism was accompanied by a full-scale Renaissance triumph, which culminated in the young prince being proclaimed amidst 'triumph and joy'.[9]

---

[5]   For the gift of the sword of state by Pope Julius II to James IV in 1507, see Charles Burns, 'Papal Gifts to Scottish Monarchs: The Golden Rose and the Blessed Sword,' *The Innes Review* 20 (1969), 163-67, 172-83, 189-93; for the 'Honours' more generally, see Thomas, 'Crown Imperial,' 55-61.

[6]   *The Hamilton Papers. Letters and Papers Illustrating the Political Relations of England and Scotland in the XVIth Century*, ed. Joseph Bain, 2 vols. (Edinburgh: H.M. General Register House, 1890-92) 33.

[7]   It is possible that the crown may have been used by James V at the time of the coronation of his second queen, Mary of Guise, in Feb. 1540: Thomas, 'Crown Imperial,' 63.

[8]   Cited in Lyall, 'Medieval Scottish Coronation Service,' 9; Cf. J. A. Guy, *My Heart is My Own: The Life of Mary Queen of Scots* (London: Fourth Estate, 2004) 17, 27.

[9]   Michael Lynch, 'Queen Mary's Triumph: The Baptismal Celebrations at Stirling in December 1566,' *Scottish Historical Review* 69 (1990): 10-13.

What happened at Stirling in December 1566 was a direct copy of some of the spectacles acted out at Bayonne in the far south-west of France eighteen months before, in June 1565.[10] The purpose and the message were much the same. At Bayonne, after a bitter civil war between Protestants and Catholics, the message was simple: only the Valois monarchy, represented by the young Charles IX and his mother Catherine de Medici, could rescue France and restore peace and order to the realm. At Stirling, the message was repeated for were not the two situations very similar? Mary, like her cousin Charles IX, had survived a Protestant putsch — in fact two conspiracies in 1565 and 1566, the so-called Chaseabout Raid and the murder of her secretary, David Riccio. What she offered was the prospect of peace, a stable monarchy which would lead Scotland out of civil war and the danger of a war of religion, and the prospect of a secure succession, with a male heir.

The birth and baptism of a male heir was the culmination of a renewed cult of monarchy, deeply imbued with imperial imagery and centred in the royal court. It was particularly evident from 1565 onwards, following Mary's marriage to Lord Darnley. As in France, the cult was designed to show two things: it was a demonstration of the power and divine status of the monarchy and it was proof of its role as the bringer of peace and harmony to a nation ravaged by civil war. This was ambitious and heady propaganda, performed in verse, song, dance, and chronicle, and culminating in the three-dimensional rhetoric of a Renaissance fête.[11] In it, Mary was Astraea. She was the focal point of a cult of honour, celebrating her as the 'daughter of a hundred kings', fulfilment of the prophecy of Merlin of an 'age of gold' to come in which the folly of civil war and religious strife would be brought to an end.[12] Her son and heir, it was claimed, was the new 'Arthur', king of Britons to come.[13]

---

[10]   Victor E. Graham and William McAllister Johnson, *The Royal Tour of France by Charles IX and Catherine de' Medici: Festivals and Entries, 1564-6* (Toronto: University of Toronto Press, 1979) 38-42, 343-56; Roy C. Strong, *Art and Power: Renaissance Festivals, 1450-1650* (Woodbridge: Boydell Press, 1984) 103-09; Jean Boutier, Alain Dewerpe and Daniel Nordman, *Un tour de France royal: le voyage de Charles IX 1564-1566*, Collection historique (Paris: Aubier, 1984) *passim*.

[11]   The significance of this period, following the royal marriage, has been highlighted in the work of Professor MacDonald, most notably in his re-dating of the collecting of the Bannatyne Miscellany, from its self-confessed gathering 'in time of pest', during an outbreak of plague in 1568, to the more likely time for a celebration of love in lyric and vernacular verse: see A. A. MacDonald, 'The Bannatyne Manuscript-A Marian Anthology,' *Innes Review* 37 (1986); A. A. MacDonald, 'The Printed Book that Never Was: George Bannatyne's Poetic Anthology,' *Boeken in de Late Middeleeuwen: Verslag van de Groningse Codicologendagen 1992*, eds. Jos M. M. Hermans and Klaas van der Hoek (Groningen: Forsten, 1994).

[12]   Frances Amelia Yates, *Astraea: The Imperial Theme in the Sixteenth Century* (London: Routledge & Kegan Paul, 1975) 59-87.

[13]   Patrick Adamson, *Serenissimi ac Nobilissimi Scotiae, Angliae, Hybernię Principis: Henrici Stuardi inuictissimi herois, ac Mariae Reginae amplissimae filij Genethliacum* (Parisiis: Apud Carolum Perier, 1566); Lynch, 'Queen Mary's Triumph,' 13. Cf. Boutier, Dewerpe and Nordman, *Un tour de France royal* 322-23.

This was compelling propaganda which had to be countered after Mary's fall, which had taken the dubious form of a voluntary abdication. The coronation of the young, godly prince, which took place five days later, had to offer an alternative version of the future — a *Protestant* future. It has sometimes been claimed that the ceremony lasted only a short time, for fear of an attack by Mary's supporters. It is certainly true that there were fears of an attack. Some 150 armed men had been sent to Stirling eleven days before the ceremony on 29 July. Yet the coronation in fact lasted fully three hours. The reason for that was the need to put on a ceremony full of meaning and convincing in its attention to precedent. The organisers of the coronation in the Holy Rude went to considerable lengths to make the ceremony not only the symbol of the new Protestant Scotland but also a guarantee of the continuity of a relationship between king and people which stretched far into the past.

Despite considerable gaps in the evidence, enough survives to show that all the standard ingredients of a medieval Stewart coronation, save one, were there.[14] They included the formal procession, bearing the 'Honours', with prominence accorded to the sword of state, a gift by a warrior Medici pope to James IV, now given a new lease of life in a Protestant realm; the acclamation by Lyon King of Arms, the chief heraldic officer of state; a sermon; the king's oath; the formal rite of anointing, enjoyed by every king since 1331, wrung by King Robert Bruce (1306-29) as a concession from the pope; the investiture or coronation rite and the inauguration, a much older rite of passage; the actual act of crowning; and oaths of fealty made by each of the three estates.

No account mentions a recital of the king's genealogy, which was also a standard part of medieval coronations and a throwback to the much older rite of inauguration. In the circumstances of 1567, when Mary's claim to be the successor of a hundred kings had to be countered, as it would be in the writings of George Buchanan which surfaced elsewhere in the months and years after James' coronation, it seems certain it would have had a place in the ceremony.[15] As will be seen, some of these standard

---

[14]   There is, however, also no record of the 'crowning' of Lyon King of Arms and his 'Declaration', which usually took place the day before the coronation itself. See Sir Francis. J. Grant, *Court of the Lord Lyon: List of His Majesty's Officers of Arms and Other Officials, with Genealogical Notes, 1318-1945* (Edinburgh: Scottish Record Society, 1945) 1; C. J. Burnett, 'Early Offices of Arms in Scotland,' *Review of Scottish Culture* 9 (1995-96): 3-13; Thomas, 'Crown Imperial,' 52.

[15]   It is likely that both John Lesley, bishop of Ross, and Buchanan had by 1565 begun to cultivate the origin legends of Scottish monarchy as part of the cult of honour surrounding Mary: see Lynch, 'Queen Mary's Triumph,' 16n Buchanan would also implicitly have to counter the notion of a 'golden age', to which he himself had subscribed in 1564-65: see his poems 'D. Gulatero Haddono Magistro libellorum supplicum Serenissimae Reginae' in George Buchanan, *The Political Poetry*, eds. Paul J. McGinnis and Arthur H. Williamson, Scottish History Society (Series) (Edinburgh: Scottish History Society, 1995) 150-53, 316-17, which hailed the two 'goddesses', Elizabeth Tudor and Mary, and his 'Genethliacon', celebrating

ingredients were put in a different order and there were some other rearrangements yet, viewed overall, great efforts were made to make the ceremony seem like a re-enactment of past rites of passage.

In one sense, the sequence of events in the immediate days and weeks before 29 July is a story simple in outline, even if the details of individual loyalties are complex and shifting.[16] On 15 June Mary and her husband, the Earl of Bothwell, were confronted on the battlefield of Carberry, just outside Musselburgh, by the coalition sometimes known as the 'Confederate Lords'. Mary surrendered to the Lords and Bothwell fled. A little more than twenty-four hours later Mary was taken to the island prison of Lochleven, by order of the privy council, a decision endorsed by no less than twelve earls and fourteen lords. Here complications begin to emerge. That consensus was intent, it seems, only on removing Bothwell. It had also been agreed to put Mary out of harm's way until the next move could be decided. That came five weeks later, on 24 July, when a delegation led by Lord Lindsay of the Byres travelled to Lochleven and persuaded or, more likely, forced the Queen to sign three acts of demission: one involved abdicating the crown in favour of her son; the second agreed to the regency of her half-brother, Lord James Stewart, Earl of Moray; and the third consented to a council of regency in the interim or if Moray declined the invitation. Five days later, the coronation took place. And a little more than three weeks after it, on 22 August, just eleven days after he returned to Edinburgh, Moray was invested as regent. In the meantime, the young Prince was kept secure in Stirling Castle by the Earl of Mar, hereditary keeper of the Castle, one of the earls who had a central place in the coronation ceremony.

It seems a fairly straightforward story — of a coup (displacing Bothwell as the Queen's consort); of a coup within a coup in which the radicals took charge, removing Mary to a remote island prison, sacking the Palace of Holyroodhouse and stripping Mary's private chapel of its Catholic furnishings; and, in parallel, a story of the Kirk seizing its chance a few days later, with the Catholic queen safely out of the way, to repair what it called the 'decay and ruin' of the Kirk, push forward with its programme of evangelization, and root out all 'superstition and idolatry'.[17]

---

the birth of Prince James, in which 'a golden age and the end of warfare' with England also figured, though with none of Adamson's Stewart triumphalism: *ibid.*, 154-62, 317-19.

[16] See Gordon Donaldson, *All the Queen's Men: Power and Politics in Mary Stewart's Scotland* (London: Batsford Academic and Educational, 1983) 84-86.

[17] *Booke of the Universall Kirk of Scotland: Acts and Proceedings of the General Assemblies of the Kirk of Scotland*, ed. Thomas Thomson, 3 vols. (Edinburgh: Bannatyne and Maitland Clubs, 1839-45) I, 94-95 [*BUK*]; *The Acts and Proceedings of the General Assemblies of the Church of Scotland, 1560 to 1618*, ed. Duncan Shaw, Scottish Record Society, 3 vols. (Edinburgh: Scottish Record Society, 2004) I, 119-25 (25-28 June).

Put another way, the tensions and dynamic of the situation in the summer of 1567 may be better understood if one thinks of Mary, not as a prisoner but as a hostage, held by the sixteenth-century equivalent of a radical militia group, which had secreted its captive in a remote location. What remained uncertain was the price Mary's abductors wanted or whether she would ever come out of the crisis alive. The fear that she would be quietly disposed of was certainly expressed in the reports made by Throckmorton, the English envoy based in Edinburgh from 12 July onwards.

The crisis which followed Mary's imprisonment at Lochleven is one example of the general point that very little in reality was as it first appears. One can count, assess and analyse events, such as the deduction that this was a coup within a coup; or one can probe what did *not* happen; or one can try to deduce what was intended to happen but did not, or what was supposed to happen after the coronation. One facet of these alternative means of analysis is either to examine who attended the coronation or to try to weigh up who were absent and why.

THE DRAMATIS PERSONAE

As has been seen, twelve earls and fourteen lords had formed the confederation which had confronted the Queen and Bothwell at Carberry and had sent her to Lochleven on the following day. Yet only five earls and eight lords were present at the coronation, along with just one bishop, five commendators, various minor commissioners, and the representatives of only eight burghs.[18] It was probably the worst attended coronation in Scottish history. It was also almost certainly the cheapest. The approximate cost of the baptismal triumph of December 1566 was £30,000 Scots and the total expenditure for that year, as revealed in the treasurer's accounts, was over £67,000. The total for the eight months which began with the coronation of 1567 was a mere £10,324. The only recorded expenditure for the coronation was £115 spent on clothes and robes for the infant prince, £29 to pay the expenses of the Lyon King of Arms and the undisclosed number of heralds who attended, and £8 to pay three trumpeters.[19]

---

[18]   Commendators were the heads of religious houses which had been secularized before or after the Reformation of 1560. Donaldson, *All the Queen's Men* 85-86, confuses the sederunt of the convention of estates which met in the Castle on the morning of 29th and the list of those attending the coronation: two commendators attended the former and five the latter. *RPC*, I, 537-38.

[19]   Lynch, 'Queen Mary's Triumph,' 1-2; *Accounts of the Lord High Treasurer of Scotland*, eds. Sir James Balfour Paul and Thomas Dickson, 12 vols. (Edinburgh: H.M. General Register House, 1877) XII, 1-61 (1566-74), 67-100 (July 67 – Feb. 68). There were other sources of both income and expenditure, such as the accounts of the comptroller. Taking these into account, the total for 1566 was over £106,000 and for 1567 over £54,000. I owe this information to Dr Julian Goodare.

Who was not there? None of Scotland's three premier noble families was in attendance — the Hamiltons, the Gordons of Huntly or the Campbells of Argyll. Only one of the three surviving conforming bishops was there and only two of the five Protestant superintendents of the kirk. The English ambassador, Throckmorton, remained in Edinburgh, having refused an explicit invitation to attend, anxious (as his instructions from Queen Elizabeth dictated) not to be seen to condone an illegal act.[20]

The same caution had manifested itself in the poor attendance at two successive meetings of the General Assembly in Edinburgh in the six weeks prior to the coronation. The first session, held over four days between 25 and 28 June, sent out letters demanding better attendance at the next meeting.[21] On 25 July, just four days before the coronation, the next session of the Assembly subscribed a set of ten articles, ratifying the acts of the Reformation parliament of 1560, demanding the punishment of all crimes and vices, promising 'to root out, destroy and alluterly subvert all monuments of idolatry', seeking the blood of the murderers of Darnley and promising to defend the son of the dead king. The articles endorsed a 'band and contract mutuall and reciprocal between the prince and God and between the prince and the faithful people'. The subscribers, however, included just three earls and seven lords, followed by a phalanx of minor lairds and the commissioners for only five burghs.[22] So poor was the attendance that the Assembly again decided to send out the articles to those who had absented themselves, ordering them to subscribe under pain of excommunication.

Another clue to the mood of these two assemblies was the declaring of a general fast for 20 July. This was a tactic used only once before, in late 1565. It should not be taken as a sign of the strength and dynamic of the radical preachers. Rather the opposite. Typically, a fast was called when the godly felt their backs to the wall, threatened not only by a resurgent Catholicism but also, more seriously, by what Knox in 1565 had condemned as 'pseudo-Christians' or 'hollow hearts' — what others, by contrast, regarded as moderate Protestantism.[23]

In the coup within a coup, it may be deduced, the revolutionaries were divided in their strategies. Initially, even before the marriage of Mary to Bothwell, it had been rumoured that part of the Confederate Lords wanted to depose the Queen and crown

---

[20]   Throckmorton sent two reports about the forthcoming coronation on 26 July: in the one addressed to Elizabeth, he wrote that the rebel lords had 'desired him to assist'; in that to the Earl of Leicester, he reported that he had been 'required to assist' but 'refused'. *CSP Scot*, II, 364, 365.

[21]   *BUK*, I, 93-95; *Acts and Proceedings*, 122-23.

[22]   *BUK*, I, 106-10; *Acts and Proceedings*, 140-41; Calderwood, *History of the Kirk* II, 382-83.

[23]   W. I. P. Hazlett, 'Playing God's Card: Knox and Fasting,' *John Knox and the British Reformations*, ed. R.A. Mason (Aldershot: Ashgate, 1998) 187-90, 193.

her son.[24] After Carberry and Mary's forced imprisonment, these rumours became reality. Knox and the radicals in the Assembly wanted Mary *deposed*. In contrast, the hardliners amongst the Confederate Lords wanted to hide behind the pretence of Mary giving up the throne *voluntarily*. That was the reason why, at the coronation, the three deeds of demission, each with the royal seal affixed, were presented, read out and read into the record of the privy council. Others ostensibly within the same faction which had seized the initiative, such as William Maitland of Lethington, the Queen's secretary, who had been one of those who had subscribed the General Assembly's articles, saw the coronation as stalling manoeuvre, a necessary step to prevent a worse outcome such as the assassination of the Queen.[25] Many of those who had taken part only in the first coup — the capture of Mary at Carberry — had since defected and had refused to attend meetings of both the privy council and the General Assembly in the vital six weeks before the coronation.[26]

Amidst this confused situation, English policy contrived to face two ways. Throckmorton, the English ambassador, arrived in Edinburgh with two sets of instructions which contradicted each other: Queen Elizabeth wanted Mary released; her secretary, William Cecil, wanted her deposed. In his private thoughts, Cecil went further. In the formal instructions to Throckmorton, Cecil parroted the royal line but in his own archival copy he revealed his own agenda when he annotated the document at its end: '*Athalia 4 Regum, inteterempta per Joas Regem*'.[27] This was a cryptic but telling reference to Queen Athalia, deposed and killed by her son Joash in the second Book of Kings – the same passage that Knox would later use in his sermon at the coronation. Elizabeth, however, wanted more than Mary's release. She also expected an agreement that the young prince be taken into safe custody in England, without recognition of his claim to the English succession. English policy, divided and self-contradictory, threatened to antagonize the hard-liners amongst the Scots nobility, who since 1560 had made up the core of the pro-English faction committed to the notion of a Protestant driven 'amity' between the two realms, and to force further splits amongst them.

---

[24] This allegation was made in a series of reports made by William Drury to Cecil in the two weeks before the marriage. The plot depended on possession of the infant prince so Mar, Keeper of Stirling Castle, was central to it. *CSPF Eliz, 1566-68*, nos. 1161, 1170, 1173, 1175, 1203. See also The National Archives, SP59/13, fo. 64r, Drury to Cecil, Berwick, 5 May 1567. I owe this reference to Dr Julian Goodare.

[25] To be precise, this was Maitland's later position. At the time, he described the coronation as an unfortunate necessity: *CSP Scot*, II, 358-59. He was also implicated in the earlier plot based in Stirling.

[26] Such as Argyll; see Jane E. A. Dawson, *The Politics of Religion in the Age of Mary Queen of Scots: The Earl of Argyll and the Struggle for Stability in Britain and Ireland*, Cambridge Studies in Early Modern British History (Cambridge: Cambridge University Press, 2002) 150-52.

[27] *CSP Scot*, II, 342; Guy, *Mary Queen of Scots* 363.

This helps explain the need for Maitland and others like him to play for time. For Throckmorton, repeatedly refused access to the Queen, it was all deeply frustrating. Within five days of his arrival, he was pleading for permission to return home and virtually every dispatch he sent after that repeated the plea.

What if — the unspoken question on the lips of many — the young prince should die? It was the same issue of a weak succession which had dominated Scottish politics since the early death of James IV in 1513 had left only one direct male successor, and that an infant. In the minds of most, if reluctantly, it was the Hamilton claim which predominated: in 1567, as in 1543, the next in line was the Earl of Arran, now duke of Châtelherault. In another view, again in 1567 as in 1543, it was the Lennox Stewarts who had the better claim: in 1543 this was vested in the Earl of Lennox and in 1567, in practice, in Lennox's younger son, Charles. This claim, however, required some creative thinking. Charles was the younger brother of Darnley. His claim was stronger if Darnley was thought of as a 'king' even if he had not been awarded the crown matrimonial, which had been the bribe with which he had been snared by the Riccio conspirators early in 1566. Some of the revolutionaries deduced that their case was stronger if they affected to be in the pursuit of the assassins of a real king rather than the murderers of a mere king consort.

Significantly, neither Châtelherault nor any of his considerable extended family, nor the grieving Lennox, grandfather of the infant king, were present at the coronation. Châtelherault was still in France but a Hamilton envoy was sent to Stirling to lodge a formal protest at a meeting of a convention of estates in the morning before the ceremony, that the coronation should not prejudice the Hamilton claim to the succession. Lennox had other, more immediate concerns: he was by now in Southampton, desperately short of money, still urging Elizabeth to finance his return to Scotland, press the Lennox Stewart claim to the throne, and to pursue Bothwell for his son's murder.[28] The two main sets of vultures were not at the coronation.

The revolutionaries had taken heed of the lesson of the Reformation parliament of 1560 which had abolished the Mass and adopted a Protestant Confession of Faith. It had later been claimed that this body had not been a legal assembly because it had not been properly 'fenced'; the Honours had not been displayed and so the monarch had been symbolically absent. That was probably the reason why the revolutionaries of 1567 did all they could to make sure that the formal paraphernalia of state were on hand for the coronation. The Honours were made a central feature of the ceremony. Awkwardly, however, two of the three officers of state who had a key role in medieval coronations were not. The Lord Lyon King of Arms, Sir Robert Forman, who had held the office since 1555, was there but the Marischal and the Constable were conspicuous

---

[28] *CSP Scot*, II, 330-31, 338.

by their absence. Their particular roles in the coronation ceremony were historically very precise, as will be seen in the table below.[29]

In one sense, driven by the familiar argument that in Scotland kin and kinship networks counted for more than religion, whether Catholic or Protestant,[30] it might be expected that the behaviour of these two officers of state, would be similar. They were related by marriage: the son of the Earl Marischal was married to the daughter of the Constable. Yet George Hay, 7th earl of Errol, Lord High Constable, was not involved in any of the key events of 1567, even though he had been reported to be at Mary's 'devotion' the day before her marriage to Bothwell on 15 May.[31] It was not until the parliament of December 1567 that he resurfaced, agreeing that Mary should remain in her island prison. By contrast, the revolutionaries might have expected more of William Keith, 4th Earl Marischal. He was linked to the revolutionaries by both marriage and religion. He was a committed Protestant and was related to Moray by marriage, as his father-in-law. Yet he, too, pleaded ill health, although he had been in Edinburgh regularly between April and June of 1567. More telling may have been his trait, which had been noted as early as 1561 by an English agent, as 'fearful and loath to enter into any matter of controversy'.[32]

With a depleted cast of the usual *dramatis personae*, the need of the revolutionaries to mount a semblance of continuity was so pressing that, remarkably, they turned to the Catholic primate of the realm, Archbishop John Hamilton of St Andrews, to officiate in the ceremony. If he could be persuaded to officiate, as primates before him had traditionally done, not only continuity but also the apostolic succession would be secured. Although it had been the archbishop who had baptized the infant Prince by Catholic rites in December 1566, he had been flirting with the reformers ever since 1560. By the summer of 1567, he was said to be 'showing himself now a conformable man both in apparel and outward orders of religion'.[33] He declined. Both religion and family, given the Hamilton interest in the succession, dictated otherwise.

The revolutionaries turned instead to Adam Bothwell, bishop of Orkney, a Protestant with impeccable family connections and close connections to the court, to take the central role in the coronation, or at least its traditional centrepiece, the rite of anointing.

---

[29] The absence of the Constable and Marischal may also have posed problems at the various meetings of a convention of estates in 1567. Both certainly had a prominent role in the meeting of full parliaments: R. K. Hannay, 'Observations on the Officers of the Scottish Parliament,' *Juridical Review* 44 (1932): 130-32, 137.

[30] Donaldson, *All the Queen's Men* 8, 151, *passim*.

[31] *CSPF Eliz, 1566-68*, 230-31.

[32] *Registrum Magni Sigilli Regum Scotorum*, eds. John Maitland Thomson, *et al.*, 11 vols. (Edinburgh: H.M. General Register House, 1882) IV, nos. 1782, 1798, 1800; *CSP Scot*, II, 460-61. It is unclear as to whether he had been at Carberry; cf. Donaldson, *All the Queen's Men* 80; *CSP Scot*, II, 333-34.

[33] *CSP Scot*, II, 371.

Bothwell has been called the 'most middle class' of all the bishops of the 1560s. He was the son of a provost of Edinburgh, the grandson of a chancellor of Scotland and his various relations amongst the judiciary included the Justice Clerk, Bellenden of Auchnoule, who was one of the key officers of state at the ceremony. He was a man with impeccable social credentials, a dubious past and some suspiciously moderate traits in religion. Described by Knox as 'ane enemy to God', he had been a very late convert in 1560 and the reformation which he had pushed through in his diocese of Orkney had been a mild one, marked by continuity of personnel and an absence of iconoclasm. Tellingly, for Knox and many of the radicals, he was tainted by his role in officiating at the marriage of Mary to the Earl of Bothwell, by Protestant rite, just two months before.[34]

A quartet of clergymen participated in the coronation. They represented a rather incongruous gang of four. It comprised Knox, the Genevan radical who had always been implacably hostile to the Queen and had been criticized for it, even in the General Assembly; John Erskine of Dun and John Spottiswoode, superintendents of Angus and Lothian respectively, who were both early Protestants but of a more moderate stamp than Knox, in their relations with the Queen as well as in theology; and the bishop of Orkney. Bothwell was an establishment figure and a late convert, who five months after the coronation, would be suspended from office for his failings, including his role in the marriage of Mary and Bothwell. Yet, personal faults or no, Adam Bothwell was a bishop and that is the reason why he was needed at the coronation.

Who else were conspicuous by their absence? As has been seen, none of the three peers who might have been expected to carry the crown, sword and sceptre — Châtelherault, Moray and Argyll — was in attendance. Nor was the Chancellor, the earl of Huntly. The two main families who were next in line in the succession — the Hamiltons and Lennox Stewarts — were not represented. Moray, the prospective regent, was still in France. He may have been awaiting a formal invitation to accept the office of regent. Alternatively, he may have been waiting to hear from Cecil how much his English pension would be before he agreed to take on the regency.

The revolutionaries of 1567 were divided, either wanting different things or taking different strategies or adopting different rationales. The official stance of the remnant of the privy council in power was that Mary had demitted office. Knox saw her as a Jezebel and a Queen Athalia who should be executed, Old Testament style, for her moral failings. For the future theorist of the king's party in the civil war which broke out in 1568, George Buchanan, busy rewriting both history and the chronicle tradition, she had broken the contract between ruler and ruled and could therefore be deposed. As always, however, the revolutionary guard was in the minority. Most of the

---

[34]   Gordon Donaldson, *Reformed by Bishops: Galloway, Orkney and Caithness* (Edinburgh: Edina Press, 1987) 19-52, esp. 21, 34.

rest of the political establishment was caught in the headlights of the succession crisis, either undecided or uncertain what to do for the best — either the best for the kingdom or for themselves. For most, reactions to the crisis took various forms: shuffling to the back of the queue when political stances had to be taken, diplomatic illnesses, or a hedging of bets. What else might be expected? Revolutions typically produce only a few revolutionaries. The coronation was designed to convince the ranks of the absentees more than the few who chose to risk attending.

THE CEREMONY

There were twelve key ingredients in the coronation of 1567.

Medieval	*1567*
Procession	**Procession**
Constable & Earl Marischal support the monarch; senior peers carry the crown, sceptre and sword	Earl or Countess of Mar carries the child; Earls of Athol, Morton and Glencairn carry the crown, sceptre and sword
Acclamation by Lyon King	**Acclamation by Lyon King**
	Reciting of Mary's deeds of demission
Sermon	**Sermon?**
By bishop or archbishop of St Andrews	by John Knox
	King's oath
Anointing	**Anointing**
oil carried by Lyon, given to Constable and Earl Marischal; unction administered by two bishops	by Adam Bothwell, bishop of Orkney, assisted by the superintendents of Angus and Lothian
Investiture and Inauguration	**Investiture and Inauguration**
robing by Constable and Marischal; spurs put on by Marischal	Earl of Mar held crown over infant's head
Reciting of genealogy by Lyon King	**Reciting of genealogy?**
Coronation	**Coronation**
by senior bishop present; crown removed by Constable	by Bishop of Orkney; subsidiary role for the two superintendents
	King's oath
Oaths of fealty	**Oaths of fealty**
	Asking of instruments
	by Knox, Erskine of Dun and Kinzeancleuch

The standard procession and acclamation were followed by a novel addition. It was, in effect, a ritual termination of the reign of Mary, Queen of Scots. A good part of the three hours which the ceremony lasted must have been taken up with a solemn recital of the three deeds of demission which the Queen had been forced to sign five days earlier on her island prison. As recorded now in the record of the privy council, the deeds run to five closely printed pages, amounting to some 4,000 words, and would have taken perhaps three quarters of an hour to recite. The acts of abdication were read out by Lord Lindsay of the Byres, who affected that they had been entered into voluntarily by the Queen during his visit to Lochleven. Lindsay's ruthlessness should come as no surprise. He had been a prominent member of the murder gang which had killed the Queens' secretary, David Rizzio, in her privy chamber sixteen months before. At the outset, the rationale for the coronation taken by the radical rump of the privy council which remained in power was established: Mary had demitted office and she had authorized the succession of her son.

It was conventional at medieval coronations for there to be a sermon, given by the senior churchman present, usually the bishop or, latterly, the archbishop of St Andrews. In 1567 the task fell to the 'trumpeter of God', as he called himself, John Knox. The precise point in the ceremony when Knox preached is not recorded but it probably came immediately after the reading of the three deeds of demission. It is likely to have taken fully an hour to deliver. The text is known of only a small handful of Knox's sermons. In August 1565, he had preached in St Giles', with Darnley in the congregation, on the prophecy of Isaiah (Isaiah, 26, verses 13-21): 'O Lord our God, other lords than You rule over us'. In it, he had railed against the government of wicked princes who, for the sins of the people, had been sent as tyrants and scourges to plague them. Crucially, he complained that 'God sets in that room, for the offences and ingratitude of the people, boys and women'.[35] A little less than two years later, Knox went from Isaiah to the second Book of Kings to find an infant prince, Joash, as the deliverer of God's people from the cruelty of an adulterous Queen.[36]

The Old Testament passage was the same as that to which Cecil had alluded in a postscript to his memorandum for Throckmorton: '*Athalia 4 Regum, interempta per*

---

[35] John Knox, *John Knox's History of the Reformation in Scotland*, ed. W. Croft Dickinson, 2 vols. (London: Nelson, 1949) II, 159; John Knox, *The Works of John Knox*, ed. David Laing, 6 vols. (Edinburgh: Wodrow Society, 1846-64) VI, 221-73.

[36] The covenant forged at the time of the inauguration of Joash had briefly been alluded to by Knox in his debate with Maitland of Lethington in the General Assembly in 1564: Knox, *History* II, 126; Athalia had predictably figured in Knox's *First Blast of the Trumpet against the Monstrous Regiment of Women* (1558): see Knox, *Works* IV, 363-420; Roger A. Mason, 'Knox on Rebellion,' *Kingship and the Commonweal: Political Thought in Renaissance and Reformation Scotland* (East Lothian: Tuckwell Press, 1998) 151.

Joas[h] Regem' and had been cited in the General Assembly's declaration of 25 July. This was Athalia, Queen of Israel, who had been killed in the sixth year of her reign, deposed by the high priest of Israel and her nobles for moral degeneracy and her young son, Joash, put in her place. With it, a double covenant was made — between the high priest Jehoidah and all the people and between the people and the king — that they should be the Lord's people and put the seven-year old Joash on the throne.[37] In the Geneva Bible of 1560, there follows the passage: 'For the sons of Athaliah, that wicked woman, had broken up the house of God; and also all the dedicated things of the house of the LORD did they bestow upon Baalim.' The passage has a footnote: 'The scriptures call her wicked because she was a cruel murderer and a blasphemous idolater.' Knox's sermon, sanctioned by the General Assembly in advance of the coronation, gave a different justification for Mary's abdication: she had been righteously deposed as an adulteress and an enemy of God's people and His true church. Here, it is as well to remember the lament of the General Assembly, meeting only days after the Queen had been imprisoned, of the 'decay and ruin' of the true church during her personal reign.

Next came the coronation oath, which was the central feature of the whole ceremony. Previously, it came after the coronation — a Scottish variant on practice in both England and the Holy Roman Empire. In 1567, it came before. The words of the coronation oath had been varied by parliament in 1445, but remained a straightforward 180 words. It began:

> I shall be loyal and true to God, and Halie Kirk, and to the three estates of my realm, and ilk estate I will keep, govern and defend in their awn freedom and privilege at my goodlie power, after the laws and customs of the realm …

and it ended: 'Sua helpe me God and this halydoume'.[38] In 1567, however, the king's oath, as recited by Morton, was twice as long. It began conventionally enough:

> I, James Prince and Steward of Scotland, promise faithfully, in the presence of the eternall my God, that I, induring the haill course of my life, shall serve the same Eternall my God, to the uttermost of my power …

but after that it descended into something of a rant, ending:

---

[37] 2 Chr. 24:7.
[38] Lyall, 'Medieval Scottish Coronation Service,' 9-10, 15-16, 18-20; *Records of the Parliaments of Scotland to 1707*, eds. K. M. Brown and Scottish Parliament Project Team (St Andrews: University of St Andrews, 2007-10) 1445/4 [*RPS*].

> And out of all my lands and empire I shall be careful to root out all heretics and enemies
> to the true worship of God, that shall be convicted by the true Kirk of God, of the fore-
> said crimes. And these things above-written, I faithfully affirm by my solemn oath.[39]

As delivered, it was less an oath than the speech of a godly prince. There were two sets
of aspirations embedded within it. The word 'empire' was a coded signal of the historical continuity of the ambitions of the revolutionaries: it recalled and further
embellished claims made by Stewart kings since the reign of James III (1460-88).[40]
Parliament had asserted in 1469 that the teenage king had 'ful jurisdictione and free
impire within his realm' and a closed or arched imperial crown had been depicted
on his coinage. The image was given physical reality in the actual closed imperial
crown commissioned by James V in 1540. Equally, it affected to be at one with Knox's
claim that the new fledgling church in Scotland was purer than any other. Further, it
tried to match the extravagant claims to an imperial monarchy implicit in the cult of
Mary as Astraea, which had been prominent at the baptism of her son only seven
months before.[41] The lineage and sovereignty of the Stewart monarchy was recast
alongside a new version of a patriotic national church which was its chief ally and supporter. A Protestant realm, with deep links with the past, and a godly church stood
side by side.

There may be a clue to the authorship of the speech. Throckmorton reported shortly
after his arrival in Edinburgh that Knox and other ministers meeting in the General
Assembly were culling histories and the ancient laws of the realm as well as Scriptures
for their arguments.[42] Another who undoubtedly had a hand in the framing of the
ceremony was the humanist and former court poet, George Buchanan. Usually the
king's oath was delivered after the crowning had taken place. In 1567, the oath came
before:

> After the solemn oath and promise, the Lords of the Nobility, Spirituality and Commis-
> sioners of Burghs, as the Estates of the Realm, be the ministration of the said Reverend
> Father Adam bishop of Orkney, anointed the said most excellent prince, in King of this

[39] *RPC*, I, 542.
[40] See Roger A. Mason, 'This Realm of Scotland is an Empire? Imperial Ideas and Iconography in Early
Renaissance Scotland,' *Church, Chronicle and Learning in Medieval and Early Renaissance Scotland*, ed. B.
E. Crawford (Edinburgh: Mercat Press, 1999).
[41] *The Acts of the Parliament of Scotland*, eds. Cosmo Nelson Innes and Thomas Thomson, 12 vols.
(Edinburgh: s.n., 1814-75) II, 95 [APS]; Knox, *History* II, 3; Ian Halley Stewart, *The Scottish Coinage*
(London: Spink, 1955) 67-74; Thomas, 'Crown Imperial,' 59-61, 66; Julian Goodare, *State and Society
in Early Modern Scotland* (Oxford: Oxford University Press, 1999) 11-12, 33-37; Yates, *Astraea: The
Imperial Theme in the Sixteenth Century* 29-38. James II was either 17 or 18 in 1469: see Christine
McGladdery, *James II* (Edinburgh: John Donald, 1990) 76.
[42] *CSP Scot*, II, 355.

Realm, investit and inaugurit his Grace therein, delivered in his hand the sword and sceptre, and put the crown royal upon his head.[43]

The implication was that the crowning and inauguration took place at the authority of the three estates and was conditional on the new monarch swearing to adhere to the terms of the oath, which came close to Buchanan's view that kings were elected by the people and a mutual pact was forged at the coronation between King and people. Thirty years later, James VI in later life as a philosopher king, would agonize, philosophize and dispute in his political tracts, and especially in his *Trew law of free monarchies* of 1597, the meaning of that oath, taken on his behalf by the Earl of Morton.[44]

Next came the anointing. Despite the protests of Knox and some other unnamed ministers, the ceremony in 1567 included the full rite of anointing, first used in 1331, at the crowning of the young David II (1329-71). The infant's head, shoulder-blades and hands were anointed with holy oil by Bishop Bothwell, with the two superintendents in attendance. Much the same protest against the rite of unction would be repeated in 1590 by Andrew Melville, the self-appointed spokesman of the next generation of radical ministers, at the coronation of James VI's wife, Queen Anne. Both the revolutionaries of 1567 and the adult James VI clung to medieval forms despite vocal opposition.

It was explicitly said in the record that the king was 'investit and inaugurat'. In other words, the ceremony was not only a coronation but also an inauguration, reminiscent of a much older rite. Typically, an inauguration would be followed, as it had been for many centuries, by a recital of the forebears of the current king. In the form recorded for 1633, the recitation was only of the past six generations. In 1633, of course, this would have been of the previous six Jameses, ignoring Mary, perhaps taking its cue from James VI's formal entry into Edinburgh in 1579, when portraits of the five successive Stewart kings called James who had gone before him were nailed to the market cross and his mother featured nowhere.[45] It is unclear in 1567 whether the ceremony was a forerunner of 1579 in the sense of limiting the roll call or whether there was a full recital of the line of more than a hundred kings of Scots who had, myth and medieval chronicles insisted, preceded the young Prince. Either way, whatever route to legitimacy and nostalgia was taken, here again was proof of the existing status of kings of Scots which had to be preserved.

---

[43] *RPC*, I, 542.

[44] R. A. Mason, 'George Buchanan, James VI and the Presbyterians,' *Scots and Britons: Scottish Political Thought and the Union of 1603*, ed. R. A. Mason (Cambridge: Cambridge University Press, 1994) 36.

[45] Lyall, 'Medieval Scottish Coronation Service,' 6; Michael Lynch, 'Court Ceremony and Ritual During the Personal Reign of James VI,' *The Reign of James VI*, eds. Julian Goodare and Michael Lynch (East Linton: Tuckwell Press, 2000) 76.

It was only at this point, following both the investiture and the inauguration, that the imperial crown was placed on the infant's head and the sword and sceptre put into his hands. Oaths of fealty by the members of the three estates followed, though it is doubtful that they would have done so on their knees, as in past ceremonies. In 1567, they touched the infant's head rather than the crown, as had been done in 1543, probably to emphasize the mutual contract between the people and the person of the king rather than a compact between subjects and the institution of monarchy. Alternatively, touching the infant's head allowed a distraction away from the customary procedure, which was to touch the papal cap gifted by Pope Julius II in 1507 along with the sword of state.[46]

The ceremony concluded with a final novelty. Bellenden, the Justice Clerk, Knox and the long-standing Protestant laird from Kyle, Robert Campbell of Kinzeancleuch, 'asked instruments'.[47] In other words, they formally asked for the fact of the ceremony to be duly recorded by a notary. And so it was, in the record of the privy council. Little is known of subsequent events. The same procession that had wound its way down from the Castle made its way back, with the Earl of Mar, hereditary keeper of the Castle, now formally charged with the role of guardian of the young King. It was claimed that there were the 'great feasts' in the Castle after the ceremony 'to the nobility and gentlemen'.[48] No descriptions of any specific festivities survive and there is nothing in the accounts of the Treasurer to show how much was spent on entertainments.

This was a coronation in which every effort had been made to include nearly all the standard ingredients of the medieval coronation ceremony; each had been scrutinized and moulded to fit the extraordinary circumstances of 1567. Despite various potential embarrassments, including the absence of a number of the traditional key players in the coronation ritual, much was done to try to lend dignity to the occasion and the infant king. One was addressing the child as 'your Majestie', which was done in the formal proclamation after the coronation, as well as 'your Grace'. This was distinctly new. It was only in 1563 that the Scottish parliament had regularly begun to use the form of address, 'the Quenis majestie'.[49] Both the abdication of the Queen and the crowning of her son were revolutionary acts. Ritual was used to affect that the more things had changed the more they had stayed the same. In later life James himself maintained that 'by the law of nature the king becomes a natural father to his lieges at his coronation'.

---

[46] Thomas, 'Crown Imperial,' 57; Burns, 'Papal Gifts,' 160-68, 172-79.

[47] This was a device sometimes used to record a formal protest, as it was by radical ministers against the passage through parliament in May 1584 of the so-called 'Black Acts' limiting the powers and privileges of the Kirk before fleeing into exile in England. The status of the three supplicants is unclear: they could only partly claim to represent the three estates.

[48] *CSP Scot*, II, 370.

[49] *RPC*, I, 543-44; Goodare, *State and Society* 34.

Buchanan and later constitutional theorists in pursuit of contract law, in contrast, maintained that the coronation had produced a contract between the king and his people. As such, it becomes possible for historians, if so minded, to claim that much of the outline script for the tensions and struggles between Stewart kings and their subjects for the next 120 years was written in Stirling in 1567.

Viewed through a prism which concentrates on the near rather than the distant future, it is possible to deduce that the coronation of the infant, now godly, prince did two things: at one and the same time, it covered up the internal differences amongst the revolutionaries yet it also revealed something of the hybrid nature of Scottish Protestantism in its early years, even at the moment of its greatest triumph to date. Three facets, if subjected to closer scrutiny, highlight the rival impulses which both united and divided the new Protestant establishment in 1567. Three questions, in turn, suggest themselves. Why call a general fast, only the second in the history of Scottish Protestantism? Why was it felt necessary to have not one but three deeds of demission, to turn an abdication into an approved succession, rather than a coup capable of being justified by a combination of historicity, Old Testament justice or *realpolitik*? And why was it felt necessary to re-enact so much of the medieval — and very Catholic — elements of the coronation ceremony?

THE GENERAL FAST

The first meeting of the General Assembly after Mary's fall had taken place in Edinburgh, on 25 June, nine days after the Queen had been removed to her island prison. The atmosphere in which it convened — a combination of crisis, exultant expectation and profound alarm — needs to be borne in mind in assessing its actions, as does the fact that Buchanan sat in the chair as moderator. The Kirk had set as its agenda the need to 'repaire the decay and ruine of … this ruinous hous of God within this realme', begun 'so vertuouslie' in 1560. Despite this, the meeting was poorly attended. Another session was arranged, again in Edinburgh, for 20 July, with a general fast called to coincide with it. Strongly worded letters threatening exclusion from the 'bosom of the Kirk' were sent to the 'unsubscribing professors', demanding that they attend the next meeting of the Assembly: the letters reveal that a total of seven earls, nineteen lords, six lairds and half a dozen commendators had absented themselves. One of them, the Earl of Argyll, protested that the June meeting had lacked a mandate and was in clear breach of precedent laid down since 1560.[50] In the meantime, the capital remained an

---

[50]   *BUK*, I, 101; *Acts and Proceedings*, 129-30; Calderwood, *History of the Kirk* II, 369-70.

armed camp, guarded by 450 harquebusiers; 150 more had been sent to both Stirling and Perth to prevent intervention from the Marian strongholds in the west and north.[51]

The purpose of the general fast of July 1567 was strongly reminiscent of its predecessor, called in the dark days of late 1565 when radical Protestantism was in disarray and many of its supporters in self-imposed exile. Published as an authorized tract of the Assembly, that Order of Fast was imbued with a heady radical Biblicism which proposed that Scotland was bound by God's covenant to Israel. It was addressed not to the nation as such but to the true believers, defined as 'the saints' and 'the elect'. It anticipated resistance amongst fellow Protestants, castigating sceptics or critics as 'atheists' or 'pseudo Christians', and it urged: 'Let not the godly be offended by the brocardes [lampoons] and lardoons [gibes] of such godless people'.[52]

There was no time, in the breakneck sequence of events in the summer of 1567, for the authorized text of an Order of Fast to be published, but the record of the General Assembly makes clear that the same uncompromising stance which informed its meeting in June also prevailed in the days of its main session on 24 and 25 July, which coincided with the Queen's forced abdication. Again, the General Assembly was less general than it hoped. It received a series of excuses for non-attendance. The objections made by Argyll expressed surprise that grave decisions had been made which lacked 'common consent' about the 'differences … presently in this realm'. The complaints made by three commendators were even more pointed: they objected to the unprecedented circumstances of being summoned to an armed camp, 'kept strictly by one part of the nobility and men of war of their retinue to whose opinion we are not adjoined as yet'. The rejoinder made by Lord Boyd, probably echoed the silent thoughts of many fellow Protestant veterans of the Wars of the Congregation: his agreement was conditional only so far as 'it might stand with the law'.[53]

The shrillness of the Assembly's response to these qualms was revealing. Citing the second chapter of the Book of Kings as justification for its actions, it echoed in advance Knox's text for the forthcoming sermon at the Stirling coronation. So were its threats, provoked by a frustratingly low turnout, to brand the absentees as no longer 'members of their body'. Although the roll recorded sixty-three members of the landed classes as in attendance, the normal power-brokers were few and the nonentities were many. Only three earls, six nobles and representatives of five burghs turned up. The rest were

---

[51] *CSP Scot*, II, 356.

[52] Hazlett, 'Playing God's Card,' 47. In this sense, 'atheist' did not mean not believing in God; rather, it meant behaving as if one did not believe in God: see Christopher Haigh, *The Plain Man's Pathways to Heaven: Kinds of Christianity in Post-Reformation England, 1570-1640* (Oxford: Oxford University Press, 2007) 68, 169, 170.

[53] *BUK*, I, 101-02; *Acts and Proceedings*, 129-31; Spottiswoode, Napier and Russell, *History* II, 65. See also Donaldson, *All the Queen's Men* 96-97.

made up of office holders from the privy council and a motley collection of lairds, mostly from Ayrshire and other parts of the west. Even then, attendance at the Assembly was no guarantee of presence at the coronation. The conclusion to be reached is that the abdication crisis had galvanised many of the radicals in the Kirk but, viewed as a whole, the dilemmas of 1567 had split rather than united Scottish Protestantism. Knox might claim that 'in religion thair is na middis'. The events of 1567 has revealed a large but very confused centre ground, in both politics and religion.

Legitimacy and the deeds of demission

The second remarkable facet of the crisis was the resort to chop-logic legalism to underpin the issue of legitimacy, seen in the sustained focus in the coronation ceremony on the three deeds of demission forced upon the imprisoned Queen. The task was a delicate legal balancing act with many half-hidden pitfalls. In the first of the deeds, the Queen had to agree that she was unfit to rule but it also had implicitly to be recognized that she was fit enough to nominate her infant son as her successor. As such, authority was granted by the Queen to:

> Plant, place and inaugurat him in the kingdome, and with all ceremonies requisite to putt the crown royall upon his head, in signe and tokin of the establishing of him therein; and, in his name, to make and give to the said nobilitie, clergie, burgesses, and others our lieges, his princelie and kinglie oathe debtfullie and lawfullie … and to receave their oaths.

The deeds were recorded in the register of the privy council as 'allowit and apprevit' by 'the Lordis of the Secreit Consall and utheris of the Nobilitie, Prelattis, Baronis and Commissaris of Burrowis'. This suggests a convention of the estates and the first of the deeds was copied, word for word, into the records of the books of parliament, with the preamble in the form of an addition made in the margin of the copy.[54] This, however, is where difficulties begin. The other two deeds do not appear in the parliamentary record, no sederunt of the convention is given and there is no record of the formal calling of a convention. The implication seems clear: the first act of abdication was copied into the record sometime later, perhaps only at the time of the next entry, the formal appointment of Moray as regent on 22 August.[55]

The reason that the convention met when it did is readily explained. The key figures amongst the revolutionaries, including Glencairn and Mar, and the enforcers, 'many

---

[54] *RPS*, 1567/7/25/1.
[55] *Ibid.*, 1567/8/1.

gentlemen of the west', arrived in Edinburgh on 23 July. Edinburgh was then, in Throckmorton's words, 'a town guarded by men-of war', a further reason for those who did not wholeheartedly support a forced abdication to stay away.[56] On the same day Lindsay was dispatched to Lochleven on his mission to force Mary's hand. He returned two days later. It was on that very day that three bodies met, in the same place, the Edinburgh tolbooth — privy council, convention of estates and General Assembly. Their respective actions — and the *legitimacy* of their actions — were blurred as a result. It seems safe to assume those who attended the convention matched the sederunt which was recorded for the Assembly, which had a preponderance of mostly obscure names from the west country. Here, chop logic ensued. Mary had abdicated. The effective date of the end of her reign was 24 July, the day she had signed the deeds of demission, as was the appointment of a single regent or a council of regents. What was the role of the three overlapping bodies which met the next day? The conventional verbiage of sixteenth-century institutions reflect the internal discrepancies: the convention of estates, as recorded in the record of the privy council, 'gladlie aggreit' to the Queen's deeds but it also 'allowit and apprevit' them. Legislation passed by a convention was usually only of a temporary nature.[57] Yet the subsequent act of parliament of December 1567 did not allude to the meeting of the convention on 25 July but claimed that the Queen's commission 'was and is and shall be in all times coming … advised and admitted'. Meantime, however, it was necessary in the intervening five months that a convention be recorded as having met.

However, the Assembly also had a key role. The terms of the coronation approved by the Queen, and ratified by the convention, described the king's oath as coming after the crowning. The resolution made by the General Assembly prescribed that the traditional sequence of crowning and oath be reversed:

> That all kings, princes and magistrates, which hereafter in anie time to come sall happin to raigne and beare rule over this realme; at their first entrie, *before* they be crowned and inaugurated, sall make their faithfull league and promise to the true kirk, that they sall mainteane and defend, and by all lawfull meanes sett fordward, the true religion of Jesus Christ, presentlie professed and established within this realme, even as they are oblished and astricted by the law of God, in Deuteronomie, and in the second chapter of the First Book of Kings; as they crave obedience of their subjects. So the band and contract to be mutuall and reciprock, in all times coming, betwixt the prince and God, and also betwixt the prince and the faithfull people, according to the Word of God.[58]

---

[56] *CSP Scot*, II, 368-69; Keith, *History* II, 694-700.
[57] Robert S. Rait, *The Parliaments of Scotland* (Glasgow: Maclehose, 1924) 151-53.
[58] *BUK*, I, 108-10; *Acts and Proceedings*, I, 138; Calderwood, *History of the Kirk* II, 381 (my emphasis).

There were further legal complications. The terms of the second deed of abdication, as endorsed by the convention on 25 July, prescribed eight 'regents' (including Moray) who would have charge of the young king and his government until Moray was formally acclaimed regent, with five needed to make a quorum. There were difficulties here for three of the nominees — Châtelherault, Lennox and Argyll — were either absent or refused to comply and Moray was out of the realm. The provisional government, as a result, was inquorate. Moray himself, immediately after his appointment on 22 August, had to enact a series of blocking measures to deflect Hamilton claims of maladministration.[59] A series of legal confusions remained to be cleared up. The full parliament which met in December 1567 'fundit and declarit' that the Queen's abdication in favour of her son had been 'lauchfull and perfyte'.[60] It thus took another legal fiction finally to establish the new king's legitimacy.

There can be little doubt that the hand of George Buchanan is to be seen in this rearrangement of the order followed in coronation ceremony and the placement of the oath. He had acted as moderator of the General Assembly which met on 25 June yet, oddly, did not figure in the record of the July meeting. The suspicion must be that he was busy elsewhere, drawing up the Assembly's resolution as regards the form the coronation ritual should follow. In this context, it is perhaps relevant that Buchanan finished a draft of his tract, *De Jure Regni*, first published in 1579, by the end of 1567, five months after the coronation. Much was made in subsequent years, not least by the philosopher king himself, that the placing of the king's oath before the crowning entailed a contract between king and people. The fact that this change in the coronation ritual rested on the authority of the General Assembly rather than the convention of estates has been missed — perhaps understandably by contemporaries but also by constitutional historians.

In the frenzied circumstances of 1567 — amidst what Throckmorton called a 'broken world'[61] — this sleight of hand was, at best, a delayed action grenade. In reality, the activists in 1567 had little confidence that any assertion by the General Assembly would carry much weight. More significant for the time being was the fact of the need felt for the three separate deeds of demission signed by Mary. The text of the three deeds has been subjected to surprisingly little detailed study and the deeds, when set in context, complicate rather than clarify the central issue of sovereignty. Yet the key change in the coronation ritual — placing the king's oath before the investiture — was not included in the Queen's first act of abdication nor, as such, sanctioned by the

---

[59] *CSP Scot*, II, 387.
[60] *APS*, III, 11, *c*. 1; Julian Goodare, *The Government of Scotland, 1560-1625* (Oxford: Oxford University Press, 2004) 37 But cf. *RPS*, 1567/12/104.
[61] *CSP Scot*, II, 368-69.

convention of estates. And no record exists to show that the meeting of the estates on 25 July was properly called. The succession of meetings of a convention — on 25 and 29 July followed by another on 22 August — strained legal forms to their limit; even Calderwood wryly admitted that 'the like had not been seen … in the memorie of man'.[62] Perhaps tellingly, the revolutionaries felt the need to add to the record when Moray's appointment was effected on 22 August: the proclamation of the new regent cited not only Mary's commission but also a claim that she had signified her 'deliberat will and mynd … alswa be hir awin mouth and voce' *since* the coronation.[63]

Legitimacy was established in 1567, not by resort either to Old Testament precedents or to a fledgling aristocratic constitutionalism, but rested four square on a legal justification of consent — by the Queen herself. The deeds of demission forced on Mary were an attempt to copper bottom both the abdication and the coronation. Despite them, the revolutionaries remained vulnerable to three charges. One was simple enough: how could the infant James 'evir be justlie king when his mother livis', however adroitly the act of abdication was framed?[64] The second was the same charge as made against the Reformation parliament of 1560, that the acts of the convention of estates were not legal.[65] The last was widely held for some considerable time after the flurry of legislative enactments in the summer of 1567: the Queen had acted under duress. The claim that Mary had personally repeated her consent since the coronation demonstrates that many remained unconvinced. More needed to be done to give both abdication and coronation a better semblance of legality. That in turn required a parliament called five months later both to endorse and to cast a veil over the highly dubious actions of July 1567.[66] That parliament added a further afterthought: the coronation had been 'orderly done and executed' as if 'her grace … had been departed out of this mortal life' or, alternatively, as if she had personally appeared before a parliament to confirm her will.[67] The conjuring up of a Doppelgänger-style consent was legal dexterity indeed. Even then, some doubt remained that the legislation of December

---

[62] Calderwood, *History of the Kirk* II, 385.

[63] *RPS*, 1567/8/3, 'Proclamation of the regentrie'.

[64] Richard Bannatyne and Robert Pitcairn, *Memoriales of Transactions in Scotland, 1569-73* (Edinburgh: Bannatyne Club, 1836) 126-27.

[65] See Knox, *History* II, 81.

[66] The legislation of the parliament of Dec. 1567 was long-winded and contorted. It deserves separate study. It included fresh justification for Mary's detention (1567/12/30), a shortened version of the new coronation ritual first mooted by the General Assembly in July (1567/12/35), and a repetition of the three deeds of demission (1567/12/104), which was placed first in the record. Even more dubiously, the legislation affected it 'expedient' to bar all women from the 'public authority of the realm' (1567/12/31). All references are to the versions in *RPS*. Cf. *APS*, III, *c*. 1 (11-12), *c*. 2 (13-14), *c*. 30 (14-15), *c*. 8 (23-4), *c*. 20 (38) and *c*. 21 (38).

[67] *RPS*, 1567/12/104.

1567, ratifying the acts of the Reformation parliament, was retrospective: words used such as 'of new' suggested that it was not. That, in turn, left collateral ambiguity over the acts of the three successive conventions of estates in the summer of 1567.[68]

THE RITE OF INVESTITURE

The third remarkable feature of the ceremony of 1567 must have seemed as obvious to contemporary witnesses as it is surprising to later observers. Why, it may be asked, were these Protestant revolutionaries so intent on a rite which was so obviously Catholic and which had originally needed the explicit permission of a pope? Why did they feel they needed the paraphernalia of the Honours of Scotland which included two papal gifts — the sword of state and the sceptre? Why did they invite a Catholic archbishop to officiate? Why did they implicitly accept and even enhance the vocabulary of an imperial monarchy? One answer, as has been seen was that the Protestant establishment felt vulnerable to claims that the legislation of the Reformation parliament of 1560 was not legal because the parliament had not been properly fenced. Another response might be that, as yet, the new Church did not have a 'usable past' to lend it historical legitimacy. Knox's 'History of the Reformation of Religion within the Realm of Scotland' started in 1422 and, in the space of little more than 1,000 words, reached the 1520s. Until it did, with the later claims made by Buchanan and others that its roots lay in the pre-Roman Celtic church, other means had to be used to effect the Kirk's claim to be a *national* church.[69]

There is another explanation. It is to do with the value placed by the revolutionaries and their contemporaries on the past and is, as such, distinctly subjective and difficult to pin down. Yet the explanation goes to the heart of the emerging status of Stewart monarchs in the fifteenth and early sixteenth centuries. Their standing was variously endorsed by other monarchs, not least in the escalating prestige of their foreign consorts from James II (1437-60) onwards: the royal brides in the next four reigns were drawn from the royal houses of Burgundy, Denmark, England and France respectively. The imperial imagery used by parliament and the imperial crown depicted on such key icons of monarchy as the coinage and the new, enhanced royal arms designed by

[68]   P. G. B. McNeil, '"Our Religion, Established by Neither Law Nor Parliament": Was the Reformation Legislation of 1560 Valid?,' *Scottish Church History Society Records* 35 (2005): 88-89. The legislation of 1581, which revisited the issues of abdication and coronation, in contrast, was unequivocal and retrospective: see *APS*, III, 221-22; *RPS*, 1581/10/20.
[69]   Knox, *History* I, 7-11; Roger A. Mason, 'Usable Pasts: History and Identity in Reformation Scotland,' *Scottish Historical Review* 76.1 (1997): 57.

Sir David Lindsay, poet and Lord Lyon in the reign of James V, represent two strands
of a new assertiveness of royal authority. Another facet lay in the fact that every reign
since that of James III had seen a concerted effort to enhance the power of the monarchy at the expense of the papacy: control of ecclesiastical appointments, heavier taxa-
tion of the church and a creeping capture of monastic income all pointed towards a
shift in the balance of power between Rome and the royal house of Stewart.[70] Nevertheless, the relationship remained mutually supportive, evidenced by a succession of
gifts made by various popes to James IV and James V.

The status of Scottish kings was measured by their relationship to the Holy Roman
Emperor as well as to the pope. Visible proof of this is to be found in the well-known
painted heraldic ceiling of St Machar's Cathedral in Aberdeen, which dates to *c.* 1525.
Alongside the arms of the king of Scots and his nobility were those of the Emperor, the
pope and the kings and leading nobles of Europe.[71] If this was the domestic view of
Scotland's increasingly important role in the Empire and Christendom, it can be
matched furth of Scotland. The celebration of one particular event showed its new-
found role in sharp relief. The investiture of the Emperor Maximilian I (1515-19) in
1515 saw the production of a representation of an enormous triumphal arch in the
style of Roman emperors in the form of a woodcut print, made up of 192 separate
wood blocks. Designed by the Nuremberg printmaker, Albrecht Dürer, and intended
for display on the walls of city halls or princely palaces, it was one of the largest prints
ever produced. This elaborate tribute to the power and the jurisdiction of the Emperor
took three years to produce. Its iconography was intricate and overwhelming. Three-
quarters of the way up the arch, there were depicted sculptures of the twelve Caesars.
Opposite them were representations of the twelve most prestigious kings of Europe. In
first place, of course, was the Emperor himself and he was followed immediately by the
five other kings of Europe who enjoyed the rite of anointing. The first in that line after
the Emperor himself was the king of Scots, followed by the kings of England, France,
Portugal and Corsica. *Arrivistes*, such as the king of Spain, were relegated to the far end
of the line.[72] This, it might be deduced, was the reason why the revolutionaries of 1567
risked what Knox decried as a Jewish and papist ceremony. The rite of anointing

[70] Roger A. Mason, 'Renaissance Monarchy? Stewart Kingship (1469-1532),' *Scottish Kingship, 1306-
1542*, eds. Michael Brown and Roland Tanner (Edinburgh: John Donald, 2008); Carol Edington, *Court
and Culture in Renaissance Scotland: Sir David Lindsay of the Mount* (Amherst: University of Massachusetts
Press, 1994) 37-39; Goodare, *State and Society* 29-33.

[71] David McRoberts, *The Heraldic Ceiling of St. Machar's Cathedral, Aberdeen*, Occasional papers (Aberdeen: Friends of St. Machar's Cathedral, 1976).

[72] Sven Lüken, 'Kaiser Maximilian I. und seine Ehrenpforte,' *Zeitschrift für Kunstgeschichte* 61.2 (1998):
50-53. I am grateful to Professor A.A. MacDonald for drawing my attention to this work. The original
print measured 295cm by 371cm. New editions were produced in 1526-8 and 1559.

reflected more than tradition in ritual; it also underpinned the European status of the Scottish monarchy — a mythical status which Scottish chroniclers had worked so hard to invent over the previous two centuries and which had been heavily embellished during Mary's personal reign.

Scottish Protestantism would come to be wary of imperial monarchy, especially in the 1590s and after, triggered by suspicions of both English chauvinistic propaganda and the theological aspirations of its own king, yet it felt in its early days in power the need to drink from some of these waters.[73] The aspiration of the revolutionaries of 1567 was a godly prince, a new Joshua. As yet, that model remained vague and ambiguous. It needed enhancement to convince a deeply conservative establishment. The Buchanan formula, even if briefly alluded to in the coronation oath, was largely put to one side; the clashes between James VI and the kirk over the terms of the oath lay some thirty years in the future, as did the lending of a history and a historical legitimacy to the Kirk by Buchanan's works.[74] A more compelling alternative of a godly prince, with firmer foundations in the past, was available. It rested on a cult of honour, which had become increasingly prominent in both Mary's reign and that of her father.

LEGITIMACY AND NOSTALGIA: THE ROLE OF THE CULT OF HONOUR

The most public face of the revived cult of honour was the stress on ceremony, ritual and display. The first public demonstration of the new Protestantism, the Reformation parliament of 1560, had seen neither a display of the Honours nor a 'riding' of parliament — a formal procession of the three estates.[75] The coronation of 1567, however, was careful to include both a ritual procession and central role for the Honours. The members of the Estates present processed to and from the ceremony and were given their accustomed place in the formal oaths given at its end. It was the first example of a new stress on ceremony.

---

[73] Goodare, *State and Society* 36; Arthur H. Williamson, *Scottish National Consciousness in the Age of James VI: The Apocalypse, the Union and Shaping of Scotland's Public Culture* (Edinburgh: John Donald, 1979) 5, 39-47.

[74] Cf. Mason, 'Usable Pasts,' 54, 57, 68.

[75] The riding of parliament had probably existed since the 1520s, if not before. It became more elaborate in the 1580s. See Thomas Innes, 'The Scottish Parliament: Its Symbolism and Ceremonial,' *Juridical Review* 44 (1932); A. J. Mann, 'The Scottish Parliament: The Role of Ritual and Procession in the Pre-1707 Parliament and the New Parliament of 1999,' *Rituals and Parliaments: Political, Anthropological and Historical Perspectives on Europe and the United States*, eds. E. Crewe and M.G. Müller (Frankfurt am Main: Peter Lang Frankfurt, 2006) 40-41.

It was followed, within less than four weeks, by the formal appointment of Moray as regent on 22 August. He was proclaimed as such 'with great pomp' at Edinburgh's market cross, the symbolic centre of the kingdom. Yet the occasion saw much the same mixture of legalities, absentees, ambiguities and ceremony as had marked the coronation itself. The same three members of the council of regency stayed away. Moray, keen to have it emphasised that he was the deposed Queen's own choice rather than 'elected', as Buchanan would claim, had Mary's 'commission' re-presented to a convention of estates before accepting office.[76] Then, in addition to repeating the same oath taken on the infant king's behalf at his coronation, Moray gave an unaccompanied rendering of Psalm LXXII, 'Give the king thy judgements, O God, and Thy righteousness unto the king's son'. For an Augustinian abbot, trained in plainsong and patron of a string of talented musicians, the task of rendering this hymn to the Biblical King David could not have been onerous, but it also highlighted once again the uneasy juxtaposition of legalism and Biblical self-justification involved in the deposing of a living and divinely sanctioned monarch.[77]

Ceremony was the most obvious of the key features linking the culture of the personal reigns of James V, Mary and James VI across and despite a change of religion. Others, if less ostentatious, were equally important, many resting on conventional notions of classicism and Biblicism, most notably the Nine Worthies and the Ages of Man. Particularly influential in the reign of James V and in the work of David Lindsay, poet and royal herald, had been the notion of the Cardinal Virtues. Lindsay in his poem, *The Dreme*, advised the King:[78]

> And vse counsale of nobyll dame Prudence.
> Founde the fermelie on faith and fortytude:
> Drawe to thy courte Iustice and Temporance;
> And to the commoun weill haue attendance. [1065-8]

Prudence, Fortitude, Justice, Temperance, the four Cardinal Virtues, formed the basis of this poem, which is firmly set in the genre of advices to princes literature. Much of Lindsay's other work belongs to this genre. In *The Complaynt of Schir Dauid Lindesay*, written in 1530, he urged James, having rid the court of the Douglas faction, to rule with 'The foure gret verteous Cardinalis' — the four Cardinal Virtues (l. 379). Twenty-two years

---

[76] Calderwood, *History of the Kirk* II, 385, *RPS*, 1567/8/1-2.

[77] The setting for Psalm LXXII may have been that of David Peebles, a canon of St Andrews, who had been commissioned by his former abbot, Moray, to compile a collection of four-part harmonizations of psalm tunes from the Geneva psalter of 1561, or of the better known ex-monk of Lindores, Thomas Wode, who was also involved with the project.

[78] Sir David Lindsay, *The Works of Sir David Lindsay of the Mount, 1490-1555*, ed. Douglas Hamer, STS 3rd ser. 1, 2, 6, 8, 4 vols. (Edinburgh: Blackwood & Sons Ltd, 1931-36) I, 36.

later, in *Ane Satyre of the Thrie Estaitis*, performed first at Cupar, near St Andrews, in 1552, and again at the Greenside in Edinburgh in 1554 before the new regent, Mary of Guise, in a rather different atmosphere, Lindsay urged 'Gude Counsell' with 'Lady Vertue' to inform the process of royal government. In short, good governance should embrace all the eternal verities, as represented by the four Cardinal Virtues and the three Christian theological Virtues of Faith, Hope and Charity, associated with the seven Ages of Man. It should come as little surprise that the overriding theme of the James VI's formal entry into Edinburgh in 1579 was the Ages of Man. Then rising fourteen, and himself passing from the second to the third Age of Man, the young King was greeted at the tolbooth by Peace, Justice, Plenty and Policy, a variant on the Cardinal Virtues.[79]

Three other sets of historical processes played upon the mindset of the nobility in the years before and after the Reformation. One was process of the feuing of kirklands which left the Church's holdings, amounting to a third of the agricultural land of Scotland, vulnerable to take-over; the peak of the movement came in the ten years either side of 1559-60. The transformation of the profile of the landed classes by feuing in turn triggered a scramble for status amongst the nobility, both new and old. Established noble families affected to distance themselves from the *arrivistes*. Newly ennobled houses sought out a claim to antiquity. In either case, there was a resort to a revived cult of honour, seen in a heightened enthusiasm for heraldry and for history, both of the nation and of family. Picture galleries displaying noble ancestors became fashionable, as did architectural totems such as emblem pictures and viewing platforms atop tower houses, offering the spectacle of a landed estate. On the walls and the ceilings of noble houses and in commissioned armorials and family histories similar iconic messages of lineage were displayed, in which classical heroes rubbed shoulders with mythical and biblical kings and with their living counterparts, Scotland's king and his nobles.[80]

Yet much of this quest for a cult of honour had to take place during two royal minorities. Scotland had a royal court for only six years between the death of James V in 1542 and the entry into the limelight of the young King James in 1579. It was only

---

[79] Douglas Gray, 'The Royal Entry in Sixteenth-Century Scotland,' *The Rose and the Thistle: Essays on the Culture of Late Medieval and Renaissance Scotland*, eds. Sally Mapstone and Juliette Wood (East Linton: Tuckwell, 1998) 28, 30; Lynch, 'Court Ceremony and Ritual,' 76.

[80] Aonghus MacKechnie, 'James VI's Architects and Their Architecture,' *The Reign of James VI*, eds. Julian Goodare and Michael Lynch (Edinburgh: John Donald, 2008) 56, 60; Deborah Howard, *Scottish Architecture: Reformation to the Restoration, 1560-1660*, The Architectural History of Scotland (Edinburgh: Edinburgh University Press, 1995) 50-57, 83-84, 86-90; Charles John Burnett, 'The Officers of Arms and Heraldic Art under King James Sixth & First 1567-1625,' University of Edinburgh M.Litt., 1992 24, 28.

in the brief six years of Mary's personal reign that a direct focus and stimulus for court culture prospered. The reduced activity of the royal court during the two long minorities meant that a country house culture grounded on a cult of honour was largely self-sustaining. As such, it became deeply ingrained in the psyche of a landed class which had become even more conservative in its cultural instincts as it prospered from the feuing of kirklands and expanded.

It is tempting in the age of the Reformation to see religion as the predominant influence on all other facets of politics, life and culture. It may often be more profitable to view the second half of the sixteenth century as an age of anxiety, which fuelled moral uncertainty and social conservatism as much as new levels of piety, whether Catholic and Protestant.[81] To concerns about the social forces unleashed by widespread iconoclasm[82] and the uncertainties and ambiguities provoked by a sudden but far from comprehensive change of the official religion of the realm were added new tensions with the return of Mary to her realm in 1561. Sovereignty was complicated by the dilemmas which stemmed from owing obedience to a Catholic monarch who was both patron of a fledgling Protestant church and the object of frequent criticism by it. Yet replacing a divinely ordained monarch provoked more rather than fewer anxieties. The result was an uneasy quest for legitimacy, which was closely allied to a nostalgic yearning for a seemingly simpler past. The new order sought legitimacy by claiming to be like the old order, only more so.

Scotland's belated reformation was largely driven from above. It is telling that the revolutionaries of 1559-60 called themselves 'The *Lords* of the Congregation'. It was as a result a remarkable 'revolution', in which almost no one — either in state or local office — was displaced. Continuity went hand in hand with religious change. In 1567, by contrast, for many amongst the nobility, already fretting regularly about the status of the 'ancient blood', the forced abdication of 1567 must have provoked much the same alarm as felt by a courtly audience when the character 'John the Commonweill' jumped onto the throne vacated by 'King Humanitie' in Lindsay's *Satyre of the Thrie Estatis*. However much the abdication was cloaked in the language of legitimacy, it must have seemed that 'Iustice and Temperance' — the watchwords of the commonweal — had been abandoned and chaos loomed in a 'broken world'. An alternative, more colourful view of the chaos of July 1567 came from the pen of the

---

[81]   William J. Bouwsma, 'Anxiety and the Formation of Early Modern Culture,' *After the Reformation: Essays in Honor of J.H. Hexter*, eds. Barbara C. Malament, William J. Bouwsma and J. H. Hexter (Philadelphia: University of Pennsylvania Press, 1980) 20-22; William J. Bouwsma, *The Waning of the Renaissance, ca. 1550-1640*, The Yale Intellectual History of the West (New Haven, CT: Yale University Press, 2000) 121-22, 124, 191-92.

[82]   David McRoberts, 'Material Destruction Caused by the Scottish Reformation,' *Essays on the Scottish Reformation, 1513-1625*, ed. David McRoberts (Glasgow: J.S. Burns, 1962) 429-40, 445-49.

pro-Marian courtier, James Melville of Halhill: Scotland was in as much of a mess as a Welshman's hose.[83]

In the confusions of the crisis of 1567, for most within this class two reactions predominated. Firstly, sovereignty counted for more than religion, whether Protestant or Catholic; the caveat that action to depose a divinely sanctioned queen should proceed only if 'it might stand with the law', as Lord Boyd had carefully stipulated, predominated. And secondly, most convinced Protestants, even if they were intent on purging the 'dregs of papistry', were anxious to preserve the cultural treasury of the past, if sometimes in a new or disguised form — as in the recast version of the Bannatyne Manuscript[84] or as a new-style imperial monarchy. As a direct result, a new version of the national and Stewart past was reclaimed, with Biblicism and classicism as its handmaidens. The coronation of 1567 was arguably the first chapter in the reclamation process.

---

[83] *CSP Scot*, II, 368-69 (31 July); 347 (8 July).

[84] A. A. MacDonald, 'Poetry, Politics, and Reformation Censorship in Sixteenth-Century Scotland,' *English Studies* 64 (1983).

Bibliography

PRIMARY LITERATURE

Accounts of the Lord High Treasurer of Scotland. Eds. Sir James Balfour Paul and Thomas Dickson. 12 vols. Edinburgh: H.M. General Register House, 1877.

The Acts and Proceedings of the General Assemblies of the Church of Scotland, 1560 to 1618. Ed. Duncan Shaw. Scottish Record Society. 3 vols. Edinburgh: Scottish Record Society, 2004.

The Acts of the Parliament of Scotland. Eds. Cosmo Nelson Innes and Thomas Thomson. 12 vols. Edinburgh: s.n., 1814-75.

Adamson, Patrick. *Serenissimi ac Nobilissimi Scotiae, Angliae, Hybernię Principis: Henrici Stuardi inuictissimi herois, ac Mariae Reginae amplissimae filij Genethliacum*. Parisiis: Apud Carolum Perier, 1566.

Adelard of Bath. *Conversations with his Nephew. On the Same and the Different, Questions on Natural Science and On Birds*. Ed. Charles Burnett, trans. Charles Burnett, et al. Cambridge: Cambridge University Press, 1998.

Ady, Thomas. *A Candle in the Dark: or, A Treatise Concerning the Nature of Witches & Witchcraft*. London: printed for R.I. to be sold by Tho. Newberry, 1656.

Alan of Lille. *Plaint of Nature / De planctu naturae*. Trans. J. J. Sheridan. Toronto: Pontifical Institute, 1980.

Albertus Magnus. *De animalibus libri XXVI nach der Cölner Urschrift*. Ed. Hermann Stadler. 2 vols. Münster: Aschendorff, 1916-1920.

—. *Albertus Magnus On Animals. A Medieval Summa Zoologica*. Trans. Kenneth F. Kitchell Jr and Irven Michael Resnick. 2 vols. Baltimore: Johns Hopkins UP, 1999.

Alexander Montgomerie, Poems. Ed. David J. Parkinson. STS 4th series 28, 29. 2 vols. Edinburgh: Scottish Text Society, 2000.

An Alphabet of Tales: An English 15th Century Translation of the Alphabetum narrationum of Étienne de Besançon. From Additional MS. 25,719 of the British Museum. Ed. Mary Macleod Banks. EETS, OS 126, 127. 2 vols. London: Kegan Paul, Trench, Trübner, 1904.

Altenglische Legenden, Neue Folge. Ed. Carl Horstmann. Heilbronn: Henninger, 1881. Hildesheim: Olms, 1969.

Analecta Hymnica Medii Aevi. Eds. Clemens Blume and Guido Maria Dreves. 30 vols. Leipzig: Fues, 1886.

Ancient Criminal Trials in Scotland Compiled from the Original Records and MSS. Ed. Robert Pitcairn. 3 vols. Edinburgh: Bannatyne Club, 1833.

Anderson, James. *The Winter Night*. Ed. Andrew Bonar. Edinburgh: John Greig, 1851.

Aristotle. *The Complete Works of Aristotle. The Revised Oxford Translation*. Trans. Jonathan Barnes. Vol. 1. 2 vols. Princeton, NJ: Princeton University Press, 1995.

The Assembly of Gods or the Accord of Reason and Sensuality in the Fear of Death. Ed. O. L. Triggs. EETS ES 69. London: Oxford University Press, 1896.

Babrius and Phaedrus. Ed. Ben Edwin Perry. Loeb Classical Library. Cambridge: Harvard University Press, 1965.

The Bannatyne Manuscript Writtin in Tyme of Pest 1568. Ed. W. Tod Ritchie. STS 2nd ser. 22, 23, 26; 3rd ser. 5. 4 vols. Edinburgh: Scottish Text Society, 1928-34.

The Bannatyne Manuscript. National Library of Scotland, Advocates' Library MS.1.1.6. Introduced by Denton Fox and William A. Ringler. Aldershot: Scolar, 1980.

Bannatyne, Richard. *Memoriales of Transactions in Scotland, 1569-73.* Ed. Robert Pitcairn. Edinburgh: Bannatyne Club, 1836.

Barbour, John. *Barbour's Bruce.* Eds. M. P. McDiarmid and J. A. C. Stevenson. STS, 4th series, 15, 12, 13. 3 vols. Edinburgh: Blackwood, Pillans & Wilson, 1980, 1981, 1985.

Bartholomaeus Anglicus. *On the Properties of Things: John Trevisa's Translation of 'Bartholomaeus Anglicus De Proprietatibus Rerum' A Critical Text.* Trans. J. Trevisa. Ed. M. C. Seymour. 3 vols. Oxford: OUP, 1975.

Beau Chesne, Jean de, and John Baildon. *A Booke Containing Divers Sortes of Hands.* The English Experience. Amsterdam: Theatrum Orbis Terrarum, 1977.

Beda Venerabilis. *Opera exegetica 1. Libri quatuor in principium Genesis usque ad nativitatem Isaac et eiectionem Ismahelis adnotationum.* Ed. C. W. Jones. CCSL 118A. Turnhout: Brepols, 1967.

Bellenden, John. *The Chronicles of Scotland, Compiled by Hector Boece.* Eds. R. W. Chambers, et al. S.T.S. 3rd ser., 10, 15. 2 vols. Edinburgh: W. Blackwood, 1938-41.

Blundeville, Thomas. *The Fower Chiefyst Offices Belongyng to Horsemanshippe.* London: VVyllyam Seres dwellyng at the west ende of Paules churche, 1566.

Boguet, Henry. *An Examen of Witches Drawn from Various Trials.* Trans. E. Allen Ashwin. Ed. A. J. A. M. Summers. 1971 ed. London: John Rodker, 1929.

Bonaventure, Saint. *Bonaventuræ… Opera omnia.* Ed. Adolphe Charles Peltier. 15 vols. Paris, 1864-71.

Booke of the Universall Kirk of Scotland: Acts and Proceedings of the General Assemblies of the Kirk of Scotland. Ed. Thomas Thomson. 3 vols. Edinburgh: Bannatyne and Maitland Clubs, 1839-45.

Bower, Walter. *Scotichronicon.* Ed. D. E. R. Watt. 9 vols. Aberdeen: Aberdeen University Press, 1987-98.

Brinton, Thomas. *The Sermons of Thomas Brinton, Bishop of Rochester, 1373-1389.* Ed. Sister Mary Aquinas Devlin. Camden Third Series. 2 vols. London: Royal Historical Society, 1954.

Buchanan, George. *The Political Poetry.* Eds. Paul J. McGinnis and Arthur H. Williamson. Scottish History Society (Series). Edinburgh: Scottish History Society, 1995.

Caesarius of Heisterbach. *The Dialogue on Miracles.* Trans. H. von E. Scott and C. C. Swinton Bland. 2 vols. London: Routledge, 1929.

Calderwood, David. *The History of the Kirk of Scotland.* Ed. Thomas Thomson. 8 vols. Edinburgh: Wodrow Society, 1842-49.

Calendar of State Papers, Foreign Series, of the Reign of Elizabeth. Eds. Joseph Stevenson, et al. 25 vols. London: Longman & Co., 1861-1950.

Calendar of the State Papers Relating to Scotland and Mary, Queen of Scots, 1547-1603. Eds. Joseph Bain et al. 13 vols. Edinburgh: H.M.S.O., 1898-1969 .

Calendar of the State Papers Relating to Scotland. Eds. William Kenneth Boyd and Henry W. Meikle. Edinburgh: H.M. General Register House, 1936.

Catholic Tractates of the Sixteenth Century, 1573-1600. Ed. Thomas Graves Law. STS 1st ser. 45. Edinburgh: William Blackwood and Sons, 1901.

Caxton, William. *Caxton's Eneydos, 1490: English from the French Liure des Eneydes, 1483*. Eds. Mathew Tewart Culley, Frederick James Furnivall and Jean Jacques Salverda de Grave. EETS, ES 57. London: N. Trübner & Co., 1890.

—. *The Prologues and Epilogues of William Caxton*. Ed. W. J. B. Crotch. EETS, OS 176. London: Oxford University Press, 1928.

Chartier, Alain. *Le Quadrilogue invectif*. Ed. Eugénie Droz. Les Classiques français du moyen âge. 2 ed. Paris: H. Champion, 1950.

Chartulary of the Cistercian Priory of Coldstream with Relative Documents. Ed. Rev. Charles Rogers. Grampian Club publications. London: Grampian Club, 1879.

Chaucer, Geoffrey. *The Riverside Chaucer*. Ed. Larry D. Benson. Oxford: Oxford University Press, 1987.

—. *The Canterbury Tales*. Ed. Jill Mann. Penguin Classics. London: Penguin, 2005.

Christine de Pisan. *The Epistle of Othea*. Trans. Scrope Stephen. Ed. C. F. Bühler. EETS, OS 264. Oxford: Oxford University Press, 1970.

The Chronicle of Perth, a Register of Remarkable Occurrences, Chiefly Connected with that City, from the Year 1210 to 1668. Ed. James Maidment. Maitland Club. Edinburgh: s.n., 1831.

The Cloud of Unknowing and the Book of Privy Counselling. Ed. Phyllis Hodgson. EETS, OS 218. Oxford: Oxford University Press, 1944, repr. 1981.

A Compendious Book of Godly and Spiritual Songs Commonly known as The Gude and Godlie Ballatis, Reprinted from the Edition of 1567. Ed. A. F. Mitchell. STS 1st ser. 39. Edinburgh: William Blackwood and Sons, 1897.

The Complaynt of Scotland, c. 1550. Ed. A. M. Stewart. STS 4th ser. 11. Edinburgh: Scottish Text Society, 1979.

County Folklore. Printed Extracts No. 5: Examples of Printed Folklore Concerning the Orkney and Shetland Islands. Eds. G. F. Black and N. W. Thomas. Publications of the Folk-lore Society. London: David Nutt, 1903.

Descartes, René. *Oeuvres de Descartes*. Eds. Charles Adam and Paul Tannery. 13 vols. Paris: Léopold Cerf, 1897-1913.

—. *The Philosophical Works of Descartes*. Eds. Elizabeth S. Haldane and G. R. T. Ross. 2 vols. New York: Dover, 1931.

Devotional Pieces in Verse and Prose from MS. Arundel 285 and MS. Harleian 6919. Ed. J. A. W. Bennett. STS 3rd ser. 23. Edinburgh: Scottish Text Society, 1955.

The Dialoges of Creatures Moralysed. Eds. Gregory Kratzmann and Elizabeth Gee. Leiden: Brill, 1988.

Le dialogue des créatures. Traduction par Colart Mansion (1482) du Dialogus creaturarum (XIVe siècle). Trans. Colart Mansion. Ed. Pierre Ruelle. Académie Royale de Belgique. Classe des lettres et des sciences morales et politiques. Collections des anciens auteurs Belges. Brussels: Palais des Académies, 1985.

Dialogus creaturarum moralisatus. Dialog der Kreaturen über moralisches Handeln. Lateinisch-Deutsch. Eds. Birgit Esser and Hans-Jürgen Blanke. Würzburg: Königshausen & Neumann, 2008.

Disticha catonis. Ed. Marcus Boas. Amsterdam: North-Holland Publishing, 1952.

A Diurnal of Remarkable Occurrents that have passed within… Scotland since the Death of King James IV till the Year M.D.LXXV. Ed. Thomas Thomson. Edinburgh: Bannatyne Club, 1833.

Douglas, Gavin. *Virgil's Aeneid Translated into Scottish Verse by Gavin Douglas, Bishop of Dunkeld.* Ed. D. F. C. Coldwell. STS 3rd series 25, 27-28, 30. 4 vols. Edinburgh: William Blackwood & Sons, 1957-64.

—. *The Shorter Poems of Gavin Douglas.* Ed. Priscilla J. Bawcutt. STS 5th series, 2. 2nd ed. Edinburgh: Scottish Text Society, 2003.

Dunbar, William. *The Poems of William Dunbar.* Ed. Priscilla Bawcutt. 2 vols. Glasgow: Association for Scottish Literary Studies, 1998.

Duns Scotus, John. *Opera Omnia.* Ed. Luke Wadding. 26 vols. Paris: Vivès, 1895.

The Early English Carols. Ed. Richard Leighton Greene. 2nd ed. Oxford: Oxford University Press, 1977.

The Exchequer Rolls of Scotland. Rotuli Scaccarii Regum Scotorum. Eds. John Stuart, et al. 23 vols. Edinburgh: H.M. General Register House, 1878-1908.

Gerald of Wales. *Giraldi Cambrensis. Opera VIII: De principis instructione liber.* Ed. George F. Warner. Rerum Britannicarum Medii Ævi scriptores. London: H.M.S.O., 1891.

Gilte Legende. Eds. Richard Hamer and Vida Russell. EETS, OS 327, 328. Oxford: Oxford University Press, 2006-07.

The Gude and Godlie Ballatis see *A Compendious Book…*

Guillaume d'Auvergne. *Opera omnia.* Orléans & Paris: F. Hotot, 1674. Facsimile edition, Frankfurt am Main: Minerva, 1963.

Guillaume de Lorris, and Jean de Meun. *Le Roman de la Rose.* Ed. Félix Lecoy. 3 vols. Paris: Champion, 1983.

—. *The Romance of the Rose.* Trans. Frances Horgan. World's Classics. Oxford: Oxford University Press, 1994.

The Hamilton Papers. Letters and Papers Illustrating the Political Relations of England and Scotland in the XVIth Century. Ed. Joseph Bain. 2 vols. Edinburgh: H.M. General Register House, 1890-92.

Hay, Gilbert. *Gilbert of the Hay's Prose Manuscript (A.D. 1456), vol. I, The Buke of the Law of Armys or Buke of Bataillis.* Ed. J. H. Stevenson. S.T.S. 1st ser. 44. Edinburgh: Blackwood, 1901.

Henryson, Robert. *The Poems of Robert Henryson.* Ed. Denton Fox. Oxford: Clarendon Press, 1981.

Henryson, Robert. *The Poems of Robert Henryson.* Ed. Robert L. Kindrick. Middle English Texts. Kalamazoo: Medieval Institute Publications, 1997.

The Historie and Life of King James the Sext being an Account of the Affairs of Scotland, from the Year 1566, to the Year 1596; with a Short Continuation to the Year 1617. Ed. Thomas Thomson. Edinburgh: Bannatyne Club, 1825.

Hugh of Fouilloy. *The Medieval Book of Birds: Hugh of Fouilloy's Aviarium*. Trans. Willene B. Clark. Ed. Willene B. Clark. Binghamton: MRTS, 1992.

Isidore of Seville. *Etymologiae XII / Etymologies Livre XII Des Animaux*. Ed. Jacques André. Paris: Belles lettres, 1986.

—. *The Etymologies of Isidore of Seville*. Trans. Stephen A. Barney, et al. Cambridge: Cambridge University Press, 2006.

Jacob's Well, an English Treatise on the Cleansing of Man's Conscience. Part I. Ed. Arthur Brandeis. EETS, OS 115. London: Kegan Paul, Trench, Trübner, 1900.

Jacques de Vitry. *The Exempla or Illustrative Stories from the Sermones vulgares of Jacques de Vitry*. Ed. T. F. Crane. London, 1890.

Jacobus de Voragine. *The Golden Legend or Lives of the Saints as Englished by William Caxton*. Ed. F. S. Ellis. 7 vols. New York: AMS Press, 1973.

John Ireland. *The Meroure of Wyssdome Composed for the Use of James IV., King of Scots Books I & II*. Ed. Charles MacPherson. STS 2nd ser. 19. Vol. 1. 3 vols. Edinburgh: Blackwood, 1926.

—. *The Meroure of Wyssdome Composed for the Use of James IV., King of Scots, A.D. 1490*. Ed. F. Quinn. STS 4th ser. 2. Vol. 2. 3 vols. s.n.: Scottish Text Society, 1965.

—. *The Meroure of Wyssdome Composed for the Use of James IV., King of Scots Vol.III, Books VI & VII*. Ed. Craig McDonald. STS 4th ser. 19. Vol. 3. 3 vols. Aberdeen: Aberdeen University Press, 1990.

Josephus, Flavius. *The Latin Josephus*. Ed. Franz Blatt. Acta Jutlandica, Humanistisk Serie 44. Aarhus: Universitetsforlaget, 1958.

Kalendars of Scottish Saints with Personal Notices of Those of Alba, Laudonia, & Strathclyde, an Attempt to fix the Districts of their Several Missions and the Churches where they were Chiefly had in Remembrance. Ed. A. P. Forbes. Literature of Theology and Church History. Edinburgh: Edmonston and Douglas, 1872.

Kennedy, Walter. *The Poems of Walter Kennedy*. Ed. Nicole Meier. STS 5th ser. 6. Woodbridge: Scottish Text Society, 2008.

Kirk, Robert. *The Secret Common-Wealth & A Short Treatise of Charms and Spels*. Ed. Stewart Sanderson. Mistletoe series. Cambridge: D.S. Brewer, 1976.

Knox, John. *The Works of John Knox*. Ed. David Laing. 6 vols. Edinburgh: Wodrow Society, 1846-64.

—. *John Knox's History of the Reformation in Scotland*. Ed. W. Croft Dickinson. 2 vols. London: Nelson, 1949.

Laing, David, ed. *Early Metrical Tales Including the History of Sir Egeir, Sir Gryme, and Sir Gray-Steill*. Edinburgh: W. & D. Laing, 1826.

Langland, William. *Piers Plowman: the B version*. Eds. George Kane and E. T. Donaldson. London: Athlone Press, 1975.

Legends of the Saints in the Scottish Dialect of the Fourteenth Century. Ed. W. M. Metcalfe. STS 1st ser. 13/18; 23/25; 35/37. 3 vols. Edinburgh: Blackwood and Sons, 1888-96.

The Letters of James V Collected and Calendared by R. K. Hannay. Ed. Denys Hay. Edinburgh: H.M.S.O., 1954.

Lindsay, Sir David. *The Works of Sir David Lindsay of the Mount, 1490-1555*. Ed. Douglas Hamer. STS 3rd ser. 1, 2, 6, 8. 4 vols. Edinburgh: Blackwood & Sons Ltd, 1931-36.

Llull, Rámon. *The Book of the Ordre of Chyualry*. Trans. William Caxton. Ed. A. T. P. Byles. EETS, OS 168. London: Oxford University Press, 1926. New York: Kraus Reprints, 1971.

Longer Scottish Poems Volume One 1375-1650. Eds. Priscilla Bawcutt and Felicity J. Riddy. Edinburgh: Scottish Academic Press, 1987.

Ludolphus de Saxonia. *Vita Jesu Christi: ex Evangelio et approbatis ab Ecclesia Catholica doctoribus sedule collecta*. Ed. L. M. Rigollot. 4 vols. Paris: Apud Victorem Palme, 1878.

Lydgate, John. *The Minor Poems of John Lydgate*. Ed. Henry N. MacCracken. EETS, ES 107; OS 192. 2 vols. London: Oxford University Press, 1911, 1934.

Lyndsay, Sir David. *Sir David Lyndsay. Selected Poems*. Ed. Janet Hadley Williams. Glasgow: Association for Scottish Literary Studies, 2000.

Mair, John. *Exponibilia*. Paris, 1503.

—. *In Secundum Sententiarum*. Paris, 1510.

—. *In quartum Sententiarum questiones utilissimae*. Paris, 1516.

A Medieval Book of Beasts: The Second-Family Bestiary. Commentary, Art, Text and Translation. Ed. Willene B. Clark. Woodbridge: Boydell, 2006.

Medieval English Lyrics. Ed. Theodore Silverstein. York Medieval Texts. London: Edward Arnold, 1971.

Melville, James. *The Autobiography and Diary of Mr. James Melvill*. Ed. Robert Pitcairn. Edinburgh: Wodrow Society, 1842.

Middle English Debate Poetry. Ed. J. W. Conlee. East Lansing: Colleagues Press, 1991.

Minor Latin Poets. Ed. & transl. J. Wight Duff and A. M. Duff. Loeb Classical Library. rev. ed. Cambridge, MA: Harvard University Press, 1982.

The Minor Poems of the Vernon MS. Ed. F. J. Furnivall. EETS, OS 117. Vol. 2. London: Kegan Paul, Trench, Trübner, 1901.

Monumenta Ritualia Ecclesiae Anglicanae. The Occasional Offices of the Church of England according to the Old Use of Salisbury the Prymer in English and Other Prayers and Forms with Dissertations and Notes. Ed. William Maskell. 3 vols. Oxford: Clarendon Press, 1846.

Of Shrifte and Penance: The Middle English Prose Translation of 'Le Manuel des péchés'. Ed. Klaus Bitterling. Middle English texts. Vol. 29. Heidelberg: C. Winter, 1998.

The Oxford Book of Late Medieval Verse and Prose. Ed. Douglas Gray. Oxford: Oxford University Press, 1989.

The Oxford Dictionary of Nursery Rhymes. Eds. Iona Opie and Peter Opie. Oxford: Clarendon Press, 1952.

Pieces from the Makculloch and the Gray MSS together with the Chepman and Myllar Prints. Ed. George S. Stevenson. STS 1st ser. 65. Edinburgh: W. Blackwood and Sons, 1918.

Pliny the Elder. *Naturalis historiae libri XXXVIII*. Ed. Karl Friedrich Theodor Mayhoff. Bibliotheca Scriptorum Graecorum et Romanorum Teubneriana. 6 in 7 vols. Leipzig: Teubner, 1870-1880.

—. *Natural History III Books VIII-XI*. Ed. H. Rackham. London: Heinemann, 1983.

The Poems of James VI of Scotland. Ed. James Craigie. STS, 3rd ser. 22, 26. 2 vols. Edinburgh: Blackwood, 1955.

The Quest of the Holy Grail. Trans. P. Matarasso. Harmondsworth: Penguin, 1979.

Records of the Parliaments of Scotland to 1707. Eds. K. M. Brown and Scottish Parliament Project Team. St Andrews: University of St Andrews, 2007-10.

Registrum Magni Sigilli Regum Scotorum. Eds. John Maitland Thomson, et al. 11 vols. Edinburgh: H.M. General Register House, 1882.

The Register of the Privy Council of Scotland. Eds. John Hill Burton, et al. 36 vols. Edinburgh: H.M. General Register House, 1877-1933.

Religious Lyrics of the XIVth Century. Eds. Carleton F. Brown and G. V. Smithers. 2nd ed. Oxford: Clarendon Press, 1952.

Religious Lyrics of the XVth Century. Ed. Carleton Brown. Oxford: OUP, 1952.

Sacrobosco, Joannes de. *The Sphere of Sacrobosco and its Commentators*. Trans. Lynn Thorndike. Chicago: University of Chicago Press, 1949.

Satirical Poems of the Time of the Reformation. Ed. James Cranstoun. STS 1st ser. 20/24, 28/30. 2 vols. Edinburgh: W. Blackwood and Sons, 1891, 1893.

Scott, Alexander. *The Poems of Alexander Scott*. Ed. Alexander Scott. Edinburgh: Saltire Society, 1952.

Secular Lyrics of the XIVth and XVth Centuries. Ed. Rossell H. Robbins. Oxford: Clarendon Press, 1952.

The Sex Werkdays and Agis. Ed. L. A. J. R. Houwen. Groningen: Forsten, 1990.

Sinclair, George. *Satans Invisible World Discovered*. Reprinted Edinburgh: T.G. Stevenson, 1871.

State Papers of Henry VIII. 11 vols. London: His Majesty's Commission, 1830-52.

The Towneley Plays. Eds. A. C. Cawley and Martin Stevens. EETS SS 13, 14. 2 vols. Oxford: Oxford University Press, 1994.

Walter of England. *The Fables of 'Walter of England'. Edited from Wolfenbüttel, Herzog August Bibliothek, Codex Gualferbytanus 185 Helmstadiensis*. Ed. A. E. Wright. Toronto: Pontifical Institute, 1997.

Wedderburn, Robert. *The Complaynt of Scotlande, wyth ane Exortatione to the Thre Estaits to be vigilante in the Deffens of their Public Veil. A.D. 1549. With an Appendix of Contemporary English Tracts, viz.: The Just Declaration of Henry of Henry VIII; the Exhortacion of James Harrysone, Scottisheman (1547); the Epistle of the Lord Protector Somerset (1548); the Epitome of Nicholas Bodrugan, alias Adams (1548)*. Ed. J. A. H. Murray. EETS ES 17, 18. 2 vols. London: N. Trübner, 1872-73.

White, Gilbert. *The Natural History of Selborne*. Eds. James Fisher and Claire Oldham. London: Cresset Press, 1960.

The Works of Geoffrey Chaucer and The Kingis Quair: A Facsimile of Bodleian Library, Oxford, MS. Arch. Selden. B.24. Introduced by Julia Boffey and A. S. G. Edwards, appendix by B. C. Barker Benfield. Cambridge: D.S. Brewer, 1997.

SECONDARY LITERATURE

A New Index of Middle English Verse. Eds. Julia Boffey and A. S. G. Edwards. London: British Library, 2005.

Abeele, Baudouin van den, et al., eds. *Bartholomaeus Anglicus, De Proprietatibus Rerum I*. De Diversis Artibus 78. Turnhout: Brepols, 2007.

Abeele, Baudouin van den. 'Une version moralisée du De animalibus d'Aristote (XIVe siècle).' *Aristotle's Animals in the Middle Ages and Renaissance*. Ed. Carlos Steel. Leuven: Leuven UP, 1999. 338-54.

Abercrombie, David. 'A Phonetician's View of Verse Structure.' *Linguistics* 6 (1964): 5-13.

—. *Studies in Phonetics and Linguistics*. Language and language learning. Oxford University Press: London, 1965.

Adrados, Francisco Rodríguez. *History of the Graeco-Latin Fable*. Trans. Leslie A. Ray. Mnemosyne: Bibliotheca Classica Batava. Dijk, Gert-Jan van ed. 2 vols. Leiden: Brill, 1999-2003.

Aitken, A. J. 'Variation and Variety in Written Middle Scots.' *Edinburgh Studies in English and Scots*. Eds. A. J. Aitken, Angus McIntosh and Hermann Pálsson, 1971. 177-209.

Anglo, Sydney. *Spectacle, Pageantry, and Early Tudor Policy*. Oxford-Warburg studies. Oxford: Clarendon Press, 1969.

Asúa, Miguel J. C. de. 'The Organization of Discourse on Animals in the Thirteenth Century: Peter of Spain, Albert the Great, and the Commentaries on *De animalibus*.' Ph.D. thesis. University of Notre Dame, 1991.

Bakhtin, M. M. *The Dialogic Imagination: Four Essays*. Trans. Michael Holquist and Caryl Emerson. Ed. Michael Holquist. University of Texas Press Slavic Series. Austin: University of Texas Press, 1981.

Bardgett, Frank D. 'Families and Factions: The Scottish Reformation in Angus and the Mearns.' Ph.D. University of Edinburgh, 1987. 2 vols.

—. *Scotland Reformed: The Reformation in Angus and the Mearns*. Edinburgh: John Donald, 1989.

—. 'John Erskine of Dun: a Theological Reassessment.' *Scottish Journal of Theology* 43 (1990): 59-85.

Bartlett, Anne Clark. *Male Authors, Female Readers. Representation and Subjectivity in Middle English Devotional Literature*. Ithaca: Cornell University Press, 1995.

Bawcutt, Priscilla, and Janet Hadley Williams, eds. *A Companion to Medieval Scottish Poetry*. Cambridge: D.S. Brewer, 2006.

—. *Gavin Douglas: A Critical Study*. Edinburgh: Edinburgh University Press, 1976.

—. 'Dunbar's Use of the Symbolic Lion and Thistle.' *Cosmos* 2 (1986): 83-97.

—. 'A Song from *The Complaynt of Scotland*: "My Hart is Leiuit on the Land".' *N&Q* 247 (2002): 193-97.

—. 'Religious Verse in Medieval Scotland.' *A Companion to Medieval Scottish Poetry*. Eds. Priscilla J. Bawcutt and Janet Hadley Williams. Cambridge: D.S. Brewer, 2006. 119-31.

—. 'The Contents of the Bannatyne Manuscript: New Sources and Analogues.' *Journal of the Edinburgh Bibliographical Society* 3 (2008): 95-133.

Bernau, Anke. 'Gender and Sexuality.' *A Companion to Middle English Hagiography*. Ed. Sarah Salih. Woodbridge: D.S. Brewer, 2006. 104-21.

Bestul, Thomas H. *Texts of the Passion: Latin Devotional Literature and Medieval Society*. Middle Ages series. Philadelphia, PA: University of Pennsylvania Press, 1996.

Bitterling, Klaus. Rev. of *Barbour's Bruce*, ed. M. P. McDiarmid and J. A. C. Stevenson, 3 vols., STS, 4th Series, 15, 12, 13 (Edinburgh: Blackwood, Pillans & Wilson, 1985). *Anglia* 107 (1989): 203-06.

—. 'Language and Style in *The Complaynt of Scotland*.' *Scottish Language* 20 (2001): 86-98.

Black, William George. *Folk-Medicine: A Chapter in the History of Culture*. Publications of the Folklore Society. London: E. Stock, 1883.

Blamires, Alcuin. *Chaucer, Ethics, and Gender*. Oxford: Oxford University Press, 2006.

Blayney, Margaret S., and Glenn H. Blayney. 'Alain Chartier and *The Complaynt of Scotlande*.' *Review of English Studies* 9 (1958): 8-17.

Blind, Karl. 'Discovery of Odinic Songs in Shetland.' *The Nineteenth Century* 5 (1879): 1091-113.

Boardman, Steve. 'The Cult of St George in Scotland.' *Saints' Cults in the Celtic World*. Eds. Steve Boardman, John Reuben Davies and Eila Williamson. Woodbridge: Boydell Press, 2009. 146-59.

Boffey, Julia. 'The Early Reception of Chartier's Works in England and Scotland.' *Chartier in Europe*. Eds. Emma J. Cayley and Ashby Kinch. Cambridge: D. S. Brewer, 2008. 105-16.

Borland, Catherine R. 'Catalogue of the Mediaeval Manuscripts in the Library of the Faculty of Advocates at Edinburgh.' Edinburgh: Department of Manuscripts, National Library of Scotland, 1906-08.

Boutier, Jean, Alain Dewerpe, and Daniel Nordman. *Un tour de France royal: le voyage de Charles IX 1564-1566*. Collection historique. Paris: Aubier, 1984.

Bouwsma, William J. 'Anxiety and the Formation of Early Modern Culture.' *After the Reformation: Essays in Honor of J.H. Hexter*. Eds. Barbara C. Malament, William J. Bouwsma and J. H. Hexter. Philadelphia: University of Pennsylvania Press, 1980. 215-46.

—. *The Waning of the Renaissance, ca. 1550-1640*. The Yale Intellectual History of the West. New Haven, CT: Yale University Press, 2000.

Bower, R. H. 'Three Middle English Poems on the Apostles' Creed.' *PMLA* 70 (1955): 210-22.

Brinkmann, Hennig. 'Der Prolog im Mittelalter als literarische Erscheinung: Bau und Aussage.' *Wirkendes Wort* 14 (1964): 1-21.

Briquet, C. M. *Les filigranes: dictionnaire historique des marques du papier dès leur apparition vers 1282 jusqu'en 1600. A Facsimile of the 1907 Edition with Supplementary Material […]*. Ed. Allan Henry Stevenson. 4 vols. Amsterdam: The Paper Publications Society, 1968.

Broadie, Alexander. 'Scotus on God's Relation to the World.' *British Journal for the History of Philosophy* 7 (1999): 1-13.

—. 'Scotistic Metaphysics and Creation *ex nihilo*.' *Creation and the God of Abraham*. Eds. David B. Burrell, et. al. Cambridge: Cambridge University Press, 2010. 53-64.

Brown, Mary Ellen. 'Balladry: A Vernacular Poetic Resource.' *The Edinburgh History of Scottish Literature. Volume One: From Columba to the Union (until 1707)*. Eds. Thomas Owen Clancy and Murray Pittock. Edinburgh: Edinburgh University Press, 2007. 263-72.

Bühler, Curt. 'Prayers and Charms in Certain Middle English Rolls.' *Speculum* 39 (1964): 270-78.

Burnett, C. J. 'The Officers of Arms and Heraldic Art under King James Sixth & First 1567-1625.' University of Edinburgh M.Litt., 1992.

—. 'Early Offices of Arms in Scotland.' *Review of Scottish Culture* 9 (1995-96): 3-13.

Burns, Charles. 'Papal Gifts to Scottish Monarchs: The Golden Rose and the Blessed Sword.' *The Innes Review* 20 (1969): 150-94.

Burrow, J. A. 'Henryson: The Preaching of the Swallow.' *Essays in Criticism* 25 (1975): 25-37.

Buuren, Catherine C. van. 'John Asloan and his Manuscript: An Edinburgh Notary and Scribe in the Days of James III, IV and V (c. 1470-c. 1530).' *Stewart Style 1513-1542. Essays on the Court of James V*. Ed. Janet Hadley Williams. East Linton: Tuckwell Press, 1996. 15-51.

Calin, William. *The French Tradition and the Literature of Medieval England*. Toronto: University of Toronto Press, 1994.

Carruthers, Ian Robert. 'A Critical Commentary on Robert Henryson's *Morall Fabillis*.' Ph.D. thesis. University of British Columbia, 1977.

Cherry, T. A. F. 'The Library of Henry Sinclair, Bishop of Ross, 1560-1565.' *The Bibliotheck* 4.1 (1963): 13-24.

Chibnall, Marjorie. 'Pliny's *Natural History* and the Middle Ages.' *Empire and Aftermath: Silver Latin II*. Ed. T. A. Dorey. London: Routledge & Kegan Paul, 1975. 57-78.

Clark, Stuart. 'Protestant Demonology: Sin, Superstition, and Society.' *Early Modern European Witchcraft: Centres and Peripheries*. Eds. Bengt Ankarloo and Gustav Henningsen. Oxford: Clarendon Press, 1990. 45-81.

Cooper, Helen. *Pastoral: Mediaeval into Renaissance*. Ipswich: D.S. Brewer, 1977.

Cowan, Ian B., David Edward Easson, and Richard Neville Hadcock. *Medieval Religious Houses: Scotland. With an Appendix on the Houses in the Isle of Man*. 2nd ed. London [etc.]: Longman, 1976.

Dawson, Jane E. A. *The Politics of Religion in the Age of Mary Queen of Scots: The Earl of Argyll and the Struggle for Stability in Britain and Ireland*. Cambridge Studies in Early Modern British History. Cambridge: Cambridge University Press, 2002.

Dickson, Robert, and John P. Edmond. *Annals of Scottish Printing: From the Introduction of the Art in 1507 to the Beginning of the Seventeenth Century, with Analytical Descriptions of Books Printed and an Index of Names, Subjects and Titles*. Cambridge: Macmillan and Bowes, 1890.

A Dictionary of the Older Scottish Tongue. Eds. Sir William Craigie, et al. Chicago, Aberdeen, Oxford, 1937-2002. Online at http://www.dsl.ac.uk/.

Dictionary of the Scots Language on-line at http://www.dsl.ac.uk/.

Dijk, Gert-Jan van. *ΑΙΝΟΙ, ΛΟΓΟΙ, ΜΥΘΟΙ: Fables in Archaic, Classical, and Hellenistic Greek Literature: with a Study of the Theory and Terminology of the Genre*. Mnemosyne, Bibliotheca Classica Batava 166 (Supplementum). Leiden: Brill, 1997.

Dilworth, Fr. Mark. 'Monks and Ministers after 1560.' *RSCHS* 18 (1974): 201-21.

—. 'Sinclair, Henry (1507/8–1565).' *Oxford Dictionary of National Biography*. Oxford: Oxford University Press, 2004.

Ditchburn, David. *Scotland and Europe: The Medieval Kingdom and Its Contacts with Christendom, 1215-1545*. East Linton: Tuckwell, 2001.

Donaldson, Gordon. *The Scottish Reformation*. Birkbeck Lectures. Cambridge: Cambridge University Press, 1960.

—. 'Scottish Presbyterian Exiles in England, 1584-8.' *RSCHS* 14 (1960-2): 67-80.

—. *All the Queen's Men: Power and Politics in Mary Stewart's Scotland*. London: Batsford Academic and Educational, 1983.

—. *Reformed by Bishops: Galloway, Orkney and Caithness*. Edinburgh: Edina Press, 1987.

—. *Scottish Church History*. Edinburgh: Scottish Academic Press, 1985.

Doody, Aude. 'Pliny's *Natural History*: *Enkuklios Paideia* and the Ancient Encyclopedia.' *Journal of the History of Ideas* 70.1 (2009): 1-21.

—. *Pliny's Encyclopedia: The Reception of the Natural History*. Cambridge: Cambridge University Press, 2010.

Duffy, Eamon. *The Stripping of the Altars: Traditional Religion in England, c.1400-c.1580*. New Haven: Yale UP, 1992.

Durkan, John, and Anthony Ross. *Early Scottish Libraries*. Glasgow: John S. Burns & Sons, 1961.

Durkan, John, and Julian Russell. 'Further Additions (Including Manuscripts) to J. Durkan and A. Ross, *Early Scottish Libraries*, at the National Library of Scotland.' *The Bibliotheck* 12.4 (1985): 85-90.

Durkan, John. 'The Observant Franciscan Province in Scotland.' *Innes Review* Autumn (1984): 51-57.

Eade, J. C. *The Forgotten Sky: A Guide to Astrology in English Literature*. Oxford: Clarendon Press, 1984.

Edington, Carol. *Court and Culture in Renaissance Scotland: Sir David Lindsay of the Mount*. Amherst: University of Massachusetts Press, 1994.

Edmondston, Rev. Biot, and J. M. E. Saxby. *The Home of a Naturalist*. 2nd ed. London: James Nisbet & Co., 1889.

Fawcett, Richard. *Scottish Architecture from the Accession of the Stewarts to the Reformation, 1371-1560*. Architectural History of Scotland. Edinburgh: Edinburgh University Press in association with Historic Scotland, 1994.

Finucane, Ronald C. *Miracles and Pilgrims: Popular Beliefs in Medieval England*. London: J. M. Dent, 1977.

Gaunt, Simon. *Gender and Genre in Medieval French Literature*. Cambridge Studies in French. Cambridge: Cambridge University Press, 1995.

George, Wilma, and Brunsdon Yapp. *The Naming of the Beasts: Natural History in the Medieval Bestiary*. London: Duckworth, 1991.

Gerke, Robert S. 'Studies in the Tradition and Morality of Henryson's *Fables*.' Ph.D. thesis. University of Notre Dame, 1969.

Gerould, G. H. *Saints' Legends*. Boston: Houghton Mifflin Company, 1916.

Gieben, Servus. 'Traces of God in Nature according to Robert Grosseteste, with the Text of the Dictum "Omnis creatura speculum est".' *Franciscan Studies* 24 (1964): 144-58.

Good, Jonathan. *The Cult of Saint George in Medieval England*. Woodbridge: Boydell Press, 2009.

Goodare, Julian. *State and Society in Early Modern Scotland*. Oxford: Oxford University Press, 1999.

—. *The Scottish Witch-Hunt in Context*. Manchester: Manchester University Press, 2002.

—. *The Government of Scotland, 1560-1625*. Oxford: Oxford University Press, 2004.

—. 'How Archbishop Spottiswoode Became an Episcopalian.' *Renaissance and Reformation /
Renaissance et Réforme* 30.4 (2006-7): 83-103.

—. 'The Attempted Scottish *Coup* of 1596.' *Sixteenth-Century Scotland: Essays in Honour of
Michael Lynch.* Eds. Julian Goodare and A. A. MacDonald. Leiden: Brill, 2008. 311-36.

Goodich, Michael. 'A Note on Sainthood in the Hagiographical Prologue.' *History and Theory*
20.2 (1981): 168-74.

—. *Lives and Miracles of the Saints: Studies in Medieval Latin Hagiography.* Variorum collected
studies series. Aldershot: Ashgate/Variorum, 2004.

Gopen, George D. 'The Essential Seriousness of Robert Henryson's *Moral Fables*: A Study in
Structure.' *Studies in Philology* 82.1 (1985): 42-59.

Graham, Victor E., and William McAllister Johnson. *The Royal Tour of France by Charles IX and
Catherine de' Medici: Festivals and Entries, 1564-6.* Toronto: University of Toronto Press,
1979.

Grant, Sir Francis. J. *Court of the Lord Lyon: List of His Majesty's Officers of Arms and Other
Officials, with Genealogical Notes, 1318-1945.* Edinburgh: Scottish Record Society, 1945.

Gray, Douglas. 'Notes on Some Middle English Charms.' *Chaucer and Middle English Studies in
Honour of Rossell Hope Robbins.* Ed. Beryl Rowland. London: George Allen & Unwin, 1974.
56-71.

—. *Robert Henryson.* Medieval and Renaissance Authors. Leiden: Brill, 1979.

—. '"Of sunne ne mone had they no need": Notes on the Imagery of Light in the Middle English
Text.' *Essays in Honor of Edward B. King.* Eds. Robert J. Benson and Eric W. Naylor. Sewanee,
TN: The University of the South, 1991. 87-108.

—. 'The Royal Entry in Sixteenth-Century Scotland.' *The Rose and the Thistle: Essays on the
Culture of Late Medieval and Renaissance Scotland.* Eds. Sally Mapstone and Juliette Wood.
East Linton: Tuckwell, 1998. 10-37.

—. '"A Fulle Wyse Gentyl-Woman of France": *The Epistle of Othea* and Later Medieval English
Literary Culture.' *Medieval Women: Texts and Contexts in Late Medieval Britain. Essays for
Felicity Riddy.* Ed. Jocelyn Wogan-Browne. Turnhout: Brepols, 2000. 237-49.

—. 'Jean de Meun (Meung).' *The Oxford Companion to Chaucer.* Ed. Douglas Gray. Oxford:
Oxford University Press, 2003. 257-58.

—. '*Roman de la Rose.*' *The Oxford Companion to Chaucer.* Ed. Douglas Gray. Oxford: Oxford
University Press, 2003. 419-20.

Greentree, Rosemary. 'The Debate of the Paddock and the Mouse.' *Studies in Scottish Literature*
26 (1991): 481-89.

Gudger, E. W. 'Pliny's *Historia naturalis.* The Most Popular Natural History Ever Published.'
Isis 6.3 (1924): 269-81.

Guy, J. A. *My Heart is My Own: The Life of Mary Queen of Scots.* London: Fourth Estate, 2004.

Guynn, N. D. '*Le Roman de la Rose.*' *The Cambridge Companion to Medieval French Literature.*
Eds. Simon Gaunt and Sarah Kay. Cambridge: Cambridge University Press, 2008. 48-62.

Hadley Williams, Janet, ed. *Stewart Style 1513-1542. Essays on the Court of James V.* East Linton:
Tuckwell Press, 1996.

Haigh, Christopher. *The Plain Man's Pathways to Heaven: Kinds of Christianity in Post-Reformation England, 1570-1640*. Oxford: Oxford University Press, 2007.

Hannay, R. K. 'Observations on the Officers of the Scottish Parliament.' *Juridical Review* 44 (1932): 125-38.

Haws, Charles H. *Scottish Parish Clergy at the Reformation, 1540-1574*. Scottish Record Society. Edinburgh: printed for the Society by Smith and Ritchie, 1972.

Hay, Father Richard Augustine. *Genealogie of the Sainteclaires of Rosslyn*. Ed. James Maidment. Edinburgh: T. G. Stevenson, 1835.

Hazlett, W. I. P. 'Playing God's Card: Knox and Fasting.' *John Knox and the British Reformations*. Ed. R.A. Mason. Aldershot: Ashgate, 1998. 176-98.

Heffernan, Thomas J. 'Dangerous Sympathies: Political Commentary in the *South English Legendary*.' *The South English Legendary: A Critical Assessment*. Ed. Klaus P. Jankofsky. Tübingen: A. Francke, 1992. 1-17.

Higgitt, John. *The Murthly Hours. Devotion, Literacy and Luxury in Paris, England and the Gaelic West*. The British Library Studies in Medieval Culture. London: British Library, 2000.

—. '*Imageis maid with mennis hand*': Saints, Images, Belief and Identity in Later Medieval Scotland*. Whithorn lecture. Whithorn: Friends of the Whithorn Trust, 2003.

Hill, Thomas D. '"Hirundines habent quidem prescium": Why Henryson's *Preaching of a Swallow* is Preached by a Swallow.' *Scottish Literary Journal* 26 (Supplement) (1987): 30-31.

Houwen, L. A. J. R. 'The Beast Within. The Animal-Man Dichotomy in the *Consolation of Philosophy*.' *Boethius Christianus? Transformationen der Consolatio Philosophiae in Mittelalter und früher Neuzeit*. Eds. Reinhold F. Glei, Nicola Kaminski and Franz Lebsanft. Berlin: Walter de Gruyter, 2010. 247-60.

Howard, Deborah. *Scottish Architecture: Reformation to the Restoration, 1560-1660*. The Architectural History of Scotland. Edinburgh: Edinburgh University Press, 1995.

Innes, Thomas. 'The Scottish Parliament: Its Symbolism and Ceremonial.' *Juridical Review* 44 (1932): 87-124.

Keiser, George R. 'The Middle English *Planctus Mariae* and the Rhetoric of Pathos.' *The Popular Literature of Medieval England*. Ed. Thomas J. Heffernan. Knoxville, TN: University of Tennessee Press, 1985. 167-93.

Keith, Robert, John Parker Lawson, and C. J. Lyon. *History of the Affairs of Church and State in Scotland from the Beginning of the Reformation to the Year 1568*. 3 vols. Edinburgh: Spottiswoode Society, 1844.

Keith, Robert. *An Historical Catalogue of the Scottish Bishops, Down to the Year 1688*. Edinburgh: Bell & Bradfute, 1824.

Kelly, J. N. D. *Early Christian Creeds*. 3rd ed. Harlow: Longman, 1972.

King, Anne. 'The Inflectional Morphology of Older Scots.' *The Edinburgh History of the Scots Language*. Ed. Charles Jones. Edinburgh: Edinburgh University Press, 1997. 156-81.

Kirk, James, ed. *Visitation of the Diocese of Dunblane and Other Churches, 1586-1589*. Scottish Record Society. Edinburgh: Scottish Record Society, 1984.

Kitson, P. R. 'Swans and Geese in Old English Riddles.' *Anglo-Saxon Studies in Archaeology and History* 7 (1994): 79-84.

Laing, David. 'Inquiries Respecting Some of the Early Historical Writers of Scotland (1846 and 1847).' *Proceedings of the Society of Antiquaries of Scotland* 12 (1878): 72-87.

Laroche, Rebecca. 'Elizabeth Melville and Her Friends: Seeing "Ane Godlie Dreame" through Political Lenses.' *Clio* 34.3 (2005): 277-95.

Lawlor, J. H. 'Note on the Library of the Sinclairs of Rosslyn.' *Proceedings of the Society of Antiquaries of Scotland* 32 (1897-1898): 90-120.

Lewalski, Barbara Kiefer. *Protestant Poetics and the Seventeenth-Century Religious Lyric*. Princeton, NJ: Princeton University Press, 1979.

Lindsay, Maurice. *History of Scottish Literature*. rev. ed. London: Robert Hale, 1992.

Linn, Irving. 'If All the Sky Were Parchment.' *PMLA* 53 (1938): 951-70.

Long, Mary Beth. 'Corpora and Manuscripts, Authors and Audiences.' *A Companion to Middle English Hagiography*. Ed. Sarah Salih. Woodbridge: D.S. Brewer, 2006. 47-69.

Lüken, Sven. 'Kaiser Maximilian I. und seine Ehrenpforte.' *Zeitschrift für Kunstgeschichte* 61.2 (1998): 449-90.

Lyall, R. J. 'The Medieval Scottish Coronation Service: Some Seventeenth-Century Evidence.' *The Innes Review* 28 (1977): 3-21.

—. 'Books and Book Owners in Fifteenth-Century Scotland.' *Book Production and Publishing in Britain 1375-1475*. Eds. J. Griffiths and Derek Pearsall. Cambridge: Cambridge University Press, 1989. 239-56.

—. 'Alexander Allan (Alesius) and the Development of a Protestant Aesthetics.' *The European Sun: Proceedings of the Seventh International Conference on Medieval and Renaissance Scottish Language and Literature*. Eds. Graham D. Caie, et al. East Linton: Tuckwell Press, 2001. 368-80.

—. 'Henryson's *Morall Fabillis*: Structure and Meaning.' *A Companion to Medieval Scottish Poetry*. Eds. Priscilla J. Bawcutt and Janet Hadley Williams. Cambridge: D.S. Brewer, 2006. 89-104.

Lynch, Michael. 'Queen Mary's Triumph: The Baptismal Celebrations at Stirling in December 1566.' *SHR* 69 (1990): 1-21.

—. 'Court Ceremony and Ritual During the Personal Reign of James VI.' *The Reign of James VI*. Eds. Julian Goodare and Michael Lynch. East Linton: Tuckwell Press, 2000. 71-92.

MacDonald, A. A. 'Poetry, Politics, and Reformation Censorship in Sixteenth-Century Scotland.' *English Studies* 64 (1983): 410-21.

—. 'Catholic Devotion into Protestant Lyric: The Case of the *Contemplacioun of Synnaris*.' *Innes Review* 35 (1984): 58-87.

—. 'The Bannatyne Manuscript-A Marian Anthology.' *Innes Review* 37 (1986): 36-47.

—. 'Religious Poetry in Middle Scots.' *The History of Scottish Literature Volume 1: Origins to 1660*. Ed. R. D. S. Jack. Aberdeen: Aberdeen University Press, 1988. 91-104.

—. '*Gude and Godlie Ballatis*.' *Dictionary of Scottish Church History and Theology*. Eds. Nigel M. de S. Cameron, et al. Edinburgh: InterVarsity Press, 1993. 379-80.

—. 'The Latin Original of Robert Henryson's Annunciation Lyric.' *The Renaissance in Scotland. Studies in Literature, Religion, History and Culture*. Eds. A. A. MacDonald, Michael Lynch and I. B. Cowan. Leiden: Brill, 1994. 45-65.

—. 'The Printed Book that Never Was: George Bannatyne's Poetic Anthology.' *Boeken in de Late Middeleeuwen: Verslag van de Groningse Codicologendagen 1992*. Eds. Jos M. M. Hermans and Klaas van der Hoek. Groningen: Forsten, 1994. 101-10.

—. 'Contrafacta and the *Gude and Godlie Ballatis*.' *Sacred and Profane: Secular and Devotional Interplay in Early Modern British Literature*. Eds. Helen Wilcox, Richard Todd and Alasdair A. MacDonald. Annual Bibliography of English Language and Literature. Amsterdam: VU University Press, 1996. 33-44.

—. 'The *Gude and Godlie Ballatis* (1597): A Ghost no More?' *Edinburgh Bibliographical Society Transactions* 6.4 (1998): 115-31.

—. 'Passion Devotion in Late-Medieval Scotland.' *The Broken Body. Passion Devotion in Late-Medieval Culture*. Eds. A. A. MacDonald, H. N. B. Ridderbos and R. M. Schlusemann. Groningen: Forsten, 1998. 109-31.

—. 'Lyrics in Middle Scots.' *A Companion to the Middle English Lyric*. Ed. T. G. Duncan. Woodbridge: D.S. Brewer, 2005. 242-61.

—. 'On First Looking into the *Gude and Godlie Ballatis* (1565).' *Older Scots Literature*. Ed. Sally Mapstone. Edinburgh: John Donald Publishers, 2005. 230-42.

—. 'Political and Religious Instruction in an Eschatological Perspective: The *Contemplacioun of Synnaris* of William of Touris.' *Calliope's Classroom. Studies in Didactic Poetry from Antiquity to the Renaissance*. Eds. Annette Harder, Alasdair A. MacDonald and Gerrit J. Reinink. Leuven: Peeters, 2007. 269-92.

MacKechnie, Aonghus. 'James VI's Architects and Their Architecture.' *The Reign of James VI*. Eds. Julian Goodare and Michael Lynch. Edinburgh: John Donald, 2008. 154-69.

MacQueen, John. *Complete and Full with Numbers: The Narrative Poetry of Robert Henryson*. Scottish Cultural Review of Language and Literature. Amsterdam: Rodopi, 2006.

Mann, A. J. 'The Scottish Parliament: The Role of Ritual and Procession in the Pre-1707 Parliament and the New Parliament of 1999.' *Rituals and Parliaments: Political, Anthropological and Historical Perspectives on Europe and the United States*. Eds. E. Crewe and M.G. Müller. Frankfurt am Main: Peter Lang Frankfurt, 2006. 135-58.

Mantello, F. A. C., and A. G. Rigg. *Medieval Latin: An Introduction and Bibliographical Guide*. Washington, D.C.: Catholic University of America Press, 1996.

Mapstone, Sally. *Scots and Their Books in the Middle Ages and the Renaissance. An Exhibition in the Bodleian Library, Oxford 10 June – 24 August 1996*. Oxford: Bodleian Library, 1996.

Marrow, James. 'Circumdederunt Me Canes Multi: Christ's Tormentors in Northern European Art of the Late Middle Ages and Early Renaissance.' *Art Bulletin* 59 (1977): 167-81.

Mason, Roger A. 'George Buchanan, James VI and the Presbyterians.' *Scots and Britons: Scottish Political Thought and the Union of 1603*. Ed. R. A. Mason. Cambridge: Cambridge University Press, 1994. 112-37.

—. 'Usable Pasts: History and Identity in Reformation Scotland.' *SHR* 76.1 (1997): 54-68.

—. 'Knox on Rebellion.' *Kingship and the Commonweal: Political Thought in Renaissance and Reformation Scotland*. East Lothian: Tuckwell Press, 1998. 139-64.

—. 'This Realm of Scotland is an Empire? Imperial Ideas and Iconography in Early Renaissance Scotland.' *Church, Chronicle and Learning in Medieval and Early Renaissance Scotland*. Ed. B. E. Crawford. Edinburgh: Mercat Press, 1999. 73-92.

—. 'Renaissance Monarchy? Stewart Kingship (1469-1532).' *Scottish Kingship, 1306-1542*. Eds. Michael Brown and Roland Tanner. Edinburgh: John Donald, 2008. 255-78.

Maxwell Scott, M. M. 'Barbour's Legends of the Saints.' *Dublin Review* 3rd ser. 34 (1887): 265-77.

Maxwell-Stuart, P. G. *Satan's Conspiracy: Magic and Witchcraft in Sixteenth-Century Scotland*. East Linton, Scotland: Tuckwell Press, 2001.

McCrie, Thomas. *The Life of Melville*. 2 vols. Edinburgh: Blackwood, 1819.

McGavin, John J. 'The Dramatic Prosody of Sir David Lyndsay.' *Of Lion and of Unicorn. Essays on Anglo-Scottish Literary Relations in Honour of Professor John MacQueen* Eds. R.D.S. Jack and Kevin J. McGinley. Edinburgh: Quadriga, 1993. 39-66.

McGladdery, Christine. *James II*. Edinburgh: John Donald, 1990.

McNeil, P. G. B. '"Our religion, established by neither law nor parliament": Was the Reformation Legislation of 1560 Valid?' *Scottish Church History Society Records* 35 (2005): 68-89.

McRoberts, David. 'Material Destruction Caused by the Scottish Reformation.' *Essays on the Scottish Reformation, 1513-1625*. Ed. David McRoberts. Glasgow: J.S. Burns, 1962. 415-62.

—. *The Heraldic Ceiling of St. Machar's Cathedral, Aberdeen*. Occasional papers. Aberdeen: Friends of St. Machar's Cathedral, 1976.

Meier, Nicole. 'Protestant Censorship in 16th-Century Scottish Manuscripts: The Case of Walter Kennedy's "Leif luve, my luve, no langar it lyk".' *Anglistentag 2008 Tübingen: Proceedings*. Eds. Lars Eckstein and Christoph Reinfandt. Trier: WVT, 2009. 159-66.

Middle English Dictionary. Eds. Hans Kurath, Sherman M. Kuhn and Robert E. Lewis. Ann Arbor: University of Michigan Press, 1952-2001. On-line at http://quod.lib.umich.edu/m/med/.

Minnis, A. J., and A. B. Scott, eds. *Medieval Literary Theory and Criticism c.1100-c.1375*. Oxford: Clarendon Press, 1991.

Mitchell, William Smith. *A History of Scottish Bookbinding: 1432 to 1650*. University of Aberdeen. Edinburgh: Oliver and Boyd for University of Aberdeen, 1955.

Murphy, Trevor. *Pliny the Elder's Natural History: The Empire in the Encyclopaedia*. Oxford: Oxford University Press, 2004.

Nall, Catherine. 'William Worcester Reads Alain Chartier: *Le Quadrilogue invectif* and Its English Readers.' *Chartier in Europe*. Eds. Emma J. Cayley and Ashby Kinch. Cambridge: D. S. Brewer, 2008. 137-47.

National Library of Scotland. *Catalogue of Manuscripts Acquired Since 1925*. 8 vols. Edinburgh: H.M.S.O., 1938-92.

Neff, Amy. 'The Pain of *Compassio*: Mary's Labor at the Foot of the Cross.' *Art Bulletin* 80 (1998): 254-73.

Nicolson, William. *The Scottish Historical Library Containing a Short View and Character of Most of the Writers, Records, Registers, Law-books, &c. which may be Serviceable to the Undertakers of a General History of Scotland, Down to the Union of the Two Kingdomes in King James the VI*. London: T. Childe, 1702.

Normand, Lawrence, and Gareth Roberts, eds. *Witchcraft in Early Modern Scotland: King James VI's Demonology and the North Berwick Witches*. Exeter Studies in History. Exeter: University of Exeter Press, 2000.

North, J. D. *Chaucer's Universe*. Oxford: Oxford University Press, 1988.

Opie, Iona, and Moira Tatem. *A Dictionary of Superstitions*. Oxford: Oxford University Press, 1990.

Oram, Richard D. 'Seton, George, fourth Lord Seton (c. 1508–1549).' *Oxford Dictionary of National Biography*. Oxford: Oxford University Press, 2004.

The Oxford English Dictionary. Ed. J.A. Simpson and E.S.C. Weiner. 2nd edn. Oxford: Oxford University Press. 3rd edition online http://www.oed.com/).

Parkinson, D. J. '*The Legend of the Bishop of St Androis Lyfe* and the Survival of Scottish Poetry.' *Early Modern Literary Studies* 9.1 (May, 2003): 5.1-24<URL: http://purl.oclc.org/emls/09-1/parkscot.html> (2003).

Patrick, Millar. *Four Centuries of Scottish Psalmody*. London: Oxford University Press, 1949.

Pedersen, Olaf. 'In Search of Sacrobosco.' *Journal of the History of Astronomy* 16.3 (1985): 175-220.

Perry, B. E. 'Demetrius of Phalerum and the Aesopic Fables.' *Transactions and Proceedings of the American Philological Association* 93 (1962): 287-346.

Pittock, Malcolm. 'Animals as People — People as Animals: The Beast Story with Reference to Henryson's *The Two Mice* and *The Preaching of the Swallow*.' *Critical Studies: Language and the Subject*. Ed. Karl Simms. Amsterdam: Rodopi, 1994. 163-72.

Purdie, Rhiannon. 'Medieval Romance in Scotland.' *A Companion to Medieval Scottish Poetry*. Eds. Priscilla J. Bawcutt and Janet Hadley Williams. Cambridge: D.S. Brewer, 2006. 165-77.

Rait, Robert S. *The Parliaments of Scotland*. Glasgow: Maclehose, 1924.

Reames, Sherry L. 'Artistry, Decorum and Purpose in Three Middle English Retellings of the Cecilia Legend.' *The Endless Knot: Essays on Old and Middle English in Honor of Marie Borroff*. Eds. M. Teresa Tavormina and Robert F. Yeager. Cambridge: D. S. Brewer, 1995. 177-99.

Reichl, Karl. 'Disticha Catonis.' *Lexikon des Mittelalters*. Vol. 3. Munich: Artemis, 1995. 1123-27.

Reid-Baxter, Jamie. '*Philotus*: The Transmission of a Delectable Treatise.' *Literature, Letters and the Canonical in Early Modern Scotland*. Eds. Theo van Heijnsbergen and Nicola Royan. East Linton: Tuckwell Press, 2002. 52-68.

—. 'Calvinism and the Lyric Voice in Jacobean Scotland: The Case of Elizabeth Melville.' *New Developments in the Literary Culture of the Reign of James VI and I*. Ed. D. J. Parkinson. Leuven: Peeters, forthcoming.

Ringler Jr, William A. *Bibliography and Index of English Verse in Manuscript, 1501–1558. Prepared and Completed by Michael Rudick and Susan J. Ringler*. London: Mansell, 1992.

Roberts, Jane, Christian Kay, and Lynne Grundy, eds. *A Thesaurus of Old English*. 2 vols. London: King's College, 1995.

Rouse, Mary A., and Richard H. Rouse. 'The Texts Called *Lumen Anime*.' *Archivum Fratrum Praedicatorum* 41 (1971): 5-113.

Salih, Sarah. 'Introduction: Saints, Cults and Lives in Late Medieval England.' *A Companion to Middle English Hagiography*. Ed. Sarah Salih. Woodbridge: D.S. Brewer, 2006. 1-23.

Salih, Sarah, ed. *A Companion to Middle English Hagiography*. Woodbridge: D.S. Brewer, 2006.

Sanderson, Margaret H. B. 'Mark Ker 1517-18, Metamorphosis.' *Mary Stewart's People: Life in Mary Stewart's Scotland*. Edinburgh: J. Thin, 1987. 166-78.

Scahill, John, and Margaret Rogerson. *Middle English Saints' Legends*. Annotated Bibliographies of Old and Middle English Literature 8. Woodbridge: D.S. Brewer, 2005.

Scheibe, Regina. 'Aspects of the Snake in the *Legends of the Saints*.' *Bryght Lanternis: Essays on the Language and Literature of Medieval and Renaissance Scotland*. Eds. J. Derrick McClure and Michael R.G. Spiller. Aberdeen: Aberdeen UP, 1989. 67-89.

Schultz, James A. 'Classical Rhetoric, Medieval Poetics, and the Medieval Vernacular Prologue.' *Speculum* 59 (1984): 1-15.

Scott, Hew. *Fasti Ecclesiae Scoticanae: The Succession of Ministers in the Parish Churches of Scotland, from the Reformation, A.D. 1560, to the Present Time*. 10 vols. Edinburgh: W. Paterson, 1866-.

Scottish Libraries. Ed. John Higgitt. Corpus of British Medieval Library Catalogues 12. London: British Library in association with the British Academy, 2006.

Secor, John Rennell. '*Planctus Mariae*: The Laments of Mary as Influenced by Courtly Literature.' Ph.D. dissertation. The University of North Carolina at Chapel Hill, 1985.

Sharpe, Kevin. *Sir Robert Cotton, 1586-1631: History and Politics in Early Modern England*. Oxford Historical Monographs. Oxford: Oxford University Press, 1979.

Shaw, Duncan. 'Montgomerie, Robert (d.1609x11).' *Oxford Dictionary of National Biography*. Oxford: Oxford University Press, 2004.

Siertsema, Gijsbert J. 'Translation and Genre in the European Renaissance: Psalms.' *Übersetzung/ Translation / Traduction: ein internationales Handbuch zur Übersetzungsforschung / An International Encyclopedia of Translation Studies / Encyclopédie internationale de la recherche sur la traduction*. Eds. Harald Kittel, Juliane House and Brigitte Schultze. Vol. 2. Berlin: W. de Gruyter, 2004. 1454-59.

Simpson, Grant G. *Scottish Handwriting 1150-1650*. Aberdeen: Aberdeen University Press, 1986.

Simpson, Jaqueline. 'The Nightmare Charm in *King Lear*.' *Charms, Charmers and Charming: International Research on Verbal Magic*. Ed. Jonathan Roper. Basingstoke: Palgrave Macmillan, 2009. 100-07.

Spitz, Lewis William. *Conrad Celtis: The German Arch-Humanist*. Cambridge, MA.: Harvard University Press, 1957.

Spottiswoode, John, Mark Napier, and M. Right Russell. *History of the Church of Scotland, Beginning the Year of Our Lord 203 and Continuing to the End of the Reign of King James VI*. 3 vols. Edinburgh: The Spottiswoode Society, 1847.

Stanbury, Sarah. 'The Virgin's Gaze: Spectacle and Transgression in Middle English Lyrics of the Passion.' *PMLA* 106 (1991): 1083-93.

Stewart, A. M. 'Adam Abell's "Roit or Quheill of Tyme".' *Aberdeen University Review* 44 (1971): 386-93.

—. 'Adam Abell, Martin of Valencia, Pedro de Gante, Andrea da Spoleto: or Jedburgh, Mexico, Yucatan and Fez in 1532.' *Bulletin of the Scottish Institute of Missionary Studies* 11 (1972): 4-10.

—. 'Neues zum Macbeth-Stoff.' *Anglia* 92.3/4 (1974): 387-94.

—. 'Sapiens, Dominabitur Astris: Wedderburn, Abell, Luther.' *Aberdeen University Review* 46.1 (1975): 55-62.

—. 'The Tale of King Lear in Scots.' *Aberdeen University Review* 46.2 (1975): 205-10.

—. 'Think and Drink Tobacco.' *Aberdeen University Review* 47.3 (1978): 261-64.

—. 'Alain Chartier et l'Écosse.' *Actes du 2e Colloque de langue et de littérature écossaises (Moyen Age et Renaissance): Université de Strasbourg, 5-11 juillet 1978.* Ed. Jean-Jacques Blanchot. Strasbourg: Institut d'études anglaises de Strasbourg et l'Association des médiévistes anglicistes de l'enseignement superieur, 1979. 148-61.

—. 'Die europäische Wissensgemeinschaft um 1550 im Spiegel von Wedderburns *The Complaynt of Scotland.' Geschichtlichkeit und Neuanfang im sprachlichen Kunstwerk: Studien zur englischen Philologie zu Ehren von Fritz W. Schulze.* Eds. Peter Erlebach, Wolfgang G. Muller and Klaus Reuter. Tübingen: Narr, 1981. 91-103.

—. 'The Final Folios of Adam Abell's *Roit or Quheill of Tyme*: An Observantine Friar's Reflections on the 1520s and 30s.' *Stewart Style 1513-1542. Essays on the Court of James V.* Ed. Janet Hadley Williams. East Linton: Tuckwell Press, 1996. 227-53.

Stewart, Ian Halley. *The Scottish Coinage.* London: Spink, 1955.

Sticca, Sandro. *The Planctus Mariae in the Dramatic Tradition of the Middle Ages.* Trans. Joseph R. Berrigan. Athens GA: University of Georgia Press, 1988.

Strong, Roy C. *Art and Power: Renaissance Festivals, 1450-1650.* Woodbridge: Boydell Press, 1984.

Thomas, Andrea. 'Crown Imperial: Coronation Ritual and Regalia in the Reign of James V.' *Sixteenth-Century Scotland: Essays in Honour of Michael Lynch.* Eds. Julian Goodare and A. A. MacDonald. Leiden: Brill, 2008. 43-67.

Thorson, Stephanie M. 'Abell, Adam (1475x80?–1537?).' *Oxford Dictionary of National Biography.* Oxford: Oxford University Press, 2004.

Todd, J. 'Jedburgh Friary.' *Discovery and Excavation in Scotland.* Ed. Edwina Proudfoot. Edinburgh: Council for British Archaeology (Scotland), 1985.

Tuve, Rosemond. *Allegorical Imagery: Some Mediaeval Books and Their Posterity.* Princeton: Princeton University Press, 1966.

Twomey, Michael. 'Editing *De proprietatibus rerum*, Book XIV, from the Sources.' *Bartholomaeus Anglicus, De proprietatibus rerum. Texte latin et réception vernaculaire / Lateinischer Text und volkssprachige Rezeption.* Eds. Baudouin van den Abeele and Heinz Meyer. Turnhout: Brepols, 2005. 221-44.

Walther, Hans, ed. *Proverbia sententiaeque latinitatis medii aevi. Lateinische Sprichwörter und Sentenzen des Mittelalters in alphabetischer Anordnung.* 6 vols. Carmina medii aevi posterioris Latina. Göttingen: Vandenhoeck & Ruprecht, 1963-67.

Wenzel, Siegfried. *The Sin of Sloth: Acedia in Medieval Thought and Literature.* Chapel Hill: University of North Carolina Press, 1967.

Wheatley, Edward. 'Scholastic Commentary and Robert Henryson's *Moral Fabillis.' Studies in Philology* 91 (1994): 70-99.

Whiting, B. J. *Proverbs, Sentences, and Proverbial Phrases from English Writings Mainly Before 1500.* Cambridge: Harvard University Press, 1968.

Williamson, Arthur H. *Scottish National Consciousness in the Age of James VI: The Apocalypse, the Union and Shaping of Scotland's Public Culture*. Edinburgh: John Donald, 1979.

Wolpers, Theodor. *Die englische Heiligenlegende des Mittelalters: Eine Formgeschichte des Legendenerzählens von der spätantiken lateinischen Tradition bis zur Mitte des 16. Jahrhunderts*. Tübingen: Niemeyer, 1964.

Woods, M. Curry, and Rita Copeland. 'Classroom and Confession.' *The Cambridge History of Medieval English Literature*. Ed. David Wallace. Cambridge: Cambridge University Press, 1999. 376-406.

Wright, D. F. 'Erskine, John, of Dun (1509?1590).' *Oxford Dictionary of National Biography*. Oxford: Oxford University Press, 2004.

Yates, Frances Amelia. *Astraea: The Imperial Theme in the Sixteenth Century*. London: Routledge & Kegan Paul, 1975.

Yeager, Peter. 'Dispute Between Mary and the Cross: Debate Poems of the Passion.' *Christianity & Literature* 30 (1981): 53-69.

Zim, Rivkah. *English Metrical Psalms: Poetry as Praise and Prayer, 1535-1601*. Cambridge: Cambridge University Press, 1987.

Mediaevalia Groningana New Series